CIVIL WAR AMERICA

Voices from the Home Front

CIVIL WAR AMERICA

Voices from the Home Front

JAMES MARTEN

A B C 🌓 C L I O

Santa Barbara, California
Denver, Colorado   Oxford, England

7/22/03

Library of Congress Cataloging-in-Publication Data

Marten, James Alan.
    Civil War America : voices from the home front / James Marten.
        p. cm.
Includes bibliographical references (p.   ) and index.
    ISBN 1-57607-237-1 (hardcover)—ISBN 1-85109-502-0 (e-book)
    1. United States—History—Civil War, 1861–1865—Social aspects. 2.
United States—History—Civil War, 1861–1865—Personal narratives. I.
Title.

E468.9.M127 2003

                                                973.7'1—dc21

07   06   05   04   03   9   8   7   6   5   4   3   2   1

This book is also available on the World Wide Web as an e-book. Visit abc-clio.com for details.

ABC-CLIO, Inc.
130 Cremona Drive, P.O. Box 1911
Santa Barbara, California 93116-1911

This book is printed on acid-free paper ∞ .
Manufactured in the United States of America

To my parents

Roy and Mary Lou Marten

Contents

Acknowledgments

A number of graduate students funded by Marquette University have aided my research over the years, and some of it appeared in new forms in this volume, so I would first like to thank the research assistants who helped on those earlier projects: Henry Blanco, James Bohl, Annie Chenovick, Brian Faltinson, Jason Hostutler, Frank Keeler, and Patricia Richard. In addition, I want to thank Joan M. Sommers of Memorial Library at Marquette University for running the best interlibrary loan department in the country! I have had the honor to receive research support from Marquette University on a number of occasions; most have gone in some small or large way into the making of this book, necessitating, once again, my sincere thank you to the university's Office of Research and Sponsored Programs. Also at Marquette University, I would like to thank Father J. Patrick Donnelly S.J. for translating the Latin passage in Chapter 8. At ABC-CLIO I would like to thank Alicia Merritt for asking me to write the book and for providing encouragement and enthusiasm along the way.

Finally, this book is dedicated to my father and mother, Roy and Mary Lou Marten. My childhood memories are sprinkled with happy vignettes of their encouraging participation in my becoming a historian: going over family photos and family histories; going to tiny South Dakota theaters to see movies based on historic events (a happy trip to see *Custer of the West* and a less happy—and abbreviated—outing to see *The Good, the Bad, and the Ugly* when I was nine and a little too young, my father decided, to see the bad and ugly parts); the famous family vacation in which we visited Gettysburg and Washington, mainly because those were the places this thirteen-year-old history buff wanted to go. There were—and are—other, more profound ways in which they supported me—and my own family. Dedicating this book to them is a small but heartfelt way of saying thanks.

Introduction:
"A People's War"

On May 18, 1861, leaders of the New York City medical establishment and philanthropic community met to discuss how they could help the U.S. effort to put down the fledgling rebellion in the Southern states. The conflict could hardly be called a war yet. The last state to secede from the Union—North Carolina—would not do so for two days, and the biggest battles so far had been street riots in St. Louis and Baltimore. In pro-slavery, pro-secession Baltimore a month earlier, a mob had confronted the 6th Massachusetts as it marched from one train depot to another on its way to Washington; four soldiers and twelve others died in the melee. In St. Louis, pro-Union volunteers and regular army units had disarmed and arrested secessionist militiamen just a week before the meeting in New York. Attacked on their way back to the post with their prisoners, the soldiers opened fire, killing thirty people. Here and there throughout the three-month-old Confederacy, ragtag units occupied Federal facilities; throughout the divided country, men gathered on town squares to begin the tedious process of teaching themselves how to be soldiers.

Nevertheless, representatives of the Woman's Central Association of Relief for the Sick and Wounded of the Army, the advisory committee of the Boards of Physicians and Surgeons of the Hospitals of New York, and the New York Medical Association gathered to try to determine "the best means of methodizing and reducing to practical service the already active, but undirected benevolence of the people toward the Army." They composed a letter to Secretary of War Simon Cameron, asking for the authority to establish a central organization "which the people at large can use to manifest their goodwill toward the comfort, security, and health of the Army." They got their wish and in a few weeks the United States Sanitary Commission would be created.

The letter to Secretary Cameron articulated a vision of the coming clash of North and South as "essentially a people's war. The hearts and minds, the bodies and souls, of the whole people and of both sexes throughout the loyal States are in it. The rush of volunteers to arms is equalled by the enthusiasm and zeal of the women of the nation," and Americans "vie with each other in their ardor to contribute in some manner to the success of our noble and sacred cause." This conflict, the authors sensed, would link battlefront and home front in ways unimagined five weeks earlier, before Confederates bombarded Fort Sumter.

Although the scale of destruction and hardship brought on by the war and the extent to which the Americans would be forced to participate in it no doubt astonished these men and women over the next four years, their words in the early days of the conflict had, indeed, been prophetic. The Civil War did become a "people's war," drawing into it every man, woman, and child in both the North and the South. These are the stories *Civil War America: Voices from the Home Front* seeks to tell.

The Civil War changed the United States forever: it irrevocably altered the political system, eradicated slavery, and helped set in motion events that sparked a vast expansion and industrialization of the American economy. The war was also an agent of change in the lives of individual Americans as dreams were fulfilled and deferred; as new opportunities were created and new burdens assumed; and as participants experienced the extremes of excitement and terror, witnessed stirring incidents of benevolence and hatred, submitted to new layers of bureaucracy, and began to see their country in exciting, disturbing new ways.

Civil War America describes the Civil War home front through the lives of individuals and through the histories of events and institutions representing the myriad ways in which the war affected Northern and Southern civilians. Some of the subjects are well known—Edmund Ruffin and Booker T. Washington, for instance—while others, like George Templeton Strong, were important actors little known to modern Americans. Most of these witnesses to war will be men, women, and children unknown to anyone but their families and friends.

The sources produced by and about these people suggest the ways in which the Civil War was a crucible of changes large and small. Each of the stories will display some element of change: the destruction of old racial relationships, the challenge to Southern whites' assumptions and complacency, the centralization of benevolence, the expansion of government power and responsibility. In more personal terms, the changes include shifting notions of personal worth, efforts to fit personal motivations and opinions into the national crisis, and the recognition of the centrality of wartime experiences to individual lives.

The book's organization reflects the fact that Americans experienced the war in vastly different ways. The section called "Southern Civilians under Siege" emphasizes the pressure that the war exerted on Southern society, the proximity of the armies of friends and foes alike, the hard choices forced on civilians, and the extent to which the story of the Southern home front is the story of Southern women. On the other hand, "Northern Society at War" offers a very different view of the home front, one characterized by distance from the war, by a constant drive on the part of home front Northerners to gather information and to find ways to contribute to their country's war effort. The particular experiences of children—as actors and victims, playmates and consumers—find expression in "The Children's Civil War," while the challenges faced by slaves and former slaves in the wartime South appear in "African Americans and the War." Finally, and importantly, "Aftermaths" extends the story of the Civil War home front far beyond the close of the fighting, as the legacies and recollections of the war continued to help shape American culture for generations after the Confederacy died.

Battles and wars come and go, but the changes they foment, the sacrifices they inspire, the losses they extract carry forward the story of the conflict in diverse and sometimes unexpected ways. The home front men, women, and children whose stories comprise "A People's War" certainly saw their lives—not just the lives of the men they supported, worried about, and mourned—as vital components of the great war raging around them. This volume does not pretend to offer a comprehensive history of civilian experiences in either the Union or the Confederacy, but it does present case studies of some of the many ways in which the Civil War was, indeed, a people's war.

SOURCE:

Bellows, Henry W., et al. *U.S. Sanitary Commission Report No. 1: An Address to the Secretary of War.* May 18, 1861. Posted at http://www.disabilitymuseum.org/lib/docs/686.htm. Accessed April 26, 2002.

PART I

Southern Civilians
under Siege

Chapter One

The Last Fire-Eater: Edmund Ruffin

"I here declare my unmitigated hatred to Yankee rule—to all political, social & business connection with Yankees—& to the Yankee race" (Scarborough, *Diary of Edmund Ruffin II*, 949). So wrote Edmund Ruffin, the infamous fire-eater of Virginia, on his last day on earth. Ruffin was relatively unknown for most of his long life—he was born in 1794 and died a few months after the end of the Civil War—although he had won local and even regional recognition as a pioneering agronomist. The 1850s had been a difficult decade for Ruffin: three of his four daughters had died, and the remaining one who had cared for him after the death of his wife married at the age of thirty-two, breaking his heart and worsening his already despondent mood. He retired from managing Marlbourne, his plantation, in 1855 (selling it later in the decade to his surviving children) to become, as he said, a "missionary of disunion" (Mitchell, 2). Yet his efforts had won few converts, especially among his fellow Virginians. That would all change as the country hurtled toward Civil War in the late 1850s. When John Brown mounted his ill-conceived and ill-fated "invasion" of the slave South in October 1859, the South recoiled in horror, then lashed out at the North. Northern peddlers, tutors, and itinerant ministers were driven out. Young Southerners withdrew from Northern colleges. Suddenly Edmund Ruffin's dire warnings about Northern extremism and aggressiveness began to make sense to increasing numbers of Southerners.

As the crisis escalated to secession and then to war, Ruffin seemed to be everywhere: witnessing John Brown's execution, speaking at the Florida secession convention, pulling the lanyard on the first gun to fire at Fort Sumter, marching with an elite company of South Carolina volunteers to the First Battle of Bull Run. His fame exploded and he became a nearly mythic figure in a South that had finally come around to his way of thinking. The photograph of Ruffin seated in a chair, musket in hand, white hair flowing over his shoulders, eyes in a steel-hard gaze at the camera is one of the most famous photographs of a civilian from the Civil War era.

A famous portrait of the warlike, fire-eating Edmund Ruffin (National Archives)

The Last Fire-Eater: Edmund Ruffin

The scion of an old and wealthy Virginia family, Ruffin had had a troubled, alcohol-soaked career as a student at the College of William and Mary, had married, and had served an uneventful six months in the army during the War of 1812—all before turning nineteen in 1814. His father settled him and his young bride on a modest plantation on the James River. Its played-out land forced him to learn how to rejuvenate it scientifically, and the young man quickly became a successful planter and the owner of dozens of slaves. Ruffin fit uneasily into planter society. He was a religious freethinker with an explosive temper; his prickly sense of personal honor collided with his penchant for brutal honesty. He was also an unabashed elitist who believed Thomas Jefferson had forsaken the Republican ideal to which Ruffin was devoted. As a member of the Virginia upper crust, he expected to lead his fellow Southerners. Yet when he went to the state senate in 1823, he only lasted three years before he resigned—after he became disgusted with the process and his constituents became disgusted with his absolute opposition to most government programs. For a number of years he published the well-thought-of *Farmer's Register,* a scientific agricultural journal in whose columns he advocated the use of natural fertilizers and, when he turned to politics from time to time, waged campaigns against such federalist atrocities as banks. When he tired of farming, he lived for a time in Petersburg, but moved back to the country in 1844, when he purchased Marlbourne on the Pamunkey River, sixteen miles from Richmond.

Ruffin identified with the cause of the South completely and irrevocably. His Southern nationalism was nurtured by his association with James Henry Hammond, the radical South Carolinian; by a defensiveness sparked by the growing abolitionist attacks on slavery; by his own deeply held convictions about slavery, agriculture, and race; and by the passage of the temperate but frustrating Compromise of 1850. By late in the 1850s, he was publicly advocating reopening the slave trade.

The slave trade was never reopened, but Ruffin got the war he hoped would separate his beloved South from the "perfidious North," and he cut a wide swath through its early months. In addition to his contributions during the bombardment of Fort Sumter and the First Manassas Campaign, he was consulted by officials of at least three different states regarding the disposition of guns and ammunition, toured Richmond's Tredegar Iron Works to determine its capacity for supplying the Confederacy with ordnance, and inspected a fortification on the James River.

Ruffin seemed pleased and gratified to be recognized, finally, after his long exile in the political wilderness. On his way back to Virginia from Charleston after he helped launch the war, crowds gathered at train stations to applaud the troops. "I also was called for whenever the people learned I was along," he

5

wrote, adding that he "was forced to utter a few sentences" at several stops (Scarborough, *Diary of Edmund Ruffin I*, 5). Back in Richmond, he noticed a "complete & wonderful change" since he had left, with most of the people suddenly supporting secession. "My reception," he reported, "seemed to approach to something like the kind & friendly & favorable appreciation evinced for me in Charleston"—a far more radical place than Virginia—which "is in marked contrast to the treatment I have generally received in my own country" (ibid., 8). He scoffed but took silent pleasure in the sudden conversion of former enemies. One such, William Rives, "a complete union-worshipper & submissionist to all northern oppressions," sought Ruffin out and offered his hand and his compliments. Ruffin answered "merely by expressing my gratification at his & the general present position" (ibid., 11). Complete strangers approached him and congratulated him on being the first to fire at Fort Sumter; three declared that the news had caused their wives to weep with joy.

His last active participation in the military events of the war occurred during the First Battle of Bull Run, where he joined his old friends from Fort Sumter, the Palmetto Guards, the 2d South Carolina Infantry regiment. His diary detailed the confusing skirmishing and maneuvering that preceded the battle, the unpreparedness of most of the troops, and the lack of infrastructure and experience in the Confederate command structure. Ruffin seems to have wandered around at his leisure, borrowing horses, hitching rides on artillery caissons, and hobnobbing with officers and other soldiers. At one point, he was convinced that the Confederates had lost the battle. He discovered soon after, however, that it was the Union army in retreat. He got into the action in fits and starts and never seems to have felt in any particular danger. Late in the battle, he once again played a role at a key point when he fired one of the shots into the retreating Federals that helped cause their infamous rout. His businesslike prose goes on to describe the aftermath of battle: a thirty-acre field strewn with dead, "clotted blood" lying below bodies, faces stretched into painful contortions, brains oozing from head wounds, and white froth gathered on dead lips (ibid., 92–93).

When his son entered the army in the late spring of 1861, Ruffin, the only white man remaining on the plantation, took to sleeping with a loaded gun. Yet sometimes he seems to have gotten bored. "Dull & wearisome time," he wrote in September 1861, "nothing to engage or employ me, or to amuse" (ibid., 134). Throughout the war, Ruffin complained of his uselessness and the encroachments of age. His hearing was dwindling, his patience for writing and reading was declining, his energy lagged, and he was easily annoyed. When he was around other people, he could not hear anything clearly because of his deafness. "Thus, the larger the company, & the more cheerful & talkative they are, the more lonesome & unamused . . . I am" (ibid., 199). All that interested him was "the progress of the war, & all connected matters . . . And to know the issue is the only thing now left for me to desire my life to be continued longer." Given the choice to die on a battlefield or not, Ruffin would have preferred to die at Bull Run: "If a cannonball . . . had then been the means" of his death, "it would have been the most desirable termination of my life" (ibid., 139).

> *When his son entered the army in the late spring of 1861, Ruffin . . . took to sleeping with a loaded gun.*

Not surprisingly, Ruffin's diary is filled with calumny aimed at Northerners. Toward the beginning of 1862, he digressed from a catalog of recent events to remark that, although the North had a superiority in resources, the Confederacy's

> superiority to our enemy is in the much higher moral & intellectual grade of the Southern people, & of the superior principles by which they are actuated, & the holy cause which supports their patriotism & courage. The Southern people are defending their just & dearest rights, their property, their families, their very existence, against the fierce & violent assault of enemies who are impelled mainly by the greedy desire to rob us of all that we possess. . . . Their impulses . . . are but those which actuate banditti & pirates in their pursuit of plunder by means of murder. (ibid., 278–279)

So contemptuous was he of the North that he once declared that he would rather "our despotic ruler & master should be any power of Europe, even Russia or Spain, rather than the Northern States" (ibid., 291–292). Ruffin loved to indulge in the worst rumors of Yankee atrocities: the garrison at Washington, D.C., regularly plundered shops, raped women, and murdered Southern sympathizers; letters found on numerous battlefields indicated that Northerners would be allowed to claim Southern land and Southerners' possessions if they won the war.

Ruffin was not above recording the most titillating rumors regarding the abolitionists he loved to hate. In March 1864, he quoted the New Hampshire *Patriot,* which had rather dubiously reported that sixty-four of the Northern women who had gone South to teach African Americans had been forced to return to the North after becoming pregnant. Ruffin assumed the fathers were black, which would simply confirm his own suspicions that these ladies were "truly what they claim to be, philanthropists, i.e., loving, or ready to bestow their love on, all of mankind" (Scarborough, *Diary of Edmund Ruffin II,* 373).

Although it occurred only a little more than a year after the war began, the central event in Ruffin's wartime existence was the massive Peninsula

Campaign, launched in mid-March 1862, with the arrival of the advance units of the Army of the Potomac at the tip of The Peninsula formed by the James and the York Rivers. Marked in turn by savage fighting and frustrating inaction, the campaign culminated in the Seven Days' Battles outside Richmond at the end of June and, in mid-August, with the evacuation of most of the Union army back to northern Virginia. Although the campaign ended with a convincing Confederate victory and the rise to command of Robert E. Lee, it played havoc with Ruffin's life and property and signaled a turning point of sorts in his view of the war.

Marlbourne lay east and a little north of Richmond; Edmund Jr.'s place, Beechwood—where Ruffin was actually living for most of this time—occupied choice land below Richmond on the James River. Union troops overran Beechwood on their way to the Battle of Malvern Hill; foragers and scouts frequently roamed the neighborhood around Marlbourne. Both men lost several slaves, many of whom ran away as soon as Northerners appeared.

As Union troops crept up The Peninsula in April and May, Ruffin began to worry about his and his family's property. Reports of slaves deserting downriver plantations began arriving in the middle of May. "I fear & expect," wrote Ruffin, "that Marlbourne will be as much exposed to the depredations of the invaders, & large loss of slaves" (Scarborough, *Diary of Edmund Ruffin I*, 306). True to Ruffin's prediction, Yankee cavalry first came near Marlbourne a few days later and, "very soon after, larger bodies of troops followed & spread through every public road leading towards Richmond & to almost every farm in that neighborhood." Ruffin's slaves had acted normally, right up to May 18, when a dozen young men and boys "went off to the enemy." The next day, all the remaining slaves refused to work (ibid., 317). Ruffin's son-in-law, who managed the plantation (his wife Elizabeth had died in childbirth in 1860), convinced that nothing could be done in the present state of affairs, and assuming that he would be taken prisoner if Union troopers appeared, took off, leaving behind Robert E. Lee's wife and two daughters who had been living in the mansion! The three women stayed until well into June, despite the frequent appearance of Federal patrols, who stripped the plantation of all its mules, corn, and fodder.

Slaves began to leave Beechwood, too, just after Ruffin and the rest of the family had evacuated it. The only men who stayed were "two cripples & a dwarf" who were not required to do any serious work anyway (ibid., 338). Slaves continued to leave, even after the white folks returned to Beechwood on June 17. By that time, it was not just men who were leaving, but women and children, too— three entire families (twenty-one people) left the night after Ruffin reoccupied the plantation. Ruffin dismissed the deserting slaves as delusional: "it appears they have been promised enormous wages, plenty to eat, & no work to do" by

U.S. forces burn one of Ruffin's properties during the Peninsula Campaign.
(Library of Congress)

the Yankees (ibid., 346). Nevertheless, Edmund Jr. lost nearly 100 slaves during the campaign.

Through much of the Peninsula Campaign, Ruffin was in Richmond hanging about the capitol, the state library, and anywhere else he believed he could pick up scraps of news and listening, despite his deafness, for the sound of guns that would signal the resolution of the crisis. He fretted about finances—especially of his children and their families; he seemed truly not to care much about his own comfort but was sincerely concerned that the war would destroy the futures of his offspring.

The big fight outside the gates of Richmond finally came on June 1, at Malvern Hill. Always curious, as soon as the sound of firing began to fade, Ruffin dashed out to view the battlefield, fighting crowds of slightly wounded men or "skulkers" fleeing the battle, roads turned into quagmires by recent rains, and crowds of other "visitors" touring the battlefield. "I could not understand anything of the movements of the troops," Ruffin wrote of his journey through the backwash of battle, "the design or the results of our or the enemy's operations—nor even whether we had gained or lost by all the fighting of the day" (ibid., 330). The Confederates had gained the advantage, of course, although the worst of the fighting would take place later in the month at the

Seven Days' Battles, as the Army of the Potomac continued its grudging withdrawal down The Peninsula.

Despite the victory, nothing would be the same for Ruffin or the South. Indicative of this was the destruction that occurred at Beechwood, which had been occupied by Yankees for some time. Although the buildings and grounds had not been burnt, they had been damaged nearly beyond recognition. Furniture was smashed, floors were strewn with litter and garbage, walls were stained with tobacco juice. All of the provisions and livestock were gone. Metal hooks, screws, and bells had been carted off, along with a magic lantern—a Civil War–era slide projector normally used to illustrate public lectures and to entertain schoolchildren—and most of the library's hundreds of books; Ruffin's personal papers were scattered or stolen. Perhaps more deflating were the examples of soldierly graffiti scratched onto the plaster of paris walls. Soldiers had written their names "& sometimes their opinions" with charcoal. Many were insults directed toward Ruffin or his son: Ruffin defiantly wrote in his diary that "I take the scurrilous abuse thrown upon myself very complacently—as being the only compliment or eulogism that a low-bred Yankee can bestow on me." He took the trouble to record some of the scribblings in his diary: "We pity but do not hate the rebels"; "This house belonged to a Ruffinly son of a bitch"; "Old Ruffin don't you wish you had left the Southern Confederacy to go to Hell, (where it will go,) & had stayed at home?"; and "You did fire the first gun on Sumter, you traitor son of a bitch" (ibid., 419–420).

In many ways the rest of the war was an anticlimax for Ruffin and, although he did not actually admit it, his confidence must have been shaken. Confederate forces had driven the invaders from The Peninsula, but at high cost and only after the enemy had nearly captured the capital. Ruffin's property had been severely damaged during the campaign and his personal life continued to deteriorate for the rest of the war. He worried about his far-flung family, many of whom were in the path of invading armies or in the Confederate forces. Although a grandson, Thomas, survived a stint as a prisoner of war, Ruffin mourned for a son and a grandson, both named Julian, killed in battle in 1862 and 1864, respectively.

Yet Edmund Ruffin never wavered in his commitment to the South or to the values he had fought for his entire adult life. He remained fundamentally and passionately committed to slavery. To him, the Northerners, to whom he sarcastically referred as those "philanthropical abolitionists," were trying to destroy a practical, humane, and reasonable economic system. Ruffin laid the blame for all the hardships endured by former slaves—especially those who cast their lots with passing Union army units and ended up in contraband camps or near military posts—on the Northern policy of emancipation and the "atrocious manner of Yankee warfare." The war had created "more privation & suffering than would have otherwise occurred in all the cases of a century . . . unprecedented previously in all our land." The war had thus brought extraordinary hardship to "what was previously the best fed & clothed, the most easy-conditioned, comfortable, & happy of all the laboring & lowest classes on the face of the globe." He predicted that within ten years, less than half of the former slave population would still be alive and that within the course of a century, "hunger, cold & consequent diseases, with extreme suffering & misery, will have nearly extinguished the race, and also the early dreams of abolition philanthropy" (ibid., 506–507).

His commitment to Southern values and honor . . . did not dull his criticism of Confederate leaders and policies.

His commitment to Southern values and honor, however, did not dull his criticism of Confederate leaders and policies, not to mention the lack of constancy of his fellow Southerners. Indeed, it is difficult to determine who Ruffin hated more: Northern "aggressors" or weak-willed Confederates. Early in 1864, he complained that "one of the evil consequences" of the government's "lenient treatment of deserters, & of the many thousands still evading service" were the "thousands who are in hiding, & in small parties, or singly, live by plundering." Pardons and easy treatment for those who were actually captured by the army were too common for the tough old Virginian: "all ought to have been put to death" (Scarborough, *Diary of Edmund Ruffin II*, 373).

Of course, Ruffin still reserved his most violent diatribes for the hated Yankees. In February 1864, he ridiculed Northerners for supporting an expensive, bloody, and thus far—at least in Ruffin's opinion—unsuccessful war, and their likely support of their "miserable vulgar fool" of a president in the upcoming presidential campaign. Later in the war he argued that it would be better for Lincoln, "an unlettered fool, & a low blackguard & vulgar buffoon," to defeat the Democratic candidate, George B. McClellan, apparently because the latter was not only "able & more respectable," but a man of "sense & education" and the "manners . . . of a gentleman." In other words, the South would have a better chance to prevail against Lincoln than against the more able McClellan. There would be a downside to a Lincoln victory, however, mainly in the damage it would do to "the cause of free government, & popular election, in the opinion of the world"—especially "the most sensible & discreet portion." There once was a time, Ruffin asserted, when American politics actually sustained the "theory of democratic government"—"that the people will always, or generally, elect . . . good & competent, if not the best men eligible." Ever the elitist, Ruffin complained that that theory had been bastardized over the years in the United States by "universal suffrage & election of executive & judicial officers by popular votes." He blamed the "pernicious doctrines of Jefferson" and of practices begun in New England and New York, which resulted in the election, not of the best, but often of the worst "men of the community." Lincoln's reelection, Ruffin seemed to be saying, would pound the final nail into the coffin of American-style democracy (ibid., 577).

It is clear that Ruffin did not necessarily equate the Confederacy with the perfect world he had envisioned as a fire-eating secessionist in the decades before the war began. Ruffin still took a perverse pleasure in being a loner. He almost relished the lack of acclaim and distinction that his controversial views had, until the last years of his life, earned him. "I do not claim, & do not flatter myself with having the merit," he wrote early in 1864, not quite three years after the crisis had finally brought his name before the masses, "that I had any important influence in inducing the secession of the Southern states, or of Virginia. But this I may truly claim—that for eleven years before any such actual movement, I had labored zealously & earnestly for that effect—when standing almost alone (in Va.,) & incurring thereby general odium, & without the avowed approbation or thanks of any of my countrymen" (ibid., 375).

Not quite a year later, in a long, depressing diary entry, Ruffin took a weird kind of solace in his notoriety among Northerners since the war had begun. Before the war, he had been unknown there, but since April 1861 his name "has been bruited there, far & wide, as that of the traitor & zealous rebel who fired the first gun against Fort Sumter, & against northern domination." He had heard so many threats uttered against him, that he believed that if he were captured, "the peculiar malignant hatred, & thirst of vengeance, felt for me" would result in "the worst sufferings that can easily be inflicted on a helpless & unprotected prisoner" (ibid., 704).

As the war wound down in late 1864 and 1865, his diary entries became more bitter and reflective of a deep and abiding depression. When he turned seventy-one in January 1865, he penned an agonized jeremiad into the depths of his own wilderness. "If I had died ten years ago," he began, "I should have escaped my suffering from all these misfortunes." As if his personal trials were not enough, "I can no longer be of any use either to myself, my family, or my country." His war-induced poverty, age-induced deafness, and growing dissatisfaction with his place in the world and the world's place in his life had rendered him superfluous. "My part in the drama of life, whether well or ill, has been played out & is finished." Ruffin displayed his characteristic candor and more than the usual amount of self-awareness when he wrote of the way that his personal thoughts must have been shaping his outward demeanor. "My company & conversation can afford no pleasure to any associates," he admitted, concluding that "the sooner that my death shall occur, the better will it be for me, & for all" (ibid., 702).

12

The Last Fire-Eater: Edmund Ruffin

Even in this dark hour in the winter of 1865, Ruffin could muster a defiant patriotism to his beloved South. "There remains but a single object for which [I] would now wish any extension of my life—which is, that I may witness the success & triumph of my country in the conclusion of the war, which is now waged against us, in the most atrocious manner, by the vilest & most malignant people & government in Christendom." Yet "every passing month seems to leave the attainment" of such a result "less hopeful." He described the chaos and destruction that would ensue after a victory by "a government, a people, & armed forces, all of which have, through-out this war, shown themselves more unjust & cruel, & more regardless of all obligations of the laws of civilized war-

"The fate which I would most desire for myself would be to be shot dead . . ."

fare, as well as of morality, mercy, & religion, than has before occurred in any case of war in modern times, carried on by a people professing to be Christian" (ibid., 705).

Unable to bear the notion of witnessing such a defeat, Ruffin longed for some form of honorable death: "The fate which I would most desire for myself would be to be shot dead in giving my feeble aid to some of the last defenders of our country against its assailing foes." But that was unlikely, he admitted, and he hoped that "natural decay" or an accident would soon put an end to his sorry state (ibid., 705).

Ruffin's demise came not on a battlefield, nor from accidental or natural causes. He survived the war, returned to his son's battered plantation, and waited for a squad of Yankees to arrest him—but they never came. He then planned a different ending to the story of his life, applying to it the same rational, if at times obsessive and self-ratifying, approach he had brought to his work and to his politics. "One of the many subjects in regard to which a close examination of the words of the Bible would serve to correct mistaken popular opinion of the supposed contents is suicide," he began in an entry he composed over three days in the middle of June 1865. Using his favorite adjective for ideas different from his own, he wrote that "vulgar belief" had it that suicide was considered a sin and a crime. He continued on this track for several pages, providing biblical exegesis, interpretations of Jewish law and history, and supporting evidence from ancient and medieval times. He con-cluded that if a man's "death would cause no service to be left unperformed to his family or country, & would increase to none either privations, losses, or physical sufferings, its being produced by his own act should not be deemed criminal, or as disobedience to God." In this lengthy treatise Ruffin justified the decision that he had reached: if the Yankees would not kill him, he would kill himself (ibid., 935–940).

He planned and explained it carefully. His long, last diary entry described the fairness with which he had, over the years, distributed his property to his family. He recounted his efforts as an agricultural reformer, "which have induced the production of millions of dollars of abiding value." He had tried to make Southerners aware of the threat posed to them from the North and had attempted to support the valiant but failed Confederacy with the limited resources at his disposal. Now, however, weary of mind and body, with "nothing left for my support & no means for aiding others . . . I can do no good in any way. I am now merely a cumberer of the earth, & a useless consumer of its fruits, earned by exertions of others." Of course, Ruffin's self-awareness was limited to the extent that his slaves may have noticed an irony in his words that he failed to detect, but Ruffin went on to describe the process by which he had come to make the decision to end his life (ibid., 940–941).

In fact, he had planned to do so two months earlier, but logistical and personal obstructions had intervened. He wanted some of his extended family to move to other houses, so as not to have too many people nearby when he finally ended his life. He waited so as not to detract from the celebration of his nephew's marriage and made sure his son would be at home to take care of the funeral arrangements, careful instructions for which he had recorded. He wanted to see how certain things turned out—the war in the West (after Lee's surrender), the continuing controversy between the United States and Great Britain over the CSS *Alabama* claims, the U.S. expedition to the border of Mexico, where French forces still occupied part of the country. Of course, not all of these issues were resolved by mid-June 1865—and would not be for months or even years. As a result, Ruffin, tired of waiting, penned these famous— almost—last words:

> I here declare my unmitigated hatred to Yankee rule—to all political, social & business connection with Yankees—a& to the Yankee race. Would that I could impress these sentiments, in their full force, on every living southerner, & bequeath them to every one yet to be born! May such sentiments be held universally in the outraged & down-trodden South, though in silence & stillness, until the now far-distant day shall arrive for just retribution for Yankee usurpation, oppression, & atrocious outrages. (ibid., 949–950)

After hurling a few more insults at his nearly lifelong enemies, Ruffin completed his final diary entry with "The End." He then scribbled a several-paragraph letter to his son, Edmund Jr., in which he asked for a simple burial within a few hours of his death, with no coffin and no service, like the simple funerals of "our brave soldiers who were slain in battle." He asked his family not to wear mourning clothes, gave his son the "possession & charge" of his manuscripts, and bequeathed his watch to his grandson George. And then he wrote, "with my latest writing & utterance, & with what will be near to my latest breath . . . my unmitigated hatred to Yankee rule." Finally, he wrote one more sentence: "Kept waiting by successive visitors to my son, until their departure at 12:15 P.M." (ibid., 949–950).

He immediately sat down in a chair, placed the muzzle of a musket in his mouth, and pushed the trigger with a forked hickory stick. Only the cap exploded. In what must have been a nearly superhuman effort of will, Ruffin replaced the cap, resettled himself, and tried again. This time the musket fired and the most famous fire-eater in the Confederacy was dead.

PRIMARY SOURCES:

Scarborough, William Kauffman, ed. *The Diary of Edmund Ruffin: Volume I: The Years of Hope, April, 1861–June, 1863.* Baton Rouge: Louisiana State University Press, 1976.
———. *The Diary of Edmund Ruffin: Volume II: A Dream Shattered, June, 1863–June, 1865.* Baton Rouge: Louisiana State University Press, 1989.

SECONDARY SOURCES:

Mathew, William M. *Edmund Ruffin and the Crisis of Slavery in the Old South: The Failure of Agricultural Reform.* Athens: University of Georgia Press, 1988.
Mitchell, Betty L. *Edmund Ruffin: A Biography.* Bloomington: Indiana University Press, 1981.

Chapter Two

Times to Try a Woman's Soul

Happily scribbling a note to his father, who was away in the Union army, Gene Spalding wrote about a funny little habit that his mother had begun. She "has your photograph in her trunk where she can see it" whenever she opened it to retrieve a piece of linen or clothes. Each time, "she kisses it and talks to it just as if you could hear every word she says" (Culpepper, 286). Gene quickly turned to other more interesting topics, but this brief mention of one mother's quiet coping mechanism highlights an important story of the Civil War home front: the way that men's absence and its accompanying material, physical, and psychological strains challenged the will and even the sanity of women in both the North and the South.

Civil War women were sometimes subject to debilitating fear, loneliness, and weariness that could lead to fights with in-laws and landlords, to short tempers and impatient outbursts, and to depression so deep that they became ill, lost sleep, and withdrew from their children. Of course, many, if not most, women persevered admirably.

A comforting toughness of character surfaced in one Southern mother, lovingly described years after the war by her son. Widowed early in the war, she nevertheless "supported . . . privation like a Roman matron," William MacCorkle boasted many years later. Going hungry so her three little children could eat, she finally moved them into a nearby town, garrisoned by Union troops, and opened a millinery store to eke out her family's subsistence. Through it all, "she valiantly worked . . . without one complaint," to make a bare living. Her son would "never forget her heroic attitude" (MacCorkle, 11–12, 14). Other parents had more difficulty conquering their fears and worries. Perhaps for the first time in their lives, many children saw their parents worry about money. When one Georgia girl imagined aloud what she would do with a hundred dollars in the fall of 1864, her father bitterly handed her a Confederate $100 bill and snarled, "There! Take it down the street and see if you can buy a stick of candy" (Miers, 91).

The conditions that strained the Confederate home front surfaced repeatedly in the life of a Texan named Lizzie Neblett, whose letters to her husband, Will, chart the course of her anguish, fear, and despair. Lizzie never saw a Union soldier during the course of the war, her plantation was never threatened, and her children remained more or less healthy. She felt the stress of isolation and uncertainty that infused the lives of Southerners living in even the most secure corners of the Confederacy. "I never was a good amiable woman," admitted Lizzie Neblett in early 1864, "always had too much of the evil." But the war had caused her to become even "worse than I ever was before," she warned her husband Will, "and if you cease entirely to love me I cannot wonder at it" (Neblett; Lizzie to Will, January 9, 1864). Will remained faithful and Lizzie apparently recovered her equilibrium once he returned from the Confederate army. As the engrossing letters from Lizzie to Will plainly suggest, the war could upset an entire household, especially if the mother in charge was having a hard time grappling with the challenges of war.

Lizzie exemplifies how distraught some Confederate women became as a result of the proximity of the war. Born Elizabeth Scott in Mississippi in 1833, Lizzie was well educated and articulate. At the age of nineteen she married William Neblett, a lawyer and editor who, when the war broke out, owned a plantation near Anderson, in Grimes County, Texas. Halfway through the war, Will joined the Confederate army. Although his post on the Texas coast kept him out of combat, her demanding children, increasingly independent slaves, and a growing sense of despondency about the future nearly overwhelmed her. In long, demanding, and sometimes angry letters, she betrayed a deep unhappiness that verged at times on suicidal.

Many of her problems were material, of course. A town girl most of her life, she seem to have been somewhat unused to working on a farm, let alone managing it. She was proud of her flock of chickens, but fretted that Will did not "know how heavily the burden, & responsibility rests upon me of having things done which are highly necessary outside of the farm and my fear that these negros [sic] will not support themselves, and I know so little about farming" (April 26, 1863). Less than a year after Will left home, the children's clothes had become ragged and too small and their shoes were disintegrating. "I am in rags," Lizzie wrote. "I try to shut my eyes to it all, but the work I have, in hands, the doleful talk, of subjugation[,] being overrun, by the invading foe, and, the idea that you are lost to me forever on this earth, almost turns my brain" (January 9, 1864). After Lizzie told Will on a particularly bad day in the spring of 1864 that several young pigs had died, the corn might have to be replanted, and the oxen were wearing out, she declared, "I don't think I can stand a farm life another year" (March 18, 1864).

Another nagging problem was the behavior of the slaves. "I could not begin to write you," she complained to Will late in 1863, "how our negroes do all the

Widowhood was only one of the hardships facing Southern women.
(Currier & Ives, 1863/Library of Congress)

little things." She could trust only a few of them—the war had apparently inspired most of them to close ranks and to present a silent, suspicious front to the white people, and only two would give her any news from the quarters at all. They became surly and reluctant to do their work: "I find I must think continually for them" (November 4, 1863). Several slaves resisted whippings from the overseer—who Lizzie was none too fond of either—or ran away for days at a time, part of a disturbing trend of insolence and misbehavior among slaves in

"I try to shut my eyes to it all, but the work I have . . . almost turns my brain."

the county. The situation had gotten so bad that "a great many" of her neighbors "are actually afraid to whip the negroes." One slave, threatened with a beating by an elderly man living nearby, "cursed the old man all to pieces, and walked off in the woods." Lizzie believed that if she ordered the overseer to whip the slaves "they would resist & it would make matters no better so I shall say nothing, and if they stop work entirely, I will try & feel thankful if they let me alone" (August 13, 1863). As that remark indicated, the much-vaunted Southern confidence in the loyalty and contentedness of their slaves began to crumble during the war, and perhaps for the first time in her life, Lizzie began to fear her bondspeople. "I won't sleep with my doors open, any more, & if they break open either door or window I'll have time to be better prepared for them & will fight til I die." Later, she wrote, "I would not care if they killed me, if they did not do worse" (August 18, 1863).

Obviously, thoughts of mortality plagued Lizzie, and she frequently wrote about death in her letters. Her brother, Garrett, had died earlier in the war, and Lizzie frequently expressed nearly frantic—and understandable—concern about Will's well-being. Lizzie's wartime situation combined with her naturally melancholy demeanor to create a state of mind that often led her to wish for her own death. At one point early in 1864, with problems mounting and her fears running wild, she told Will that, "I often pause in my sad, & distracting thoughts and in heart felt misery exclaim, 'why did I not die in my infancy'" (January 9, 1864). A few months later, she "had the blues most awfully" and claimed that, "if I did not believe in the bible, I would end this continual war-fare"—an apparent reference to the conflict within her own impassioned mind—"and do both you and myself a service, by leaving this world" (March 20, 1864).

Mid-nineteenth-century medical care hardly inspired confidence in patients, and mainstream religious beliefs tended to be rather fatalistic about the tenuous grip most people had on life. Even before the war, days before the birth of her fourth child—she would bear six altogether—Lizzie wrote to Will what she considered, "may be for the last time." Lizzie's pessimism must have been a bone of contention between her and Will, for she admitted, "I know you think not, for yours is the brave good heart that hopes always *for the best*." But she could not put from her mind the perfectly reasonable fear, given the mortality rates for mothers and babies during the antebellum era, that she might not survive "this bitter cup of suffering." She also worried about the health of the baby, claiming that "it almost distracts me when I dwell upon the probabilities of its being deformed physically or mentally or it coming dead" (April 26, 1860). The baby arrived safely and seems to have remained relatively healthy, but the war provided more than enough challenges and discouragement to keep Lizzie swimming upstream for its duration.

Just a month after Will left for the army, Lizzie, whose fifth baby was nearly due, complained that "I do feel so utterly wretched & hopeless at times, when I think that you may never return and my being left a widow with five little helpless dependent children, to raise & educate." She confessed, "If it was not for them, I might end my own life." A short period of elation followed the baby's birth. "The mountain of anxiety & dread has been removed," she wrote, "the time of exquisite suffering has been passed, and I this morning lie on a bed of ease a free unshackled woman once more" (May 27, 1863). The chipper mood soon passed. When little Bettie had trouble nursing, cried incessantly, and generally proved to be a handful, she reported shedding "bitter tears, over the work of last August"—the month in which the baby had been conceived. She could "take no pleasure" in little Bettie. "The very sight of her is a pain to me" and "I can't help feeling that her death would be a blessing, to me & her" (June 9, 1863). Her mood had hardly brightened by six months after Bettie's birth. Whenever she cried or fussed, Lizzie immediately fell into "a bad humor . . . for the first thought that comes up is, if I had not been the biggest fool in the world that child would never have been here, to molest me as she does" (February 12, 1864). Although Lizzie may well have been suffering from what doctors now call "postpartum depression," the symptoms also fit into her lifelong and somewhat fatalistic tendency to focus on the negative facets of her life, which the war and Will's absence would naturally magnify.

The innocent irritations of Bettie was one thing, but Lizzie also had to deal with the older children. When little Walter one day grabbed her favorite comb and broke out three of its teeth, "I was provoked beyond measure." She "whipped him good, & wished a little stronger than usual that I never had been cursed with children" (January 3, 1864). Her oldest, Billy, was much worse. Showing the strain of his father's absence and other family pressures, Billy was a constant source of frustration and anger. He refused to do his chores and constantly bullied his younger brother Walter. "He grows worse all the time," Lizzie announced to Will. He was "so hateful, such a mean, bad child, and you can't appeal to his feelings, he is too flinty to care for any thing." Lizzie threatened to

An unsympathetic engraving entitled "Sowing and Reaping" shows Southern women persuading their husbands to join the rebellion (left) and the same women rioting for bread later in the war. (Hulton Archive)

"whip him every day" and predicted that Billy would "be a thorn in my heart as long as he lives." Although the other children missed their father, Billy "never speaks of you voluntarily." Bob was no prize either; he chewed tobacco at school, mistreated the horses, and once called Billy a "God damned liar" within earshot of his mother. That Bob was lapsing into preteen angst frustrated and saddened Lizzie, who believed that he "is the best child we have naturally, and if he is led astray so easily, what may we not expect of the others?" (May 29, 1864). Lizzie remarked once with obvious understatement, "children have lost their charm for me." Stronger words appeared in another letter. "I tolerate them less & less—they have been the bane of my life & will be so 'till I die, here to fore I have lived in dread of more coming—now, I live in horror of what I have— I'll never have another, & I'll stick as close to that as a mason ever did to his oath" (January 3, 1864).

A perceptive and self-aware woman, Lizzie knew that her moods set her apart from other women and mothers. "Like all crazy people," she wrote once, "I must

& will talk of that which affects my mind, temper, heart, & life most intimately" (May 29, 1864). She referred to "this gloomy, desponding, hopeless feeling that almost kills me at times" and wished "most heartily" late in the war "that I had no one in the world to care for but myself" (January 3, 1864). She blamed her lack of affection for her children on her own childhood, "which mentally from my youth up" is "more like some poor stray dog's fate than any thing you can liken it to" (April 26, 1863 and January 3, 1864).

There is a danger of focusing solely on Lizzie's nearly paralyzing fears and unhappiness. Her letters also included news from the neighborhood, juicy gossip from her dysfunctional family (her siblings seemed to be competing with one another for their mother's good graces, angling for bigger inheritances), and mundane comments about plantation affairs and goings-on in the slave quarters, and the tender passages in her letters suggest that she allowed herself to lapse into such wholehearted and eloquent complaints because she knew Will could take it. Her love for him—and his for her—shows clearly. In the same letter in which she wishes he could show her more sympathy for her depression, even though it could not "relieve me of one single bodily pain," she assured him that she could "never feel sufficiently thankful—I know that I have a true loving, tender, and noble husband" (April 26, 1863).

And yet she sometimes lashed out at him. Apparently unsatisfied at his letters' emotional content, she wrote angrily a few months after he left home, "If you were not my husband, & worthy the love I have so fully expressed in all my letters, I would feel ashamed of what I have written, when the crumbs in return have been so scanty." Their separation, and the unequal level of devotion appearing in their correspondence, had forced her to realize something she had never thought of before. "It is . . . a course of great mortification to me, that, I have failed to inspire, even one fourth of the love that I feel—I feel & know that is my fault." Although his absence had "made my heart grow fonder," apparently just the opposite had occurred to him. "The humiliating truth was forced upon me that, you felt, no more than you wrote, nor wrote no more than you felt." It struck her that that had been the case when he had been home, too; whenever she poured out her fears and concerns and miseries to him, "you immediately grew taciturn, closed your eyes, & no doubt your ears, & wandered off" into his own thoughts. Even when she stood "on the brink of a great suffering"—childbirth—a suffering "that claims you as the unintending originator," he refused to admit any anxiety and, in fact, failed to attempt to come home and be with her (May 14, 1863).

> *"It is . . . of great mortification to me, that, I have failed to inspire, even one fourth of the love that I feel . . ."*

The letter goes on in the same vein for some time, but apparently served as therapy for Lizzie, who in her next letter issued a kind of apology—at least an explanation—of her state of mind. Physical problems (breast-feeding had been painful), a medicine with uncomfortable side effects, and other elements of this "season of suffering" had gnawed at her mood and her love for Will for weeks; she had finally had enough and spilled her thoughts into the letter. Now she felt better—like Noah when he "stepped from the Arc, on dry land, & saw the waters of the flood retreating, and the rainbow of promise"—and regretted sending the letter. Yet, she defended herself; "you with your hopeful disposition can never know how ingenious a despairing mind can become in inflicting torture, by warping all our just & true ideas" (May 30, 1863).

Lizzie would not stay happy though. By Christmas 1863, she was deep in another bout of depression. Will's holiday at Corpus Christi, which he had reported in a cheerful Christmas letter home, was a cozy and carefree day. After listening to Lizzie read Will's letter, one of their sons declared "why Pa had a better Christmas than we had!" Lizzie agreed. "Mine was a gloomy bitter & dissatisfied spirit that bore me company & entertained me all day long, and far into the night." As she wrote her weekly letter a few days later, "the same spirit occupies his seat." She nearly decided not to write this time, for "I know you derive very little pleasure from reading what I write when I feel as I do at present," but she also knew that if she did not write he would worry about the children. "For that reason I continue the doleful strain, better that perhaps than be kept in uneasiness & suspense about the welfare of your children" (January 3, 1864).

Lizzie could apparently say almost anything to Will. At one point, she wrote about an acquaintance, "Now if you want a chance to marry, when I am gone, think of her, but always think that I would never be willing for you to marry her, so long as one of my children are alive, and under age. I know she would not suit you, for [as] a wife [she] would cause you more trouble than even I do" (April 26, 1863). In the same letter in which she promised him that "I long so ardently to see you, & talk with you, and be near you," even to "risk impregnancy," she tries to get him to agree to use some sort of birth control—an unusual and possibly disruptive request from a nineteenth-century woman (May 29, 1864).

It is hard to know what Will made of the long, demanding letters he received almost each week from Lizzie, although her own letters indicate that he responded temperately and patiently. She clearly suffered, at least temporarily, from depression; her brief periods of brightness suggest that she may have been manic-depressive. If so, that she managed to retain her sanity and keep her family well in the face of these problems was indeed a major accomplishment. Although her particular psychological profile may have made her reactions to the hardships of war and the absence of her husband more extreme than most, they differ only in degree, not in kind, from the thoughts of hundreds of thousands of women whose husbands were in the Confederate army.

Of course, most women managed to hold themselves and their households together despite the difficulties and hardships spawned by the war. Will came home safely, and after his death Lizzie wrote a loving, admiring biography of him that she never published.

"I have given up all hopes of the better time coming . . ."

Even though she once wrote during the war that "I have given up all hopes of the better time coming" (January 9, 1864), Lizzie Neblett survived the conflict and lived into old age in Anderson, Texas, dying in 1917. As Lizzie's letters show, the distress experienced by Civil War women was an important dynamic on the Civil War home front. Lizzie Neblett's cousin, Jennie Teel, once complained that Confederate newspaper editors were constantly writing that "these are the times to try men's souls." With little money, a houseful of young children, and a husband about to go off to war, she would "always mentally add—woman's too, for if my soul is not sorely tried then I do not know anything about it!" (Neblett; Jennie Teel to Lizzie, March 23, 1862).

PRIMARY SOURCES:

MacCorkle, William A. *Recollections of Fifty Years of West Virginia.* New York: G. P. Putnam's Sons, 1928.

Miers, Earl Schenk, ed. *When the World Ended: The Diary of Emma Le Conte.* New York: Oxford University Press, 1957.

Neblett, Lizzie. Papers. Austin: Center for American History, University of Texas at Austin. Unless otherwise cited, all quotations are from this collection. An edition of Lizzie's letters has recently been published in Murr, Erika L., ed. *A Rebel Wife in Texas: The Diary and Letters of Elizabeth Scott Neblett, 1852–1864.* Baton Rouge: Louisiana State University Press, 2001.

SECONDARY SOURCES:

Culpepper, Marilyn Mayer. *Trials and Triumphs: Women of the American Civil War.* East Lansing: Michigan State University Press, 1991.

Faust, Drew Gilpin. "Confederate Women and Narratives of the War." In *Divided Houses: Gender and the Civil War.* Edited by Catherine Clinton and Nina Silber, pp. 171–199. New York: Oxford University Press, 1992.

Rable, George C. *Civil Wars: Women and the Crisis of Southern Nationalism.* Urbana: University of Illinois Press, 1989.

Chapter Three

A Miserable, Frightened Life: Southern Refugees

At the dawn of the new century, Kate Stone Holmes sat in her Tallulah, Louisiana, home and opened the faded pages of a diary. She had begun writing in the diary nearly forty years before when, as a young woman, she was determined to record her experiences as the war between states burst into violence. Copying the diary into two big ledger books, she added a reflective introduction she called "In Retrospect." "How the old life comes back," wrote the fifty-nine-year-old pillar of the community, "the gay, busy life . . . at Brokenburn" (3). She inventoried the happy household living on the prosperous, 1,200-acre plantation near Delhi, Louisiana, just upriver from Vicksburg: her indomitable thirty-seven-year-old mother, Amanda Ragan Stone, a widow managing the plantation while at the same time raising her many dependents; Kate's twenty-one-year-old brother Will, just home from college and ready to take over the planting operation; teenagers Coley, seventeen, and eager to go to the University of Virginia; Walter, sixteen, and Jimmy, fourteen, the middle brothers; Johnny, just thirteen when the war began; and "Little Sister," only nine, "the pet and plaything of the house." Uncle Bo, her mother's carefree and beloved brother, also lived with the family. This extended family was joined at any given time by friends and relatives, "for the people of those times were a sociable folk and the ties of kindness were closely drawn" (4).

Kate was nineteen in 1860, had just graduated from Dr. Elliott's Academy in Nashville, "and was of course the much indulged young lady of the house" (3). Her description of peacetime life at Brokenburn reads like an early chapter of *Gone with the Wind*. Their home lay in Madison Parish on the Mississippi River floodplain, which was one of the richest places in the United States—nine out of ten people living there were slaves. Although a real mansion had not yet replaced their temporary quarters, it was still a grand life. From the long galleries bracketing the eight-room affair, the Stones could see the neatly laid-out slave quarters and the substantial log cabin where the overseer and his family lived. The house nestled in a proud grove of water oak, sweet gum, and sycamore, while the yard sprouted thick Bermuda grass. Life was good, and plans were being made for a grand tour of the North in the summer of 1861 and of Europe the following year. The Stones could afford it; Amanda had nearly paid off her debts and the family's slaves alone were worth $120,000.

In addition to offering the nuts and bolts of plantation life and of the Civil War home front, Kate's diary is valuable for revealing the mindset of a young, well-to-do Southern woman. Kate was a fairly introspective person, and frequently described her own attitudes and shortcomings. In the same paragraph in which she calls an acquaintance "a regular witch of an old lady with the most apologetic, deprecating air," she scolds herself: "now is not it mean of me to write in that way of that harmless old lady . . . She may be in her daily life an uncannonized saint" (89). She was also more than a little self-aware: on a nice, warm Sunday, the entire family stayed home from church—the driver was not feeling well and the horses were lame or indisposed. "It is strange how little it takes to keep one from going to church," she wrote, "and how much to keep one from attending a party" (33). She was a bookworm—"I do not remember the time when I could not read," she claimed. She believed herself to be fairly plain looking, that she was her father's favorite, and popular among other family members, more for her quick mind than for her beauty. Indeed, she believed that "Father and all the family petted and encouraged me because they thought me so ugly." Early in the book, the burden of considering herself an ugly duckling is lifted by a "long, sweet talk" with her mother, who, to Kate's great surprise, told her how pretty she was. By the age of twenty, she was "tall, not quite five feet six, and thin," with "an irregular face, a quantity of brown hair, a shy, quiet manner, and talk but little" (34–35).

Fortunately for historians, her shyness did not carry over into her diary, which is a crisply edited and straightforward account of one family's experiences during the Civil War. Yet it is much more than a simple chronicle of that family. Stone's articulate writing style, her wide interests, and her sometimes surprisingly balanced point of view have attracted historians ever since the diary's publication in 1955. *Brokenburn* is dominated by several topics: Kate's family, their slaves, and the effects of the war on the upper-crust society to which she belonged. The diary is a wonderful source for studying the trials and tribulations on the Confederate home front during a war that changed every facet of life for most Southerners, white and black alike. It offers graphic glimpses of the way that the war uprooted tens of thousands of Southern families from their homes and from one another.

Although she does not dwell on the issue, Kate occasionally writes about the 150 African Americans who served her family as servants, laborers, and property. "In Retrospect" includes detailed descriptions of the lives of the slaves and

Union refugees (Library of Congress)

especially of the kindly and loyal house servants who filled the Stones' lives with leisure. She also asserts that her "first recollection is of pity for the Negroes and desire to help them." She admitted that, even under the best owners—like her mother—"it was a hard, hard life . . . to be absolutely under the control of some-one until the last breath was drawn."

"The runaways are numerous and bold. . . . [T]he Negroes are suspected of an intention to spring on the fourth of [July]."

She claimed to have "always . . . felt the moral guilt of it, felt how impossible it must be for an owner of slaves to win his way into Heaven." It may have been easier for Kate, as a matriarch in her own right entering old age two genera-tions after the end of slavery, to write such words; such examples of overt guilt and kindness appear only rarely in the diary itself (7–8).

Like many Southerners throughout the war, Kate feared that the family's slaves would, from the whites' points of view, become troublesome, even to the point of a revolt. Early in the war, while sitting on the gallery one summer evening, "a runaway Negro passed just in front of the house." The boys vainly gave chase, and Kate reported that "the runaways are numerous and bold. . . . [T]he Negroes are suspected of an intention to spring on the fourth of [July]." But the neighborhood was vigilant—"our faith is in God" (28). A few days later, Kate reported that the house servants "have been giving a lot of trouble lately—lazy and disobedient." They were threatened with being sent to the fields (33). Apparently, Kate thought, the "Negroes looked for a great upheaval of some kind," but when nothing out of the ordinary occurred on July 4th, Kate hoped that the house servants would "settle to their work now" (37).

Despite their occasional concern about the loyalty of their bondspeople, until the war actually entered their lives in 1862, Kate and her privileged siblings and relatives lived a life of leisure. The entry from May 23, 1861, reports that "Mamma" was busy ordering the slaves around, getting carpets replaced and summer curtains hung. "Of course," Kate complained, "the house was dusty and disagreeable." The tutor and the younger children escaped by holing up in the schoolroom until supper time, "but Uncle Bo wandered aimlessly around, seek-ing rest and finding none. I retired to the fastness of my room with a new novel and a plate of candy and was oblivious to discomfort." Later there was a walk with the boys and dogs down by the bayou. The evening was spent in front of a "little fire" listening to the war news read from the newspaper (13–14). Throughout the first year or two of the war, there is a constant round of visiting, shopping, and other social occasions.

Kate's inactivity and isolation occasionally drove her a little crazy. "When qui-etly our days are passing, when the whole planet is in such a state of feverish excitement and everywhere there is the stir and mob of angry life—Oh! To see and be in it all. I hate weary days of inaction. Yet what can women do but wait and suffer" (24). Yet hints of the growing excitement turned up in nature, as a comet appeared during the summer, "a long train of light seen dimly as through a mist"—an unexpected omen (33). Then during the second summer of the war, when it was clear that Brokenburn might be in the path of the Union armies approaching Vicksburg, the tension mounted considerably. The boys "cannot settle to work and who can blame them," declared Kate, "it seems useless to have a teacher" (109). As it turns out, Kate would endure enough action and excitement to last a lifetime when the Union army drove into the Vicksburg region in the summer of 1862.

In the meantime, daily life took on a rougher complexion. By early summer of 1862, Kate reported that the household was on a "strict 'war footing,'" with "cornbread and home-raised meal, milk and butter, tea once a day, and coffee never." Not long before, "we would have considered it impossible to get on for a day without the things that we have been doing without for months." Clothes also became "a secondary consideration. Fashion is an obsolete word and just to be decently clad is all we expect" (122). The war obviously slowed the social whirl of Vicksburg, the nearest big town. When visiting the Confederate citadel in the fall of 1862, Kate complained that "nothing was going on there and I was glad to get home as quiet as it now is and will be, I suppose, until the close of the war." Many of her friends had left town; she optimistically suggested that the Confederacy would soon win the war and society would return to its gay self in Vicksburg and elsewhere (142).

In the spring of 1862, the Stones could hear the booming of artillery at Vicksburg—it turned out to be just Confederate gunners testing their guns, but it foreshadowed the moment when invading Federal troops would actually appear. On June 25, Kate wrote, "well, we have at last seen what we have been looking for [sic] weeks—the Yankee gunboats descending the river. . . . They are polluting the waters of the grand old Mississippi." Called outside by one of the slaves, the family watched a "dark, silent, and sinister" gunboat glide round the bend near their plantation, followed by three more and a troop transport—whose passengers "had the impudence" to wave at their resentful audience. When one of the hated boats turned toward the Stones' landing, the family hightailed it into a nearby cornfield, despite an officer's shouting at them to come back. The boat soon rejoined the tiny convoy, however, and "we turned back to the house, a hot excited lot of people, and the dinner cold on the table." "Oh, how we hated" them "deep down in our hearts," seethed Kate, "not the less that we were powerless to do [them] any harm" (122–123).

Within a fortnight slaves had begun running away to the nearby Union encampments, where they were put to work on fortifications and on building a canal around Vicksburg's earthworks. Kate reported that "there has been no attempt at resistance" by the locals, but a few plantations had been burned by foraging parties anyway. Others, depending on the "temper of the officer in charge," were spared. Amanda made plans to have the male slaves taken into the backcountry, "if she can get them to go. Generally when told to run away from the soldiers, they go right to them and I cannot say I blame them" (128).

A few plantations had been burned by foraging parties . . .

With the Vicksburg Campaign approaching its climax in the spring of 1863, Kate described "the life we are leading now" as "a miserable, frightened one—living in constant dread of great danger, not knowing what form it may take, and utterly helpless to protect ourselves." On March 22, Federal troops raided Brokenburn for the first time, taking Kate's favorite horse. As if the arrival of the invaders wasn't bad enough, the nearly constant rain during the months since Christmas cast a pall over everything. Some of their neighbors believed that the heavy cannonading at Vicksburg caused the rain. "It is seldom we hear the cannon that it is not succeeded by showers or a downpour," admitted Kate. Even beyond the immediate scene of fighting, the country was "in a deplorable state. The outrages of the Yankees and Negroes are enough to frighten one to death. The sword of Damocles in a hundred forms is suspended over us, and there is no escape." A neighbor's slaves ran off to the Yankees, then returned with a squad of soldiers who carried off "every portable thing." Some of the runaway slaves who camped near Lake Providence had been armed by the Union officers, "and they are a dreadful menace to the few remaining citizens." The countryside "seems possessed by demons, black and white." The leisure activities with which the family members had filled their peacetime lives seemed hollow and supercilious now: "We beguile the time sewing and reading well-thumbed books, starting at every sound, and in the evening play backgammon or chess" (184–185).

After delaying for several months, once Kate's mother made the decision to leave the plantation, the family quickly packed and headed for the relative safety of Monroe, Louisiana, a three-week journey that was made all the harder by the news that Walter had died of fever. The eighteen-year-old had been in the army for only a few months before dying, with his African American servant "the only familiar [face] near him." Kate agonized over the circumstances and tragedy of Walter's death, comforting herself with religious bromides: "Happy boy, free from the toil and turmoil of life, safe in the morning of life in a glorious immortality" (187). By the time Coley became the second casualty of the family late in 1863—he died in Mississippi after being crushed by his falling horse—the family was living in Texas.

Cover of History of the United States, *showing men, women, and children traveling with soldiers, wagons, oxen, and horses (Library of Congress)*

Walter's death rocked the tight-knit family, but they could ill afford to dwell on it. They were at the beginning of the toughest journey of their lives. It had begun with a ride through a swamp and six-hour trip on a dugout to Delhi, on the Mississippi, with seven white people, assorted slaves, dogs and cats, and a little baggage. The smoke from burning cotton—planters were ordered by the Confederate army to keep their crop from falling into Union hands—clogged their lungs. They wilted in the stifling heat, one of the slaves was sick, and the little boat was so crowded that, once ashore, they welcomed the chance to stretch their legs during the wearying mile-long walk into town. Delhi was crammed with fellow refugees:

> such crowds of Negroes of all ages and sizes, wagons, mules, horses, dogs, bag-gage, and furniture of every description, very little of it packed. It was thrown in promiscuous heaps—pianos, tables, chairs, rosewood sofas, wardrobes, parlor sets, with pots, kettles, stoves, beds and bedding, bowls and pitchers, and every-thing of the kind just thrown pell-mell here and there, with soldiers, drunk and sober, combing over it all, shouting and laughing. (191)

All the escaping throng "have lost heavily," and "all had their own tales to tell of the Yankee insolence and oppression and their hairbreadth escapes." They filled the air with their stories of woe and hardship. "Nearly everybody took his trials cheerfully, making a joke of them, and nearly all are bound for Texas." The good cheer would be fleeting, and, for the Stones, Texas would hardly be a panacea (191).

But first they had to float, walk, and ride through northern Louisiana. In addi-tion to the normal discomforts of nineteenth-century travel, they encountered refugees, flee-bitten hotels, crude food, and a company of black men—it is unclear from Kate's rather hysterical recounting of the incident whether or not they were actually Union soldiers—who spent two hours terrorizing the party of refugees staying in a hotel in Trenton. One of them gestured wildly with a pistol and threatened Kate, her mother, her sister, and anyone else in view. No one was hurt, but many of the fleeing Southerners lost most of their personal belongings. Outside, there were other "strange Negro men standing around." They remained silent, but "looked at us and grinned and that terrified us more and more." The estate of some friends was sacked by a crowd of such men, and the Stones felt lucky to get out of town before a full-fledged race riot broke out (195–197).

As Kate would later recall "In Retrospect," everything in the Stones' lives had turned upside down, from the comfortable beds and chairs they had left behind to the awful food they choked down on the road, from the uncertainty of everyday life to the shocking lack of respect shown them by African Americans. Once the family reached Texas, they sojourned for a few weeks here and there until finally, after nearly four months in the state, they found an acceptable place near Tyler, a bustling town near the Louisiana border where a fairly large community of refugees had landed. The slaves were, by and large, hired out to local planters and farmers, and the white members of the household settled in for the duration of the war.

One of the side effects of the war was the great responsibility it placed on youngsters, especially teenaged boys whose fathers and older brothers were away with the army. Walter and James Stone became men in fact, if not in age, during the war. They managed the slaves, conducted plantation business, and undertook wearying journeys through the dangerous countryside. Even as the Yankees bore down on Brokenburn, seventeen-year-old Walter traveled eighty miles to Monroe, Louisiana, to purchase the year's supplies (128).

There were, it turned out, limits to Walter's maturity. When he went off to the army in the autumn of 1862—before turning eighteen—he displayed hints of the boy he still was. On the day he left, Kate recorded his deep feeling. "He could hardly speak to Mamma in all the time we were in Vicksburg without his voice quivering and his eyes filling with tears. . . . Poor little fellow, it is his first parting from home and going among strangers, and he feels so lonely and cut adrift from us all" (151).

In his older brother's absence, fifteen-year-old Jimmy became, as Kate called him, "Mamma's right hand" and de facto man of the house. He journeyed to Mississippi to obtain leather for the slaves' shoes and, his proud sister reported, became "a 'cute' little trader"—meaning a shrewd bargainer (153). Once the family was safely away, Jimmy went back for the slaves. He recovered virtually all of them, skirting Union patrols, wading bayous, and hiding out in cane fields during the day. Brokenburn had been taken over by the Yankees. The slaves considered themselves free and were working for themselves and for the Union. Jimmy got them off under cover of night, at gunpoint. Later, in Texas, Jimmy was sent off with only a few slaves and a wagon for a seven-week trip to Navasota to buy salt and other provisions. The youth seemed to flourish in the face of adversity and responsibility. When he returned, according to his sister, he was "looking very well, much improved by the trip" (240). Still later, Jimmy and his mother had to take the place of their overseer, Mr. Smith, who was periodically taken away to serve in the militia in Texas.

At one point during their trek to East Texas, Mrs. Stone, worn out by worry and travel, laid her head in Jimmy's lap, where she slept soundly. On the road, in the emergency, the roles of parent and child had been reversed. Stranger things would happen during the Stones' two-year absence from Brokenburn.

To a certain extent, once the Stones were settled more or less comfortably in Tyler, they returned to their normal roles and pastimes. The boys and "Little

Sister" attended a local school, and the women managed the home and went visiting. Once Kate mildly rebuked—in her diary—another refugee because she "still clings to her river custom of riding every day" (256). Kate still occupied her time reading, sewing, gossiping, visiting, and receiving visits from an attentive young lieutenant named Henry Bry Holmes. The social scorecard kept in peacetime was maintained during the war; one day in late 1864, even as the Confederacy entered its last gasp, Kate happily remarked that she and her mother "Have paid up all our calls" (308). Indeed, Kate admitted once that the last year in Texas was the most pleasant of her young life.

But there were rough spots in their lives, particularly in their relationships with their new neighbors. The extraordinarily unself-conscious arrogance that the wealthiest refugees exhibited toward the less fortunate Southerners with whom they came into contact shone through in Kate's opinions about the residents of Tyler, Texas. "The more we see of the people," she wrote shortly after the Stones settled in, "the less we like them, and every refugee we have seen feels the same way." She chalked the Texans' attitude up to "envy, just pure envy. The refugees are a nicer and more refined people than most of those they meet, and they see and resent the difference." She did add, "that is the way we flatter ourselves," but the Stones clearly did not relish their contact with the great unwashed (238). Shortly after arriving in Texas and while they were staying for a day or two with a family of strangers, Kate disgustedly recorded seeing a servant wash the dishes—dishes on which they would be expected to eat later—in the duck pond "right out in the yard." When it was time to eat, "half a dozen dirty, unshaven men took their seats in their shirt sleeves at the dirtiest tablecloth and the coarsest ware" (226). Nearly a year later they attended a barbecue, but a friend complained that it "was not clean enough to eat" and asked, "'why should we dine with plebians?'" After making an appearance and seeing "the animals feed," in the memorable words of Kate's mother, the Stones returned to their home and enjoyed their own, presumably more sanitary, dinner (292).

Other local habits amused or distressed the Louisianans. When the Stones attended a large "Baptist meeting," Kate noticed among the "country-looking congregation" only "a sprinkling of nice people." The loud worshipers, with their "anxious, excited faces, crowding and surging around the altar; the exalted, earnest mien of the minister; the groans and shrieks and wild prayers of the mourners," the thunderous hymn singing, was enough "to thrill and interest anyone," Kate admitted. Yet, she sniffed, "I must take my religion more quietly" (241).

Texas never really seemed like home to the Stones. It "seems like a hard land for women and children," Kate wrote soon after reaching the relative safety of the Lone Star State. "They fly around and work like troopers while the men loll on the galleries and seemingly have nothing to do" (227). Kate felt like she was in a different world, where "we hear no news . . . but accounts of murders done and suffered by the natives. Nothing seems more common or less condemned than assassination." Within one week she heard of four or five murders; worse, "no one . . . seems surprised or shocked, but take it as a matter of course that an obnoxious person should be put to death by some offended neighbor" (227).

> *"No one . . . seems surprised or shocked . . . that an obnoxious person should be put to death by some offended neighbor."*

The antipathy was hardly one-sided, at least according to Kate. Nearly as soon as the family settled in Tyler, Jimmy and a few other refugee boys became the object of scorn and physical threats at the school they attended. Apparently set off by the fact that the refugees were better off—Jimmy wore black broadcloth clothes and "a little strand of gold" for a watch chain—the Texans began sticking pins in Jimmy and his friend during church. In good Southern style, Jimmy issued a challenge to one boy, which was refused. Soon the boy's father got into the mess, demanding that Jimmy be expelled and warning Mrs. Stone that Jimmy had to stop wearing his "fancy" clothes. The drama continued for several days, with Jimmy claiming that several of his enemies were actually wearing pistols to class. Eventually Jimmy had to leave the school (249–250). Jimmy's problems with his Texan neighbors ended when he went off to join the army at the age of seventeen, but his little brother Johnny also ran into trouble with the locals from time to time, most notably in March 1865, when he had a fistfight "with a Tyler boy" and "came off decidedly second best." He was sore and stiff and squinted through a huge black eye, but, unlike the controversy of a year and a half before, a larger confrontation between refugees and "natives" did not ensue (325).

Despite the hardships and tragedy experienced by the Stones, they were hardly representative of most Southerners, or even of most Southern refugees. Most of the poor, sad Southerners forced away from their homes had far fewer resources at their disposal than the Stones. A *Charleston Courier* correspondent reported the bitter comments of a poor woman he encountered on the road in Tennessee. "It's a hard lot, gentlemen, to have to leave your house in this way and look for another among strangers" (Merrill, 152–153). A diary less famous than Stone's but no less useful to historians, Cornelia Peake McDonald's shows another family headed, for a lengthy part of the war, by a woman, who bounced around Virginia for most of the conflict. She and her children were often sick, her husband died in the army, a baby died shortly after birth, and they endured extraordinary poverty. Encountering unfriendly Union troops at every step, sometimes unable to find food, Cornelia barely made ends meet by teaching. Her sons also brought in a little money cutting firewood for the Confederate government, but sometimes Cornelia was forced to borrow money from friends. She steadfastly counted pennies, but was stunned to find that $100 in Confederate money bought only poor bacon, three candles, and a pound of nearly rancid butter. She would have relished living as well as the Stones, even in their reduced circumstances.

The war ended with the Stones still trying to figure out the Texans among whom they lived. The family and most of their now-freed slaves made the "sad journey to the old scenes" on the Mississippi in the autumn after the war ended—with "no money, no credit, heavily in debt, and an overflowed place"— and for two years fought floods, boll weevils, sagging prices, and rising labor costs. They found the house to be in better repair than most of the dwellings overrun by Yankees, but the absence of beloved brothers and cousins and friends left sentimental corners empty and sad. By 1868, the family had moved to a new, rented place called Rose Hill, and Kate was cautiously optimistic. She was proud of her surviving siblings—"what splendid fellows my brothers are"— and relieved that her mother retained her "bright hopeful spirit" (377).

Yet the war changed everything for the Stones. As Kate recalled in her introductory reflection, the struggle "swept from us everything and life since '65 has been a long struggle for the necessaries of life." From the baggage they lost in their initial flight from Brokenburn to the deaths of Walter, Coley, and countless other friends and relatives, to the collapse of their way of life, the war years were, by and large, lost years for the Stones. Kate took some comfort, she wrote, in the emancipation of the slaves. "The great load of accountability was lifted, and we could save our souls again" (8). Yet she mourned the passing of the old days. "Life seemed so easy and bright before us when in the winter of 1861 commenced the great events that swept away this joyous future and set our feet in new and rugged paths." Forty years later, she sadly commented, "we are still walking the same rough path, laden with heavy burdens" (11).

Kate seemed to have learned something about herself, however. Looking back at her life before the war, she realized "what an unthankful, wicked girl I was not to be supremely happy. With youth, health, and everything surrounding me for comfort and happiness, with unmistakable blessings, I was yet an unsatisfied, discontented girl." The war had "taught me my faults, and how earnestly I try now to enjoy instead of repine, to be thankful instead of fault-finding. I will try always to see the silver lining to the cloud" (378).

We do not know if she lived up to her promise to be more self-aware and optimistic. We do know that Kate finally married in 1869—the Lieutenant Holmes who had courted her (vainly, at first) in Texas—bore several children (two of whom survived to adulthood), and became a respectable wife, mother, and citizen of her little town, active in the United Daughters of the Confederacy and in the local book club. She never traveled to the North or, it appears, anywhere else. She died in 1907.

PRIMARY SOURCES:

Anderson, John Q., ed. *Brokenburn: The Journal of Kate Stone, 1861–1868.* Baton Rouge: Louisiana State University Press, 1955. Unless otherwise cited, all quotations are from this source.

McDonald, Cornelia Peake. *A Woman's Civil War: A Diary, with Reminiscences of the War, from March 1862.* Edited by Minrose C. Gwin. Madison: University of Wisconsin Press, 1992.

Merrill, James M., ed. "'Nothing to Eat but Raw Bacon': Letters from a War Correspondent, 1862." *Tennessee Historical Quarterly* 17 (June 1958).

SECONDARY SOURCES:

Campbell, Randolph B. *A Southern Community in Crisis: Harrison County, Texas, 1850–1880.* Austin: Texas State Historical Association, 1983.

Massey, Mary Elizabeth. *Refugee Life in the Confederacy.* Baton Rouge: Louisiana State University Press, 1964.

Chapter Four

"A Species of Passionate Insanity": Women of Vicksburg

When she arrived in Vicksburg on a beautiful spring day in 1863, toward the beginning of the final campaign against that Confederate stronghold, Mary Ann Loughborough asked a friend living in the disputed city, "How is it possible you live here?" The friend answered, "After one is accustomed to the change," she answered, "we do not mind it; but becoming accustomed, that is the trial." This reminded Mary Ann "of the poor man in an infected district who was met by a traveler and asked, 'How do you live here?' 'Sir, we die,' was the laconic reply. And this is becoming accustomed." Comparing the civilians of Vicksburg to the victims of a plague seemed particularly appropriate to Mary Ann, who asked herself on that sunny and glorious April morning if "I could believe that over this smiling scene . . . the blight of civil warfare lay like a pall—lay over the fearful homesteads . . . lay by the hearthstones, making moan in many a bereaved heart looking forward with vague fears to the coming summer" (Loughborough, 12).

The campaign of that summer would blight more homesteads, interrupt in awful and irrevocable ways thousands of families, and further fray the already thin veil between the battlefront and the Mississippi Delta home front. In Vicksburg, as in other Southern cities besieged later in the war, including Atlanta and Petersburg, Southern civilians became casualties, experienced extraordinary hardships, and witnessed the sharp end of war in ways that few Americans have ever endured. The three women who produced the documents considered in this chapter reveal a mixture of hope and honor, despair and res-ignation, and pluck and courage shared by many Southerners. Through their eyes the six-week-long siege of Vicksburg becomes a microcosm of the Southern home front.

Although the actual siege of Vicksburg lasted for only the month and a half prior to July 4, 1863, the day on which the city was surrendered to General Ulysses S. Grant, the campaign for the "Gibraltar of the Confederacy" had begun more than a year earlier. Because the guns of Vicksburg commanded the river, the city was one of the most imposing obstacles to Northern control of the Mississippi. In addition, as long as Vicksburg remained in Confederate hands, supplies and men from Confederate states west of the river—particularly Texas and portions of Louisiana—could con-

" 'How do you live here?'
'Sir, we die.' "

tinue to flow into the hard-pressed eastern Confederacy. Vicksburg became the chief target for Union forces after the fall of New Orleans in April 1862 and of Memphis two months later. A flotilla of riverboats appeared below the city in May 1862; after Confederates refused to surrender, the Yankees staged a halfhearted attempt to shell the city into submission but retreated back to New Orleans late in the summer.

Even as the Federals pulled back, the defenders got busy building fortifications; eventually an army of 30,000 men with over 170 cannon would protect the city. Late in 1862, two separate land forces under Grant and General William T. Sherman approached the city, but Confederate raiders cut Grant's supply line and Sherman's men were badly defeated at Chickasaw Bayou northeast of Vicksburg. The following spring, Grant marched his army down the west bank of the river, and Union gunboats forced their way past the Vicksburg batteries. The land- and river-based forces met below Vicksburg, where Grant crossed the river on May 1, marched inland to Jackson, defeated several small Confederate forces, and bottled up Vicksburg from the east. By May 19, the Union army was on the outskirts of the city, and although two frontal attacks against the Confederate defenses failed, they would sustain a short, tight siege that would sap the energy and will of the defenders and of the civilians trapped among the bluffs and streets of the sprawling city.

The battles for Vicksburg were a nightmare for everyone involved. The frequent skirmishing, punctuated by major assaults and the occasional explosion of huge mines placed in tunnels that were dug under Confederate lines by Union soldiers; the stench of rotting flesh—of horses and humans alike—broiling in the Mississippi heat; and the nearly constant shelling of the city created nearly unbearable conditions. Dysentery and malaria struck the troops on both sides as well as the civilians crowded into the city, many of whom huddled in caves burrowed into the many hillsides. Supplies dwindled steadily, and by the end of June, Confederate soldiers subsisted on rationed water and tiny amounts of rice and peas. Not surprisingly, the nightly bombardments from Federal guns monopolized everyone's attention. "Shells were plainly seen," a girl wrote years later, "with their tiny flames of light shooting through the air, making that peculiar scream that the old darkies used to say meant, 'Whar is you? Whar is you?' and when they exploded 'Dar you is'" (Broidrick). Mrs. W. W. Lord described the "horrible shells roaring and bursting all around" her family and neighbors,

Union forces attacking Confederate entrenchments at Vicksburg (Library of Congress)

"the concussion making our heads feel like they would burst." Her own four children were quite young, and one of the women with whom she shared a cave had a ten-day-old baby. She proudly reported that her "children bear themselves like little heroes." Every night, "when the balls begin to fly like pigeons over our tent and I call them to run to the cave, they spring up . . . like soldiers, slip on their shoes without a word and run up the hill" (Lord, 3–4).

No amount of courage could offset the misery spawned by the siege. A series of letters from her sisters to a woman living in San Antonio provided excruciating details of the cost to the civilians of Vicksburg, including the diphtheria deaths of four of her youngest siblings during the opening days of the Union attack. The letter also reported that at least three women had been decapitated by Union shells, that a little boy had died in a cave, and that the young son of an Irish couple living nearby was killed during the shelling. Lavinia Shannon wrote to Emmie Crutcher that a neighbor had "heard screams down [in the kitchen] one morning and ran down there. A piece of shell had passed through the bed where the child was laying cutting it in two and its legs were sticking out of the wall where the shell had driven them and still kicking." The horrifying scene had "killed" the sick mother, "and the Father rushed all about town screaming and going on terribly" (Crutcher-Shannon Family Papers, Lavinia Shannon to Emmie Crutcher, July 13, 1863).

A Southern wife prays in a makeshift home during the bombardment of Vicksburg.
(Library of Congress)

Three documents—a diary and two memoirs—offer a sampling of the experiences and attitudes of women who survived the civilians' ordeal at Vicksburg. Although obviously quite similar in the topics their authors broach and in the facts of the battle that find their way into the documents, they do show how three different women responded to the greatest challenge of their lives. Emma Balfour's diary shows a young woman making the best of the situation with poise and equanimity; a memoir about a soldier's wife, Madge Brown, reveals the demands made on Vicksburg women who responded in ways that transcended gender and many other of society's conventions; and a book-length memoir by Mary Ann Loughborough presents the most complete description of the daily tension and strain faced by besieged civilians.

Forty-three-year-old Emma Balfour was the mother of five children between the ages of one and ten and the wife of a prominent local doctor when her hometown became the target of one of the great campaigns of the Civil War. Her guests witnessed a dramatic scene straight out of a romance novel when her 1862 Christmas ball was interrupted by the appearance on the river of the first Yankee invasion force. Her diary, which she kept from May 16 through June 2, 1863, began with defeated Confederate troops falling back on Vicksburg and the start of the incessant shelling that dominated the memories of most Vicksburg

A Confederate soldier and two women dodge a Union shell in Vicksburg. Painting by the turn-of-the-century illustrator Howard Pyle, who was a small boy during the Civil War (Hulton Archive)

civilians. Her worst moment came early in the siege, when she had taken refuge in a cave with a number of friends and neighbors. "Just as we got in several machines exploded, it seemed, just over our heads," she wrote a couple of days after the experience, "and at the same time two riders were killed in the valley below us by a twenty-four pound shell . . . so you see we were between two fires. As all this rushed over me and the sense of suffocation from being underground, the certainty that there was no way of escape, that we were hemmed in, caged:— for one moment my heart seemed to stand still—then my faith and courage rose to meet the emergency, and I have felt prepared since and cheerful" (Balfour, May 20, 1863).

This attitude prevailed through the rest of the period covered in her diary. Despite frequent descriptions of houses torn apart and of civilians and soldiers alike being killed and wounded, Emma retained her calm. Indeed, a little over a week into the siege, she recorded—with a certain amount of humor—a night in which, although the barrage remained heavy and explosions occurred quite near the house, she and her family went to bed "and slept as if we were in safety. Now and then when a shell exploded nearer than usual or the house shook more than usual we would listen for a while and then sleep again." Her husband commented that "he begins to realize now that we can get used to anything." Not everyone faced danger in the same way: "Poor Mrs. Crump does not get used to it and it is pitiable to see her at every shell jumping up and crouching with fear" (ibid., May 27, 1863).

Emma gained something of a reputation around town for the calmness with which she faced the siege. She was already taking care of a sick officer when the chaplain of an artillery battery stopped to ask if she could take in a badly wounded lieutenant who was "in a highly excited nervous state." The chaplain had "heard I was the coolest lady in town, never discomposed by the shelling and he thought my calmness would keep him cooler and so prevent any future effects." Emma "could but laugh but I told him I would take him with a great deal of pleasure and do my best for him." The officer never appeared, but Emma appreciated the compliment and exhibited that coolness on many occasions: feeding troops during their retreat into Vicksburg; refusing to panic when a servant cried that the Yankees had overrun nearby Confederates, believing—correctly, it turned out—that the soldiers dashing over a nearby hill were actually reinforcements rushing toward rather than away from the enemy; and calmly explaining the physics and psychology of ducking artillery shells: "You must understand that it was not in the usual way we walked down the street," she wrote. Pedestrians "had to take the middle of the street, when we heard a shell and watch for it, and this was about every half minute. You may imagine our progress was not very fast. As soon as a shell gets over your head you are safe for even if it approaches near, the pieces fall forward and do not touch you, but the danger is that sometimes while watching one—another comes and may explode or fall near you 'ere you are aware" (ibid., May 23, 1863).

Although Emma Balfour's story focused on the perils of the bombardment of the city, another brief memoir about a soldier's wife named Madge Brown, written for a collection of wartime memories by Mrs. Lou Clarke of Vicksburg, presented the whole gamut of experiences of Vicksburg women and was meant as a testament to Southern women's steady support of the Confederate war effort. Madge's story began with the departure of her husband with one of the first contingents of Confederate troops to leave the city early in 1861. As cars full of soldiers departed the station, wives, daughters, sweethearts, and mothers saw them off with baskets of food and clothes and with more intimate keepsakes. Mrs. Clarke reported that "their hearts seemed crushed, their eyes were filled with tears and their lips quivered with deep emotion"—except for one young wife and mother, who was asked, "Why did you shed no tears?" She replied: "Because my storeroom is empty and my pocketbook is empty, and he knows it. I had to seem brave to keep him from breaking down" (Clarke, 444).

That brave and independent woman was Madge Brown, whose wartime career Mrs. Clarke portrayed as demonstrating the best qualities of Vicksburg women in particular and of Confederate women in general. She made ends meet by sewing uniforms for the soldiers early in the morning and late in the evening and by teaching school in between. Her clients paid her with pumpkins, potatoes, butter, and firewood. Later, once the siege began, she earned a little extra money making hats from palmetto leaves; with the Confederate army fallen back on Vicksburg, and "ambitious to help the Cause as well as maintain herself," she also went to work baking bread and pastries for the soldiers (ibid., 444). Her husband was fighting with one of the artillery units defending the city, and, like a Civil War Molly Pitcher, Madge borrowed a horse and traveled the three dangerous, shell-pocked miles between her home and the front every day, carrying food to the several men of his battery. She eventually lost the horse, but replaced it by setting out in the morning with a bridle and simply catching the first loose horse she could find, dodging shells all the way. Madge's exploits resembled many of the adventures and attitudes of home front women in the South. She nursed back to health a soldier with pneumonia and confronted a speculator who was charging hundreds of dollars for barrels of flour. Through it all she frequently came under fire, barely missing serious injury when shrapnel from a shell ripped her dress and, on another occasion, when she slipped through a floor partially destroyed by a shell.

Even when the siege finally ended, Madge's trial was not over. Her husband was quite ill and, through a loophole in the surrender agreement, could not be immediately paroled. As a result, he was sent to Memphis and then St. Louis—accompanied by Madge, who forced her way into Federal offices and onto military steamboats to argue her husband's case. The siege of Vicksburg and its aftermath pulled young Madge far beyond her routine existence to a time and place where she had to deal with Yankees shooting at her, eke out a meager living with no help from her husband or family, and confront, in decidedly unusual situations, both Confederate and Union officials.

Mary Ann Loughborough was a Missourian married, like Madge Brown, to a Confederate soldier. She came into Vicksburg twice, once for a short visit early in the campaign, later to take refuge. She first traveled from her house in Jackson to the river town in mid-April 1863, when the delightful spring scenes of the countryside and the anticipation of seeing friends inspired "a very happy heart and very little foreboding." She wrote that she "had been planning a visit to Vicksburg for some weeks, and anticipating pleasure in meeting our friends. How gladly, in a few days, we left it, with the explosions of bombs still sounding in our ears!" On the way into town they had passed peaceful scenes of plantations so far untouched by war: young colts and mares standing in meadows, milk cows trudging home on ancient cow paths, a girl reading the newspaper to her father on a veranda (Loughborough, 9–10).

Knowing of the shelling by Union gunboats a year earlier, Mary Ann anticipated more damage to the streets and buildings than she actually saw, "though very few houses are without evidence of the first trial of metal." She was awestruck by a house in which it could clearly be seen that a cannonball had passed first through a window and a door and then after clipping the corner of a piano had passed through the far wall (ibid., 11).

Coincidentally, the first night of Mary Ann's visit was also the night that Union transports and gunboats ran the batteries of Vicksburg on their way south to rendezvous with Grant's troops. Mary Ann had been sound asleep, worn out after a "delightful" ride. In the middle of the night a booming cannon shook her awake, and she dashed to the veranda overlooking the Mississippi, where hours before she had spent a pleasant evening listening to military bands playing in the Confederate entrenchments. There she and her hosts watched the hulking black masses of Union navy vessels churning past the city, illuminated by fires set on the far shore. They returned the fire of the Confederate batteries, and shot and shell soon began falling among the houses on the river bluffs. Mary Ann soon found herself dashing—sliding, actually—down the hill behind the house to the cave. Part of her had wanted to remain, but when a shell exploded at the side of the house, "fear instantly decided me," and she scrambled down the hill, avoiding yet another near miss. She reached the cave mouth "breathless and terrified" and without one of her slippers, which was still somewhere out on the dark hillside. Mary Ann's slight loss of dignity matched a sheepishness over her anxiety: "I was sorry to find myself slightly fluttered and in a state of rapid heart-beatings, as shell after shell fell in the valley below us" (ibid., 16–17).

Mary Ann had "seen the elephant"—as the soldiers would say about their first combat—and survived, but she was glad to get back to her home in Jackson. However, Grant's rapid and dramatic move into the interior soon placed the capital city at risk. Although fortifications were constructed

One night the Southern sky was lit with the fires set by Union forces . . .

and a battery was placed near the house in which she lived, Mary Ann doubted that the city would be defended—especially after she found out that the commanding general's wife had been sent to safety in Mobile. Mary Ann and several other friends decided to go to Vicksburg, where the danger from gunboats seemed less than the threat posed by the Union soldiers and "the rabble that usually followed a large army" who were flooding the countryside. Mary Ann journeyed to Vicksburg a second time, without incident, and she settled into a quiet, genteel life of sewing in the morning, riding in the evening, and reading reassuring newspaper reports that "all was right." Everyone believed that the "matter would be decided some distance from Vicksburg" (ibid., 34–35).

Nothing could have been further from the truth, of course, and one night the Southern sky was lit with the fires set by Union forces in Warrenton, a little town near the river. Worse news began to arrive, and when Confederate wagons, horses, and dusty and despairing soldiers began to pass through town, the residents crowded the sidewalks, asking the soldiers what had happened. "We are whipped," one replied, "and the Federals are after us." Some of the crowd began to heckle the defeated boys and men. "I could not but feel sorry for the poor worn fellows," wrote Mary Ann, "who did seem indeed heartily ashamed of themselves" (ibid., 42–43). The city was soon stifled with a blanket of "dejected uncertainty," and the final siege of Vicksburg had begun.

Like many of her fellow besieged, Mary Ann spent much of her time in a cave hollowed out of a convenient hill. Hers had three rooms—a six-feet-deep entrance, fitted with a cloth "door," branching into a "T" with a bedroom on one side and a dressing room on the other. Although she had to crouch in the front room and bedroom, enough earth had been scooped out in the other room for her to stand upright. In this little space she "went regularly to work, keeping house under ground," fixing meals of corn bread and bacon, and slowly growing accustomed to her "shell-expectant life" (ibid., 60–62).

From time to time Mary Ann reported on the casualties of the siege: the little boy crushed by a shell that entered a nearby cave, the frightened and starving horses belonging to the army and to private citizens, the mangy wild dogs that hovered just outside the ring of light cast by cooking fires (who soon disappeared into Confederates' stews!), and soldiers falling to disease and gunfire in the rebel lines. "How very sad is this life in Vicksburg," she wrote (ibid., 81). "I endeavored by constant prayer to prepare myself for the sudden death I was almost certain awaited me. My heart stood still as we would hear the reports from the guns, and the rushing and fearful sound of the shell as it came toward us." As it descended to earth, "the noise became more deafening; the air was full of the rushing sound; pains darted through my temples; my ears were full of the confusing noise; and, as it exploded, the report flashed through my head like an electric shock, leaving me in a quiet state of terror." The physical sensations were matched by psychological pain, as Mary Ann held "my child to my heart—the only feeling of my life being the choking throbs of my heart, that rendered me almost breathless." The "terrible fright" returned again and again through a typical night of shelling, after which "morning found us more dead than alive, with blanched faces and trembling lips" (ibid., 56–57).

But the heavy ordnance had its own particular brand of beauty, too. A few nights later, Mary Ann sat at the mouth of her cave, "watching the brilliant display of fireworks the mortar boats were making—the passage of the shell, as it traveled through the heavens, looking like a swiftly moving star" that, as it fell, "seemed to leave behind a track of fire." The shells on this night were passing safely over her refuge, which certainly helped create the illusion that it was all simply a fireworks show. "The incendiary shells were still more beautiful in appearance. As they exploded in the air, the burning matter and balls fell like large, clear blue-and-amber stars, scattering hither and thither" (ibid., 64).

The calm that such a night inspired in Mary Ann could vanish in the instant of a near miss. One morning the shells fell "so thickly" around her yard that she feared an explosion would collapse the cave. As a result, she, her little girl, and the servants left the cave and found shelter in the exposed roots of an ancient tree that stretched over the bank into which the cave had been dug. Almost immediately a shell fell in the opening of the cave. Although there was no serious physical damage, the psychological damage was clear, as Mary Ann found that "my past resolution having forsaken me, again were the mortar shells heard with extreme terror, and I was many days recovering the equanimity I had been so long attaining" (ibid., 67).

The dreary and terrifying days were brightened by little things: a soldier bearing the gift of a pair of apples, as exotic to the besieged young mother as a pineapple; "little trinkets" carved from bullets by a friendly and skilled major from Texas, including a tiny armchair and a plough; the singing that drifted over from a nearby headquarters whenever officers gathered to make out their reports. One original piece was set to the tune of "Listen to the Mockingbird," with "Listen to the Parrott shells" substituting for the traditional chorus (ibid., 107, 119).

One of Mary Ann's worst moments, perhaps because her two-year-old daughter witnessed it, occurred toward the end of the siege. A young soldier named Henry had often stopped by to see the little girl, bringing her flowers, apples, or other small presents. His visits had lightened the girl's days. Whenever she saw him, she would "call his name, and clap her hands gleefully," and exclaim about his beautiful black horse. One day Mary Ann heard an explosion down the ravine and saw a horrific sight: one man dead, and Henry staggering about, "holding out his mangled arms—the hands torn and hanging from the bleeding, ghastly wrists—a fearful wound in his head—the blood pouring from his wounds." Stunned and in shock, he cried to unnamed comrades, "Where are you, boys? O boys, where are you? Oh, I am hurt! I am hurt! Boys, come to me . . . Almighty God, have mercy!" Henry and his friend had been trying to remove the powder from an unexploded shell when it had blown up—and Mary Ann's little daughter had seen it all. She "clung to my dress, saying, 'O mamma, poor Henny's killed! Now he'll die, mamma. Oh, poor Henny!'" She was right; the maimed boy died by nightfall (ibid., 128–129).

Mary Ann and her daughter survived the siege; they left the city when the Yankees moved in, waiting for her husband to be paroled. A Northern press published her account of the siege, dramatically and anonymously named *My Cave Life in Vicksburg*—"by a Lady"—while the war still raged. Following the war, in addition to raising four children, Mary Ann published several other books and served as editor of the *Southern Ladies Journal*.

The chronicler of Madge Brown's wartime adventures noted that "History will never record the privations endured" by the women of Vicksburg, "because they will never tell them—they endured and were silent" (Clarke, 444). That may have been true for a time, but among the most popular genres of Civil War writing over the years have been the memoirs of Southern women from the Civil War era and, during the last ten or twenty years, books about Southern women during the war. These sources are important for a number of reasons—including their insights into gender relations, child rearing, and women's roles in the nineteenth-century South—but perhaps most importantly for revealing just how thin the line between combatant and civilian could become when Northern forces broke through Southern defenses. C. Vann Woodward, the great Southern historian, wrote in *The Burden of Southern History* that the South's history was different from the North's in a number of ways, not least of which was its experience with invasion and defeat. The women of Vicksburg knew that nearly a century before Woodward articulated it, and their experiences reflect the most destructive and dangerous element of the Confederate home front.

PRIMARY SOURCES:

Balfour, Emma. Diary. Mississippi Department of Archives and History, Jackson, MS.

Broidrick, Annie Laurie. "A Recollection of Thirty Years Ago." Chapel Hill: Southern Historical Collection, University of North Carolina.

Clarke, Mrs. Lou. "The Siege of Vicksburg." *Our Women in the War: The Lives They Lived, The Deaths They Died.* Charleston, SC: News and Courier Book Presses, 1885.

Crutcher-Shannon Family Papers. Center for American History, University of Texas at Austin, Austin, Texas.

Lord, W. W. Journal. Library of Congress, Washington, DC.

Loughborough, Mary Ann. *My Cave Life in Vicksburg.* New York: D. Appleton and Co., 1864.

SECONDARY SOURCES:

Arnold, James R. *Grant Wins the War: Decision at Vicksburg.* New York: John Wiley & Sons, 1997.

Bearss, Edwin C. *The Campaign for Vicksburg,* 3 vols. Dayton, OH: Morningside, 1985–1986.

Miers, Earl Schenck. *The Web of Victory: Grant at Vicksburg.* Baton Rouge: Louisiana State University Press, 1984.

Schultz, Duane P. *The Most Glorious Fourth: Vicksburg and Gettysburg, July 4, 1863.* New York: W. W. Norton, 2002.

Winschel, Terrence J. *Triumph & Defeat: The Vicksburg Campaign.* Mason City, IA: Savas Publishing, 1999.

Woodward, C. Vann. *The Burden of Southern History.* Baton Rouge: Louisiana State University Press, 1960.

Chapter Five

Culture Clash: Invaders and Rebels in the Occupied South

Their encounter began like thousands of others, as Northern armies paused in Southern towns and villages. Whenever officers established their headquarters in civilians' houses and soldiers went foraging, they never failed to meet terrified, curious children. After cautious glances and half smiles, despite childish patriotism and jaded soldierly habits, young and old alike nearly always called a quick truce. When Union troops passed through a little Florida town, not long after the Battle of Olustee, a young Southerner and a Union officer came upon each other.

At first, little Eddie Bradford was eager to meet the stranger, especially when he asked him to "come and talk to me awhile, I have a little son at home just your size." Eddie climbed into the kindly man's lap and they chatted pleasantly, until the youngster asked him, "Don't you hate Yankees?" Taken aback, the officer confessed that he was a Yankee. Eddie burst into tears, jumped to the ground, and ran to his grandfather. "I sat in his lap and just a month ago they killed my . . . dear uncle Mack," he sobbed. "Do you think, grandpa, that this Yankee killed him?" Of course, the young Northerner, who understandably hurried away after Eddie's outburst, had nothing to do with the death of Eddie's beloved Confederate uncle, but even that remote possibility caused the little boy to question his own loyalty to the South and his love for his uncle (Eppes, 272–273).

As Eddie's experience shows, deep ambivalence characterized the relationships that formed between civilians in the occupied South and Northern soldiers, who demonstrated both cruelty and compassion toward the child and adult Southerners they met. A striking example of that disturbing combination occurred very late in the war, when Union troops stormed into Columbia, South Carolina. Despite the excitement, a small girl continued playing with her puppy on the front steps of her home. A Union soldier, in an act of astonishing meanness, brained the dog with the butt end of his rifle as he ran by. The girl naturally burst into tears. Moments later, another soldier stopped, consoled the child, made a tiny coffin out of a cigar box, and dug a grave for the martyred pet.

Out of such conflicting images and attitudes sprang the legacy of soldier-civilian relationships in the Civil War South, relationships that called into question notions about the character of Northerners and Southerners, the rights of civilians living in occupied territory, and even the nature of "womanhood." In addition, white Northerners and Southern African Americans met one another in large numbers, really for the first time, forcing each group to scout new trails through the confusing terrain of American race relations.

Not surprisingly, the stereotypical response to the invasion of the South was hostility on the part of Southern whites and relief and celebration on the part of Southern African Americans. Often bemused and sometimes angry Yankees routinely wrote home about the steadfast Confederate patriotism of the women they met. During the war, most Northerners believed that most Southern females acted to a greater or lesser extent in the same way that the ladies of New Orleans greeted General Benjamin Butler's forces when he took over the captured city in the spring of 1862. On at least one occasion, a woman dumped the contents of a chamber pot out of a window and onto the head of a passing Union general. So virulent was their hatred, so insulting was their behavior, so contemptuous was their demeanor toward Yankees that Butler issued his famous order comparing them to prostitutes. Indeed, during the first year of the war, the intransigence of Southern civilians—many of whom President Lincoln and other members of his administration had assumed were still largely Unionists—convinced the government to establish martial law and to treat residents of occupied territory as conquered enemies rather than fellow Americans. The reception of Union troops by black Southerners inspired a very different but corresponding set of images in popular prints, in pictures produced in the illustrated weeklies, and in songs and speeches. Smiling crowds of freedmen and women crowded around their liberators, who, in turn, welcomed the chance to help drive a stake through the heart of slavery, the wicked cause of the rebellion.

In both cases, the reality was far more complex—and more interesting—than these stereotypes. As one journalist touring the defeated South just after the war reported of Southern women, they "are very polite to Yankee officers in particular, but very bitter against Yankees in general" (Silber, 27), and that is a key point: human nature seems to demand that people respond to other people at different levels—as members of a group and as individuals. It is easy for us to believe the worst—or the best—about a person we have never met, as long as he or she belongs to a group whose salient characteristics we already believe we understand. When we actually meet a person belonging to that group though, when a more complicated reality intrudes on easily digested assumptions, everything changes. Myths are exploded and illusions are challenged. That process also occurred countless times throughout the Confederacy, becoming one of the constants of the Southern home front experience.

Northerners encountered the whole spectrum of Southern civilians during the war, ranging from wealthy aristocrats, middle-class professionals and small farmers, and poor whites, to say nothing of the slaves and free blacks who constituted over a third of the Confederacy's population. The demographics of most towns and counties occupied by Federal forces had changed dramatically from the beginning of the war. A

A woman dumped the contents of a chamber pot out of a window and onto the head of a passing Union general.

motley crew of Southerners remained in any given town or region by the time Federals occupied it. The Confederate army had, of course, evacuated a place before the Yankees arrived, but so had high-ranking civil officials; even local politicians feared arrest or worse if they were captured by Union troops. Most of the healthy men between the ages of eighteen and fifty were in the army by the end of the war; the boys, old men, and invalids remaining nevertheless often departed before they could be seized by Northerners ferreting out saboteurs or spies. Wealthy residents were the most likely civilians to leave, taking with them as much movable property as they could carry and many of their slaves. So, in many parts of the South, the society that Federal forces encountered was probably not quite what they expected: poor whites, middling sorts, those trying to protect their property from the invaders, and others who for one reason or another found it impossible to leave. As a result, most of the civil and social leaders of Southern communities were gone, leaving the rest to their own designs.

The challenges of living in an occupied region were many. Without fail, personal property, livestock, and food stores became fair game for Northern foragers. Although property rights were far more likely to be respected by soldiers serving garrison duty than by soldiers who were just passing through—it was safer to live in occupied Memphis, for instance, than to live along the path of Sherman's March—Southerners could rarely feel totally secure in their possessions. Of course, having hundreds, if not thousands, of young armed men living away from home, always on the lookout for something to do when they were off duty, and freed from the anxieties of combat, did not make for a particularly quiet or secure atmosphere for Southern civilians to endure. Economic distress, plunging morale caused by the presence of an enemy from which their own army was supposed to protect them, worry over absent fathers and brothers and sons, and countless other sources of stress and disappointment wearied people living in occupied territory. The uncertainty of who was in charge—their own civil authorities or the U.S. military—also weighed heavily on Southern civilians, who often had to swear oaths to the United States to be allowed to move about the country, conduct business, or execute legal documents.

There was, moreover, always the threat of personal danger. Although violence abounded in border states and in the hill and brush country of the South, where guerrillas and vigilantes warred on each other and on civilians alike, relatively few noncombatants were actually harmed intentionally by volunteers in the Union armies. That was small consolation to Southern women and children, and the idea of violence, the knowledge of their vulnerability, was a painful worry for most Southerners in occupied areas. The author of the most thorough account of the relationship between Southerners and Yankees in the occupied South suggests that, although Southern women feared the worst, few were actually assaulted sexually. More common was an experience he calls "symbolic rape," which was especially prevalent whenever troops moved into a new region (Rable, 158). They would storm into houses, paw through personal possessions, destroy photographs, parade about with lingerie thrown over muddy uniforms, force women out of their beds, and ogle them as they scrambled to find decent clothing. Some spewed obscenities; a few exposed themselves to women and children. The experience was devastating, inspiring anger, fear, and resentment. "It makes my blood boil," one woman wrote, "when I remember that our private rooms, our chambers, our very inner sanctums, are thrown open to a ruthless soldiery" (Ash, 201).

Inevitably, Northern soldiers sometimes viciously attacked Confederate women and children. Rumors flew around the South of alleged atrocities, some involving children. An unverified newspaper story claimed Union troops had murdered a toddler because he was named for a noted Confederate general, a Confederate officer in Florida passed along a story that three Yankees had taken a ten-year-old girl into the brush and raped her, and a Louisiana woman reported that soldiers abused a girl so badly that she never regained her sanity. Yankee deserters and stragglers raided a Virginia plantation in June 1864; two of the men locked themselves in a room with the family's thirteen-year-old daughter until she offered to show her attackers where the family's valuables were hidden. Perhaps 600 Union soldiers were court-martialed for raping black and white civilians, mainly in the South, and the army executed at least twenty-two men for sex crimes. The historian Thomas P. Lowry sampled 5 percent of all Civil War court-martial records in the National Archives, finding at least thirty cases in which the defendants had committed or attempted sexual assault.

Southern women did not necessarily simply accept abuse when it came their way. When a Northern officer crudely teased one woman by suggesting that "we sometimes divest Southern women of their clothes," the woman stood her ground, declaring that if he tried it, he would never ride a horse again (Rable,

161). When threatened, women could protect themselves with loud screaming; at least one, in a scene straight out of *Gone with the Wind,* fired two shots at a soldier who had exposed himself.

One of the more complex relationships in the occupied South developed between Northern whites and Southern African Americans. With the most to gain from the appearance of Northern troops, blacks had a different point of view of the occupation experience—at least at first. Like their white counterparts, slave children did not quite know how to sort through the rumors and gossip about the nature of these Yankees and often awaited the appearance of Union troops anxiously. "I didn't know if they was varmints or folks," recalled Alice Johnson (Rawick, vol. 9, pt. 4, 60). On a Georgia plantation, black children longed for the Northerners to show up. "We wanted 'em to come," said one former slave, "we knowed 'twould be fun to see 'em" (ibid., vol. 13, pt. 3, 116). When Union troops did appear, some of the smallest slave children, whose masters had said all manner of bad things about the approaching army, were surprised that they were men rather than monsters, and gathered around to see the bright uniforms and polished buttons of the invaders and to listen to the blaring brass and sounding drums of their bands.

One of the more complex relationships in the occupied South developed between Northern whites and Southern African Americans.

As African Americans soon discovered, however, not all—or perhaps even most—Union soldiers worried about the plight of the African Americans. They were fighting to save the Union, not free the slaves, and although they cared little either way about the issue of slavery, they held many of the same racial attitudes as the secessionists against whom they fought. Not surprisingly, many African Americans' experiences with Northern soldiers displayed the sharp divide between the races.

Yankees often played pranks and committed careless cruelties against freedpeople. One company locked terrified black youngsters in a dark room, laughed when a pan of burned beans scalded a hungry boy's mouth, and repeatedly dunked a small child headfirst into a barrel of molasses. They teased young children with promises of gifts that never came and frequently forced slaves of all ages to perform improvised minstrel shows, apparently taking their cue from the blackface entertainments popular throughout the North. One reluctant boy finally danced when soldiers made him stand barefoot on a sheet of hot tin. Others threatened slaves when they refused to show them where jewelry and other valuables were hidden. Eager for plunder, soldiers rarely worried about what would happen after they continued on their march. On one plantation, a young girl finally told her inquisitors where her mistress's valuables were hidden. When he discovered this betrayal, her master hanged her for disloyalty. Adult slaves were often forced into work by Yankees setting up camp near Southern plantations. Worse cases of abuse occurred when soldiers reenacted one of the most demeaning facets of the slave system: raping slave women.

Although most atrocities were committed by individuals or small squads of soldiers detached from the main bodies of Northern troops, one of the most infamous cases of mass abuse of black Southerners by Union troops occurred during the famous March to the Sea. Despite their treatment at the hands of the men in blue—the Yankees frequently stole what little property slaves owned and deprived them of even the most meager provisions when they raided farms and plantations—hundreds of black refugees nevertheless attached themselves to General William T. Sherman's army. They survived by eating leftover rations and huddling under torn and discarded tents. The disdain with which Sherman's force considered the people they had freed became clear when the XIV Corps crossed Ebenezeer Creek between Augusta and Savannah, Georgia. Once the Union troops were across, its commander ordered the pontoon bridge taken up immediately, before the column of contrabands could cross. This doomed them to recapture or death. Many drowned trying to swim the creek, while others were killed by the Confederate cavalry and Southern guerrillas trailing the army. Similar, if less dramatic, demonstrations of racial antipathy occurred all over the South.

Incidents like these demonstrate the terrible hold of race on nineteenth-century Americans. Too often, encounters between slaves and Northern soldiers veered into the senseless violence and casual cruelty that characterized the period's race relations. However, the relationships that developed between Yankee invaders and Southern civilians they met sometimes transcended expectations and sectional hatred.

Southern children commonly described meeting Northern soldiers; indeed, first encounters became a set piece scene in many postwar reminiscences. They naturally expressed fear at first, likening the prospect of invasion to the terrifying stories of pioneer children captured by "savage" Indians that appeared in books like Peter Parley's popular *Child's History*. "My hair 'stood on end,'" remembered Sallie Hunt, "when I thought of the Yankees tying the children up in bags and knocking their brains out against a tree" (Hunt, 41, 45). A different but equally terrifying set of images plagued a little girl in New Orleans, who could think only of scenes of "captured cities of the Bible where men and women were cut through with spears and swords, and children were dashed into walls" (King, 5). An older girl, upon hearing that Yankees had been spotted not far from her home, wrote, "I am like a prisoner awaiting his doom!" (Rable, 156). After such harrowing, if imaginary, buildups, initial meetings were often

58

A sketch by Alfred Waud depicts women grudgingly lining up to receive rations from the U.S. Army in occupied Richmond, Virginia. (Library of Congress)

a bit of a letdown. A young Missourian was amazed to find that the Yankees were men, for she had feared they would "be some dreadful kind of animals" (Shippery, 136–137).

Many black Southerners recalled sympathetic soldiers among the Yankees they met. Most Northern soldiers had never seen a slave and many had never encountered black people. Some handed out sugar or candy and struck up conversations with old and young alike. Caroline Richardson, who was about ten when the war ended, recalled a conversation with a member of one of the Union regiments passing by her North Carolina home. He asked her how many shoes she received each year and what she wore during the summer. "When I tells him dat I ain't wear nothin' but a shirt, an' dat I goes barefooted in de summer, he cusses awful an' he damns my marster" (Rawick, vol. 5, pt. 3, 270–271). Other soldiers seemed to enjoy their roles as agents of freedom. One soldier ordered a young girl to never let anyone call her a "nigger" again. "You tell 'em dat you is a Negro and your name is Miss Liza Mixon," he said (ibid., vol. 6, 125). Slave boys went for rides on Union cavalry horses, earned money fetching water for companies camped near plantations, and showed soldiers where caches of money and liquor were hidden. Foraging parties sometimes gave the clothes and even the food they looted from plantations to the slaves.

White children also found themselves drawn to the dangerous-looking but surprisingly friendly strangers. Groups of boys would creep up near the encampments of Union soldiers, checking out their guns, their horses, and their demeanors. The well-dressed and orderly Union soldiers setting up camp outside Gallatin, Tennessee, greeted Opie Read and his playmates good-naturedly. A Wisconsin soldier spun tales of bear hunting in return for a slice of homemade peach pie, while when Opie later heard a Yankee sergeant reciting a Shakespearean quote from *McGuffey's Reader,* the boy gave him an old hen for supper.

As Northern soldiers and Southern children mingled, they often became fast friends, although some youngsters made a point of confirming their continuing loyalty to the rebel cause. When asked if she was afraid of the Yankees, an Alabama girl quipped, "No sir, not when they talk right." After Union troops reached Savannah, Georgia, late in 1864, a one-armed officer on General Sherman's staff took three-year-old Juliette Low on his knee. When she asked how he had lost his arm, he playfully replied, "Got it shot off by a Rebel." "I s'pose my father did it," Juliette forthrightly declared. "He shot lots of Yankees" (Low, 4).

A key to the readiness with which enemy soldiers befriended children was their desperate loneliness for their own sons and daughters, which perceptive Southern youngsters took as proof of their kindliness and trustworthiness. Dosia Williams's valiant attempts to remain aloof from the alarmingly friendly enemies who occupied her plantation collapsed in the face of an offer she could not refuse: an officer promised to show her the contents of a gold locket in return for a kiss. "I must have descended from Pandora," wrote Dosia years later, "for I could not stand it." She pecked him on the cheek and he showed her a "miniature of a lovely little girl about my age." Eventually, even Dosia's sister—who, apparently made of sterner stuff, at first refused the Yankee's offer—softened, and the colonel and the Williams girls became "great friends, and his aides brought us candy and made much of us." Knowing how much the Yankees "wanted to see their children back up North"—and, no doubt, appreciating the candy—the Williams girls "excepted these particular Yankees from our fear and hatred" (Wells, 21–22).

A few older girls and young women also were tempted by the forbidden fruit of intersectional flirtations, much to the disgust of their more loyal peers. Young ladies in occupied Natchez were quick to slight classmates spied walking with Union soldiers. The teenaged Nannie Haskins endured the Federal occupation of her Tennessee hometown with gritted teeth, sprinkling her diary with the usual complaints about the arrogance and cruelty of Federal officers as well as the fraternization by some of her schoolmates with the occupiers.

A sketch from Frank Leslie's Illustrated Newspaper *depicting contrabands trailing General W. T. Sherman's troops in Georgia (Library of Congress)*

One remarkable case of intersectional fraternization that sounds as though it came straight out of a dime novel was recorded by Russell H. Conwell, a former Union soldier who traveled through the South a few years after the war. His dispatches from Southern battlefields and cities were published in the *Daily Evening Traveller,* a Boston newspaper, in 1869. He visited battlegrounds and cemeteries, talked with former Unionists and Confederate veterans, and interviewed prominent rebel officers. One day in southeastern Virginia, near the scenes of great carnage and destruction during the Peninsula Campaign seven years before, he went to a country wedding.

His account of the wedding was a little condescending: the sophisticated Yankee describing the hopeful "darkeys" waiting for an "old-time feast"; the "lank, grisly-haired, mud-colored white men" leaning on the rail fence, "actually too lazy to hold up their hands"; the backwoods preacher stretching the ceremony "to a doleful length by prayers and exhortations"; the brawl of a dance called the "Virginia Reel," with "men laughing, women screaming, fiddle screeching until at last, all out of time and breath, they tumble into one mass of squirming humanity. Then the men all take a drink and the women fix their hair."

But the back story to this wild country affair was a romance born of a wartime encounter between a Yankee and a young Southern girl. The groom had been a member of the 31st New York and had been wounded during the fight at White House during the Peninsula Campaign in June 1862. Shot in the leg and unable to walk, he had been left on the field. Although counterattacking Confederates had passed nearby several times, he was incapable of reaching his own lines and, believing that he was dying, he began "hallooing" for help, but no one came. The next morning, faint from the loss of blood, he finally saw a young girl who shrieked when she saw him and began to run away. With his last ounce of strength, the wounded Yankee rose to one elbow and cried "For God's sake, Miss, don't leave me to die."

She hesitated, then turned. By the time she reached the soldier, he had fainted. Her dilemma was acute: on the one hand, "she feared that when he became sensible he might prove to be the monster she had heard the Yankees were." On the other, something had to be done for him "or his last words would haunt her all the days of her life." She could not tell her father, who had "threatened to shoot the first Yankee he saw." Instead, she sought the help of an old black woman, who, over the next several days, helped to conceal the soldier right under the nose of the girl's father. His wound worsened though, and the soldier convinced the girl and the African American woman to go to find help. They found a picket guard and convinced him that an ambulance must be sent for the wounded Yankee, who was taken back to Union lines and recovered, although his leg would be maimed for life.

After the war, the young soldier, "determined to find out what had become of . . . his benefactor," returned to Virginia. Although the black woman had since died, he did find the white girl, now twenty-one and so changed in appearance that he at first failed to recognize her. However, they fell in love, despite the woman's father, who still threatened to shoot the first Yankee he saw. After a brief correspondence, using African Americans as messengers, the father finally capitulated to his daughter's ultimatum and allowed the wedding to take place. Conwell concluded the romance by quoting Thomas Moore, "maids are best in battle woo'd," and by admitting that "we suppose it was so in this case!" (Carter, 48–53).

Romances like this one were fairly rare, of course, and most Southerners were not won over so easily. Some learned to hate Northerners with astonishing passion: "Yankee, Yankee, is the one detestable word always ringing in Southern ears," a Georgia girl declared late in the war. "If all the words of hatred in every language under heaven were summed up together into one huge epithet of detestation, they could not tell how I hate Yankees. They thwart all my plans, murder my friends, and make my life miserable" (Rable, 155). That was one side of the home front response to invasion and to the invaders. As always, real-life relationships on the Southern home front between loyal Confederates, African Americans, and Union soldiers reflected the ambiguities that arise whenever the immediate passions of war and deeper human instincts collide.

PRIMARY SOURCES:

Carter, Joseph C., ed. *Magnolia Journey: A Union Veteran Revisits the Former Confederate States*. Tuscaloosa: University of Alabama Press, 1974.

Eppes, Susan Bradford. *Through Some Eventful Years*. Macon, GA: J. W. Burke, 1926.

Hunt, Sallie. "Boys and Girls in the War." *Our Women in the War: The Lives They Lived; The Deaths They Died*. Charleston, SC: News and Courier Book Presses, 1885.

King, Grace Elizabeth. *Memories of a Southern Woman of Letters*. New York: Macmillan, 1932.

Low, Juliette. "When I Was a Girl." In *Juliette Low and the Girl Scouts: The Story of an American Woman, 1860–1927*. Edited by Anne Hyde Choote and Helen Ferris. Garden City, NY: Doubleday, Doran & Co., 1928.

Rawick, George P., ed. *The American Slave: A Composite Autobiography*. 19 vols. Westport, CT: Greenwood, 1972–1974; supplement, ser. 1, 12 vols., 1978; supplement, ser. 2, 10 vols., 1979.

Shippery, Eliza Freleigh. "Some War Experiences." Missouri Division, UDC, *Reminiscences of the Women of Missouri during the Sixties*. Jefferson City, MO: Hugh Stephens Printing, n.d.

Wells, Carol, ed. *War, Reconstruction, and Redemption on the Red River: The Memoirs of Dosia Williams Moore*. Ruston, LA: McGinty, 1990.

SECONDARY SOURCES:

Ash, Stephen V. *When the Yankees Came: Conflict & Chaos in the Occupied South, 1861–1865*. Chapel Hill: University of North Carolina Press, 1995.

Grimsley, Mark. *The Hard Hand of War: Union Military Policy toward Southern Civilians, 1861–1865*. New York: Cambridge University Press, 1995.

Lowry, Thomas P. *The Story the Soldiers Wouldn't Tell: Sex in the Civil War*. Mechanicsburg, PA: Stackpole Books, 1994.

Rable, George C. *Civil Wars: Women and the Crisis of Southern Nationalism*. Urbana: University of Illinois Press, 1989.

Silber, Nina. *The Romance of Reunion: Northerners and the South, 1865–1900*. Chapel Hill: University of North Carolina Press, 1993.

Chapter Six

A Lukewarm People: Home Front Dissenters in the Confederacy

At daylight on October 1, 1862, armed squads fanned out across Cooke County, Texas. Their movements were shielded by a heavy rain. They grimly approached dozens of houses and farms in the gray dawn, pounded on doors, and arrested perhaps 150 men "in the name and by the authority of the people of the County of Cooke, State of Texas." Some houses, one chronicler of the raid claimed, yielded "large quantities" of guns and ammunition, concealed in beds, ladies' clothes, and "every conceivable secret place." Wives sobbed, the men were hustled off to Gainesville, the county seat, and a general migration, sparked by "intense excitement," of guards, prisoners, citizens, and "screaming women and children" began toward the town. In other parts of the county, groups of men gathered to arm themselves and plan a rescue; at the same time, loyal men "grasped their guns and organized for defense." Throughout this corner of north Texas, "all were active and fully alive to a sense of the danger & peril of the next act in the exciting drama" (Acheson and O'Connell, 361–362).

The "next act" resulted in the deaths of at least forty-two of the accused conspirators—forty were hanged and two were shot while trying to escape. The commander of the local military district, Brigadier General William Hudson—as the man mainly responsible for administering the militia, he had directed members of the early morning posse to arrest men who had failed to show up for militia duty—created a "citizen's court" that quickly convicted and executed many of the suspects (ibid.).

Although the episode at Gainesville was an extreme case, similar events took place all over the Confederacy, where declining morale wore down the resources and energy of Southerners. Some men so opposed the Confederacy that they fled the South, joined the Union army, and fought against their fellow Southerners; Union regiments were recruited in each of the Confederate states. Nonslave-owning farmers who had no stake in preserving the plantation economy and no reason—beyond a potent racism—for supporting slavery found themselves fighting for a way of life only a few enjoyed. Conscription and its accompanying exemption clauses seemed unreasonably burdensome to them. Other Southerners disliked the Confederate government for impressing their slaves and taxing their farms and plantations. Ardent states' righters, including some leading secessionists, lost their stomach for rebellion when Jefferson Davis and other Southern nationalists moved to centralize power in ways that, to them, made a mockery of states' rights. More often, however, dissent stemmed from wartime conditions that tried the souls of Southern men and women. Shortages of food and other necessary items; the loss in battle or from disease of husbands, fathers, and sons; the belief that Confederate and state officials were incompetent or corrupt or both; and simple war weariness all contributed to an epidemic of disaffection that plagued many parts of the Confederacy to an increasing degree as the war dragged on.

Some men so opposed the Confederacy that they fled the South, joined the Union army, and fought against their fellow Southerners.

Some combination of these reasons led many to turn away from the Confederacy, and disaffection sprouted and grew in every Confederate state. Disaffection took many forms, ranging from outright disloyalty—deserting from the army and trying to evade conscription, sometimes violently—to opportunistic and lucrative practices like trading with the enemy, speculating in cotton or any other commodity, and depreciating Confederate currency. While many Texans participated in such activity, Texas was probably no more or less loyal than any other Confederate state.

Texans displayed all of the typical motivations for failing to support the Confederacy, and throughout the war some military leaders criticized the weakness of support in Texas for the Southern cause. Shortly after the defeats at Gettysburg and Vicksburg, General E. Kirby Smith, commanding forces west of the Mississippi, called the residents of his department "a lukewarm people, the touchstone to whose patriotism seems beyond my grasp." North Texas, especially, teemed with deserters and other disloyalists. "Any enemies in our midst who by their acts and public expressions clearly evince their disloyalty," he wrote to the commander of that section of the state, "must be disposed of" (*War of the Rebellion*, vol. 26, pt. 2, 285). Less than six months later, however, the military commander of Texas, Major General John B. Magruder, admitted that news from north Texas was "most gloomy" and that "a large portion of the people is disloyal" (ibid., vol. 34, pt. 3, 779–780). Clearly, the Confederate war effort in Texas was weighed down by a load of dissent and disaffection that demonstrates one of the most serious and divisive facets of the Southern home front, one that

VOLUNTEERING DOWN DIXIE.

A Northern cartoon satirizing Confederate efforts to recruit reluctant Southerners
(Library of Congress)

created tensions and conditions that challenged the supposed unity with which the South had gone to war in the spring of 1861.

One of the most hated and most subversive groups in the South were those who sought to make a profit from the war, regardless of how their entrepreneurial schemes hurt the Confederate cause. The Episcopal bishop of Austin, Alexander Gregg, assailed "The Sin of Extortion" in a sermon delivered in March 1863. The war had brought great hardships, challenges, and opportunities to Southerners, the bishop declared, and, unfortunately, "the spirit of Mammon" in the form of speculation had reared its ugly head. This was "a development more dangerous to our peace, and more hostile to our welfare, than foes of flesh and blood." Gregg warned against the "insidiousness of the evil, the temptations to its indulgence," and "its radically demoralizing tendencies" (Gregg, 2). Other observers joined the attack on merchants who charged high prices for everyday necessities. A letter to a Houston newspaper demanded that Texans "mark forever with a brand of infamy" those extortionists, "who no longer crawl like the slimy reptiles that they are, but boldly stalk through your streets, grinding at every step with their iron heels, deeper and deeper down, the poor man, the widow and the orphan" (*Houston Tri-Weekly Telegraph*, February 4, 1863).

All sorts of activities came under the definition of economic disloyalty, including charging high prices for the necessities that became more and more scarce as the war dragged on, refusing to accept inflated Confederate currency, and participating in the booming cotton market in Mexican border towns, where European and Yankee traders eagerly paid top dollar for scarce raw cotton. The trade violated the official Confederate cotton embargo, a foreign policy designed to force England and France to recognize the Confederacy, and also amounted to trading with the enemy, as tons of illegally traded cotton made its way to mills in New England. As early as November 1861, just a few months after the Confederate victory at Bull Run, the *San Antonio Weekly Herald* alerted its readers to the "treason" practiced by many San Antonio merchants of refusing to exchange gold and silver for Confederate paper money (*San Antonio Weekly Herald,* November 9, 1861). A Confederate soldier complained in his diary that San Antonio was "a town noted for extravagant prices and extortion." Merchants "will not change a Confederate note unless the soldier takes one half in goods at 3 times their price. . . . Don't think there are many good honest Southern people in Town." Other towns also had their share of less-than-loyal merchants (Smith, 12). The prices of salt and flour doubled after a few Houston speculators cornered the market late in 1861. Failing to accept loan payments in Confederate currency, whose value plummeted throughout the war, was particularly unpopular. Newspapers threatened to publish blacklists of persons who refused to accept Confederate money, and a military commission meeting in San Antonio sentenced a man to thirty-five days in prison and fined him $100 for turning down Confederate paper for a $20 debt. In 1862, the San Antonio Committee of Public Safety cracked down on "every little sharper, to whom a dollar is more important than national independence, every croaker, who has no faith in the success of our cause—and every Lincoln sympathizer." Their names, occupations, and addresses would be published in order to expose them to "the sudden, summary and condign punishment to be inflicted upon them by an aggrieved and outraged people" (*San Antonio Weekly Herald,* April 26, 1862).

As the war became harder, bloodier, and more hopeless, and as military service lost its charm for the men who had eagerly volunteered in 1861, the problems of desertion and conscript evasion became even worse forms of disloyalty. Many soldiers no doubt came to the same realization as the weary Confederate who complained just a few months after joining the army, "how I wish this war was over, there ain't a bit of fun in it" (Wiley, 34).

A letter from a soldier to the *Houston Tri-Weekly Telegraph* late in 1862 outlined some of the causes of dissatisfaction among Texas soldiers. The 2d Texas Infantry—stationed on the Texas coast—had not been paid in months.

A Lukewarm People: Home Front Dissenters in the Confederacy

> When we ask why the privates are not paid, all the satisfaction we get is, "No money for the soldiers yet." Yes, the poor soldier, who finds himself far away from home and friends, who risks his life for his country, is neglected, he falls sick, is sent to the hospital with not a dime in his pocket to buy any of the luxuries that a sick man requires. Vegetables are paraded before him, No money he says, and turns over and suffers. Week after week he lingers, and then fills an unmarked grave. (*Houston Tri-Weekly Telegraph,* November 5, 1862)

For these and other reasons, well over 4,000 Texans deserted from the Confederate army.

But desertion was not simply a military problem, for the demoralization reached far behind the front lines. Deserters and men seeking to avoid army service altogether left home, fled to isolated thickets and to the hill country, and sometimes formed armed gangs for self-protection. By the summer of 1863, Colonel John S. Ford reported that large groups of armed men were preparing to resist the authorities in the counties north of Austin. Three months later, Brigadier General H. E. McCulloch, commanding the northern subdistrict of Texas, estimated that at least 1,000 deserters were hiding in the woods in north Texas. One band guarded every road leading to their camps so closely "that not a man, woman, or child goes near them" undetected. The men "have sympathizers all through their country, and, if they can't be induced to come out peaceably, we will have trouble and bloodshed enough in this section to make our very hearts sick" (*War of the Rebellion,* vol. 26, pt. 2, 344–345).

The evasion of military service, like the sharp practices of economic disloyalists, struck deep divisions in Southern society.

Those wishing to avoid conscription in Texas used a large assortment of techniques to escape military service. Some stayed off the line by securing exemptions from friendly physicians, others left temporarily—supposedly to join a regiment forming elsewhere—when conscription quotas were being filled in their own hometowns. Some scrambled to find government jobs or other positions that exempted them from conscription. Other ways of avoiding duty included bribery, securing long furloughs immediately upon entering the army, and getting "detailed" from the army to perform some sort of necessary work, such as working in a saltpeter mine, at a saltworks, or as a slave overseer.

The evasion of military service, like the sharp practices of economic disloyalists, struck deep divisions in Southern society. Publicly, politicians and editors decried the disloyalty of erstwhile Confederates and suggested various modes of punishment. The *Brownsville Fort Brown Flag* urged all government agencies to follow the lead of the General Land Office by replacing all male clerks of military age with old men, and declared that young men who refused to go to war ought to be barred from holding public office in the future. Newspapers frequently published the names and descriptions of men absent without leave, while the army offered rewards ranging from $30 to $60 for the capture of wayward soldiers. Suspected deserters' families were sometimes dropped from relief roles, while the state senate passed a bill that would have prevented deserters from voting. One newspaper went even further, suggesting that deserters should not be allowed to own property or to marry in Texas.

Little could be done, and other disaffected Texans often joined with bands of deserters to resist attempts by the Confederate government to force them into the military. Like similar bands of desperate men who gathered together throughout the Confederacy, these often preyed upon Texas civilians, Unionists and secessionists alike. In October 1863, an Austin newspaper warned against going outside the city limits unarmed, "as there are jayhawkers all around us, hiding in the mountains, who have been frequently seen close by" (*Austin State Gazette,* October 14, 1863). One former slave remembered years later that parents warned their children not to wander into the nearby woods. "Dey was deserters hidin' in de woods, an' I 'spose dey thought de chillen would tell on 'em. So dey ketch dem an' whip dem an' scare dem an' sen' dem home so dey wouldn' come back no mo!" (Rawick, supp. 2, vol. 2, pt. 1, 64). Although the civil war among Texans never grew to the proportions of the chaos in border states like Missouri, violence between competing groups of Texans was commonplace.

Not surprisingly, the largest number of lawless deserters and hangers-on centered in north Texas, where pro-secession feelings had never been strong and where relatively few residents owned slaves. Cooke County had been settled by families from the border states—Tennessee, Kentucky, Indiana, Ohio—and although, like most parts of the South, local leaders tended to come from the ranks of large property owners and slaveholders, only 10 percent of the population owned slaves. Most were small farmers with no stake in the plantation system; worse, most were Unionists who had no interest in secession. In fact, Cooke County was one of a handful of Texas counties whose voters rejected secession in the statewide referendum held early in 1861. Other sections of Texas overwhelmingly supported leaving the Union, however, and the Lone Star State joined the Confederacy in March.

But resistance to the Confederacy grew in Cooke County—as it did throughout the South—especially when the Confederate Congress initiated conscription in the spring of 1862. After thirty Cooke Countians signed a petition condemning the new policy, several leaders of the petition movement were chased out of the state. Others remained, however, and they began to form small cells of dis-

A Lukewarm People: Home Front Dissenters in the Confederacy

loyalists apparently committed to resisting the provost marshals sent to track them down. However, a few leaders had allegedly made larger, secret plans, which quickly unraveled when a drunken member of the club boasted to a loyal Confederate. The alarmed confidant notified local authorities, who organized the soggy roundup of October 1. Militia units from surrounding counties and elements of several Confederate regiments hurried to Gainesville, and soon a mob of several hundred armed men gathered outside the courthouse. After an informal "town meeting" had selected a jury, the "trial" began on October 2.

Although little evidence of actual foul play could be found, and although the "confessions" printed in one newspaper reporter's account are pretty bland descriptions of secret meetings, signs, and handshakes, the facts could not stand in the way of outraged Confederate loyalty, and the citizens' tribunal promptly tried and condemned seven defendants; a mob seized and hanged fourteen more. A lull in the executions—the court had even considered releasing the remaining prisoners—ended when unknown assailants ambushed and killed two leading Confederates. The rejuvenated and enraged jury got back to business, sentencing another nineteen to death. Three alleged members of the conspiracy, who belonged to military companies, were later court-martialed and hanged.

News of the plot flew around Confederate Texas, which learned of an elaborate and dangerous campaign to overthrow not only a government but a social system. A newspaper report alleged that the organization had three progressively treasonous levels of membership: initiates in the first "degree" pledged themselves to secrecy and to "avenge a brother member's blood," while the second degree was committed to "robbing, jayhawking, &c," and the third "contemplated the re-establishment of the old Union." One chronicler even claimed that the group actually planned to wrench north Texas out of the Confederacy and to reenter the United States, with help coming from Union army units in Kansas and from "every hostile tribe of Indians then in arms against the South, and especially against Texas." The Unionists "openly denounced the Government, and vowed organized resistance to the Conscript Law"; they refused to work for "southern men," and "became a terror to their southern neighbors . . . while their conduct evinced a spirit of hate and revenge too intolerable to be borne." They allegedly had gone so far as to plan the murders of all loyal Southerners, including women and children—except for young marriageable girls—and the division of their property (*Texas Republican,* November 1, 1862).

George Washington Diamond, a young Texas newspaperman and Confederate soldier—who was also the brother of one of the officers involved in the hangings—was commissioned to write the "official" story of the incident.

Although he completed the manuscript in the mid-1870s, it remained unpublished until 1963, a century after the hangings. It contained lengthy excerpts from testimony, but its value lies in the rhetoric Diamond employed to describe the conspirators, which suggests something of the emotion and urgency that characterized Confederate responses to perceived disloyalty.

"Their conduct evinced a spirit of hate and revenge too intolerable to be borne."

Diamond's account begins with a brief history of the region, which emphasized the conflicting interests and backgrounds of the settlers. Not surprisingly, he associates the antislavery, pro-Union settlers as interlopers, "restless and adventurous in their dispositions, manifesting an unfriendly spirit toward the older settlers." More sinister, they were apparently receptive to the plots of Northern abolitionists, who were blamed for the so-called "Troubles" in the summer of 1860: a series of unexplained fires that politicians and others believed to be the work of a slave revolt. A number of slaves were hanged, and a posse trailed a Northern Methodist minister named Anthony Bewley all the way to Arkansas, dragged him back to Fort Worth, and hanged him without a trial.

Diamond dismissed political principles as a possible motivation for the conspirators. Rather, in his view, they saw the chaos brought about by war as the perfect opportunity for personal gain: "political sentiment" was a "pretext for their movements," and "they rejoiced that the general disturbance and confusion had given them an opportunity to gratify their revenge against a neighbor and sordid lust for plunder." Their supposed plans involved all of the bogeymen feared by Confederate Texans: rebellious slaves (who had begun the work with their aborted revolt in 1860), "savage" Indians (who by attacking the frontier would draw Texas militiamen away from north Texas settlements), Northern abolitionists (who would provide inspiration, encouragement, and an appropriately honorable, if false, motivation), and Yankee soldiers (who would provide the muscle once their allies in north Texas went to work). The suggestion that the conspirators planned to kill most residents of north Texas—except for the young women they wanted to keep for themselves—was perhaps the wildest accusation, which the court and most other observers nevertheless took at face value. Little wonder that Diamond could say with a straight face that the "Order," as it was often called, undertook "a regular system of robbery, rapine and murder unparalleled in the history of this country."

The extremist rhetoric employed by Diamond makes perfect sense when one reads the reports of the Confederate officers whose job it was to evaluate the loyalty of Texans. Major General John B. Magruder, commanding the District of Texas, indicated the extent of disloyalty in Texas when late in 1863 he wrote his superior, Lieutenant General E. Kirby Smith, that "my difficulties here would be as nothing, if the troops could be made to stay in the ranks and the people true to themselves." Magruder felt himself "surrounded . . . by traitors, [and] harassed by deserters and mutineers" (*War of the Rebellion,* vol. 26, pt. 2, 528–531).

Although none were celebrated by as eloquent—if unpublished—a propagandist as Diamond, similar episodes took place elsewhere in Texas. A prominent local politician and general managed to prevent another mass lynching by persuading angry townsmen to turn their prisoners over to military authorities. A Collin County legend—unconfirmed in official documents or newspapers— tells about the capture and hanging from a cottonwood tree on the town square of forty-two "bushwhackers" and conscription evaders in 1864. Here and there individuals and small groups of men were gunned down, lynched, or otherwise eliminated by vigilantes.

Disloyalty flourished in other parts of the Confederacy, too. "Peace" plots were uncovered in Arkansas, east Tennessee, and northern Alabama, among other places. Vigilantes executed hundreds of deserters and dissenters, courts ordered thousands jailed or deported from the Confederacy, and in North Carolina the 1864 election featured a slate of candidates from a "Peace Party" that offered a platform promising to end the war.

Dissent and disloyalty were central characters on the Civil War home front. Yet, after Appomattox, most Confederates tried to ignore the chapter of the Confederate past written by dissenting and disaffected Southerners. They were generally successful, as, like the soft folds of a worn Confederate flag, the unifying rhetoric of the Lost Cause gradually covered over tensions that had plagued the South during the war. In Texas, a series of family feuds in the decades immediately after 1865 settled a few wartime grudges, and even the German community, which had generally been sympathetic to the Union—and who suffered their own persecution by Confederate authorities during the war— blended into the general population. Like most Southerners, Texans reserved their calumny and their long memories for the Reconstruction policies of the radical Republicans and took their frustrations out on African Americans. By the beginning of the twentieth century, the role of dissent and disloyalty in the Civil War South was largely forgotten.

Despite the historical whitewash, disloyalty had been a crucial factor on the home front, where hardships were complemented by hard feelings; where sacrifice was accompanied by greed; and where the loss of loved ones was juxtaposed by a desire on the part of many to save their own skins. The South had willingly gone to war in 1861, united in thought and determination. As the war dragged on, however, cracks appeared in the home front façade that would not be repaired until the selective memory of the Lost Cause erased them.

PRIMARY SOURCES:

Acheson, Sam, and Julie Ann Hudson O'Connell, eds. "George Washington Diamond's Account of the Great Hanging at Gainesville, 1862." *Southwestern Historical Quarterly* 65 (January 1963).

Austin State Gazette, October 14, 1863.

Gregg, Alexander. "The Sin of Extortion, and Its Peculiar Aggravations at a Time Like the Present." Austin: Texas Almanac Office, 1863.

Houston Tri-Weekly Telegraph, November 5, 1862, and February 4, 1863.

Rawick, George P., ed. *The American Slave: A Composite Autobiography.* 19 vols. Westport, CT: Greenwood, 1972–1974; supplement, ser. 1, 12 vols., 1978; supplement, ser. 2, 10 vols., 1979.

San Antonio Weekly Herald, November 9, 1861, and April 26, 1862.

Smith, Thomas C. *Here's Yer Mule: The Diary of Thomas C. Smith.* Waco, TX: Little Texian Press, 1958.

Texas Republican, November 1, 1862.

The War of the Rebellion: A Compilation of the Official Records of the Union and Confederate Armies. Ser. 1, Vols. 26 and 34. Washington, DC: Government Printing Office, 1880–1901.

SECONDARY SOURCES:

Buenger, Walter. *Secession and the Union in Texas.* Austin: University of Texas Press, 1984.

Lonn, Ella. *Desertion during the Civil War.* New York: Century Co., 1928.

Marten, James. *Texas Divided: Loyalty and Dissent in the Lone Star State, 1856–1874.* Lexington: University Press of Kentucky, 1990.

McCaslin, Richard B. *Tainted Breeze: The Great Hanging at Gainesville, Texas, 1862.* Baton Rouge: Louisiana State University Press, 1994.

Moore, Albert B. *Conscription and Conflict in the Confederacy.* New York: Macmillan, 1924.

Tatum, Georgia Lee. *Disloyalty in the Confederacy.* Chapel Hill: University of North Carolina Press, 1934.

Wiley, Bell I. *The Road to Appomattox.* Memphis: Memphis State College Press, 1956.

Chapter Seven

"I Ain't Ashamed of Nuthin": Bill Arp Explains the Confederate Home Front

I ain't agwine to fight no more, I shan't vote for the next war. I ain't no gurilla. I've done tuk the oath, and I'm gwine to keep it, but as for my bein subjergated, and humilyated, and amalgamated, and enervated, as Mr. Chase says, it ain't so—nary time. I ain't ashamed of nuthin neither—ain't repentin—ain't axin for no one-horse, short-winded pardon. Nobody needn't be playin priest around me. I ain't got no twenty thousand dollars. Wish I had; I'd give it to those poor widders and orfins. I'd fatten my own numerous and interestin offspring in about two minits and a half. They shouldn't eat roots and drink branch-water no longer. Poor, unfortunate things! to cum into this subloonary world at sich a time. (111)

So concluded one of the most popular Southern humorists of the nineteenth century, Bill Arp—the pen name for Charles Henry Smith, the Georgian whose periodic epistles on politics and conditions in the South during wartime are among the more entertaining sources on the Civil War home front. Written in a thick Southern dialect with odd spelling and sparkling wordplay, Smith's reports from the besieged South fit into a tradition in American letters that reached its peak during the Civil War era. The best-known representative of this genre to modern readers is, perhaps, Mark Twain, but at the time of the Civil War several men were equally prominent as humorous writers and speakers: Artemus Ward (Charles Farrar Browne), Petroleum V. Nasby (David Ross Locke), and—a favorite of Abraham Lincoln's—Josh Billings (Henry Wheeler Shaw). Using humor to entertain, to score political points, or to shame politicians and voters into pursuing social and political reform, the humorist-essayist–public speaker was a popular character in Civil War–era America.

The century and a third that has passed since the Civil War has raised barriers to understanding all the intricacies of the humor of that era—modern readers of nineteenth-century humor simply do not get many of the jokes!

Charles Henry Smith (alias Bill Arp)
(From Bill Arp from the Uncivil
War to Date, 1861–1903, *1903)*

Despite the frequent inexplicable references and the sometimes agonizing puns, however, several characteristics make Arp's wartime writings, which are liberally quoted in this chapter, useful for understanding the Southern home front: his obvious pride in the South and blind loyalty to the Southern cause, his sadness about the economic and material conditions facing the average Southerner as the war intensified and Union armies drove deeper into the South, his cynicism about politicians and government officials in both sections, and his commitment to the notion of white supremacy.

One of ten children of a Vermont-born storekeeper, Charles Henry Smith attended several schools, leaving Franklin College (later the University of Georgia) just before graduating because his father had fallen ill. His varied professional career included stints as a merchant, lawyer, judge, and farmer. He and his wife Mary, who also had ten children, resided in Rome, Georgia—the "eternal city" in Arp's bulletins—from 1851 to 1877. Smith was one of Rome's leading secessionists and in 1861 entered the Confederate army as a staff officer in General Francis Bartow's brigade. After Bartow was killed at Bull Run on July 21, 1861, Smith was transferred to General George Thomas Anderson's brigade, where he rose to the rank of major.

Although Arp could refer to his combat experiences humorously—he once quipped that he had killed about as many Yankees as they had killed of him—he did witness some hard fighting. During the Peninsula Campaign in 1862, he "saw more of the horrors of war than ever before or after." In a haunting passage that belies the ironic tone of his letters, he recalled "a soldier who sat upon the ground with his back erect against a tree, his rifle grasped with rigid hands and the muzzle resting on the ground. He was sitting just where he fell, but his head was gone, entirely gone, and the blood still oozing from his neck." Later he crossed a makeshift graveyard on a swampy portion of the Seven Pines battleground, where wagon wheels cut deep into the marshy ground, opening shallow graves and revealing swollen bodies and mutilated limbs (Parker, 14).

Although he was sent home in 1863 on a medical discharge, Smith remained a steadfast Confederate, serving in the local home guard unit and as a judge on a special Confederate court investigating treason. As it did for many Southerners, Sherman's March forced the Smiths to leave their home. They went first to Atlanta, then to Alabama, then to the home of Smith's in-laws. When the family returned to their home in Rome, they discovered that it had been seriously damaged by Union troops.

As it did for many Southerners, Sherman's March forced the Smiths to leave their home.

Smith's career as a humorist and commentator had actually begun just after the Confederate bombardment of Fort Sumter in April 1861, when President Lincoln issued a proclamation ordering the Southerners to "disperse and retire." Smith, having some fun with the Union president, wrote a satiric letter addressed to "Abe Linkhorn," in which he said, "We received your proklamation, and as you have put us on very short notis, a few of us boys have conkluded to write you, and ax for a little more time. The fact is, we are most obleeged to have a few more days, for the way things are happening, it is utterly onpossible for us to disperse in twenty days. I tried my darndest yisterday to disperse and retire, but it was no go." Written in the form of a "friendly" missive to the Union president, the letter warned Lincoln that

> The fact is, the boys round here want watchin or they'll take sumthin. A few days ago I heard they surrounded two of our best citizens, because they was named Fort and Sumter. Most of em are so hot that they fairly siz[zle] when you pour water on em, and that's the way they make up their military companies here now—when a man applies to jine the volunteers, they sprinkle him, and if he sizzes they take him, and if he don't they don't. (19–20)

Smith later recalled that he "thought the letter was right smart, and decently sarcastic," and when he read it aloud to a small group of friends and townspeople, a wiry and virtually illiterate hunter, farmer, and ferry keeper named Bill Arp asked under what name he was going to publish it. When Smith replied that he had not chosen a pen name yet, Arp offered his own—and a Southern legend was born (Smith, *From the Uncivil War to Date*, 58). Smith's letters first appeared in local newspapers but were passed throughout the South from newspaper to newspaper; Smith apparently made nothing from them, although the positive response from civilians and soldiers alike encouraged him to write more.

Arp's letters appeared more regularly after Smith returned from the army. They traced the fortunes of the Confederacy and of his own family. Some of his best columns recorded the experiences of the "runagees"—refugees—fleeing before Federal forces. A few appeared while he was still in the service. In January 1862—"Ginnerwerry" in Arp-speak—his "Second Paper" complained of the difficulty of getting messages to President "Linkhorn" through the various disasters and defeats suffered by the Union at Bull Run and Harpers Ferry and the famous foreign policy dustup between Great Britain and the United States over the boarding of the English vessel *Trent* by Union sailors in late 1861. Along the way, Arp expressed his concern to Lincoln, the Yankee leader, about the turndown in the Northern economy, the disruption of railroads and canals on the border, and the quality of his troops (24).

Arp's frequent digs at the lack of Union progress in the war, always clothed in artificial sympathy and friendly advice, reveal his own deep loyalty to the Confederate cause and his belief that Southerners would sacrifice all for their new country. In 1863, he suggested that, since the Union had apparently and vainly set its goals too high, "Hadn't you better sublet the contrak to sum Uropean nations? Shore as you are born you'll need a heap of *undertakers* before you finish." Of course, the reason for Union failure was the plucky determination and courage of the Southern people:

> Mr. Linkhorn, sur, our peepul git more stubborn every day. They go mighty nigh naked, and say they are savin their Sunday klothes to wear after we have whipped you. They just glory in livin on half rashuns and stewin salt out of their smoke house dirt. They say they had rather fight you than feed you, and swear by the ghost of [John C.] Calhoun they will eat roots and drink branch water the balance of the time before they will kernowly to your abolition dyenasty. (33)

This is not to say that Arp looked the other way when Confederate officials violated states' rights or displayed the incompetence that humorists through the ages have delighted to point out in their leaders. In his "Eighth Paper," written as a stump speech to his "f-e-l-l-e-r-sitizens," Arp skewered some of the policies of the Confederate government as well as the opposition of some Southerners to those policies. For instance, recognizing that some merchants refused to accept Confederate paper money, Arp declared it "hily necessary for the peepul to git together and take sum akshun on the KURRENSY BILL," which, he had recently determined, was the "most monstrous maulstroom which the gographers describe as aboundin on the koast of Norway, but which by sum jugglery or hokus pokus or secret session hav resently bin brought and moved into the konfedersy, to swaller up all the money in cirkulashun." This had happened when the Confederate Congress had "barred the doors, and shot the winder blinds, and let down the kurtins, and stopped up the key holes, and went into a place kalled SEKRET SESSION, . . . a thing that plots, and plans, and skemes for a few weeks and then suddenly poaks it head out like a katawampus, and says, *Booh!*" From similar origins came the "KONSKRIPSHUN BILL, which has so long deprived you of the right to volunteer, and like a vampire gnawd away at your burnin and glowin patriotism," and "HABEUS KORPUS," which is, when suspended, "the mast savagerous beest that ever got after tories and trators." Of course, many Southerners did, indeed, complain about the centralization of power in the Confederate government—Robert Toombs and Alexander Stephens of Smith's home state of Georgia led the fight against some of the more federalistic elements of Confederate war policy—and Smith seems to have had as much sympathy for those opponents of centralization as he did agreement with the Confederate government on these matters (53–58).

Among his favorite targets on the Confederate side were the cavalrymen who foot soldiers throughout time had come to hate (a famous line among Civil War infantrymen was "Whoever saw a dead cavalryman?"). "Hurray for the cavalry!" Arp declared in a column devoted exclusively to the mounted soldiers:

> When a big battle has been fout by the infantry, and inimy is runnin, how majestic and sublime the cavalry appear, as they foller up the skedaddlers and holler "go it bobtail, we're gainin on you." When they are persuin a panik struk enimy, or layin wait for a train of kars, or assaltin a karavan of waggins . . . they load themselves down with dry goods, and wet goods, and blankits, and hats, and boots, and tiklers, and canteens. (63)

Arp "once heerd a poor infantry say, as he were huntin over the ground he fout, 'Let's go home, Jim, the cavalry has done bin here and licked up evry d-a-m thing—atter we whip the fite, they cum jist a rippin and a snortin, and a dodging around" (63). In fact, toward the end of the war, Arp predicted the Confederacy would live on because the Confederate cavalry would never be caught; they had prepared the entire war for the moment when their elusiveness and refusal to actually enter into combat with the Yankees would pay off. "The truth is, that the Konfederit cavalry can fite on, and dog em, and doge em, and bushwhack em, and bedevil em for a thousan years" (106).

The cavalry were, in a way, easy targets, and Arp played their reputation for laughs. More serious were the columns that explored his own experiences as a refugee, which revealed the hardships faced by Confederate civilians as well as some of the harsh feelings Arp developed toward Yankees. The real-life adventures of the Smith family meshed closely with those of Arp's "family," bringing a vivid immediacy to the normally bemused tone of Arp's columns. He succinctly and movingly described refugee life:

> When a man is arowsed in the ded of night, and smells the approach of the fowl invader, when he feels konstraned to change his base and becum a runagee frum his home, leavin behind him all those usussury things whitch hold body and sole together; when he looks, perhaps for the last time, upon his luvly home wher he has been for many delightful years raisin children and chickens, strawberries and

pease, li soap and in-guns, and sich luksuries of this sublunnery life, when he imagines evry onusual sound to be the crack of his earthly doom; when from such influenses he begins a dignified retreat, but soon is konstraned to leave the dignity behind, and git away without regard to the order of his goin. (65–66)

The Smith family and many of their friends and neighbors in Rome were caught up in the violence and degradation of Union general William T. Sherman's campaign against Atlanta. The Confederate commander had "asshoored" residents that "Rome wer to be held at every hazard . . . and the fowl invaders hurled all howlin and bleedin to the shores of the Ohio [River]," but when push came to shove, "the militery evakuashun of our sitty was preemptorly ordered," with "no whisper of alarm, no hint of the morrer cum from the muzzled lips of him who had lifted our hoaps so high" (67). The Smiths and many others, "with reluctant and hasty steps," fled their homes in the foggy wee hours of May 17, 1864. When the sun cut through the fog,

> Then wer xhibited to our afflicted gaze a hiway crowded with waggins and teems, kattle and hogs, niggers and dogs, wimmen and children, all movin in disheveld haist to parts unknown. Mules were brayin, kattle wer lowin, hogs wer squeelin, sheap wer blatin, children wer kryin, wagginers wer kussin, whips wer poppin, and hoses stallin. . . . Everybody was kontinualy looking behind and drivin befo—everybody wanted to kno everything, and nobody knu nothing. (69)

The Smiths spent months away from their home, traveling by mule cart and by train to Atlanta, then to Alabama, and finally back to Georgia. Like many Southerners, Arp commented on a popular new book written by "Sum frog-eatin Frenchman" called "'Lee's Miserbels,' or sum other sich name"—Victor Hugo's *Les Miserables* was published in 1862. The phrase, which obviously lent itself to the kind of wordplay employed by Confederate quipsters, seemed to resonate with Arp, who supposed that it contained stories about "the misfortunes of poor refugees. . . . and if any man gived to romans [romance] would like a fit subjeck for a weepin narrativ, we are now reddy to furnish the mournful materiel" (81). First pitching their tents in the "piney woods," the family was safe from Yankees and exposed to the "mounting seenry in this romantik country," but also exposed to the elements, including rain of biblical proportions, which ruined the little crop of peas they had planted (83). They next took the train to Columbus, Georgia, but then headed for his wife's family—where, unfortunately, the railroad did not run. While Smith was looking for a wagon to carry his "large and interestin family," they were actually captured and held for a few hours by Union troops, which "skeerd my poor wife so she couldn't talk for two hours" (86). Confederate cavalrymen scouring the countryside for horses and mules to be used by the Confederate army exacerbated the difficulties faced by Southern refugees. Once the family reached safety, Arp declared, "We hav now tride Mr. Sherman's front and his flanks, and found no pease; for the future we shall rest in the reer of his army, until dislodged by kauses unknown and unfourseen" (87).

Smith took his family home a few months later, after which his alter ego promptly wrote a letter describing

> the trials and tribulashuns, the losses and crosses, the buzzards and ded hosses seen on our jurny. . . . It wer in the ded of winter, thru snow and thru sleet, over kreeks without bridges and bridges without floors, thru a deserted and deserlate land wher no rooster was left to krow, no pig to squeel, no dog to bark, wher the rooins of happy hoams adorned the way, and ghostly chimniz stood up like Sherman's sentinels a gardin the rooins he had made.

With Arp and his wife were eight of their children; none had ever been "as hungry before in their life, as on that distressin jurny" (88–89).

Although their house was still standing—and although the shade trees Arp enjoyed sitting under so much were not cut down—most of their possessions had been taken or destroyed by the Yankees who had occupied the house in the Arps's absence. In a later letter Arp asked for the return of a packet of letters written by the author to his wife while they were courting: "Them officers hav got em, and I spose hav laffed all the funny part away by this time. They contained sum fool things that boys will write when they fall in luv, and my wife sometimes used em on me as reminders of broken promises" (98). Soon other residents of the town drifted home. "It was a delightful enjoyment to greet em home, and listen to the history of their sufferins and misfortins. Misery luvs company, and atter the misery is past there's a power of kumfort in talking it over and fixin up as big a tale as enybody" (91).

Lurking beneath the equanimity of most of Smith's columns was a more sinister attitude: his notions about race. During and after the war, Arp consistently defended slavery and ridiculed African Americans, not to mention Northerners who sought to emancipate them. Although Smith never possessed a large number of slaves, he did own a half dozen men and women during the 1850s, and his racism and his belief in slavery as the most appropriate relationship between the races emerges clearly. Indeed, the introduction to a 1960s edition of *Bill Arp's Peace Papers* referred to it as a "rancid book . . . an effusion of parochial ignorance barely concealed by a pretense of yokel humor" (vi).

A couple of months after Lincoln issued the Preliminary Emancipation Proclamation, Arp took pen in hand to write his "Third Paper," which pretended to congratulate "Linkhorn." This was a great moment in time, when Africa is to be unshackled, when Niggerdom ar to feel the power of your proclamation, when Uncle Tom are to change his base and evakuate his kabin, when all the emblems of darkness are to rush frantically forth into the arms of their deliverers, and with perfumed and sented gratitude embrace your exsellency and Madam Harriet Beechers toe! What a galorious day that ar to be! What a sublime ery in history! What a proud kulmination and konsumation and koruskation of your politikul hoaps! (27)

Two years later, after the Congress had sent the Thirteenth Amendment to the states for ratification, Arp's "Fifteenth Paper"—in which "Bill Arp Filosofizes on the War, Etc."—harshly dismissed attempts to change the fundamental relationship between white and black Americans.

Well, they say that old Abe's Kongress hav finaly and forever set all the niggers free, by mendin the Konstitution. How did that free em, or how did freeing em mend the Konstitution? The darned old thing hav been broak for forty years, and it is broak yet; but spose they hav freed em, it's no more than old Abe done three or four times by his proklamashuns. What does it all amount to? I want to by a nigger, and I had jist as life by a chunk of a *free* nigger as eny other. I don't keer a darn about his bein free, if I can subjergate him; and if he gits above his nature, I'll put 39 whelks rite under his shirt, and make him wish that old Linkhorn stood in his shoes. (103)

Even worse was a diatribe about the free African Americans who had come into Rome after emancipation: "Why the whole of Afriky have cum to town, wimmin and children, and boys and baboons, and all. A man can tell how far it ar to the sitty better by the smell than the mile-post. They wont work for us, and they wont work for themselves, and they'll perish to deth this winter" (113). Less virulent but no less confident in the necessity to preserve the South as a white man's country was a letter that declared, "the nigger wasent made to keep a post offis nor set on a jewry [jury]. He wasent made for intelektual persoots. He was made to dig, and ditch, and grub, and hoe, and plow a mule, and tote things about for white foaks, and nothing else don't soot him" (Parker, 73).

Despite his continued support for slavery and states' rights, Arp—and Smith—were heartily tired of the war by the time the Confederacy's long collapse began in earnest early in 1865. Arp related a conversation with a Confederate soldier who returned home after a time as a prisoner of the Yankees: "I am at home now for good. . . . I'm agin all wars and fitins. I'm posed to all rows, and rumpuses, and riots. I don't keer as much about a dog fite as I used to" (97). As Arp himself declared just after the war, "We had killed foaks and killed foaks until the novelty of the thing had wore off, and we were mity nigh played out all over. Childern was increasing and vitels diminishin" (117).

Bill Arp Explains the Confederate Home Front

Although he had no further use for war, Arp refused to back down in his support for states' rights and the Southern way of life. Another letter declared that he would never fight again and that he meant to abide by the loyalty oath he had sworn to the United States. However, "as for my bein subjergated, and humiliyated, and amalgamated, and enervated"—as some radical Republicans claimed—"it ain't so—nary time. I ain't ashamed of nuthin neither—ain't repentin—ain't axin for no one-horse, short-winded pardon" (111).

Even eight years later, in the "Prefase" to *Peace Papers,* Arp assured readers that his "war heat" had cooled, but complained about Northern attitudes:

> They've *sorter* let us slip back into the Union, but they've put task-masters over us, and sent carpet-baggers down to plunder us. They wont let us throw flowers on the graves of our poor boys who fell on their side of the fence. They wont give our invalid soljiers, or our widders and orfins any pensions. . . . To keep in offis, they must hav votes for the party, so they manage to mix up the skum and filth of our society with the niggers, and back em up with carpet-baggers and sustain em with bayernet, and all we can do is to stand off and look on. They don't keer no more for our rights or our feelins, than a Sinsinnatty butcher does about killin a hog. (13, 15)

Just after the war, in a letter entitled "On the State of the Country," Arp had admitted that "there's a heap of things to be thankful for. I'm thankful the war is over—that's the big thing. Then I'm thankful that I ain't a black republican pup. I'm thankful that [Radical Republicans] Thad Stevens and Sumner, and Phillips, nor none of their kin, aint no kin to *me.* I'm thankful for the high privilege of hatin all sich. I'm thankful I live in Dixey, in the State of Georgy" (122).

Thirty years after he wrote those defiant words, just before he died, Smith published a mellow memoir in which he summarized his life with the following benediction. "We have had more than our share of blessings. We have been blessed with health and the comforts of life. Of course the war made an inroad upon our peace and happiness for a time, but the good Lord preserved us and we suffered no dire calamity or affliction" (Smith, *From the Uncivil War to Date,* 30).

Although the immediate postwar years were difficult ones for the Smith family, "Bill Arp" took on a life of his own. Shortly after the war a Democratic newspaper published his wartime Bill Arp letters in a book entitled *Bill Arp, So-Called: A Side Show of the War.* The small printing—1,000 copies—sold out, but before a second printing could be completed, a Republican mob broke into the newspaper office and destroyed it.

Although his column certainly broached political subjects, Smith only dabbled in politics personally, serving briefly as mayor and alderman in Rome, as a state legislator, and as a member during its first few years of the Ku Klux Klan. He became famous throughout the South—and to a lesser extent throughout the

United States—with his nearly weekly columns in the *Atlanta Constitution*. They began appearing in 1878, and although they often expressed his admiration for the modernization of the South, they also cast a nostalgic eye back to the "Old South," suggesting that Smith—through his alter ego—was somewhat uncomfortable with the changes wrought by the war, Reconstruction, and the

Arp refused to back down in his support for states' rights and the Southern way of life.

ambitious and often quixotic attempts by "New South" advocates to remake the South. These columns were published in *Bill Arp's Scrap Book* (1884) and *The Farm and the Fireside* (1891). In addition, he published *A School History of Georgia: Georgia as a Colony and a State, 1733–1893* (1893), which was widely used in Georgia schools.

Smith, through the character he created in his columns and the lectures he gave throughout the South and, ironically, the North in the 1880s and 1890s, became a beloved, even venerated figure. He reminded Southerners of earlier, simpler, grander times, but also of their valiant efforts to preserve their way of life from what they believed to be Yankee aggression. He may have had that effect during the war, too, when in his letters to "Abe Linkhorn" or in his letters to the editor detailing his outrage over the latest Yankee atrocity, the hardships faced by average Southerners, or the grit and determination of the South, residents of the Confederate home front could see a little bit of themselves in the irascible, folksy, and plucky correspondent.

PRIMARY SOURCES:

Smith, Charles Henry. *Bill Arp's Peace Papers.* New York: G. W. Carleton, 1873. Reprint, New York: Gregg Press, 1969.

Note: Although the pieces were first published in *Bill Arp, So-Called: A Side Show of the War* (New York: Metropolitan Record Office, 1866), the editors, at Smith's request, revised the spelling. The original spelling was restored in most of the wartime pieces when they were republished in *Bill Arp's Peace Papers*. Unless otherwise cited, all quotations are from this source.

———. *From the Uncivil War to Date, 1861–1903.* Atlanta: Hudgins Publishing, 1903.

SECONDARY SOURCE:

Parker, David B. *Alias Bill Arp: Charles Henry Smith and the South's "Goodly Heritage."* Athens: University of Georgia Press, 1991.

PART II

Northern Society at War

Chapter Eight

George Templeton Strong and the Serious Job of Journalizing

Journalizing is a serious job just now. We are living a month of common life every day. One general proposition to begin with. My habit is to despond and find fault, but the attitude of New York and the whole North at this time is magnificent. Perfect unanimity, earnestness, and readiness to make every sacrifice for the support of law and national life. Especially impressive after our long forbearance and vain efforts to conciliate, our readiness to humble ourselves for the sake of peace. Still, I expect to hear only of disaster for a long while yet. (187–188)

So wrote George Templeton Strong, the New York blue blood, lawyer, and ultimate insider, who kept a detailed diary throughout his adult life. The Civil War added a sense of urgency to his "journalizing," however, as Strong's nearly daily entries became more a record of the war than of his personal life.

This transition had actually occurred a few days earlier, on the heels of an extended discussion of his and his cronies' response to the Confederate shelling of Fort Sumter, when Templeton uncharacteristically called on God in capital letters in a kind of benediction to his April 16 entry: "GOD SAVE THE UNION, AND CONFOUND ITS ENEMIES. AMEN" (187). Still earlier, when the morning newspapers had confirmed that rebels had attacked the barely manned and not-quite-completed fort in Charleston Harbor, Strong had begun his entry: "Here begins a new chapter of my journal, entitled WAR—EXSURGAT DEUS *et dissipentere inimici ejus, et fugerunt que oderunt eum a facie ejus. Amen!*" ("Let God arise, let his enemies be scattered; let those who hate him flee before him!")

Historians have thanked the muse of history for Strong's dedication to keeping a personal record of the great events of his life, which reveals much about the response of the Northern middle class to the crisis, from its ambiguous attitude toward President Abraham Lincoln to its corporate approach to organizing the home front war effort, and to its contempt not only for Southerners but for the working classes in the North, especially the Irish. Through it all, it is apparent that Strong and his cadre shared at least two deeply held values: a steadfast patriotism and an abiding interest in sustaining social order during the great crisis of civil war. Their work on behalf of their country did not entail risking life or limb on the battlefield; rather, they chose to honor their loyalty by applying their businesslike approach to supporting the war effort.

Strong began his diary in 1835 as a fifteen-year-old undergraduate at Columbia University (then Columbia College) and faithfully kept it until his death forty years later. The final word count of the many volumes he filled reached the neighborhood of 4 million.

"Here begins a new chapter of my journal, entitled WAR."

His habit of writing in it virtually every evening assured the freshness of the information he recorded and the rawness of the emotions and attitudes he expressed. A lawyer all his life, he wrote about his practice and about Wall Street financial markets, but also about his family, his hobbies, and his philanthropies. He spent many afternoons at meetings of the trustees of Columbia College and of Trinity Episcopal Church. His wife Ellen Ruggles Strong—Ellie—and his three sons (all under the age of ten when the war begins) naturally occupied prominent positions in the diary. This deep well of information about New Yorkers' responses to the Civil War was all about Strong, however, who emerged as often prickly and sometimes sensitive, with attitudes running the gamut from cynicism to patriotism, and with traces of both arrogance and humility.

Sprinkled among the discussions of committee meetings, war news, and politics are descriptions of everyday life for a well-heeled New Yorker, much of which was unaffected by the war being fought in far-off Virginia. (Like many northeasterners, Strong's attention almost never strayed to the vast war raging beyond Virginia.) He rarely put in more than a few hours of work at his law firm, occupying his time instead with meetings, lunches and dinners, confidential conversations, and attending the opera, theater, and symphony. He and his wife were patrons of the arts, and he confided to his diary knowledgeable and opinionated capsule reviews of the singers, actors, and musicians he saw. One of his favorite pieces of symphonic music was Beethoven's *Eroica,* which he heard in late 1864 at the Academy of Music. Although the performance was "slovenly," the "strength and beauty of the symphony was apparent nevertheless. . . . From beginning to end, it is an intense manifestation of that highest art which cannot be embodied in rules or canons of art" (254). Indeed, on another occasion, upon hearing Beethoven's Second Symphony, he recalled that "for one hour I forgot all about the war and . . . was conscious of nothing but the marvelous web of melodic harmony and pungent orchestral color that was slowly unfolding" (215–216).

But the war refused to be put aside for long, and most of Strong's wartime diary entries are about the war. Perhaps his most frequent entries revolved around his constant search for war news. He regularly scanned the headlines of the many newspapers published in New York, Republican and Democratic alike, although he often referred to newsboys' cries of some great breaking story as "puffery" and resisted buying the "bogus extras" put out by the major papers in between editions. Most days he checked in with friends and colleagues at various clubs and offices for the latest telegrams from Washington or the front.

Like many civilians on both sides, he fancied himself an expert in military affairs, tossing out jargon and comments on tactics and strategy like a West Pointer. During the Fredericksburg Campaign, Strong reported that Union general Ambrose "Burnside, having established himself on the right bank of the Rappahannock, seems to have engaged the Rebels at nine this morning, advancing his left under General Reynolds." In the meantime, the Confederates "have been throwing cavalry round his right, threatening Aquia Creek and the vital umbilical cord of railway on his rear. I knew and predicted they would do it," wrote the forty-two-year-old who had never heard a gun fired in anger, "and I would bet that there is not a gun or a regiment in position to block that old dodge of theirs, so often successful" (226).

Perhaps his newfound interest in the military, combined with his own steadfast loyalty, led him to the rather harsh conclusion that the only thing lacking in the Northern army was backbone. "God alone can give us good generals," he averred, "but a stern and rigorous discipline visiting every grave military offence [sic] with death" would "make us strong enough to conquer without firstrate generals" (201). Later he complained that "want of discipline in the army is our great danger, and that is due to want of virility in those who should enforce it. . . . At all our battles, nearly one man out of three has shirked and straggled, and not one man has been shot down by his commanding officer" (226).

Although he cited no sources for this bold claim, Strong often blamed the commander in chief for the absence of tough leadership in the army, and his love-hate relationship with Abraham Lincoln is one of the diary's most interesting elements. Just before the 1860 general election, Strong complained, "I don't feel like voting for Lincoln," but he saw no other honorable course of action (157). The gathering storm nurtured his conviction, however, and a few days later he approvingly described a procession of "Wide-Awakes"—pro-Lincoln activists—who packed the streets around the Palace Gardens, listening to Senator William Henry Seward deliver a rousing stump speech. "The show in the street was brilliant—rockets, Roman candles with many colored fire balls, Bengal lights, the Wide-Awakes with their lanterns and torches" and singing, interestingly, "Dixie." In the next paragraph he wrote firmly, "Think I will vote the Republican ticket next Tuesday. One vote is insignificant, but I want to be able to remember that I voted right at this grave crisis. The North must assert its rights, now, and take the consequences" (159). When election day came, Strong had to wait in line for an hour to cast his ballot.

Strong was hardly an abolitionist, although he was even less a supporter of slavery. African Americans appear as decidedly secondary characters in his diary, which is sprinkled here and there with the term "nigger" but really never confronts the issue of race. (Indeed, in this way he represents many Northerners.) For him, the war was about the relationship between the states and the Union—between the North and the South—and he believed that the time had come for the North and the U.S. government to stop giving in to the whims and demands of the slaveholding South. This is the standard against which he measured Lincoln and most other Northern politicians, and if at any time during the war he felt the president was not prosecuting the war harshly enough, he felt free to criticize him.

Strong's duties as treasurer of the United States Sanitary Commission frequently took him to Washington, where early in the war he sat in on a meeting with the president. In his characteristically forthright way—some would say harsh—he described the president's physical features and intellectual abilities with a mixture of contempt and perception. Lincoln was "lank and hard-featured, among the ugliest white men I have seen. Decidedly plebeian. Superficially vulgar and a snob, but not essentially. He seems to me clear-headed and sound-hearted, though his laugh is the laugh of a yahoo, with a wrinkling of the nose that suggests affinity with the tapir and other pachyderms" (192). On another occasion, Strong and a few colleagues "enjoyed an hour's free and easy talk with him," during which the rail-splitter told several interminable anecdotes in that Western dialect that set Strong's teeth on edge. "He is a barbarian," wrote the more sophisticated and proper easterner, "Scythian, yahoo, or gorilla, in respect of outside polish . . . but a most sensible, straightforward, honest old codger. The best President we have had since old Jackson's time, at least . . . His evident integrity and simplicity of purpose would compensate for worse grammar than his, and for even more intense provincialism and rusticity" (195).

Nevertheless, Strong occasionally fumed about Lincoln's appointments and policies. Democratic generals Lincoln believed to be "spineless"—George B. McClellan, among others—were a pet peeve of Strong's. He particularly hated General Henry Halleck, who served as chief of staff of the army during much of the war and whose politically motivated caution and penchant for red tape were obstacles to the work of the Sanitary Commission. Lincoln's refusal to enforce strictly normal military discipline annoyed Strong deeply. Upon hearing that the president had rather pathetically admitted he could not bring himself to have stragglers shot, Strong wrote bitterly, "It's an army of lions we have, with a sheep for commander-in-chief. O for a day of the late Andrew Jackson!" (226).

But Strong generally awarded Lincoln high marks for his performance as wartime leader, and when American voters reelected him over the Democratic McClellan in 1864, thus rejecting the Democrats' peace plans, Strong's normally icy cynicism melted and he exulted to his diary, "The crisis has been past, and the most momentous popular election ever held since ballots were invented has decided against treason and disunion. My contempt for democracy and extended suffrage is mitigated. The American people can be trusted to take care of the national honor" (261). A few months later Strong found himself in the White

> *"The American people can be trusted to take care of the national honor."*

House again, attending the East Room funeral of the assassinated president. Somewhat awed by the surroundings and the ceremony—although he mustered a caustic criticism of the "vile and vulgar" religious service—he humbly filed past the open coffin to say good-bye to "our great and good President." Strong counted it "a great privilege to have been present. There will be thousands of people ten years hence who would pay any money to have been in my place" (298–299).

Although Strong's ambiguity toward Lincoln was ultimately overcome by his belief in the president's basic honesty, competence, and determination to save the Union—traits he shared with the New York lawyer—no ambiguity marked his attitudes toward either Southerners or the Confederacy. Although he never mentioned the words "slave power conspiracy," Strong certainly seems to have been a proponent of this Northern belief that the South, despite its minority status, had somehow succeeded in dominating the political and economic life of the United States for many decades, controlling even Northern-born presidents like Franklin Pierce and James Buchanan, stifling the debate over slavery, and blocking government economic policies like the high import duties on manufactured goods vainly desired by northeastern businessmen and politicians.

He frequently complained about the folly of Southern arrogance. "If they were not such a race of braggarts and ruffians, I should be sorry for our fire-eating brethren, weighed down, suffocated, and paralyzed by a nigger incubus 4,000,000 strong, of which no mortal can tell them how they are to get rid, and without a friend escept [*sic*] the cotton buyers who make money out of them. . . . The sense of the world is against them" (162).

Southern attitudes, Strong had argued before Lincoln's election, would lead inevitably to ever more radical actions and ultimately to secession, which "would do fatal mischief to one section or another and great mischief to both. Amputation weakens the body, and the amputated limb decomposes and perishes. Is our vital center North or South? Which is Body and which is Member? . . . We are not a polypoid organism that can be converted into two organisms by mere bisection." However, he wrote grimly, "if the only alternative is everlasting submission to the South, it must come soon, and why should it not come now?" He ended the thought with a little shrug: "I feel Republican tonight" (158). Submission would be tantamount to admitting "that our federal government exists chiefly for the sake of nigger-owners. *I can't do that*" (159).

As Southern threats to secede became reality, Strong's hatred and contempt for Southerners hardened. "If these traitors succeed in dismembering the country," he wrote just before South Carolina fire-eaters celebrated their passage of an ordinance of secession, "they will have a front place in the Historical Gallery of Celebrated Criminals. No political crime was ever committed as disastrous to mankind and with so little to provoke or excuse the wrong as that which these infamous disunionists are conspiring to perpetuate" (166). A few months later, as rumors flew around New York that Charleston had been shelled by U.S. warships in retaliation for the attack on Fort Sumter, Strong, although he doubted the rumors to be true, applauded the idea: "that damnable little hornet's nest of treason deserves to be shelled. It's a political Sodom" (183). Nearly four years later, as the war wound down, he relished the shrill panic he read in Southern newspapers. "Richmond newspapers are in a special spasm of fury beyond any fit they have yet suffered," he gloated in a passage that listed yet again the worst characteristics of the Southerners he loved to hate. "We must not attach too much weight to what these sensitive, excitable, high-toned, chivalric creatures rave when in nervous exaltation, whether arising from patriotic or from alcoholic stimulus. . . . The editorial utterances are violent, desperate, incoherent, hurried, and objectless," and resemble "the death flurry of a whale" (275). A few days later, he worried that the war might end before the leaders who had brought misery to so many of their fellow Southerners—ravaged by invading armies, hunger, and lawlessness—could be punished: "I almost hope this war may last till it become a war of extermination. Southrons who could endure the knowledge that human creatures were undergoing this torture within their own borders, and who did not actively protest against it, deserve to be killed" (282).

That kind of fire and brimstone seems out of place in a diary whose writer generally displayed rationality and calm in the face of most challenges. Indeed, a third theme that emerges from Strong's diary is his devotion to the concept of order. Although he was a lifelong New Yorker, sophisticated in his tastes and thoroughly ensconced in urban pleasures, he often contrasted the messiness of wartime society in particular and democratic society in general to his own orderly routines. In December 1860, he blamed the sectional turmoil not only on Southern "ruffianism and brutality" but also "the selfishness, baseness, and corruption of the North." But his contempt for politics and politicians went even deeper: "Universal suffrage has been acquiesced in for many years. It is no longer debated. But it's at the root of our troubles. What we want is a strong government, instead of a 'government of opinion'" (168).

The notion of social or even political equality clearly annoyed Strong, who felt quite confident that he, for one, was superior to most of his fellow New Yorkers. This belief was dramatically confirmed during the New York City draft riots in July 1863. Strong witnessed at least some of the violence of the outbreak that began July 13; he hurried from one club and friend's house to another, seeking news and recording in his diary the events as he understood them. He placed the blame for the riot squarely on the shoulders of the "lowest Irish day laborers," the New Yorkers for whom he held the most contempt. His entries for the days covering the riot are littered with attacks on the Irish Catholics who did, in fact, make up a large percentage of the mobs who ruled the streets during those violent days. "The rabble," he reported, "was perfectly homogeneous. Every brute in the drove was pure Celtic—hod-carrier or loafer." He called them "beastly ruffians," referred to "the fury of the low Irish women," both "stalwart young vixens and withered old hags" (237–238). Strong attended a meeting with a number of other New York notables, who gathered to advise Mayor George Opdyke. Strong urged him to declare martial law and to enroll "all loyal and law-abiding citizens" in "a volunteer force for defense of life and property" (239). Strong also rushed a telegram to the president, asking him to send troops. Later the same day he visited a neighbor who had gathered a small force of men with muskets to protect his house from a rumored attack; Strong dismissed the neighbor's fears—"he is always a blower and a very poor devil" (240).

Still, Strong was obviously caught up in the tension and drama. He anxiously recorded the sounds of the rioting a few blocks from his house: occasional blasts of gunfire, the constant ringing of fire bells, the sound of a mob singing "a genuine Celtic howl" as they marched down the street, the hurried footfalls of a police squad rushing past the Strong brownstone, the welcome and regular steps of soldiers marching into the fray with fixed bayonets (241). He wrote—mistakenly, it turned out—of similar terrors in other northeastern cities, "each [with] their Irish anti-conscription, Nigger-murdering mob, of the same type with ours. It is a grave business . . . that must be put down by heroic doses of lead and steel" (243).

Although the draft riots certainly alarmed Strong, they really only confirmed his already negative impressions of the city's Irish population and of the Democratic leaders who he believed had encouraged them to pursue their disloyal course. A much more positive expression of his personal search for order appeared in his earnest and important work with the United States Sanitary Commission.

Between board meetings for his church and his alma mater and forays to the theater and to dinners, Strong spent much of his time helping to run the Sanitary

Soldiers killed during the Battle of Antietam (Corbis)

Commission. As treasurer, he served on the executive committee and was privy to all of the negotiations with the U.S. Army and with the numerous state and local societies that fit loosely under the USSC umbrella. He traveled to Washington for weeklong conferences from time to time and met in New York with other leaders, like the up-and-coming landscape architect Frederick Law Olmsted, who served as secretary, and the eccentric but passionate president of the organization, Unitarian minister Henry W. Bellows. Strong complained bitterly about the hidebound and overwhelmed military bureaucracy early in the war and about the lack of concern for the soldiers expressed by generals who fought their wars from desks in Washington. He was intimately involved with the commission's most important goals: influencing the appointment of army medical officials, organizing an ambulance corps, gathering and distributing supplies to army hospitals and to frontline regiments, and recruiting and supporting doctors and nurses. He occasionally was able to record gifts to the commission of thousands of dollars—contributions from California goldfields were particularly crucial at one stage of the war—but he fretted about the tendency of the commission to spend its money as fast as it came in.

The commission had paid agents in the field, but Strong also visited the front on behalf of the USSC following the Union victory at Antietam September 17 and 18, 1862. Aside from the draft riots that occurred ten months later, it was his only exposure to the violence and destruction of war. Taking advantage of his attendance at a meeting in nearby Washington, Strong traveled to the battlefield at Antietam Creek just three days after the fighting stopped. Basing himself at the home of a Maryland Unionist, Strong helped set up a hospital (rather, he paid the bills for the doctor who was actually doing the work) and spent a memorable day touring the battlefield. Jouncing over the country roads in an ambulance, he knew he had reached the scene of battle when they "entered an atmosphere pervaded by the scent of the battlefield." "Long lines of trenches marked the burial places; scores of dead horses, swollen, with their limbs protruding stiffly at strange angles, and the ground at their noses blackened with hemorrhage, lay all around." The houses in the village of Sharpsburg were "scarified with shot." He visited several hospitals, where he saw a "horrible congregation of wounded men . . . our men and rebel prisoners both—on straw, in their bloody stiffened clothes mostly, some in barns and cowhouses, some in the open air. It was fearful to see; Gustave Doré's pictures embodied in shivering, agonizing, suppurating flesh and blood." Later he walked over the battlefield, still strewn with shell fragments and spent bullets and "traced the position in which a Rebel brigade had stood or bivouacked in line of battle for half a mile by the thickly strewn belt of green corn husks and cobs, and also . . . by a ribbon of dysenteric stools just behind" (208–209).

If he was shaken by his battlefield experience, he shook it off fairly easily; he did not mention it again. He returned to work with vigor and passion. Not surprisingly, his conservative, elitist, and confident values shone through. He hoped that the commission could regularize the pay system and encourage soldiers to send their few dollars "home to their families and check the growth of pauperism instead of spending it in the sutler's tent to the detriment of their own condition, moral and sanitary" (190). His love of order led him to agree completely with the commission's insistence that all state and local societies be subservient to the national office. This was a source of much contention outside of Washington and New York and occupied much of the executive committee's attention. The commission responded to the "quasi-secession claims of the Cincinnati branch" with a unanimous vote on a resolution flatly stating that "the commission is central, federal, national, and must and will control the action of state organizations calling themselves branches of the commission." He seemed amused that the representatives from the Queen City "had supposed themselves our equals," when in fact "they are expected to be more 'hewers of wood,' and so on; that is expected to conform to a general system in the distribution of hospital and other supplies." The New Yorker dismissed them as "fair but false, governed, perhaps unconsciously, by jealousy of the East" (223). Although the East-West/national-local debate never went away, the central office of the USSC managed to maintain and, in fact, increase its influence throughout the war.

"The country is turning out raw material for history very fast . . ." Strong clearly believed that his work with the Sanitary Commission made a great contribution to the war effort. He apparently never considered military service as an option; in 1864, he paid a substitute to take his place in the draft. Unlike the Confederacy, where the overwhelming majority of men of military age served in the army (along with a good many older and younger than the law required to enroll for conscription), far fewer Northern men had to serve in the Union forces. As a result, home front men found other ways of contributing to the war effort: producing more food on their farms, buying government bonds to help pay for the war, throwing their support behind the administration's plans. Strong was deeply engaged in the war—he seems to have believed that one way to support the war effort was to educate himself about its military and political ramifications—but he truly found his niche in the Sanitary Commission. After the commission's successful support of the army during the Second Battle of Bull Run, he wrote, "Our Commission wagons were first on the ground and did good service, thank God; and the relations of our inspectors and agents with the [army] medical staff seem perfectly harmonious. All, from the Surgeon-General down, recognize the value of what we are doing, or rather of what the people is doing through us as its almoner" (202).

In September 1862, after the Union debacle at the Second Battle of Bull Run and just before the showdown at Antietam Creek, Strong began a diary entry with the rather enigmatic comment that "The country is turning out raw material for history very fast, but it's an inferior article" (201). It is hard to know what exactly he meant by that, but by the end of the war he seemed to have changed his tune regarding the worthiness of the historical "material" he and his generation were creating. When word reached New York City of the surrender of Richmond, Strong joined a throng of people before the U.S. Customs House on William Street, where for four hours they cheered impromptu speeches and sang the hymn "Old Hundred" ("Praise God from whom all blessings flow"), "John Brown's Body," and the "Star-Spangled Banner," "repeating the last two lines of Key's song—"The land of the free and the home of the brave"—"over and over, with a massive roar from the crowd and a unanimous wave of hats at the end of each repetition." The normally cynical and somewhat detached Strong was deeply moved by this demonstration of relief and patriotism. "I think I shall never lose the impression made by this rude, many-voiced chorale. It seemed a revelation of profound national feeling, underlying all our vulgarisms and corruptions" (286–287).

Long gone were the attitudes Strong voiced two and a half years before, when he wrote with feeble optimism of the latest Union campaign (which would end disastrously at Fredericksburg) and expressed "a dim foreboding of a coming time when we shall think of the war . . . as a terrible, crushing, personal calamity to every one of us; when there shall be no more long trains of carriages all along Fifth Avenue, . . . when I shall put no burgundy on my supper table. . . . The logic of history requires that we suffer for our sins far more than we yet have suffered" (222–223).

The course of the Civil War may have threatened the way of life enjoyed by upper-middle-class Northerners like George Templeton Strong, but the North's victory, in effect, confirmed everything. Although the virulent anti-Southern, anti-Irish attitudes found in his diary—and in the hearts and minds of countless other New Yorkers—would fade over the decades, Strong's commitment to strong government and to the corporate model of philanthropy, as revealed in the activities of the Sanitary Commission, would become models for the future. Strong would live only another ten years after the end of the war, but the culture that he represented—the culture that brought passion and organization and rationality to the business of patriotic philanthropy—would grow and flourish in the twentieth century, making it one of the most far-reaching consequences of the Civil War.

PRIMARY SOURCE:

Nevins, Allan, and Milton Halsey Thomas, eds. *The Diary of George Templeton Strong.* Abridged by Thomas J. Pressly. Seattle: University of Washington Press, 1988. Unless otherwise noted, all citations are from this source.

SECONDARY SOURCES:

Burrows, Edwin G., and Mike Wallace. *Gotham: A History of New York City to 1898.* New York: Oxford University Press, 1998.

McKay, Ernest A. *The Civil War and New York City.* Syracuse, NY: Syracuse University Press, 1990.

Chapter Nine

Reporting the War: Civil War Journalism in the North

July 5, 1863: "Tidings from Gettysburg have been arriving in fragmentary installments, but with a steady crescendo toward complete, overwhelming victory. If we
can believe what we hear, Lee is smitten hip and thigh, and his invincible 'Army
of Northern Virginia' shattered and destroyed. . . . I am skeptical . . . and expect to
find large deductions from our alleged success in tomorrow morning's newspapers."

Later the same day: "Private advices tend to confirm report of capture of over
fifteen thousand prisoners and one hundred guns. Lee retreating. Pleasanton holds
Potomac fords."

Still later, same day: "In rushed the exuberant Colonel Frank Howe with a
budget of telegrams. Lee utterly routed and disorganized, with loss of thirty thousand prisoners(!) and all his artillery. . . . We may be fearfully disillusioned yet."

July 6: "An extra *Herald* dispatch . . . gives us a splendidly colored picture of
Lee's retreat and tells how teamsters and artillery men are cutting their traces and
riding off for life on their draft-mules; how even Couch's [Union] militia regiments
are following up the defeated army and bagging whole brigades; and how there is
general panic . . . All of which is pleasant to read, but probably fictitious."
(Nevins and Thomas, 231–233)

These diary entries, penned by a New Yorker with more than a passing famil-
iarity with the military issues and political machinations of the war, suggest
something of the vagaries of news gathering on the military front and of newspaper reading on the home front. George Templeton Strong read every newspaper he could lay his hands on—Sunday editions, dailies, and the extras that hit
the streets as soon as type could be set after the arrival of urgent telegrams—
but still doubted if he ever got the whole truth. A cynic by nature, he also understood that, despite the vast quantities of information poured into newsprint
throughout the war, the accuracy of much of it was suspect, to say the least. As
most people know, Lee's defeat at Gettysburg was not as complete as the early

dispatches suggested, nor was his army trapped and destroyed before he crossed the Potomac River to safety in Virginia. Newspapers more interested in hopeful speculation than in precise reporting sometimes failed, however, to report those facts until days or even weeks after the events took place.

The hunger for war news demanded constant vigilance and effort, and Strong prowled the streets looking for the latest word from the front. It also resulted in frequent disappointment, crushed hopes, and, as Strong suggested, disillusionment. The pages of *Frank Leslie's Illustrated Weekly,* one of the leading sources of news for Northerners, during the drawn-out invasion of the Virginia Peninsula in the spring of 1862 and the campaign against the Confederate capital of Richmond over the next several months provides a case study of the difficulties in obtaining reliable news about the war. Even as *Leslie's* reporters and editors applied the most modern technologies and practices to the biggest news story in the United States since independence from Great Britain, they were limited by the availability of hard data and by the competitive and politically charged demand for fast reporting.

By March 1862, after a lull of nearly nine months since their embarrassing defeat at Bull Run, the main Union army in the East, now called the Army of the Potomac, had been built into perhaps the largest and best-equipped army ever assembled in North America. Commanded by Major General George B. McClellan—who also commanded all Federal armies—the 100,000-man army had gathered strength and confidence. Despite prodding from his commander in chief, McClellan refused to take the field until he believed his army was ready. The late winter and spring of 1862 had seen a sharp upturn in Union fortunes in the war against the Confederacy, with the Federals' capture of Forts Henry and Donelson, the occupation of Memphis and Nashville, the bloody but decisive victory at Shiloh, and, in April, the fall of New Orleans to Union forces. Large swaths of Confederate Tennessee and Mississippi lay under Union occupation, and many observers believed that a successful campaign against Richmond in the East would end the Confederacy's short history.

McClellan had finally acted in mid-March, when he suddenly shifted his base of operations from northern Virginia to The Peninsula between the York and James Rivers, where Union forces still held Fort Monroe at the tip of southeastern Virginia. Less than 100 miles separated the Army of the Potomac from the Confederate capital, but McClellan, believing that he was outnumbered by the Confederate army, mounted a slow and cautious campaign up The Peninsula. Despite a numbing and unnecessary siege against a small force of Confederates at Yorktown and a badly managed but successful fight at Williamsburg, by early May McClellan had the Confederates on their heals and was closing in on his objective. He dithered, though, losing momentum and confidence. The

Confederates attacked at Seven Pines on May 31; the Federal force would go no farther. Beginning at the end of June, the Confederates' new commander, General Robert E. Lee, launched furious attacks at Mechanicsville, Gaines' Mill, Savage's Station, Glendale, and Malvern Hill—the famous Seven Days' Battles. McClellan managed to fend off each of these attacks and to withdraw his force back to Harrison's Landing, near Fort Monroe. Between them, the two armies had lost 50,000 in killed and wounded during the Peninsula Campaign, with some 36,000 casualties during the Seven Days' Battles alone, and, at least on the surface, the strategic situation in Virginia remained unchanged.

The Seven Days' Battles, occurring in rapid succession after the snail-like pace of the early part of the campaign, were covered in considerable detail by the Northern press. It was the first real test for fledgling war correspondents, at least in the Virginia theater, and they did their best to accomplish their two primary—and sometimes conflicting—objectives: to inform the reading public and to sell more newspapers than their rivals. Editors sent hundreds of reporters and sketch artists to the front, and most days newspapers were filled with war news. With the great daily newspapers of the eastern seaboard and the "illustrated weeklies" that had gathered popularity and momentum before the war published in New York, Boston, Philadelphia, and other northeastern cities and with the nearly instant communication available via the telegraph, correspondents could get articles to editors on the day of the events they described.

Unfortunately, the "fog of war" was even thicker for newspaper reporters than it was for Civil War generals, who could sometimes communicate with the Secretary of War back in Washington faster than they could get word to a subordinate located a few miles away over a dangerous, smoky, and often unseen battlefield. The same technology let reporters file stories before battles were actually decided, leading to hasty reporting and hastier publication of erroneous reports. Readers like Strong were right to be skeptical about the "news" that appeared in their newspapers on any given day.

One of the leading publications of the Civil War era was *Frank Leslie's Illustrated Weekly,* founded by the Scottish immigrant and veteran illustrator Frank Leslie, who promised to bring to subscribers in New York and beyond "a weekly miscellany to be featured by news pictures." *Leslie's*—and, to a certain extent, sister publications like *Harper's Weekly*—resembled both late-twentieth-century news magazines and tabloid scandal sheets. Rather lurid accounts of local crimes, scandals, prizefights, and other sensationalistic stories earned Leslie notoriety and a fortune. By 1860, the circulation of individual issues approached 350,000. *Leslie's* was headquartered in a five-story marble building where well over a hundred illustrators, engravers, printers, and other craftsmen worked. Although for big stories the lag time could be reduced, illustrated news articles generally appeared about two weeks after the events they chronicled.

Civil War newspapers and magazines, while not exactly welcoming the onset of war, certainly sprang into action to cover the stories of their lifetimes. The compromises made and broken in Congress during the tumultuous 1850s, the sectional violence in "Bleeding Kansas," and John Brown's raid of Harpers Ferry in 1859 had provided grist for newspapers' rise to prominence as presenters of information and shapers of opinions. The secession crisis of 1860–1861, the formation of the Confederacy in February 1861, and the buildup to the Confederate attack on Fort Sumter in Charleston Harbor in April inspired newspapers and magazines to expand their staff. Some sent undercover journalists to Charleston and other Southern flash points; several major New York papers began issuing Sunday editions for the first time; most publications invested in faster, more efficient engraving equipment and printing presses; all took advantage of the 15,000 miles of telegraph wires strung by the end of the war.

The journalists' surge to war in early summer 1861 was dampened somewhat by the defeat at Bull Run, but by the beginning of the Peninsula Campaign they were ready. At least fifty reporters and artists accompanied the Army of the Potomac, including *Leslie's* crack illustrator William Waud (Winslow Homer sketched the campaign for the rival *Harper's Weekly*). Stories from the front dominated the papers at times during the long campaign. Although the fastest way to get stories back to editors was through the Western Union Telegraph Company or the U.S. Military Telegraph, military officials often sought to limit the amount of information published regarding troop movements and strategy. At one point, *Leslie's* published a cartoon of a stern McClellan as the proprietor of a tent show trying to chase away a gang of boys—pint-sized journalists with notepads— attempting to sneak a peak at the "Great Anaconda" (a metaphor for the military strategy proposed by General in Chief Winfield Scott at the beginning of the war). "No peeping," said the caption, while "Manager McClellan" cried, "Now then you boys, get away from there! Wait till the show's ready" (*Frank Leslie's Illustrated Weekly*, April 26, 1862). Notwithstanding the occasional and often inconsistent censorship, these hardy journalists provided vivid, thorough, and sometimes misleading coverage of the fighting for readers on the Northern home front.

Leslie's coverage of the Peninsula Campaign began with great confidence. On April 19, a report of heavy firing from the direction of Yorktown inspired a lead paragraph to assure readers that "news of another 'great victory'" would no doubt soon reach the North, "for with the National army now, 'there is no such word as *fail.*'" Along with other movements of Federal forces in northern Virginia and in the Shenandoah Valley, "this implies a vigorous prosecution of the war throughout Virginia and indicates a speedy overthrow of the Rebel authority in that State." Indeed, "it is safe to predict that Richmond will be brought under the National authority before the 1st of May, and that [Confederate President Jefferson] Davis and his so-called Cabinet will be, still earlier, fugitives on their road to Mexico."

Other positive signs included the continued occupation of a thin slice of coastal North Carolina by Union troops under General Ambrose E. Burnside, secret plans to meet the challenge posed by the Confederate ironclad CSS *Virginia,* and a movement in Congress to endorse President Lincoln's suggestion that Union border states (Maryland, Missouri, Delaware, and Kentucky) begin to emancipate their slaves. *Leslie's* declared,

> Altogether we may regard ourselves as having not only reached the turning point of the war, but the period of a decisive change in our National policy, in respect to Slavery. . . . A few days, or a few weeks at most, must settle the question of the supremacy of the National arm, and reduce the great rebellion to the dimensions of an incoherent, impotent insurrection, without an army or navy, or the semblance of a political organization capable of commanding obedience at home or respect abroad. (ibid., April 19, 1862)

Subsequent articles would never again exude the comforting assurance of this mid-April bulletin, and serious reservations about the commanding general's leadership and about the ramifications of the campaign would also develop later. The first order of business was, of course, to inform the Northern public about the progress of the "national" army. Although the information presented in *Leslie's* was sketchy at times, in several cases huge sections of the paper were filled with precise details of the fighting. Perhaps the most thorough came late in the campaign, after Union troops had advanced close enough to Richmond to hear the church bells ring, but then retreated in the face of furious Confederate counterattacks. The July 19 issue featured two maps, several columns packed with orders of battle, casualty figures, and accounts of each of the several separate fights that made up the Seven Days' Battles. Replete with grand overviews and arresting detail—"shot and shell flew in antagonistic directions with dangerous liveliness" reported one correspondent—the report on the last fortnight of heavy fighting was *Leslie's* most valuable contribution to the coverage of the campaign (ibid., July 19, 1862).

The Peninsula Campaign was the first major movement into Confederate territory, and *Leslie's* sought to inform its readers about Virginia and about the enemies their sons and brothers were fighting. Reporters following the army as it inched its way northwesterly toward Richmond provided a kind of travelogue of colonial Virginia. "This famous town," one story began during the siege of Yorktown, "which has twice been the theatre of great events in American history (let us hope the present will be equally glorious with the past), is a port of entry on the York river." It went on to present a brief history of its founding, its economic status (oyster harvesting had recently made up, in part, for the decline of the shipbuilding industry), and its demography, along with a description of the York River (ibid., May 3, 1862).

In addition, whenever they could, correspondents described rebel soldiers and civilians in the worst possible light. General John B. Magruder, Confederate commander at Yorktown, although "daring," was also "willful and intemperate" and "comic" when under the influence of "too much champagne." Magruder's troops, after an inflammatory speech from their commander condemning their orders to evacuate Yorktown, "enthusiastically cheered" him; "the dissatisfaction was so great as almost to amount to mutiny" (ibid., May 10, 1862). According to *Leslie's,* Confederates rarely retreated in order, often deserting guns and baggage and positions in "absolute desperation" (ibid., May 24, 1862). The panic carried over to the civilians in the Confederate capital; with the approach of Union forces, *Leslie's* declared early in June, "the city is in a state bordering on anarchy. . . . Thieves and robbers of all classes have congregated there, with the evident purpose of re-enacting the scenes of disorder and pillage that made New Orleans a hell" (ibid., June 7, 1862).

On the other hand, order, discipline, and confidence characterized Union troops. Early in April, when "the welcome order" came to break camp at Fort Monroe and advance on Yorktown, "never were orders obeyed with greater alacrity. The men were ordered to prepare five days rations, and at three A.M. the long roll sounded, summoning the troops from their sleep, and in a few minutes the lights of a thousand camp fires were burning" (ibid., May 3, 1862).

In a style common in war reporting throughout modern history, correspondents sought to dramatize the fighting by focusing on small portions of large fights or of detailed descriptions of small fights. *Leslie's* prominently featured a dramatic account—borrowed from the *Evening Post*—of a sniper finally bringing down a "seven foot" rebel who was in the habit of taunting the Yankees across no-man's-land (ibid., May 17, 1862). Another little skirmish covered intensively by *Leslie's* occurred in late April at Lee's Mills, near Yorktown, when several companies of the 3rd Vermont charged across a chest-high stream to attack a Confederate artillery battery. Firing as they went and dragging wounded comrades up to the shore, they quickly charged the nearest rifle pits, from which they drove a rebel regiment. Several companies from other regiments reinforced them, but additional Confederate troops and guns also arrived, and the New Englanders had to pull back, "carrying with them all their wounded whose condition at all promised survival of their hurts," firing from behind trees, and generally withdrawing "in good order." Many were killed while recrossing the stream—one private said the

Sketch drawn by Edwin Forbes of a Union soldier reading a newspaper
(Library of Congress)

bullet-pocked water "was just like sap-boiling . . . the bullets fell so thick"—and others were "drowned beyond all possibility of help." Perhaps half the Union soldiers engaged died or were wounded (ibid., May 10, 1862).

Although the description of the firefight at Lee's Mills withheld judgment on who was to blame for the failure of the operation, one of the developing themes of *Leslie's* coverage of the Peninsula Campaign was the heroism and valor of rank-and-file soldiers and the incompetence of many of their generals. Although never shy about focusing on generals and politicians in other contexts of their war reporting, combat reports tended to idealize the frontline soldiers and to hold their senior officers accountable for tactical and strategic failures and unnecessary deaths. One article declared that the fierce fire put down by the 10th Massachusetts was "worthy of the descendants of the soldiers of Bunker Hill" (ibid., July 12, 1862). During the hard-won and costly victory for the Union side at Williamsburg, the men fought "with unsurpassed energy . . . against overwhelming odds with a bravery and tenacity which has covered all engaged with imperishable glory." The division commander, General Samuel Heintzelman, was compared to "Napoleon at Waterloo," and the casualties suffered by some of the Northern regiments were greater than that of the Light Brigade at Balaklava, the Austrians and French at Magenta, and the English and French at the Alma. "And yet carping Englishmen and braggart Frenchmen, the idiots assume to sneer at the bravery, the pluck, the discipline and the endurance of the American Volunteers!" (ibid., May 24, 1862). A later article claimed that the victory plucked from the jaws of defeat at Williamsburg came "through the indomitable heroism of our soldiery and special Divine interposition"—not the leadership of the senior commanders (ibid., May 31, 1862). By the end of the savage

"An enemy is less to be dreaded than Sumner as a friend."

fighting that accompanied the Federal retreat back down The Peninsula a few weeks later, the army was "wearied but undismayed" (ibid., July 19, 1862).

One of the most remarkable anecdotes illuminated an incident during the retreat of the Union forces later in the campaign, when a lieutenant in charge of destroying an ammunition depot at Savage's Station, lest it fall into the hands of the Confederates, had the explosives loaded onto a train, which he then set on fire and launched toward enemy lines. "The sight was at once grand and novel, the powder, shells, etc., exploding, as the apparently infuriated train of monsters rushed along." The rocketing train plunged into the Chickahominy River—the bridge had been destroyed earlier—in what one newspaperman called the most "terrific instance of reasonless brute force dashing itself to pieces" that he had ever seen (ibid., July 26, 1862).

Although fighting generals like Heintzelman, Daniel Sickles, and Winfield Hancock were praised for their daring, leadership, and determination, their corps commander, General Edwin Sumner, in allowing those 10,000 men to fight most of a day against 30,000 Confederates, had proven himself to be "a man either triply traitor, or controlled by motives so low and vile, that it would be a compliment to call him a traitor." Sumner's inaction was detailed, analyzed, and castigated for nearly three columns, ending with the bald declaration that, as long as Sumner was "allowed to weigh down the energies and nullify the patriotic impulses of his soldiery," Confederate hero General P. G. T. Beauregard "as an enemy is less to be dreaded than Sumner as a friend" (ibid., May 31, 1862).

It should be noted that not all unsuccessful generals were so roundly attacked. Indeed, General Nathaniel Banks, a Massachusetts politico who commanded a series of Union disasters and missed opportunities throughout the war, was one of several Federal commanders outmaneuvered and defeated in battle by Confederate General Thomas J. "Stonewall" Jackson during the latter's famous Shenandoah Valley Campaign during March through June 1862. When Jackson withdrew from the valley to reinforce the Confederate capital, *Leslie's* referred to

FRANK LESLIE'S
ILLUSTRATED
NEWSPAPER

No. 269—Vol. XI.]   NEW YORK, JANUARY 19, 1861.   [Price 6 Cents.

Soldiers cutting down the U.S. flagstaff under the direction of Major Anderson at Fort Multrie, Charleston Harbor, South Carolina, on Christmas night, 1860 (Frank Leslie's Illustrated Newspaper, *January 19, 1861)*

Banks's "driving the rebels out of the Shenandoah Valley" and to the "brilliant success" of his colleague, General John C. Frémont—in actuality, Frémont was yet another victim of Jackson's superior generalship (ibid., June 7, 1862).

Daniel Sickles, who had gained command of a brigade (and later a division) due to his connections with the Democratic machine controlling New York City from Tammany Hall, was a special favorite. When his unit performed well in a large skirmish just preceding the Seven Days' Battles, *Leslie's* boasted, "It is needless to say that the Sickles Brigade, which has thus far done the hardest fighting of the war, was again, as always, in the front, and assigned to the severest duty" (ibid., July 12, 1862).

Ultimately, however, the big story of the campaign was the failure of Union leadership, and *Leslie's* laid the blame clearly on McClellan. An article fairly early in the campaign commended him for his "great activity," having recently spent nearly twenty hours in the saddle over a two-day period, visiting every position "along the whole front" (ibid., May 17, 1862), but a week later, after the near catastrophe at Williamsburg, *Leslie's* wondered why the commanding general had arrived on the field so late in the day. "His presence five hours earlier might have converted a dearly-bought into a *decisive* victory. Napoleons of the old school were always at the front!" (ibid., May 24, 1862). A similar charge was made during a long attack on the leadership of General Sumner in the next week's issue, which concluded by reluctantly admitting that, perhaps, the absence of the commander from the front had something to do with "strategy," but "quite the reverse of Napoleonism in war—at least, it does not require the Commander-in-Chief to be at the head of his army, but is content to leave the fortunes of war to the possible concurrence of bickering subordinates!" (ibid., May 31, 1862). After McClellan lost his nerve and retreated with his army in the face of repeated attacks by Robert E. Lee's Confederates—attacks that took a heavy toll on both sides—*Leslie's* rather ominously declared that "the dreadful responsibility of more than 20,000 slaughtered heroes rests upon some high official's head, and the public will yet demand a fearful reckoning from both Southern traitors and Northern incapables" (ibid., July 19, 1862).

That reckoning, at least for *Leslie's*, came six weeks later, when, in the August 30 edition, the paper reported the evacuation of most of McClellan's troops from The Peninsula and declared the campaign a dismal failure. Continuing its earlier criticism of the army's sorry leadership, the front-page article also continued to commend the rank and file for fighting "splendidly . . . and with a patience, steadiness, devotion, and courage never surpassed." But their superb performance ended in tragedy: "their enormous sacrifices of life in battle and from disease, which have reduced the most splendid army ever organized on this continent to half its original strength, have effected nothing." The campaign

*Lieutenant Colonel George D. Wells of the 34th Massachusetts (center) poses with a
pair of war correspondents. (Corbis)*

should never have happened; on The Peninsula, the "army had nothing to protect" and there was "nothing gained" in occupying it. The article ends with a
quick and approving assessment of the new strategy—returning to the old front
lines in northern Virginia—and a cautiously optimistic account of the fighting
then transpiring southwest of Washington.

President Lincoln agreed with *Leslie's* in faulting McClellan's leadership. He
replaced McClellan with General Henry W. Halleck as commanding general and
transferred many of his units to General John Pope's Army of Virginia. When
McClellan got a second chance after Pope's disastrous performance during the
Second Battle of Bull Run, he barely hung on for a hard-fought victory at
Antietam in September. His failure to pursue Lee's Army of Northern Virginia
as it withdrew back into Confederate territory was the last straw for Lincoln, and
by late November, McClellan was out of a job.

Newspapers and magazines like *Frank Leslie's Illustrated Weekly* shaped the Civil War on the home front. Each day millions of Americans poured over morning editions, tracing troop movements on battle maps, matching names of generals and far-off Southern towns with engraved images, anxiously scanning casualty lists, and nodding or shaking their heads over dubious headlines and heated editorials. Especially in the North, where few people actually witnessed a battle or saw an army on the march, these publications brought the war into living rooms to an unprecedented degree.

The process and priorities of reporting the news had also changed, inspiring one historian of journalism to write that "the whole emphasis of American journalism had changed" after the Civil War (Starr, 289). Although opinionated publishers and reformers would continue to publish editorials promoting specific points of view and shape their newspapers' and magazines' news coverage to match those points of view, a new journalistic ethos had emerged during the Civil War: that the job of a news publication was, at its most basic, to publish the news. War correspondents had altered and expanded the role of reporter, had indeed, according to another historian, created "a new profession." They accomplished this by informing the home front of the hardships and dangers faced by their sons, brothers, fathers, and neighbors, and of the heroism they displayed despite the not infrequent incompetence and callousness of their commanders. After the war, Americans would increasingly look to journalists for information and for at least an honest version of the news (Weisberger, 5).

PRIMARY SOURCES:

Frank Leslie's Illustrated Weekly (cited by date).

Nevins, Allan, and Milton Halsey Thomas, eds. *The Diary of George Templeton Strong.* Abridged by Thomas J. Pressly. Seattle: University of Washington Press, 1988.

SECONDARY SOURCES:

Dean, Eric T. "We Live under a Government of Men and Morning Newspapers." *Virginia Magazine of History and Biography* 103 (January 1995).

Gallagher, Gary, ed. *The Richmond Campaign of 1862: The Peninsula & the Seven Days.* Chapel Hill: University of North Carolina Press, 2000.

Perry, James M. *A Bohemian Brigade: The Civil War Correspondents—Mostly Rough, Sometimes Ready.* New York: John Wiley & Sons, 2000.

Sears, Stephen W. *To the Gates of Richmond: The Peninsula Campaign.* New York: Ticknor & Fields, 1992.

Reporting the War: Civil War Journalism in the North

Starr, Louis M. *Reporting the Civil War: The Bohemian Brigade in Action, 1861–1865.* New York: Collier, 1954, 1962.

Thompson, William F. *The Image of War: The Pictorial Reporting of the American Civil War.* New York: A. S. Barnes, 1959. Reprint, Baton Rouge: Louisiana State University Press, 1989.

Weisberger, Bernard A. *Reporters for the Union.* Boston: Little, Brown and Company, 1953.

Chapter Ten

Literary Nurses: Louisa May Alcott and Walt Whitman

"They've come! They've come! hurry up, ladies—you're wanted."

"Who have come? The rebels?"

This sudden summons in the gray dawn was somewhat startling . . . and as the thundering knock came at our door, I sprang up in my bed, prepared "To gird my woman's form, And on the ramparts die," if necessary; but my room-mate took it more coolly, and, as she began a rapid toilet, answered my bewildered question,—

"Bless you, no child; it's the wounded from Fredericksburg; forty ambulances are at the door, and we shall have our hands full in fifteen minutes." (Alcott, 25)

So began nurse Tribulation Periwinkle's personal experience with the Civil War. Miss Periwinkle was the alter ego of Louisa May Alcott, who, before she became the famous author of *Little Women,* spent a memorable few weeks as a nurse near Washington, D.C. Although Victorian notions of gender roles and relationships normally prohibited such intimate contact between strangers, hundreds of women applied to head U.S. Army nurse Dorothea Dix, who required, among other things, that her nurses be "plain" and unmarried. Perhaps 2,000 Northern and Southern women actually served as volunteer nurses in hospitals. Others did, of course, nurse their own relatives back to health, either at home or at the front. For instance, hundreds of women flocked to Gettysburg to take care of loved ones in private homes given over to the thousands of wounded men left behind after the armies moved back into Virginia.

Despite the fact that few women actually spent time in a military hospital, nursing was, in some ways, an extension of the kinds of duties Civil War women gladly performed as their part in the war effort. Untold thousands of girls and women at home made bandages, "picked" lint, sewed clothes, knit socks, and packed bundles and boxes with food and other supplies. A number of women also played major roles in the organization and maintenance of the vast fund-raising and distribution networks of the United States Sanitary Commission and the United States Christian Commission, even acting as agents representing those organizations in army camps. Nurses, however, were the frontline troops in the efforts by women to help win the war. Although some traveled to battle-fields for the Sanitary Commission, staffing a hospital boat during the Peninsula Campaign in southeastern Virginia in 1862, for example, and although Clara Barton occasionally came under fire during her peripatetic and lonely journeys on behalf of the soldiers, most nurses remained safely behind the lines. There they ensured that those sick and wounded soldiers lucky enough to survive the filth of field hospitals and the agonizing journey to such central locations as Washington or, later, Nashville, Vicksburg, and other major cities would come under the influence of the home front.

Nurses, however, were the frontline troops in the efforts by women to help win the war.

Of course, men also worked as nurses, and one of the most famous Civil War nurses was the poet Walt Whitman. Forty-one years old when the war began, Whitman was a vigorous supporter of the Union war effort. When word arrived that his brother George, who served as an officer in the 51st New York, was wounded at Fredericksburg late in 1862, Whitman traveled to the battlefield to nurse him back to health. It turned out that George was fine, but Walt stayed in camp for a couple of weeks, thus beginning his three-year commitment to act as, in his words, a "visitor" to wounded and sick soldiers in the hospitals that crowded the nation's capital. He was an unpaid volunteer, working as a jour-neyman printer and reporter and in various government offices by day, and roaming the hospitals and camps by night.

Like Alcott, Whitman wrote about his experiences in Civil War hospitals. There is no reason to believe either writer's experiences were particularly unique, but their commitment to communicate those experiences, to draw meaning on behalf of other Northerners, in a way brings to life an element of the Civil War home front that, like so many others, challenged long-held assumptions about midcentury life. Simply by becoming nurses, women—and men, for that mat-ter—confronted notions of gender roles, while at the same time they confirmed them. If Alcott and Whitman, admittedly more articulate than most nurses, were representative, working as nurses helped these men and women explain to them-selves the meaning of the war, helped them come to a greater appreciation of the character of Americans, and opened them up to ideas about the nature of human character—courage, piety, duty, honor—that they held so dear.

Alcott was reared in Concord, Massachusetts, where her father, Bronson, was a good friend of Nathaniel Hawthorne, and Henry David Thoreau was one of her teachers. Inspired, no doubt, by the literary world in which she grew up, she began publishing in literary and women's magazines as a teenager. She eventually wrote fiction for highly respected journals such as the *Atlantic Monthly* and the *Commonwealth,* as well as magazines for children like the *Little Pilgrim, Youth's Companion, Our Young Folks,* and *Merry's Museum,* which she edited for a time in the late 1860s. On the side, she created mystery thrillers under various pseudonyms, including A. M. Barnard.

Not surprisingly, given the environment in which she grew up, Alcott was sympathetic to the abolitionist cause. Indeed, after John Brown was hanged for his attack on Harpers Ferry, she published a poem in the abolitionist newspaper the *Liberator* entitled "With a Rose, That Bloomed on the Day of John Brown's Martyrdom." After the war began, she sewed uniforms and acted in amateur theatricals to raise money for the United

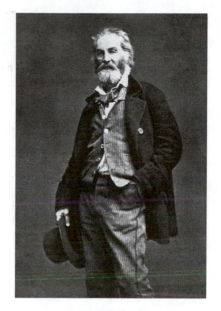

Walt Whitman
(Library of Congress)

States Sanitary Commission. She felt she had more to give, however, and convinced her parents to allow her to become a nurse. She arrived at the Union Hotel Hospital in Georgetown just in time to help receive the casualties from the Battle of Fredericksburg. After only a few weeks, she developed typhoid and was rushed back to Concord. She would remain a semi-invalid for the rest of her life.

But Alcott felt her war experiences deeply, and she spent the next several years writing books, articles, and stories about the Civil War. She placed some of her thrillers in Civil War settings, but much better known were the books she published, such as *On Picket Duty, and Other Tales* and in incidental pieces she wrote for adult as well as juvenile magazines. One of her wartime stories, "Nelly's Hospital," appeared in a new children's periodical called *Our Young Folks* just as the war ended. It told the story of a little girl who, animated by sympathy for her wounded brother, decides to create her own hospital in which she will treat all the "wounded" animals she finds in the neighborhood. Aided by the gardener's son, she gathers mice, spiders, birds, and insects into her "U.S. Sanitary Commission" wagon and nurses them back to health.

The first of Alcott's major pieces to draw on the Civil War was actually based on letters she had written while serving at the hospital. Composed as a memoir of a sometimes scatterbrained but hardworking and committed nurse with the Dickensian name of Tribulation Periwinkle, *Hospital Sketches* appeared in 1863.

Louisa May Alcott (Circer, Hayward, ed., Dictionary of American Portraits, *1967)*

Told in a rather jaunty tone—the tone of a young woman who, like Alcott, faced her first extended stay away from home with a mixture of excitement, trepidation, and good humor—the vignettes detail a somewhat whitewashed version of the life of a nurse in a big army hospital. When "Trib," as she's called by her friends and family, learns that she has been accepted into the nursing corps, she "turns military" at once, sprinkling her prose with soldiers' jargon: she calls her dinner "rations"; begins referring to clothes according to their condition—some take "picket duty" while being aired on the backyard fence, others, needing repair, go into the hospital; she calls her handbag a knapsack; and she announces to her family that "I shall march at six" (ibid., 5–6).

Her departure recalls similar scenes from soldiers' memoirs and in popular prints of volunteers leaving home: brave tears, lingering hugs, and heartfelt emotion. Trib knowingly maintains "that the soldier who cries when his mother says 'Good bye,' is the boy to fight best, and die bravest, when the time comes, or go back to her better than he went" (ibid., 7).

Trib describes her transition from civilian to nurse with a mixture of humor and pathos. Her journey to the city takes the form of a wide-eyed travelogue in which she misplaces her train tickets and snuggles up to an overweight woman during a ferry ride (believing that a large person had a better chance of floating if the boat sank). Once at the hospital, Nurse Periwinkle settles into her routine of caring for the ill soldiers who are already there. After three days she is tired of treating the unheroic sick, "washing faces, serving rations, giving medicine, and sitting in a very hard chair" while waiting for her next chore. "Having a taste for 'ghastliness,' I had rather longed for the wounded to arrive, for rheumatism wasn't heroic, neither was liver complaint, or measles; even fever had lost its charms" (ibid., 26). In the bloody backwash of the disaster at Fredericksburg, however, Nurse Periwinkle found herself up to her elbows in squalor and heroism.

At her first look down the early morning street where stewards were unloading ambulances, "My ardor experienced a sudden chill, and I indulged in a most unpatriotic wish that I was safe at home again, with a quiet day before me" (ibid., 26–27). Before she could turn and run, she was called to duty and rushed into the main hall, where "The first thing I met was a regiment of the vilest odors that ever assaulted the human nose." She had been warned about the odors, and fought back by sprinkling herself with lavender water—then she got to work. "There they were! 'Our brave boys,' as the papers justly called them, for cowards could hardly have been so riddled with shot and shell, so torn and shattered, nor have borne suffering for which we have no name" (ibid., 27).

"The first thing I met was a regiment of the vilest odors that ever assaulted the human nose."

Indeed, one of the themes—perhaps the only sustained theme—of *Hospital Sketches* is of the suffering of the soldiers. They are uncommonly polite to everyone and stoic, without being grim. A remarkably sanguine patient was the "little sergeant . . . with a curly brown mane, honest blue eyes, and a merry mouth" who had lost a leg and whose right arm was so grievously injured that he would soon lose it, too. He "was as merry as if his afflictions were not worth lamenting over," comforted her when she shed a few tears on his behalf, and assured her that he would be fine. He laughed at his own joke when he suggested that there would be quite "a scramble . . . for arms and legs, when we old boys come out of our graves, on the Judgment Day: wonder if we shall get our own again?" (ibid., 31).

The good humor with which this patient met his fate was matched only by those who greeted a far sterner destiny—death—with composure and courage. When Trib offers to help a wounded man eat his food, he shakes his head and says quietly, "Thank you, ma'am; I don't think I'll ever eat again, for I'm shot in the stomach. But I'd like a drink of water, if you aint too busy." By the time she returns, however, he has died (ibid., 35). Later, a patient lingers for days with an untreatable chest wound. A doctor orders the young nurse to inform him that he will die, for, he tells her, women were better equipped to break news like that. She finally gets her chance when, in a conversation about his brief military career, he says, "This is my first battle" and asks, "do they think it's going to be my last?" She replies, "I'm afraid they do, John." His only response: "he seemed a little startled." No tears, no outward grief, no moans (ibid., 54–55).

Alcott's descriptions of noble deaths and patient suffering are thoroughly conventional, but she does touch on the delicate topic of women treating men in such close and possibly intimate ways. Her first duty on the memorable day when the wounded came from Fredericksburg was, in the words of her supervisor, "to wash as fast [as] you can. Tell them to take off socks, coats and shirts, scrub them well, [and] put on clean shirts." Although the attendants would "finish them off"—meaning, apparently, that they would deal with other, more controversial parts of the body—Trib confesses that "if she had requested me to shave them all, or dance a hornpipe on the stove funnel, I should have been less staggered; but to scrub some dozen lords of creation at a moment's notice, was really—really—." But, she decides, this was "no time for nonsense" and she "drowned my scruples in my washbowl" and "made a dab at the first dirty specimen I saw." That happened to be "a withered old Irishman" with a head wound. He rolled his eyes, insisted on removing his own shoes and shirt, and inspired a bit of a giggling fit in his nurse. Other men were "grimly scandalized" at the idea of a woman giving them a bath, "and several of the roughest colored like bashful girls." A few, no doubt exhausted beyond shame, simply leaned against her shoulder as she worked (ibid., 29–30). Interestingly, Whitman recommended that only middle-aged and elderly women be allowed to nurse soldiers. This was partly due to the "irresistible conventions of society"—the modesty behind which so many Victorians took refuge—but also to the fact that young women had not yet reared children, which alone could teach the skills and build the character that "answer[ed] the practical requirements of nurses for soldiers" (ibid., 116).

Although Trib's "height of ambition" was to become a battlefield nurse—she even forced herself to witness several amputations to steel herself against the sights and sounds she would experience in a field hospital—she, like her author, fell ill and had to return home early in 1863 (ibid., 90). She had promised herself she would stay at least three months, but when friends and doctors kept urging her to go home and her father appeared, "my resolution melted away, my heart turned traitor to my boys, and, when he said, 'Come home,' I answered, 'Yes, father;' and so ended my career as an army nurse." She returned to her safe, civilian life (ibid., 78).

Although the Civil War certainly inspired Walt Whitman as a writer, he could never bring himself to complete a memoir of his own experiences as a Civil War nurse. Producing the light touch and determined and somewhat superficial optimism that characterized a book like Alcott's—and the kind of writing that made the horrors of war palatable for many readers—was completely beyond him. In fact, in a letter to editor and war correspondent James Redpath in which he proposed to write a book about the conflict, he declared that it would be "something worthy the time—something considerably beyond mere hospital sketches" (Lowenfels, 10). Perhaps he was referring to Alcott's work, which was published about the same time. Whatever the case, he never did produce his war memoirs. Perhaps he believed most Americans could not handle the truths that he would have to tell. There is evidence in the fragments of war writing he left behind, brought together a century later by Walter Lowenfels in *Walt Whitman's Civil War*, that he thought the war was just too big to write about.

Part of the problem was that he apparently believed that a reading public that so eagerly sought simplistic accounts of bravery and patriotism would never be drawn to the messiness and horror and complexities of "the real war" that he famously feared would "never get in the books." He seems to suggest at one point that his own conception of the war was too large to fit into a single book, that the issues it raised and values it reflected were simply too massive for most people to understand, or for him to get into prose. A "few attempts and reflections thoroughly convince me," he wrote a decade after the war, "how futile . . . are all efforts either at a full statement of the war in its origins or for writing its history—not only its military history, but . . . its vast complications, civil and domestic, diplomatic and social byplay." He had, he declared, "become accustomed to think of the whole of the Secession War in its emotional, artistic and literary relations," and he did not feel up to the task of integrating all those facets of a war that, despite its gory sorrow, was "an inside proof of [the] perennial grandeur" of the United States (ibid., 12).

Yet, he did write about the war and about his work in army hospitals. Although there are obvious differences in his and Alcott's approaches to their war writing, there are also similarities. Both reveled in relating the character and behavior of the men they observed. "I would have given much to have possessed the art of sketching," writes Nurse Periwinkle, "for many of the faces" of the men for whom she cared "became wonderfully interesting when unconscious. Some grew stern and grim, the men evidently dreaming of war, as they gave orders, groaned over their wounds, or damned the Rebels vigorously; some grew sad and infinitely pathetic, as if the pain borne silently all day, revenged itself by now betraying what the man's pride had concealed so well. Often the roughest grew young and pleasant," while sometimes the sweetest-looking men, when conscious, "grew bad and sly when the shadows came." Some talked in their sleep; one drummer boy sang delightfully. "I learned to know these men better by night than through any intercourse by day" (ibid., 43–44).

Whitman also grew very close to the patients; he corresponded with many after they left the hospital—one even named a son after him—and he sometimes visited them in their camps when he went to the front. Like Alcott's Trib, who insisted on watching amputations to make herself a better nurse, Whitman forced himself to go to the hospital housing the most serious cases to face the worst that the war had to offer. Both commented on the nonchalance with which soldiers and hospital workers alike faced death. "Death is nothing here," Whitman declared during his first exposure to an army hospital, and both noted that once a person died, he was quickly and unceremoniously covered up, hauled out, and buried (ibid., 35). Both authors complained of the occasional callousness of stewards, stretcher bearers, and even doctors. Whitman claimed that the government was "anxious and liberal in its practice toward its sick," but worried that the men actually in charge—from officers to surgeons to clerks—were too often "entirely lacking in the right qualities. There are tyrants and shysters in all positions and especially those dressed in subordinate authority" (ibid., 91). Of course, as in all walks of life, "some pompous and every way improper persons . . . get in power in hospitals, and have full swing over the helpless soldiers" (ibid., 96). Whitman's and Alcott's criticism of the system and of individuals within it reflected their shared benevolence toward the men they loved.

Despite their similarities, there are major differences in the experiences that Whitman and Alcott created for themselves and in the ways they chose to write about them. Whitman chose his own role in the war: "I do not think I quite had my match," he wrote characteristically of what exactly he did in Washington. A free agent, unbounded by the strict rules governing women like Alcott and the soldiers who worked as hospital stewards and nurses, Whitman came and went as he pleased, although he did impose a rigid self-discipline on his work. He wrote letters for soldiers; delivered fruit, jelly, tobacco, and stationery; ran errands (buying clothes for men going home on furlough, for instance); read them books; provided fellowship. He boasted of rescuing at least one young boy from the jaws of death. Ill with diarrhea, fever, and various other maladies, the young man was nearly sent to the tent where hopeless patients were taken to die. Whitman intervened and, without medicine but with quiet determination, nursed him back to health with constant attention and kindness.

"Death is nothing here."

His reasons for remaining in Washington and for going to various sites to visit friends in the army were, he believed, very different from those of the thousands of other people who jammed into the capital. "People went there for all sorts of reasons, none of which were my reasons: went to convert, to proselyte, to observe, to do good, to sentimentalize . . . and I honor them all," he wrote after the war. He, however, "went just from my own reasons, from a profound conviction of necessity, affinity, coming into closest relations—relations O so close and dear!—with the whole strange welter of life gathered to that mad focus" (ibid., 14). He was drawn by curiosity, by the desire to be helpful, but also by a sense of belonging—or the need to belong—to this great congregation of humanity. Where else could he witness so many traits, good and bad, of the people he celebrated in his poetry? Where else could he feel so at the center of things? He believed that the experience made him a better person. When he asked himself "what did I get?" he answered, "Well, I got the boys, for one thing. . . . I gave myself for them." His work made him a better poet, too: "but for this I never would have had *Leaves of Grass*—the consummated book (the last confirming word)" (ibid., 16). The war—or being close to the war—became an obsession for

Whitman. He had to feel that he was an integral part of the massive war machine, but also a member of the mass of humanity that fed it.

Although Alcott no doubt considered her account of hospital life to be fairly realistic—she does refer to oozing stumps where arms used to be, she gingerly but truthfully refers to the awkwardness of the bathing process—her prose is far more delicate than Whitman's. This is not surprising; the two authors could not have chosen more different genres or career paths. The chaos and bloodiness of war fit Whitman's style perfectly, and his war-related prose and poetry teem with gore and realism. In an article that he wrote for the *New York Times* in February 1863, Whitman described a single man's journey from the front to the hospital. He intended it to demonstrate the "candor and manliness" that he had found among the patients in the army hospitals around Washington. It also showed readers that popular conceptions about the generosity of spirit among soldiers, the patriotism of everyone associated with the war effort, and the great care taken of wounded and sick soldiers was sometimes, sadly, lacking in real life. The young man in question was from Massachusetts and had been sick for some time before the Battle of Fredericksburg, in which he fought. He collapsed soon afterward, however, and began a grinding and exhausting journey from one hospital to another, finally being sent from the regimental hospital to Washington via Aquia Creek. There was no provision made for men who were not obviously and badly injured, and he remained, only partially conscious, on the deck of the steamer, unfed, without water, and uncovered in the chill, damp winter air. Surviving the trip to Washington, he was once again deposited on a wharf, where he lay until someone finally put him in an ambulance. He nearly died from the lack of attention. He fell into a semiconscious, quiet state, refusing to talk to anyone until Whitman happened by one day, got him to talk, wrote a letter for him to his family, and gradually worked his friendly magic on yet another tired soldier. The poet believed that the young private had nearly died, not from his sickness, bad as it was, but from a broken heart, due to the "long train of exhaustion, deprivation, rudeness, no food, no friendly word or deed, but all kinds of upstart airs and impudent, unfeeling speeches and deeds from all kinds of small officials . . . cutting like razors into that sensitive heart" (ibid., 88–90). Eventually he regained the will to live and, after a long stay in the hospital, was out of danger by the time Whitman wrote his dispatch to the *Times*. Such overt callousness rarely found its way into stories of wartime efforts to aid the soldiers.

Of course, Whitman's most memorable contribution to our understanding of the war came in the form of the celebratory but frank free verse in which he cataloged the character of his country and, after the war, commemorated the struggle to reunite the Union. "The Wound Dresser" reflected both his hospital experiences and his commitment to getting the "real war" into *his* books, at least. It tells of the nurse, "with hinged knees and steady hand," making his rounds through the hospital ward, changing the bandages on the silent wounded.

> On, on I go, (open doors of time! open hospital doors!)
> The crushed head I dress, (Poor crazed hand tear not the bandage away),
> The neck of the cavalry-man with the bullet through and through I examine,
> Hard the breathing rattles, quite glazed already the eye, yet life struggles hard,
> (Come sweet death! be persuaded O beautiful death!
> In mercy come quickly.)
> From the stump of the arm, the amputated hand,
> I undo the clotted lint, remove the slough, wash off the matter and blood,
> Back on his pillow the soldier bends with curv'd neck and side falling head,
> His eyes are closed, his face is pale, he dares not look on the bloody stump,
> And has not yet look'd on it. (ibid., 129)

Even in her brief career, Alcott certainly witnessed such scenes—she was a wound dresser, herself—but nothing she wrote matches the stark honesty of Whitman's simple description of this common image of war.

Alcott and Whitman began their service at about the same time, but for different reasons. Alcott returned home after only a few weeks and, although she lived into old age, never quite recovered from her bout of wartime sickness. Whitman lasted much longer as a nurse, but he, too, fell ill in the summer of 1864. He believed years after the war that he had lost his health permanently due to "the overzealous, overcontinued bodily and emotional excitement through the years of 1862, '63, '64, and '65." Like so many Americans who fought the Civil War on the battlefield or the home front, their war experiences never left Alcott and Whitman. Although they had injured their health in the war efforts, neither seemed to regret their decisions or their sacrifices and our knowledge of the home front is richer because the war inspired them to come to grips with the sacrifices, the subtly shifting roles of men and women, and the myriad other ways that the war tested the character of American soldiers and civilians.

Primary Sources:

Alcott, Louisa May. *Hospital Sketches*. Boston: J. Redpath, 1863.
Lowenfels, Walter. *Walt Whitman's Civil War*. New York: Knopf, 1960.

Secondary Sources:

Burton, David H. *Clara Barton: In the Service of Humanity*. Westport, CT: Greenwood, 1995.

Literary Nurses: Louisa May Alcott and Walt Whitman

Elbert, Sarah. *A Hunger for Home: Louisa May Alcott and Little Women.* Philadelphia: Temple University Press, 1984.

Kaplan, Justin. *Walt Whitman: A Life.* New York: Simon & Schuster, 1980.

Loving, Jerome. *Walt Whitman: The Song of Himself.* Berkeley: University of California Press, 1999.

Morris, Roy, Jr. *The Better Angel: Walt Whitman in the Civil War.* New York: Oxford University Press, 2000.

Oates, Stephen B. *A Woman of Valor: Clara Barton and the Civil War.* New York: Free Press, 1994.

Stern, Madeleine B. *Louisa May Alcott.* New York: Random House, 1996.

Chapter Eleven

Thinking Big: Love and Advice from Civil War Fathers

"I don't pretend to understand a girl or a woman," Lieutenant Colonel James Goodnow assured his wife Nancy. He went on to promise that he would never advise Nancy on how to raise their little daughter, Belle; he considered himself simply too ignorant to have any notions about bringing up females. He had plenty to say about how to raise sons, and from the time he left home late in 1862 until he resigned his commission two years later, Goodnow maintained a remarkable correspondence with his three sons back in Jefferson County, Indiana. Although his oldest, a teenager, Sam, received the longest and most detailed letters, James often enclosed separate notes for Daniel, who was about nine, and for Johnny, who was three or four. Like nearly all Civil War fathers who had the resources, education, time, and inclination to write home, Goodnow filled his letters with love and advice (Goodnow; James to Nancy, November 20, 1862).

The Civil War placed incredible pressure on families in both the Union and the Confederacy. Fathers and brothers left home for months, years—forever. Wives and children had to take the places of men in fields and shops. Many boys and some girls quit school to take jobs or to keep farms and plantations running. The unbearable stress of separation, worry, and economic hardship was perhaps the heaviest burden for those left behind. Fathers were not, of course, merely breadwinners; they provided emotional support and guidance. Men tried to continue fulfilling those roles despite the separation, and a veritable blizzard of letters flew between the armies and home. That correspondence offers glimpses of nineteenth-century family life and reveals that the relationships between fathers, mothers, and children was already changing from the stern, parent-centered family of the eighteenth and early nineteenth centuries to the "modern," affectionate, child-centered family of the twentieth century. The stresses and strains of the Civil War may have encouraged the development of closer family bonds. At the very least, their absence gave fathers the chance to articulate their concerns and affection, to put their love in writing. The overwhelming loneliness and longing of fathers and children, heartbreaking as it was, reveal the contours of the relationships between Civil War–era fathers in ways that may not have been as clear if the war had not happened.

Communicating with loved ones was a kind of therapy for at least some men, who described homely scenes and comfortable family circles in their letters.

The stresses and strains of the Civil War may have encouraged the development of closer family bonds.

Surgeon Edward Pye lightened the dreariness of a Confederate hospital in Houston by describing for his family the cozy vision of home that he stored in his memory. "Stand aside little ones & let me edge in to your *bright fire* this dark, cold, dismal night," he wrote gently. "Ma need'nt move & *Charley & Bud* can find a *place on each knee*—so now—how cheerful & pleasant to be amongst you all again! Now how Natural it seems to me—and how glad you all seem!—So You had not got used to doing without 'Pa' all these long *long weary days!* Nor have I, Dear ones, got used to doing without you" (Vandiver, 382). Even young men, who might be expected to prefer the adventure of military service over the quiet routines of civilian life, drew on similar images to sustain themselves. "This is the sort of day I always liked to be at home," nineteen-year-old Fred Fleet wrote his little sister on a chilly fall day in Virginia, "where we could all be sitting around a large fire in the chamber, some reading, others talking, and the little ones playing." Alas, he sighed, "I am afraid those happy days are past for me now" (Fleet and Fuller, 172–173).

Such happy memories frequently infiltrated the dreams of Confederate and Union soldiers. Winston Stephens described for his wife "a regular soldiers dream" in which he "had returned home" and "Rosa called Pa Pa & smacked her lips for a kiss" (Hodges and Kerber, 55). Dreams seemed more real than the nightmare of war, "so life-like & natural," according to one Confederate, "that I could hardly realize that I was not *at home* when I awoke in the morning. I seemed not only to see *your faces*—loving faces—but I heard & distinguished the voices . . . I saw & heard you all *so plainly!*" (Glover, 358).

A three-year-old once asked his mother what his soldier-father could be thinking about in his far-off camp. "About you," she assured him. "Then tell him to think *big*," pleaded the toddler, "so I can hear" ("Anecdotes and Sayings of Children," 41). Soldiers did, in fact, think big about their boys and girls, and in their letters they expressed constant concern for the physical and mental well-being of their children. The vast distances separating them from loved ones rendered them powerless and frustrated. Most would have loved to read, like one Iowa soldier did, that baby Charlie "has no fever and runs around. He is a caution for fun" (Mills, 515). Yet most men could not be assured of such benign and happy news. After learning of his newborn daughter's crippled hand, a

A sentimental Currier & Ives print illustrating soldiers' longing for home
(Library of Congress)

Mississippi cavalryman pleaded for more information. "My imagination has given wings to my anxiety," he exclaimed, "until my sleep has been disturbed and my waking hours rendered gloomy in consequence of all kind of vague suppositions" (Cash and Howorth, 146).

No news was never good news for soldiers obsessed with their families' wellbeing. Jedediah Hotchkiss, the distinguished Confederate topographical engineer, had to wait more than a week after learning of his daughter's critical illness. When two letters came the same day, he read them "with streaming eyes by the camp fire." He wrote his wife that he had been spending "sleepless nights . . . thinking of her and your sorrowing condition." The crisis passed in a few days; he soon received a letter containing a violet from her. "I was very happy to think my little daughter was reviving and getting new life again just as the sweet flowers are opening" (Hotchkiss; Jedediah Hotchkiss to Sara Hotchkiss, March 25, 26, 27, and April 4, 1862).

The birth of a son or daughter obviously inspired elation tempered by dismay at the miles separating father from newborn. When Lieutenant Colonel James

Williams, commanding the garrison of Fort Morgan near Mobile, heard of the birth of his son, George, in May 1863, he wrote his wife that "It is well that I have some control of my very restive and excitable nerves or they might have led me into extravagancies . . . that would ill accord with the dignity of the post com-

"My heart is bursting . . . I almost fear I shall go crazy—I don't see how I can stand it."

mander." Whenever he tried to work, his "wife and the black haired babe charge into my thoughts—break my lines of battle—harass my columns and demolish my squares in four ranks in a manner unknown before to military art" (Folman, 111, 118).

The death of a child caused equally strong, if opposite, emotions. Victorians placed great importance on the family and on salvation, so the death of a family member initiated a series of ritualized responses in which fathers in the army could participate only through aching letters to their wives. During the month after Edwin Fay's oldest son William Edwin died at the age of five, the despondent Confederate sergeant could only mourn through long and sometimes harsh letters. "My heart is bursting," Fay cried, "I almost fear I shall go crazy—I don't see how I can stand it." At one point, he blamed his wife for negligently allowing the boy to run outdoors too often and to eat too much fruit. He also blamed the Yankees, whose "accursed villainy took me away from my family." He saved plenty of blame for himself: if only he had not joined the Confederate army, perhaps he could have prevented Will Ed's death. He could at least have "been at home to see him die." He pleaded with his wife to "take care of our last one, do not let it die," then almost hysterically closed, "My heart is broken—I dont deserve or crave to live. . . . My heart is bursting, my brain on fire" (Wiley, 130–131).

The urgent longing to see their children, to fulfill their duties as fathers, to rekindle home fires, led Civil War soldiers to relish their encounters with children, even children whose own fathers and brothers were fighting in enemy armies. A North Carolinian wrote his nine-year-old boy that he "would give as much to see a little boy or a baby as you would give to see Genl. Beauregard" (Blacknall; Charles Blacknall to Oscar Blacknall, August 2, 1861). "Nothing would do me more good than to see a half-dozen bright little girls at play," wrote a young member of the 7th Pennsylvania to his younger sister. Of course, he added, "it would do me as *much* good to see one or two big ones" (McLaughlin, 132). Even the stern Stonewall Jackson delighted in the afternoon visits of a little girl named Janie Corbin to his headquarters near Fredericksburg during the spring of 1863. The proud and lonely father of an infant daughter he had barely seen, Jackson visited for hours with the five-year-old, cutting the gilt band from his army cap and arranging it in her hair.

Thinking Big: Love and Advice from Civil War Fathers

When armies went into winter quarters or were assigned to garrison duty, the children of officers sometimes accompanied mothers to camp. According to Colonel Thomas Wentworth Higginson, a single child could brighten the mood of an entire regiment. When the quartermaster of Higginson's African American regiment brought his wife and six-month-old baby to winter quarters on Port Royal Island, "the new recruit" became a valued member of the regiment. Her African American nurse frequently paraded her about the camp, and the baby nearly always attended the daily drills and dress parades. Officers reported to her for "orders" every morning, mischievous drummer boys loudly entertained her, and the sergeant-major would sometimes wrap her up in the folds of the lowered flag at retreat "like a new-born Goddess of Liberty." Visiting officers, old or young, never failed to look pleased at the sudden appearance of the "little, fresh, smiling creature,—a flower in the midst of war." The childless Higginson remarked in his memoir at his surprise that he had not shouted "Shoulder babies" rather than "Shoulder arms," since he never failed to notice the little girl out of the corner of his eye. Annie left camp in the spring and, in fact, died shortly after returning to the North. Yet Higginson devoted an entire chapter of his famous memoir to her short stay. "I know . . . that her little life, short as it seemed, was a blessing to us all, giving a perpetual image of serenity and sweetness, recalling the lovely atmosphere of far-off homes, and holding us by unsuspected ties to whatsoever things were pure" (Higginson, 177–186).

Of course, the satisfaction gained from playing with other people's children faded when soldiers returned to their lonely tents, where a child's cry in the distance or the notes of a familiar tune evoked bittersweet memories. As David Coon, the father of a four-year-old boy, snacked on a concoction of stewed apples, milk, sugar, and hardtack, his thoughts wandered home. "I don't know why," he wrote to his wife, "but I thought how Johnny would enjoy it if he would sit down with Pa and help eat it" (Coon; David Coon to Isabel Coon, July 14, 1864). Similarly, a lonely Texan took stark comfort in the knowledge that the stars shining down on his cold encampment also lit the night sky over his Waco home, where his five-year-old son and toddler daughter awaited his return. He thought of "the children's favorite, 'Twinkle, twinkle, little star,'" and wondered "if Stark has taught it to Mary yet" (West, 129).

James Goodnow's letters to his three sons rarely referred to nursery rhymes; his correspondence tended toward straightforward bits of advice and manly affection. He was committed, however, to continuing his role as guide and comfort to his boys. "I want that you and I should be regular correspondents during my absence," he wrote Sam, the eldest, in his first letter home. He urged him to "tell your mind freely," in weekly letters, to "tell me all about what you are doing—and all about your cares and troubles—and you may be sure I will always feel an interest in whatever interests or affects you" (Goodnow; James to Sam, November 20, 1862). Although Sam and Daniel both wrote frequent notes to their father, their letters have not survived. The several dozen letters written by Goodnow to his sons matched the interests and needs of each son. As the oldest, Sam received most of the general news about Goodnow's unit, including information about their travels in Alabama and other parts of the Western theater, speculations about military strategy, and a detailed description of the only battle that Goodnow fought. More important, however, were the pieces of fatherly advice and compassion and affection that Goodnow freely distributed. His letters to Sam frequently, if gently, nudged him toward adulthood. "It will not be long before you will have to go out in the world to make your own way," he wrote in that first letter, "and you will then be too busy to study." He naturally urged him to work hard at school, for "your success and usefulness will altogether depend on the way you employ your time now." Sam was also to "Remember always that your Mother has a right to your help" and that he could "never do too much for her" (February 20, 1863).

Indeed, the mindful father often reminded the boys to obey their mother. On one occasion, he was uncharacteristically stern when he blamed Nancy Goodnow's poor health at least partly on the fact that "you have made her do too much work." Sam must realize how hard she had labored to care for him over the years and out of "common gratitude make up to her for what she has done for you." He and his brothers were to carry all the wood, make all the fires, milk the cow, work in the garden, help with the wash, and generally "take all work off her hands that you can do" (January 11, 1863).

Variations on these themes of duties to be fulfilled abounded. Although he expressed surprise that Sam had been temporarily suspended from school—he could not "believe you were deserving of such harsh treatment"—he advised him to go to the teacher, apologize, and promise to obey him in the future. "If he is a reasonable man that will be enough" (February 20, 1863). Ever watchful of his son's future, Goodnow wrote that, as he approached manhood, Sam must learn to value the "habits of industry and also to . . . not be ashamed of honest labor." Apparently the young man was working while he attended school, which pleased his father, who commented that even if Sam did not care for the job, he could at least have "the satisfaction of knowing that you are earning your own livelihood" (April 6, 1863).

The two younger sons received similar messages tailored to their ages and interests. Goodnow's first letter to "Master Daniel Goodnow" began with chitchat about Christmas and Saint Nicholas, but he quickly moved to more exciting information regarding his army experiences. "Well Dan," he wrote breezily, "you ought to be out here and See our big armies." He described their march out of

Officers could sometimes bring their families to live with the army; this is Brigadier General John Rawlins and his family standing in the door of their quarters at City Point, Virginia. (Library of Congress)

Memphis and their encampment. "If you would have been there you would have thought there was going to be a battle there was So much noise. The men Cheered and yelled and the mules brayed loud enough to make you jump out of your boots." Despite the excitement and drama, Goodnow was very glad that his boys were not with him, "for wherever the large armies go here they drive the people away from home and take all they have to eat and all their corn and then burn their houses and fields—and a great many little boys down here do not have enough to Eat and often have no home" (James to Dan, January 11, 1863). Dan also received advice, but of a very different sort than Sam. Whenever he felt like quarreling or crying, suggested Goodnow, "just run out into the wood Shed and Saw a few Sticks of wood and See if you don't get in a good humor before you get done" (February 20, 1863). Even Johnny, whose mother had to read his letters for him, got advice. "I have been wanting to See you for a long time," wrote James, "but I am too far away to go home often." Like countless fathers throughout the Union and Confederate armies, he promised that when he returned, "we will have a big talk." In the meantime, "I want you to be the best little boy . . . I dont want you to Say any bad words—or cry much—I want you to be a man" (James to Johnny, February 20, 1863). Dan and Johnny later received a joint letter that assured them

"I have always had confidence in you, knowing that you would do right when you reflected on your duty. . ."

that "although you are little fellows I think as much of you as I do of Sam," and emphasized the importance of their helping out around the house. "I want you to play and enjoy yourselves as much as you can," wrote their father, "but you must not forget to be at home when your Mother wants you." Johnny could baby-sit their little sister, while Dan could easily fetch wood, wash dishes, feed the cow, and "do a hundred little things that wont be much trouble to him, but will Save mother from getting tired" (James to Dan and Johnny, October 25, 1863).

The boys frequently received congratulations from their father for their good behavior, and kind words from an approving dad never failed to follow news that they were behaving themselves at school and at home. "I have always had confidence in you," he assured Sam, "knowing that you would do right when you reflected on your duty, and I am proud indeed to know that my confidence is well founded" (James to Sam, October 25, 1863). To Dan, Goodnow wrote how much he appreciated the little boy's "very good letters"; "if you will only learn to write a little plainer, you will Soon do first rate" (James to Dan, January 11, 1863). He was also immensely pleased when Nancy reported that Dan sawed and split all the wood. "I don't say go in lemons," he wrote—apparently meaning "don't let it go to your head"—"but I do say there are not many boys of your age can do that much" (February 20, 1863).

James Goodnow returned to his boys back in Jefferson County safe and sound, but many fathers did not. Some of the most poignant letters written by Civil War fathers assured young children that, as long as they behaved themselves, their fathers and brothers would remain safe. "A great many little girls like you, have lost their father in this battle," Wisconsin's Colonel Hans Heg once wrote his daughter, Hilga, who probably did not have to be reminded about the dangers her father faced. Late in 1862, Heg wrote that "When I get into Battle I might get shot, but if you are a good girl and Edmund is a good boy, God will take care of me for you" (Blegen, 157, 175). Marcus Speigel was a little more subtle when he mentioned that he had recently been in a battle with "the Cannon Balls . . . flying over my head but none hurt me; the good Lord preserved me from any harm and if you will only be right good Children, mind well and pray to the good Lord, I trust soon to see you all well and hearty" (Byrne and Soman, 80–81). Henry Abbott similarly linked his survival to the behavior of his favorite brother, five-year-old Grafton: "Now you must be good all the time & remember, when you get mad & begin to cry, it makes the rebel bullets come a good deal nearer to me" (Abbott, 117). As if the men were playing roles in sentimental and moralistic Victorian tale, all three were killed—Colonel Heg at Chickamauga, Colonel Speigel in a Confederate ambush in May 1864, and Major Abbott at the Battle of the Wilderness at about the same time—leaving Hilga and Edmund Heg, the three Speigel children, and Grafton Abbott not only to mourn their loved ones but to wonder about their own roles in the deaths of these loving but misguided men.

As the Hegs, Speigels, and little Grafton Abbott knew, the correspondence between soldiers and their families could be a two-edged sword. Letters from the front helped their readers understand what fathers and brothers, husbands and sons were going through, while at the same time they alerted the folks back home to the dangers their men faced, understandably causing them to worry. Yet the letters also clearly provided comfort in the knowledge that those men, despite the hardships and dangers they faced, still thought about their families and still wanted to be fathers in fact as well as in name. Such letters suggest that Civil War–era fathers were deeply concerned with their children and that child rearing was not simply a duty best left to mothers. Indeed, the love and advice that animated these men's letters to their children prove that the war may have driven families apart physically, while at the same time drawing them closer together emotionally.

PRIMARY SOURCES:

Abbott, Henry Livermore. *Fallen Leaves: The Civil War Letters of Major Henry Livermore Abbott.* Kent, OH: Kent State University Press, 1991.

"Anecdotes and Sayings of Children." *The Little Pilgrim* 10 (March 1863).

Blacknall, Oscar W. Papers. North Carolina State Archives, Raleigh, NC.

Blegen, Theodore C., ed. *The Civil War Letters of Colonel H. C. Heg.* Northfield, MN: Norwegian-American Historical Association, 1936.

Byrne, Frank L., and Jean P. Soman, eds. *Your True Marcus: The Civil War Letters of a Jewish Colonel.* Kent, OH: Kent State University Press, 1985.

Cash, William M., and Lucy Somerville Howorth, eds. *My Dear Nellie: The Civil War Letters of William L. Nugent to Eleanor Smith Nugent.* Jackson: University Press of Mississippi, 1977.

Coon, David. Letters. Library of Congress, Washington, DC.

Fleet, Betsy, and John D. P. Fuller. *Green Mount: A Virginia Plantation Family during the Civil War.* Lexington: University Press of Kentucky, 1962.

Folman, John Kent, ed. *From That Terrible Field: Civil War Letters of James W. Williams, Twenty-First Alabama Infantry Volunteers.* Tuscaloosa: University of Alabama Press, 1981.

Glover, Robert W., ed. "The War Letters of a Texas Conscript in Arkansas." *Arkansas Historical Quarterly* 20 (Winter 1961).

Goodnow, James Harrison. Papers. Library of Congress, Washington, DC.

Higginson, Thomas Wentworth. *Army Life in a Black Regiment.* Boston: Fields, Osgood, 1870. Reprint, New York: W. W. Norton, 1984.

Hodges, Ellen E., and Stephen Kerber, eds. "Children of Honor: Letters of Winston and Octavia Stephens, 1861–1865." *Florida Historical Quarterly* 56 (July 1977).

Hotchkiss, Jedediah. Papers. Family Correspondence. Library of Congress, Washington, DC.

McLaughlin, Florence C., ed. "'Dear Sister Jennie—Dear Brother Jacob': The Correspondence between a Northern Soldier and His Sister in Mechanicsburg, Pennsylvania, 1861–1864." *Western Pennsylvania Historical Magazine* 60 (April 1977).

Mills, George, ed. "The Sharp Family Civil War Letters." *Annals of Iowa, 3rd Ser.* 34 (January 1959).

Vandiver, Frank E., ed. "Letters from the Confederate Medical Service in Texas, 1863–1865." *Southwestern Historical Quarterly* 55 (January 1952).

West, John. *A Texan in Search of a Fight.* Waco: J. S. Hill, 1901.

Wiley, Bell Irvin, ed. *"This Infernal War": The Confederate Letters of Sgt. Edwin H. Fay.* Austin: University of Texas Press, 1958.

SECONDARY SOURCE:

Marten, James. *The Children's Civil War.* Chapel Hill: University of North Carolina Press, 1998.

Chapter Twelve

A Record of Munificence: Supporting the Troops

"This Book contains the story of seventy millions of dollars." So wrote Frank B. Goodrich, compiler of *The Tribute Book: A Record of the Munificence, Self-Sacrifice and Patriotism of the American People during the War for the Union.* Published soon after the Civil War ended, *The Tribute Book* recorded the many different ways in which Northerners supported the Union war effort. "Ordinarily," Goodrich admitted, "millions do not furnish an interesting or an instructive theme; he who writes their history has generally little to tell but a tale of selfishness and greed, or at best, of dogged industry or stubborn self-denial." The person who "collects the chronicles of dollars and cents, pounds, shillings, and pence" can rarely "lay before the reader . . . a record of self-sacrifice." But the history of the home front efforts of thousands of Northerners was "not the annals of mercantile shrewdness, of wealth heaped up by toil or avarice," but was instead "the records of money given, not money earned; of a labor of love, not of labor for hire and salary; of self-assessment, of tribute rendered always willingly, often unasked" (3).

The amount of time, sweat, and money that went into the home front support for the war effort was unprecedented. Although fairs, raffles, and bazaars had long been used as fund-raisers for churches, schools, orphanages, and other "non-profits," as they would be called today—before the war, abolitionists had raised money at fairs, including Boston's annual "Anti-Slavery Bazaar"—the sheer scale of the fund-raising, the large number of volunteers, the ambition of the organizers to create national rather than purely local campaigns, and the degree of centralization and administration all outpaced prewar philanthropy. The efforts of the United States Sanitary Commission, the United States Christian Commission, and the countless other large and small organizations that collected food and supplies for the soldiers, raised money, or bolstered morale reflected a growing, if at times controversial, confidence in corporate philanthropy, offered sometimes temporary but meaningful employment and leadership positions to women, and helped make the Civil War one of the first "modern" wars by mobilizing the economy as well as the military.

The Tribute Book highlighted the "ways and means by which" individuals and organizations throughout the United States, already "having been taxed to pay

> *The amount of time, sweat, and money that went into the home front support for the war effort was unprecedented.*

three thousand millions of dollars for the prosecution of the war . . . of their own accord, without tax or toll, collected and expended nearly seventy million more" (3). Goodrich claimed to have condensed enough material for twenty volumes into this single book, chronicled a diverse set of causes, ranging from promoting enlistments, providing supplies to the families of soldiers, caring for sick and wounded soldiers, "sustain[ing] the efficiency of the army," aiding Unionists within Confederate lines and soldiers' orphans in the North, creating "soldiers' rests," and memorializing dead and rewarding living soldiers and officers. As such, the book embraces the activities of all "those who, unable to aid the government by shouldering a musket, still wished to serve their country according to their strength[s]" (78).

Taking the place of honor in Goodrich's book, as well as in the overall fundraising machinery of the Union, was the U.S. Sanitary Commission. The explosive growth of the U.S. Army during the summer of 1861 inspired a small group of Northern civilians to develop an organization dedicated to providing medical care, supplies, and other comforts and necessities to soldiers in the field. Chartered but not funded by the War Department, the USSC was modeled at least partly on British sanitary commissions organized during the Crimean War and during the Indian mutiny. The commission and its regional and local branches set out with "scientific thoroughness" to build and administer hospitals and soldiers' lodging houses; recruit nurses, doctors, and ambulance drivers; provide blankets and stationery; deliver telegrams and letters; and help soldiers apply for disability pensions. To do this, the commission formed 7,000 aid societies, organized branches in ten cities—including the huge and semi-independent Northwestern Branch, headquartered in Chicago—and employed hundreds of paid agents.

Goodrich claimed that 2,300 soldiers were received every day by the twenty-five "soldiers' homes" established from Louisville to Washington, where soldiers going to and from the field armies received rations, a clean bed, and even medical care. Soldiers could receive help filling out pension forms, securing enlistment bounties, and recovering lost paperwork. Some men preferred to deposit their meager pay with a USSC agent rather than run the risk of spending it on cheap whiskey and prostitutes. The families of sick and wounded soldiers could

Women making rifle cartridges at the U.S. Arsenal (Library of Congress)

rely on the commission for help traveling to and from army hospitals and for lodging while attending to disabled menfolk.

In addition, the commission maintained a registry containing the names of 600,000 hospitalized men, hired sixty "of the most skilful [*sic*] surgeons and physicians in the nation" (95) to inspect army hospitals, maintain hospital ships and trains to carry men away from battlefields, and organize wagon trains of hospital supplies and ambulances so field hospitals could be quickly set up once the fighting began.

Although tens of thousands of women performed the bulk of the commission's work at the local level, it was led at the national level by men from the highest ranks of society. Its president was Henry W. Bellows, a Unitarian minister, while the conservative New York lawyer George Templeton Strong served as treasurer, and landscape architect Frederick Law Olmsted was secretary. Rejecting the idealism of antebellum reformers, the men who set commission policy insisted on practical reform, on administering an organization that paid its own way, on setting measurable, hardheaded goals. These strong, shrewd men insisted that the fuzzy-headed idealism that they believed had driven the great antebellum reform movements had no place in the massive effort required to meet the nation's greatest crisis.

The commission's methods, strict rules, and centralized administration were sometimes controversial, yet most of the men, women, and children who pitched in acted out of unabashed compassion and enthusiasm. Local women's organizations and soldiers' aid societies eagerly attached their own work to the commission's. Among the earliest efforts were the "Alert Clubs" established in towns and villages all around the North. The first club, organized by the children of Norwalk, Ohio, raised $560 in just a little over a year, which was used to purchase material and sewing supplies to make uniforms for the soldiers.

Gentlemen were asked for "as much as their good will prompted them to give."

Nationwide, members of the clubs—unlike the original "Alert Club," many were adults—were assigned certain neighborhoods to canvas. Women were asked to subscribe to the club for $.20 a month, while gentlemen were asked for "as much as their good will prompted them to give" (88). Contributions were turned in at the meetings held on the first Monday of each month, where women and girls could, if they liked, sew slippers and quilts. Apparently, however, the women and girls focused much more on raising money through a wide variety of events and campaigns. They held concerts and tea parties during the winter and strawberry festivals early in the summer; gave up money they would have spent for fireworks to buy onions in July (to prevent scurvy in soldiers whose army diets rarely included fruit and vegetables), and picked and sold blackberries in August. The younger members "held fairs on the door-step and in the front yard, whenever it did not rain; enacted charades when any one would pay to see them; and, throughout the war, worked with a zeal worthy of older heads, and an unselfishness beyond all praise" (88).

Central to the Sanitary Commission's fund-raising were the giant "Sanitary Fairs" held during the last two years of the war. Building on longtime Northern traditions of church, school, and community "fairs" to raise money for benevolent projects, the commission staged fairs in cities large and small, from Damariscotta, Maine, to Dubuque, Iowa, and from New York City and Brooklyn to Cincinnati and St. Louis. Lowell, Massachusetts, had the honor of holding the first fair to benefit the Sanitary Commission. Originally conceived as a traditional, neighborhood affair by twenty or so women, it grew into a citywide effort organized by representatives of every church in town, Catholic as well as Protestant, and many individuals. Their efforts brought $4,850 into the Sanitary Commission's treasury.

Although Lowell provided a model of civic patriotism and cooperation, the amount of money raised there paled in comparison to the vast sums brought in by the first of the really large fairs, sponsored by the Northwestern Branch in Chicago in the fall of 1863. On October 27, banks, post offices, schools, and businesses closed for the day, and tens of thousands of people, young and old, elbowed their way into the dozens of displays, exhibits, and shops. The Chicago Fair, like all the fairs, raised money in several ways: by charging admission; by soliciting cash donations; by selling a huge range of crafts, toys, and baked goods and other food products; and by sponsoring performances ranging from amateur theatricals and tableaux to singing and gymnastics demonstrations by schoolchildren. Regular features at the fairs included tables or booths displaying and selling arts, crafts, and snacks peculiar to individual Northern states. Many had "New England Kitchens," while most included displays of little girls dressed as "The Old Lady Who Lived in a Shoe" surrounded by dolls that were, of course, for sale. Rooms were packed with Union and Confederate flags; battlefield artifacts like captured guns, swords, and splinters from famous ships; and famous documents—a draft of President Lincoln's Emancipation Proclamation was auctioned off for $3,000 at the Chicago Fair in 1863. Many fairs published their own newspapers, like Albany's *The Canteen* and Brooklyn's *The Drumbeat,* which listed hundreds of contributors, ranging from the economic and political elite to lowly residents of orphanages and members of Sabbath school classes.

As Goodrich noted in his description of the Lake County delegation, children were conspicuous participants in the fairs, as attendees as well as contributors. Newspaper descriptions show why children flocked by the thousands to the fairs. The Great Central Fair in Philadelphia offered automaton rope dancers, stereopticon views, magic shows, ventriloquists, and (foreshadowing a marketing device in modern fast-food franchises) an indoor playground adjacent to the sprawling restaurant. The Children's Department of New York's Metropolitan Fair, according to *Frank Leslie's Illustrated Weekly,* was "a treasury of useful articles, toys and knick-knacks, almost realising the fables of fairyland" (*Frank Leslie's Illustrated Weekly,* June 25, 1864). Youngsters in Albany could cluster around the "very remarkable animal called the Gorilla" at the "Gipsey tent" and the "life picture" of Indian life—complete with a canoe, baskets, and ladies dressed in Native American costumes—at the "Wigwam." Boys elbowed through crowds sometimes "so immense that locomotion was well nigh impossible" at the other exhibits to get into the 1,800-square-foot "Military Department." There they admired a musket fired at the Battle of Bunker Hill, a Cornwallis pistol captured at Yorktown, and Lafayette's camp

Entire communities became involved in the campaigns to support the men at the front. A wagon train from Lake County carried 100 loads of vegetables, barrels of cider, and kegs of beer, which upon arrival were unloaded by a gang of Lake County boys. "This magnificent harvest-home brought tears to the eyes of many a spectator, and would have done, doubtless, had the onions been parsnips" (161).

kettle. Even more interesting were such items as the clothes worn by Elmer Ellsworth, friend of Abraham Lincoln and the first Union officer killed in the Civil War, when he was killed, as well as the gun that killed him and the soldier who avenged him, scores of firearms, fragments from a shell fired into Fort Sumter, the battle flags of seventy New York regiments, and a number of captured rebel banners. The "Trophy Room" offered more captured Confederate battle flags as well as metal splinters from the Confederate ironclad *Virginia* and an iron plate from a Union ironclad (*The Canteen*, February 20, 27, 29, and March 4, 1864). Children at the Brooklyn Fair cast a quick glance at William Bradford's china, George Washington's punch bowl, and Miles Standish's hoe in the "Art and Curiosity Museum," but probably devoted more attention to the "Rebel war memorials," which included "muskets, pistols, sabres, pikes, swords, and Arkansas tooth picks" (*The Drumbeat*, March 1, 1864).

Very late in the war, a Chicagoan named Alfred L. Sewell applied the principle of centrally organized giving to children's fund-raising by devising the "Army of the American Eagle" as a way to raise money for the second Chicago Fair. Sewell later wrote in *The Little Corporal*, a juvenile magazine he also founded, that he had been trying to think of a way to "marshal the children . . . and give them a chance to show how well they love their country and her brave defenders." His plan was to entice boys and girls to sell pictures of "Old Abe, the War Eagle," mascot of the 8th Wisconsin, legendary for leading his regiment into numerous battles and emerging unscathed. The Chicago attorney made children "privates" in the Army of the American Eagle simply for buying pictures for a dime each. Recruits who sold pictures to other children or to adults advanced through the "ranks" of Sewell's "army," starting with a corporal's rank for selling 10 copies and progressing up to major general for selling 4,000 copies. Other incentives included gold, silver, and bronze medals for the best-selling salesmen and saleswomen. One picture at a time, 12,000 children from all over the North raised more than $16,000 (*The Little Corporal*, July 1865).

Although the Sanitary Commission may have dominated the headlines, many other organizations also contributed mightily to the Northern war effort. The USSC's largest competitor—and they did "compete" for the energies and wallets of Northerners—was the United States Christian Commission, which first appeared when members of the New York chapter of the Young Men's Christian Association began greeting regiments as they passed through the city on their way to Washington in the spring of 1861. Although committed to distributing Bibles, religious tracts, and other items aimed at nurturing the soldiers' spiritual

The Grand Music Festival at a sanitary fair in Philadelphia (Corbis)

sides, the USCC did not neglect the temporal needs of the men fighting for the Union and also raised money to buy much-needed camp and medical supplies.

Although smaller in scope than the USSC, the Christian Commission also established local and state organizations, which, like their secular counterparts, adopted prewar methods of raising money to pay for the publications and supplies flowing to the camps. In a rare display of cooperation, Baltimore branches of the two commissions held a joint fair that opened, with President Lincoln in attendance, on April 18, 1864, one day before the third anniversary of the attack on the 6th Massachusetts as it passed through Baltimore on the way to Washington at the beginning of the war. The Maryland State Fair featured the usual array of moneymaking and entertainment activities—including a "New England Kitchen," a doll shop (called "the Cinderella" rather than the "Old Lady Who Lived in a Shoe"), and displays of battle flags and historic relics (for example, Washington's bucket, furnishings from the old state capitol at

Annapolis, chairs from the Mayflower). Not surprisingly, given the participation of the Christian Commission, there was a religious tone to some of the exhibits and booths: Jacob's Well provided soda water and lemonade with names like Adam's Ale, while Adam's Express Company employed a manager called "Mrs. Eve." There were also many raffles—still considered by some to be a close enough kin to gambling to make it distasteful, if not sinful, to many Christians—for handcrafts and gold rings hidden inside pieces of cake.

Despite the storm of criticism that greeted the Emancipation Proclamation when it was issued on January 1, 1863, many Northerners devoted their time to helping African Americans in the South. The first of the organizations dedicated to helping the freedpeople of the South appeared in Boston early in February 1862, just after Union troops' capture of Port Royal and Beaufort, South Carolina, brought thousands of slaves into Federal lines. The "New England Freedmen's Aid Society" immediately put out a call for money and clothing; the response was so great that within weeks supplies were heading for the South, soon to be followed by over thirty teachers. By the end of the war, the Society had sent more than 200 teachers to Virginia and North and South Carolina. The progress shown by the freedpeople was described in the rather condescending and confidently optimistic tone of antebellum reformers: "They are self-supporting; they are prosperous; they are valuable producers; they are profitable customers; and one out of three of the whole population has received more or less instruction in the schools" (368).

Just days after the New Englanders established their organization, the National Freedmen's Relief Association was organized in New York, with the same goals as their New England predecessors. Its mission statement, as expressed in a public call for donations, was fourfold: to clothe, shelter, and cure the sick, ragged, and orphaned freedpeople; to "aid in placing the freedmen in positions of self-sustenance" by providing jobs and implements; to create and support schools for the adults and children among the freedpeople, in order to teach them the "three Rs" as well as domestic skills and to provide religious instruction; and to help those loyal white refugees who may be in distress (370).

Unlike the Sanitary and Christian Commissions, the campaign to aid the freedmen did not achieve a national organization, and unity of purpose sometimes suffered from regional and denominational jealousies. The various organizations—Cincinnati; District of Columbia; Worcester, Massachusetts; Concord, New Hampshire; as well as New York and Boston and even London and Manchester, England—occasionally tried to organize nationally, but none of the efforts worked out.

Northerners nevertheless evinced a fair amount of goodwill toward the freedmen, and Goodrich offers a charming story of the "Bird's Nest Bank of

A Record of Munificence: Supporting the Troops

Kalamazoo" as an example of the sort of grassroots fund-raising that character-ized the Freedmen's Aid Societies as well as the Sanitary and Christian Commissions. The children of a church in Kalamazoo, Michigan, met every Sunday in a chapel called the "Bird's Nest." One day in February 1864 a sol-dier visited from a nearby encampment. Legend has it that when the collec-tion plate was passed, he dropped in a penny and said, "here is a penny I found in the bottom of my pocket, and it won't grow there; now I want to deposit it with the 'Bird's Nest,' and see if it will

Northerners nevertheless evinced a fair amount of goodwill toward the freedmen.

grow THERE." The teacher took the cue and she and her students soon estab-lished the "Bird's Nest Bank." Stockholders bought "shares" for $.10 and the children set out to solicit investors on Wednesday and Sunday afternoons. Three little girls sold eighty-nine shares in less than a month, and soldiers and chil-dren from virtually every Northern state and England and Scotland contributed. Within a year, 2,400 shares had been purchased. Sadly, the "founder" of the bank had died before the end of the war, never knowing that his spontaneous act had resulted in the mobilization of hundreds of children and adults on behalf of African Americans they had never met. In his honor, his penny was polished and hung from a red, white, and blue ribbon each Sunday in the Bird's Nest.

Fund-raising was a central component of the Northern home front. Southerners, of course, also worked for their soldiers by holding bazaars and forming soldiers' aid societies. Most Confederate efforts, however, were entirely local; there was no Confederate equivalent of the Sanitary Commission. This was partly due to the political orientation of the states' rights South; it was also due to the largely rural nature of the Confederacy, to the constant disruption caused by local military operations, and to the economic distress that plagued most fam-ilies. Southerners did their best. During its first six months of work, the Spartanburg, South Carolina, Methodist Sunday School Relief Society, organized by the Sunday scholars and their teachers, raised over $60 by selling needle-work, blackberries, and blackberry wine. Over the next two years, the Society sent boxes to the army containing clothing, towels, bedding, cooking utensils, cakes, and dried fruit, as well as a bottle of laudanum, a butter dish, a bundle of religious tracts, and a box of guava jelly.

But soaring inflation and shortages of necessities caused Southerners to raise only a fraction of the money and supplies collected by Yankees. In the North, the Sanitary Commission and other patriotic philanthropies touched virtually every civilian and became a central component of the way they thought about the war and about themselves, as three stories from the children's magazine *Our Young Folks* suggest. The spoiled children in Lydia Maria Child's "The Two

Christmas Evenings" learn the true meaning of the holiday by raising money for a local orphan asylum and for books and toys for black children in South Carolina with a year long series of tableaux, speeches on liberty and patriotism, and sales of handicrafts. A girl in another story gives the money she had hoarded to spend at the local sanitary fair to a poor soldier's orphan, while Gertie, the "Discontented Girl," finally does her share for the soldiers after her older brother calls her a "rebel" for her lazy refusal to get to work. In stories such as these, readers learned the valuable lessons that fictional characters had been demonstrating for years. Even the war effort had to include life lessons applicable to peacetime.

Indeed, the centralization of philanthropy and the bureaucratization of giving inspired by the war left its mark on Northern—and, ultimately, American— society. It is not far-fetched to suggest that, after they grew up, Northern children adapted and refined the businesslike ideas about centralization and efficiency their parents had applied to the massive mobilization of manpower and resources that won the war. Their new attitudes shifted reform and benevolence from an evangelical, individualistic footing to one of scale and pragmatism that would eventually include a willingness to allow at least a modicum of government-controlled reform. They would target outlaw trusts, the most egregious social ills, and some of the problems caused by rapid urbanization and unregulated immigration in attempting to bring order to their section. These were obviously not the precise goals of the well-meaning ladies, patriotic gentlemen, and excited children who contributed to the success of Northern wartime philanthropy. Nonetheless, the coming together of Yankee civilians to support the war effort affected the social consciousness of the society in which they lived as much as it helped the North preserve the Union.

PRIMARY SOURCES:

The Canteen (Albany, NY, February–March 1864).
The Drumbeat (Brooklyn and Long Island, NY, March 1864).
Frank Leslie's Illustrated Weekly (June 25, 1864).
Goodrich, Frank B., comp. The Tribute Book: A Record of the Munificence, Self-Sacrifice and Patriotism of the American People during the War for the Union. New York: Derby & Miller, 1865. Unless otherwise stated, all quotations are from The Tribute Book.
The Little Corporal (Chicago, IL, July 1865).

A Record of Munificence: Supporting the Troops

SECONDARY SOURCES:

Frederickson, George M. *The Inner Civil War: Northern Intellectuals and the Crisis of the Union.* New York: Harper & Row, 1965.

Gordon, Beverly. "A Furor of Benevolence." *Chicago History* 15 (Winter 1986–1987): 48–65.

Maxwell, William. *Lincoln's Fifth Wheel: The Political History of the United States Sanitary Commission.* New York: Longmans, Green, 1956.

Thompson, William Y. "Sanitary Fairs of the Civil War." *Civil War History* 4 (March 1958): 51–67.

Chapter Thirteen

"The Bloody Week": The New York City Draft Riots

It is not without a shudder that we proceed to give an account of the horrors perpetrated on the citizens of the city[,] . . . the catalogue of . . . barbarities almost
without a parallel in the dark ages, and certainly transcending anything of modern times. The bombardment of a city by a foreign foe is nothing to be compared
to it. . . . When a band of men—thirsting for blood and hungry for plunder—are
in our midst, led on by men maddened with drink, and utterly lost to every sense
of humanity and decency—and whose only ambition is plunder and murder, language fails to express the horrors of the scene.

So began one of the first published accounts of the most serious breech of
order on the Northern home front during the Civil War: the New York City draft
riots of mid-July 1863. The emotion-filled introduction continued:

No matter what was the assumed cause of the outbreak, politically, that cause was
no justification for murdering peaceful citizens—for pillaging and burning private
dwellings—and for rendering homeless innocent babes. The mind can scarcely
conceive a worse picture than this city presented during Monday, Tuesday, and
Wednesday. The howls of these barbarians and inhuman ruffians, as they marched
from one street to another, the crackling of the flames, the crash of the falling
walls, the roar of cannon and the rattling of musketry, mingled with the cries of
pain and rage from the multitude. The honest citizen knew not at what moment the
torch would be applied to his own dwelling, and his family obliged to take refuge
in the streets. Mothers wrung their hands in agony, fathers looked pale and care-
worn, while the younger members of the family were terror stricken at the sights
they beheld. (1)

The events chronicled in the thirty pages that followed were startling in their
violence—the riot still stands as the bloodiest episode of urban unrest in U.S.
history—but the unnamed compilers of the pamphlet describing them had a
broader agenda than simply relating the facts. Their title says it all: *The Bloody*

Week! Riot, Murder & Arson, Containing A Full Account of the Wholesale Outrage on Life and Property, Accurately Prepared from Official Sources, by Eye Witnesses, with Portraits of "Andrews," the Leader and "Rosa," his Eleventh Street Mistress. Here was violence and insult, treachery and crime, shady characters and sex. The rioters certainly directed their violence at the people, institutions, and property of New York, but there was even more at stake: their cowardly actions challenged the very power of the federal government and threatened to undermine the Northern war effort.

The hyperbole of the introduction barely matched the reality. Few observers could deny the massive destruction and loss of life, the savagery of the crowd and, at times, of the police response, or the ways that the riot reflected serious strains of dissent and disaffection toward the U.S. government. *The Bloody Week!,* which internal evidence suggests was rushed into print by the 18th or 19th of July, before the ashes from the hundreds of fires had cooled or all of the casualties had been counted, says as much about Northern wartime attitudes about dissent, the war effort, ethnicity, and race as it does about the actual fighting in New York City.

New York City was a Democratic stronghold in a state controlled by Democrats, a reality that led to frequent clashes with the Republican administration in Washington. In the early days of the war, some city fathers suggested that New York should remain an "open city"—neutral, in effect, in the war to save the Union—and although that idea was quickly discarded and although most New Yorkers had cheered their boys on to battle, there were still rumblings throughout the city as the war dragged into its third year in the summer of 1863.

The two main complaints of New Yorkers, especially the large immigrant, working-class population, and especially among the overwhelmingly Democratic Irish workers who dominated parts of the city, were the Emancipation Proclamation, which went into effect on January 1, 1863, and the Enrollment Act, passed on March 3, 1863. Although the Emancipation Proclamation's provisions were rather limited (only those slaves living inside Confederate lines were actually considered free, leaving out tens of thousands of slaves in Union-occupied Confederate territory and all the bondsmen and women slaves living in Delaware, Maryland, Missouri, and Kentucky, the four "border" states still in the Union), it was extremely unpopular with the Democratic Party. The New York Irish complained that emancipating slaves was not the reason the federal government had gone to war; part of their concern stemmed from the fear that freed slaves would flock into Northern cities and take away the low-paying jobs from which most Irish scraped meager livings. That rocky future seemed much closer when, in June, striking Irish dockworkers were replaced by African Americans under police guard.

"The Bloody Week": The New York City Draft Riots

A mob lynching an African American on Clarkson Street during the New York City draft riots (Harper's Weekly, *July 1863*)

The Enrollment Act posed a more direct threat to working-class New Yorkers; it allowed the federal government to conscript men directly into the Union army. States and even local communities had used similar "drafts" to reach their enlistment quotas in the past, but state procedures contained numerous loopholes, and the extraordinary manpower needs of the Union war machine threatened to overwhelm the decentralized system. (State drafts had sparked riots in far-off Wisconsin as early as 1862 and resistance in Maryland and Pennsylvania as well.) The federal law closed many of those loopholes; all able-bodied men between the ages of twenty and thirty-five and unmarried men between the ages of thirty-five and forty-five would be enrolled by government agents going door-to-door. If a congressional district failed to meet its quota, a lottery-style drawing would fill out the state's regiments. Some occupations were exempt from enrollment, but the most controversial provisions excluded African Americans from the draft and allowed men to buy exemptions for $300. Although set at a level that the Republican Party believed most men could afford, the price was out of reach for many New York workingmen hit hard by the recession of 1861–1862 and by the normal, seasonal unemployment of the winter and early spring. They resented the fact that well-off gentlemen—such as Theodore Roosevelt, merchant, Republican, and father to four-year-old and future president Teddy—could choose not to enter the military, while boys from the working-class neighborhoods in the Upper East Side's desperately poor Eleventh Ward had no choice but to submit to the draft.

In addition to the anger and excitement inspired by emancipation and conscription, the early days of July had brought other sources of tension to the Northern home front. Lee's army had invaded Maryland and Pennsylvania, and the campaign leading up to the massive battle of Gettysburg had occupied the public's attention for weeks, with militia units and "thirty-day" and "ninety-day" regiments mobilized to defend the homeland. Union forces had turned back Lee's army, of course, and when word arrived early in July that the Confederate stronghold at Vicksburg had fallen after a long, bloody campaign, the war finally seemed to be headed in the right direction for the North. Despite the good news, New York retained a hothouse atmosphere. As late as the weekend of July 3 and 4, "peace" meetings had been held around the city. The tension grew as the date for drawing names approached, the most recent in a series of postponed efforts to begin the lottery. Some opponents of conscription doubted that Democratic Governor Horatio Seymour or the Democrats running the city from Tammany Hall would allow a draft to occur.

Nevertheless, the provost marshal, an army officer charged with administering the draft, drew the first set of names on Saturday, July 11. Aside from the expected grumbling, nothing happened that day, but the public's anger simmered over the Sabbath. Newspapers reported that seething workers had gathered in small crowds on Saturday night and Sunday, complaining and, perhaps, planning an appropriate response. Some sort of action had certainly been decided upon by the morning of July 13 when the draft office reopened for business. A mass of workers left their jobs in the mills and on the docks and in the factories of the East Side and marched to the conscription office. When the morning's work of selecting names was completed, the mob promptly set the structure ablaze—the fire soon spread to other buildings—and nearly killed the superintendent. They then moved on to other targets: the pro-Republican *New York Tribune* offices, which they set afire; well-heeled gentlemen hurrying down the streets ("There goes a $300 man," someone would shout); and the homes of wealthy New Yorkers on Lexington Avenue. In addition, the mob attacked Protestant churches, factories with a reputation of hostility toward unions, and businesses that employed African Americans. By the end of the day, a number of African Americans had been beaten and lynched and the Colored Orphan Asylum on Fifth Avenue had been burned to the ground (without any loss of life).

Historians have distinguished between the rioters of the first day, who apparently intended simply to stage a one-day protest against the draft and included large numbers of artisans, native-born Protestants, and Germans, and the mobs that kept up the violence through the next several days, which were overwhelmingly Irish and were drawn from the ranks of lower-paid craftsmen and manual laborers. The latter expanded their targets to include anything related to the Republicans, middle-class reformers (including a home for aged prostitutes), and government institutions (police stations came under attack later in the week, for instance).

Men, women, and children armed with "sticks, stones, adzes, axes, saws . . ."

The chronicle of blood and destruction contained in *The Bloody Week!* focused on the spectacular scenes of property damage and carnage and ignored the possibility that any of the rioters were acting out of political principles. The first section of the pamphlet, called "The Assembling of the Mob," described the gathering of "workmen and others" on the warm and cloudy Monday morning. Small groups began moving toward an open lot near Central Park, where they met to plan their assault on the provost marshal's headquarters at the corner of Forty-sixth Street and Third Avenue. Soon they headed south, cutting telegraph lines as they went, and accumulating more supporters: men, women, and children armed with "sticks, stones, adzes, axes, saws, and some with old swords," in addition to, it was recounted later, table legs, revolvers, and bowie knives (2–3). The mob waited in the humidity for the provost marshal to read the names of that day's drafted men. After the last name was read, a rock crashed through the headquarters window, apparently signaling the beginning of the protest. Turpentine was splashed around the building and set on fire; the provost marshal was attacked, along with ten policemen assigned as security; and when two fire brigades appeared they were forced to flee the scene.

The crowd hesitated after the disruption at the provost marshal's headquarters and the dispersal of the police and firemen, until "a tall man, with large whiskers and heavy moustache and wearing a coat, vest, and striped trousers" rose to address them. He urged them to organize, denounced the president and the government, and congratulated the mob: "You have done well today. You have done nobly," but "you must organize and keep together and appoint leaders, and crush this damned abolition draft into the dust!" He vowed that "if you don't find anyone to lead, by Heaven! I will do it myself" (4). Although his identity was not immediately known, it turned out that he was a Mr. Andrews, the chief villain of the pamphlet's version of the riot.

A rush of events followed this impromptu pep rally: the crowd, now estimated at 3,000 people—with as many as 50,000 other New Yorkers gawking from sidewalks, windows, and roofs—encountered a small company of perhaps forty soldiers, who fired a single volley into the crowd, then turned and ran. The enraged mob, having suffered its first casualties of the day, pursued, beating several and picking up discarded rifles to fire after the retreating soldiers. Policemen—often coming upon the mob individually—could offer little resistance, although at least one fired into a group of attackers and allegedly killed a woman. Many policemen were savagely beaten and a number died.

Having easily dispatched the only resistance they had encountered, the mob returned to the work of destruction. They sacked and burned the Bull's Head Hotel on Lexington Avenue and Forty-third Street, then, moving down the block, rushed into the Colored Orphans Asylum, from which they pitched beds, bedding, furniture, and anything else of value before torching it. Fortunately, the children and staff escaped without injury. Other targets in this phase of the riot included the New Haven Railroad, whose tracks were torn up for several blocks, a cattle market, yet another hotel, policemen, and a reporter. Rioters stripped the shelves of all kinds of stores, acquiring weapons from gun shops and hardware stores, but also sacking clothing, shoe, cigar, millinery, and even hoopskirt establishments.

The rioting died down by evening, but by Tuesday morning "crowds of infuriated men out in resistance to the draft in all wards of the city, re-assembled and began reorganizing" (19). Employers and laborers at ironworks and shipyards were threatened with fire and beatings if they did not close down for the day; streetcars, trains, and omnibuses stopped running when the rioters appeared. The work of destruction picked up where it left off, with the crowd burning and looting mansions and beating wealthy-looking passersby and the few African Americans who fell into their hands. A horrific lynching occurred on Thirty-second Street after a short chase of a black man suspected of shooting a white rioter. The crowd "jumped upon him and pounded him with their fists and with stones until life was extinct," cut off his fingers and toes, hanged his body from a nearby tree, and burned his house. The corpse hung there for several hours, as nearby tenements housing black families burned to the ground (24–25). A sad procession of poor African Americans streamed from black neighborhoods throughout the city, throwing their few belongings on rickety carts "amid the sneers and threats and cruel assaults of the rioters, whose merciless tyranny spared neither sex nor age" (27).

As they had been from the beginning, some of the targets were chosen simply because they represented wealth and power. The mob destroyed or carried off vast private libraries, silverware, and exquisite furnishings and drapes. Other

Rioters looting the homes of affluent New Yorkers (Library of Congress)

targets were political, including the supposed boardinghouse of Horace Greeley, the editor of the pro-Lincoln, pro-Emancipation *New York Tribune;* a young man suspected of being a reporter for Greeley was kicked nearly to death.

The second day saw the police, reinforced by army units, begin to gain control of the city. After a crowd had driven a small army of 300 Eighteenth Ward policemen from the Steam Works on Second Avenue, the police, along with a squad of "regulars," mounted a full-scale attack on the building. Despite being "greeted with a perfect storm of stones, bricks and shot," the police continued their advance. "After a sharp fight, lasting some ten minutes," they "worsted the people and beat them in a terrible manner" (10). Afterward, when remnants of the mob began to jeer and throw stones at the detachment of soldiers, their captain formed his men into a rough battle line and ordered them to fire, killing and wounding more than a dozen. This cleared the streets in the vicinity of the Steam Works. A firefight erupted on Thirty-third Street between a detachment of the 11th New York Regiment—brilliant in their red, white, and blue Zouave uniforms—and snipers firing from apartment houses. Although no soldiers were killed, several rioters were slain, along with two children. Another fight occurred at Broome and Pitt Streets, where a company of soldiers fixed bayonets and charged the rioters who were taunting them, and then, when confronted by another group of rioters, shot and killed several of them.

These victories, however, did not end the warfare in the avenues and alleys of New York. Nor did an impromptu speech to a portion of the mob by Governor Seymour from the steps of city hall at noon on the second day of rioting. In the speech, which was followed up by a stronger printed version, the governor reminded his listeners that he was their friend and that, like them, he opposed the Enrollment Act. He assured them that he had asked the government to suspend the draft, but also warned them that the "only opposition to the conscription which can be allowed is an appeal to the courts," which his administration had already begun. He asked the crowd to disperse, reminded them that it "is your duty to maintain the good order of the city," and asked them "to leave all to me now, and I will see to your rights" (14–15).

Still the rioting continued. The next day, in addition to the random attacks on whites and blacks alike, the mob sacked the house of New York City Mayor George Opdyke, and only a determined defense by a mixed group of policemen, soldiers, and neighbors armed with clubs kept it from being burned. The governor proclaimed the city and county of New York "to be in a state of insurrection" and promised "the means provided by the laws of this State for the maintenance of law and order will be employed to whatever degree may be necessary" (22).

Most of the reports gathered in the pamphlet suggest that many different men were in charge of the mob, but only on a rather ad hoc basis. Indeed, "they seemed to be without any definite leader, as one man was to be seen calling them one way, and another to take an opposite direction" (18). Individuals seemed to have taken charge of specific groups of people or of attacks on specific buildings, rising out of the crowd and, it seems, fading back into it once a phase of the battle passed. As the area of the city under attack expanded, segments of the mob made decisions by group consensus: which buildings to burn, where to throw up barricades—several streets were blocked by makeshift fortifications—which neighborhood to invade next, and, in one case, not to burn a shop because it was located on a block of working-class tenements. In some parts of the city, patrols of rioters forced passersby to join them or suffer the consequences. As a result, "many peaceably disposed persons were thus mixed up with the others, and many who went with the crowd, for fear of exciting their anger, managed to slip away before the main body had decided on any definite movement" (18).

Despite the apparent decentralized leadership—historians have referred to the "committees" that made most of the decisions for small groups of a few dozen or even a few hundred rioters—*The Bloody Week!* saved its most virulent attacks for the man named Andrews, who had made the impromptu anticon-

Cartoon attacking Democratic Governor of New York Horatio Seymour for his reluctance to intervene to stop the rioting in New York; the rioters are depicted as apelike and violent, at the time, common caricatures of Irish laborers. (Library of Congress)

scription speech on the first day. Later discovered to be a Virginia lawyer with Confederate sympathies, he was specifically accused of being one of the ringleaders and, in fact, his picture appeared on the title page of *The Bloody Week!* (Curiously, "Rosa," the "mistress" mentioned in the pamphlet's title, does not appear in the text.) Andrews was actually captured on the third day of the uprising by detectives operating in disguise. The authors of the pamphlet let loose their purplest prose in describing Andrews:

For three days he has hounded on his pack of savages to their deeds of violence. An apostle of carnage, he has marched at their head and incited [them] to do deeds at which the manhood of free people should revolt. Where poor, unoffending Negroes were beaten dead, then hung, and their mangled corpses trodden in the mire by the feet of brutal men and women, where private houses of peaceful citizens have been sacked and burned, where widows and orphans have been turned almost naked into the streets, where barricades have arisen, and every infamous outrage has been perpetrated, this self-elected Virginia "gentleman" has been foremost in the fray. Mounted upon a horse, no doubt stolen from a private stable, clad in a red shirt and brandishing a saber, he has been a chosen leader of the pack of robbers and murderers. (30)

Although the authors fail to show exactly how Andrews had led or even inspired the sprawling chaos of the riot, they rarely miss the opportunity to remark that the crowd was "maddened with the liquor they had so freely imbibed during their destructive pastime" (9). During lulls in the violence, groups of a few dozen rioters "wandered through the streets, swearing, drinking wherever they could get liquor" (20). Indeed, once word raced around town of the fate of several hotels and inns, the mob found it rather easy to convince saloon owners to hand out free drinks. Even young boys prowled the streets, "flourishing and firing off pistols," and men "brandished guns, and made hoarse with passion and bad spirits, cursed and swore, and threatened every one disagreeing with them in their excesses," including "every Black Republican-nigger worshipping s____ of a b____." Others loudly threatened all Republican leaders and military officers (21). One "well-dressed man" was knocked down by a "rowdy armed with a club," who spat, "you have got $300, and I have not" (30–31).

The female members of the mob also appear in a bad light. "Prominent among those who made the first attack" on July 13 "were quite a large number of women" who cheered on their "relatives and acquaintances" and, "armed principally with bricks, and stones," broke windows and attacked "those who made any show of resistance" (3). Even worse, reported the authors, when a small detachment of invalid soldiers were overwhelmed and at least nine beaten by the mob, women took bayonets from the soldiers' rifles and "plunged them into the already wounded soldiers" (13).

Other incidents suggested that at least some of the rioters had pro-Confederate sympathies. Once led by two armed men on horseback on Third Avenue and Thirty-third Street, the crowd could be heard cheering for Jefferson Davis. A frightening rumor indicated that an attempt would be made to liberate a boatload of Confederate prisoners scheduled to arrive in Jersey City.

The Bloody Week! locates the source of the problem in the "copperhead" leadership of the state and city. Indeed, they predicted that even Andrews, "this howling fiend, this emissary and spy of the Rebels," would go free at "a sham trial on writ of habeas corpus, and speedy acquittal by a copperhead judge." They complained that "if we had a commanding General possessed of energy, a Governor thoroughly loyal, and a Mayor not absolutely paralyzed with fear," Andrews "would have been shot at the head of his rioters on Tuesday and this community spared the mortification of his subsequent career of crime" (30–31).

"The Bloody Week": The New York City Draft Riots

The open warfare finally ended when armed policemen and five regiments rushed from Pennsylvania, where they had fought at Gettysburg, and regained control of the city. The government agreed to suspend the draft for a couple of weeks, and by July 18th the riot was over. The costs were enormous: property with a value of at least $2 million was destroyed and at least 105 people were killed (although contemporary estimates of the dead ranged up to 1,000).

The introduction to this exciting—even inflammatory—tale concludes, "Would that we were better able to tell this story of ruin and desolation, but the tale is too painful and harrowing to the soul, and we hope never to be called to record a like scene" (1). Despite the damage and bloodshed, the government restored the peace and the draft started up again by August. The city government raised $300,000 to pay commutation fees for a thousand men, but for the most part, after the rioting died down, New Yorkers grimly accepted their nation's call to arms.

Resistance to the draft continued throughout the North. Ironically, conscription provided only about 5 percent of the total number of men who served in the Union army, although officials believed it encouraged others to enlist. The army rounded up draft resisters and threw a number of them in jail. The issue became a useful campaign tool for Republicans, who in local, state, and federal elections trumpeted their patriotism and somewhat unfairly attacked the Democrats as obstacles to the war effort in general and unpatriotic draft resisters in particular. Indeed, expanding on their opponents' opposition to emancipation and to conscription, Republicans linked some Democrats—called "copperheads" after the poisonous snake—to plots to free Confederate soldiers held in Northern prison camps, to aid Confederate agents operating out of Canada, and to subvert the legal functioning of state governments in the Midwest.

The Bloody Week! was compiled by reporters who literally risked their lives on the city streets. Lacking the perspective of historians with the luxury to calmly study the motivations of the participants and the subtle shadings of disaffection and economic distress, the pamphlet resembled several other sources compiled from newspaper reports published soon afterward, such as David Barnes's straightforward *The Draft Riots in New York, July 1863* (1863) and the more incendiary *Three Days' Reign of Terror, or the July Riots in 1863, in New York* (1867). Told from the point of view of the police and other metropolitan authorities, these sensational accounts shared a sense of outrage and of fear. *The Bloody Week!*, in particular, written even as the storm broke over New York, reflects the passion of crisis and the almost surreal nature of the rumors flying about the city. It does, nevertheless, exert a raw power that helps modern-day Americans understand the complexities of a Northern population surprisingly diverse in its politics and desperate in its commitment to principles and to survival.

PRIMARY SOURCE:

The Bloody Week! Riot, Murder & Arson, Containing A Full Account of the Wholesale Outrage on Life and Property, Accurately Prepared from Official Sources, by Eye Witnesses, with Portraits of "Andrews," the Leader and "Rosa," his Eleventh Street Mistress. New York: Coutant & Baker, 1863. Unless otherwise cited, all quotations are from this source.

SECONDARY SOURCES:

Bernstein, Iver. *The New York City Draft Riots: Their Significance for American Society and Politics in the Age of the Civil War.* New York: Oxford University Press, 1990.

Cook, Adrian. *The Armies of the Streets: The New York City Draft Riots of 1863.* Lexington: University Press of Kentucky, 1974.

Geary, James W. *We Need Men: The Union Draft in the Civil War.* De Kalb: Northern Illinois University Press, 1991.

PART III

The Children's Civil War

Chapter Fourteen

Rabid Partisans among Their Playmates

The Civil War was the climax of the worst political crisis in American history. In an era when upwards of 70 percent of all eligible voters trooped to the polls on election day, the sectional conflict made politics into even more of a public spectacle, with men, women, and children becoming deeply engaged in the political process. Thousands of people cheered Lincoln and Douglas in their famous debates, while Southern youngsters were avid participants in the rallies and campaigns that swirled around the secession movement of 1860 and 1861. Northern males of all ages donned oilcloth capes and proudly marched under oil lamps as Republican "Wide-Awakes." War rallies attracted entire communities, who held emotional flag presentations for local units and encouraged their men and boys to enlist.

Children were as likely as their parents to become politicized by the events leading up to the Civil War. Many years after the war ended, a Georgian named Andrew Miller remembered that, in his Civil War boyhood, "the small boy" had become "a politician, as unflinching and uncompromising in his imaginary convictions" as his father. He learned his politics at home, from which he went "forth a most rabid partisan among his playmates" (Miller, 38–39). So did the girls, of course, and through the North and the South, children of both genders played politics with name-calling and playground bickering. A Minnesotan remembered that she and her playmates knew nothing of "the tragedy and sorrow" of the war, but enthusiastically joined the politics of sectionalism. "Epithets such as 'Rebel,' 'Copperhead,' 'Black Republican,' and 'Mudsill' were flung about with the utmost freedom by the children," she recalled, "and the certainty of being able at any minute to stir up a fight simply by marching up and down aggressively and singing 'We'll hang Jeff Davis on a sour apple tree' filled one with a sense of power that was indescribable" (Furness, 116).

Although the politicization of children cut across sectional lines, the education of two Southern children, who could identify quite precisely the moments when they decided they were rebels, may have been more dramatic than most. They, like their parents, were severing ties to the only government they had known, and in both cases, parents were eager guides in their children's political journeys.

When Susan Bradford was fifteen, her father took her to the climactic moments of the Florida secession convention in the state capital at Tallahassee, an adventure she committed to her diary. Because Susan had been exposed to "all the *pros* and *cons* of this movement from both the Secession and the Union side" and was, as a result, "sometimes a little mixed as to politics," she preferred during the early weeks of the secession winter to think instead about

Children were as likely as their parents to become politicized by the events leading up to the Civil War.

Christmas, which she thought "much more interesting" (Eppes, 135). Politics intruded on the family gathering on New Year's Day, however, as her father and her Unionist brother argued over the South's appropriate response to the election of Lincoln, the imminent meeting of the Florida secession convention, and the result of the inevitable war that would follow a disruption of the Union. Susan's father and uncles attended the first days of the convention early in the New Year, and Susan could "hardly keep my mind on my books I am thinking so much of the probable action of the convention." She feared that she was too curious, that she peppered her father with too many questions, "which, of course, must be troublesome" (ibid., 139).

Apparently convinced of Susan's interest, Dr. Bradford decided to let her skip her lessons and attend the convention with him, to see "history in the making" and to become part of the great movement sweeping the lower South early in 1861. When Mrs. Bradford protested, he sternly said, "she will learn more than she can get out of books and what she hears in this way she will never forget" (ibid., 140). He was right about that. Susan shared her father's enthusiasm for secession and for the Confederate cause, and she loved her time at the convention, sporting a "Palmetto cockade"—the blue-ribboned symbol of South Carolina's secession—and listening to speeches by such fire-eating luminaries as Edmund Ruffin of Virginia and Leonidas Spratt of South Carolina. She and her father also viewed the final vote in favor of severing Florida's ties with the Union and the formal signing of the ordinance of secession. Her days at the convention were "filled to overflowing with excitement and interest," although sometimes "the language the members used is not familiar to me and some of the things they talk about are just as new." Of course, she admitted, "I am just a little girl" (ibid., 142). She wrote of the sad-looking Union men, the mass of people jammed into Capital Square, and of the solemnity of the process. By the time she returned home, Susan wondered "if I can collect my wits enough to learn my lessons" (ibid., 146).

Rabid Partisans among Their Playmates

Susan did eventually regain her focus, but having shifted her loyalty from the Union to the Confederacy, Susan never looked back. As her state mobilized for the war during the spring and summer of 1861, and as she watched local recruits drill and parade around in their uniforms, she grew "more patriotic all the time." Her older sister teased her that it was simply because she was unmarried and attracted to the young officers in their new outfits; Susan admitted that "they all look fine to me" (ibid., 157). More somberly, she wished she could go to war with her father, who had volunteered against his wife's wishes: "I wish I was a boy; even if I am young, I could go with him if only I were not a girl. It will break my heart if he goes." Her brother Amos marched off with one of the first units to leave the community, driving her sister "wild with grief" (ibid., 150).

Far across the Confederacy, in the Mississippi Delta, a little boy also found his political bearings during a dramatic midnight argument between his father and a friend. When Samuel A. Steele sat down to write what was supposed to be a two-volume account of his experiences as a boy during the Civil War, he wrote first about his father's pastoral work among the slaves on nearby plantations. Indeed, one of his earliest memories was of going to "negro meetings" with his father, an experience that no doubt inspired his own life's work as a Methodist minister. Paid by rich planters to preach the gospel to their slaves, Steele's father "was never happier than when he was telling several hundred negroes the old, old story of Jesus and His love." Yet, Steele wrote with more than a trace of bitterness as an adult, "at the very time we were trying to give the negroes the gospel, and the planters were paying to have their slaves taught the religion of Jesus, the people in New England were denouncing us as 'brutal slave-drivers,' whose chief pastime was flogging slaves, and hunting runaways with bloodhounds!" Steele claimed he never saw a bloodhound until he was thirteen—during the war—and that one was chasing a runaway Yankee! "I didn't know that while I was listening to my father's simple preaching to these negroes, and enjoying their wonderful singing," abolitionists in Boston "were telling the world we were little better than savages because we had slaves." Unfortunately for the South, "the world believed them, and three million men invaded the South with fire and sword to put a stop to what we were doing" (Steele, 16–17).

Steele's digression in defense of slavery was typical of memoirs written by Southerners long after the Civil War. He fondly recalled being taught the catechism by his mother side by side with the young slaves who lived on their farm. Later he referred to John Brown's attempt "to incite the negroes of the South to murder the white people," and argued that there was a vast difference between "slavery as it actually was, and slavery as it was represented to be in the North." Yet the war occurred anyway—a "cruel and utterly needless war waged by the

North" that "deserved to be called 'The War of the Great Misunderstanding'" (ibid., 52).

These thoughts came from a man reflecting on his life nearly sixty years after the end of that "Great Misunderstanding"; little Sam Steele was not a political animal until the war made him one. Indeed, if he'd been like most children, he would have aped the political ideals of his father, who was a staunch Union man right up until the fighting began in 1861. Sam had been converted to the Southern cause some months before, when a visiting friend drew the elder Steele into a sharp debate over the merits of secession. It was early autumn, and eight-year-old Sam had thus far paid scant attention to the outside world. His little, isolated corner of rural

If he'd been like most children, he would have aped the political ideals of his father . . .

Mississippi was all he cared about. Fishing and trapping "afforded me far more interest than the way the world was being managed. What happened in Virginia did not concern me, for Virginia, to my little mind, was as far away as the man in the moon." But that all changed on this chilly night, as Brother Crouch shifted the sands on which Sam's life stood: "I became a man in a moment," he recalled, and, like a Confederate Saul on the road to Damascus, his sudden maturity struck with the force of lightning. He would be a rebel for the rest of his life.

Steele painted a cozy picture of a warm hearth, a lamp-lit room, heartfelt conversation between two great friends, and the dutiful wife's knitting needles clacking softly from the corner. Sam had to talk his mother into letting him stay up late; she agreed, as long as he promised to remain quiet and keep still. So he did, perched on a little stool at his mother's side "with two ears wide open and eager to hear what might be said."

He heard plenty. Not surprisingly, as the 1860 presidential election approached, as each of the four candidates accused the others of threatening the Union, the talk "drifted to the condition of the country." Sam's father "expressed great uneasiness," fearing that Lincoln might be elected. This was the first time Sam had ever heard the name Lincoln, but as he had promised his mother he would be quiet, he remained silent. His father feared that if Lincoln was elected, the South would secede and war would result. This "fired me up at once"—he had just finished reading a book about Napoléon—but he could not ask "where the war would be."

The knowing visitor disagreed; Lincoln would win, the South would secede, but there would be no war. "The Constitution gave the State the right to secede, and did not give the Federal Government the right to coerce a State by force of arms to remain in the Union," he declared. With the inevitable coming to power of Lincoln, the United States would "become . . . an instrument of tyranny which no free people would endure." And even if the North had the gall and the guts to wage war against the South, "we would whip them in sixty days!" The good Reverend Steele continued to disagree. Secession may be constitutional, he admitted, but the North would fight, and with its overwhelming resources would win. "He grew eloquent," remembered Sam, "and his talk might have moved the Senate. It profoundly impressed me, and decided my wavering mind"—he moved "irresistibly" toward "his father's side of the question."

Yet Crouch pressed the issue. He and Mr. Steele "went over and over the same ground two or three times." Sam slipped out of the room to get more firewood, fearing he would miss something. When he returned, his father was insisting that if war broke out, the Union would build gunboats in St. Louis and "come down the Mississippi river and carry desolation through the heart of our country." But Sam reflected on one issue to which his father had no answer: that the election of Lincoln would mean that "the program of John Brown would be put in operation, with the President of the United States backing it up, and no home in the South would be safe." Sam felt himself swinging—along with his mother—over to the side of the persuasive visitor.

It was nearly midnight, as the "closing scene of that drama of the fireside" began. Brother Crouch had been pacing and gesturing before the hearth for some time. Now he "paused, leaned his elbow on the end of the mantel, passed his hand through his hair, and waving it as if in disdain," said, "My dear Brother Steele, you do not know what you are talking about!" Yankees may send gunboats down the river, but "we will put cannon on the bluffs at Memphis, and blow them out of the river as fast as they come around the bend!"

That sanguinary image "fixed it" with Sam, he declared. "I was a rebel from that time on, from heel to head and head to heel." He went to bed, but tossed and turned before falling into a fitful sleep filled with "gunboats coming around the bend; and as fast as they came, boom went a gun, up went a gunboat," until the river and sky were "filled with flying smokestacks and timbers, and mutilated Yankees!" It did not turn out that way, of course, "but in my imagination that night, I saw it all happening just as 'Bro. Crouch' said." The next morning, after a nighttime of dreaming of exploding gunboats, Sam "woke up . . . in a new world" (ibid., 61–69).

That "new world" did not change Sam's life immediately. Even as "the nation was rushing into the whirlpool of war, revolution shaking loose the settled order of society; drums beating, bugles blowing, captains shouting, flags flying and armies marching, with all the hellish pomp of ruthless war," the young Mississippian was "unconscious of the mighty drama." Surrounded, as he was, "by bears and wolves and panthers, and working hard from early morn till starry eve," without newspapers or contact with other knowledgeable people, "I was completely detached from the national pageant" (ibid., 83). There were some occasions, however, when the war inched closer to Sam. One of those times came after the First Battle of Bull Run, when the neighborhood held a giant bonfire and rally. Although he allowed Sam to go, the elder Steele remained at home, saddened that the war would continue and knowing that the outraged, humiliated North would now take the South seriously. "To my mother's taunt: 'I told you so,' he simply said: 'The end is not yet'" (ibid., 105).

Indeed, the end was not to come for a long time, and in the meantime this little community of Southerners celebrated. Old and young, black and white, everyone "had a Confederate flag, and were as merry as a flock of blackbirds in a rice field" (ibid., 106). There were baskets of food, courting couples, a sharply dressed, well-mounted Confederate officer who gave a rousing speech by way of recruiting new men to help finish off the Yankees. His talk attracted dozens of young men that day, and "woe to the young man who held back! The concentrated scorn of even the negroes would have scourged him as a coward" (ibid., 111). Inspired, Sam returned home to run through the manual of arms by himself in the woods and to practice his shooting. Indeed, the handsome officer in his clean uniform, with the silver sword and spurs, "captured my fancy" so deeply that "I saw everything through a golden mist of military glory" (ibid., 115).

The politicization of children like Susan and Sam occurred all over the United and Confederate States. Some children witnessed divided households. For all of his nine years, Maurice Egan of Philadelphia had watched his father and mother argue politics. As the crisis deepened, his father leaned toward Abraham Lincoln, but his mother favored Stephen A. Douglas. Even after the war began, Mrs. Egan was more "copperhead" than Unionist. Both parents tried to influence young Maurice by reading newspapers aloud at the breakfast table, and after Mr. Egan left for work, Mrs. Egan would read the controversial speeches of Ohio's Peace Democrat Clement Vallandigham from the *Congressional Record.* Maurice relished the politically inspired tension in his boyhood home. His father won the tug-of-war for Maurice's political heart; the boy cheered for Union victories and mourned the assassination of Abraham Lincoln.

Schools became perhaps the bloodiest home front political battlegrounds, with children of all ages expressing their devotion to the Union or to the Confederacy or to one political party or the other in sometimes violent ways. At times they became pawns in the political fights raging among adults. After Union troops occupied New Orleans in the spring of 1862, for instance, Generals Benjamin Butler and Nathaniel Banks attempted to quash dissent among the parents and teachers in the New Orleans public school system. The military government reopened the schools, established loyalty requirements for teachers, tried to influence course content, and on occasions such as the 1864 inauguration of a Unionist government, drafted hundreds of school children to take part in official ceremonies. Throughout the years that New Orleans was occupied by Union troops, teachers and parents of unrepentant rebels fought these plans. Federal anthems only slowly replaced Southern songs, and U.S. history only gradually subsumed "Confederate" history. The school system also continued to pay the salaries of teachers serving in the Confederate army. In a case that attracted much attention in the local press, officials expelled five children whose parents refused to let them participate in the inaugural concert.

Federal authorities also attempted to flush Confederate sympathies from the city's private schools, many of which carried on as though the Crescent City had never been captured. At Madame Locquet's school, for instance, students wore mourning ribbons on the first anniversary of the city's fall. A student named Martha Moore bitterly reported a surprise inspection by "two coarse looking" Yankees "whom, I should think from their appearance had not been washed or combed in six weeks." They had come to inspect Madame Locquet's school for "secession emblems, flags, or anything treasonable." The men ripped a few pages out of books and cast several threatening looks toward a student named Martha, then stomped out. She had drawn a small Confederate flag on a composition and another girl sat through the ordeal "hugging" a book with a flag on it, declaring that she would not give it up. Although the intrusion was meant "to restore the Union feeling," it had, of course, just the opposite effect. Afterward, Martha "hate[d] the Northerners with a deeper, and more lasting hatred, than ever before" (Moore, May 7, 1863).

Far to the North, similar passions consumed the small city of Dayton, Ohio— the hometown of Democratic congressman, gubernatorial hopeful, and dissenter Clement Vallandigham. There, Republican "Union Leaguers" wore Union army uniform buttons to school, while Democratic "Butternuts" sported halved walnut shells. This sparked confrontations among adults as well as children, particularly in the high school, where the conflict escalated into fistfights and rock throwing by the spring of 1863. "Loyal" adolescents formed clubs and sought to eliminate the "butternut charm" from their school. Efforts by administrators to end the violence by eliminating the wearing of all insignias sparked criticism from both sides, but especially among the more numerous Union parents in the city. The partisan battle raged through school yards and the columns of local newspapers, and intensified in the rioting that followed the arrest of Vallandigham in May. Eventually, the issue died down with the demise of strident antiwar feeling.

Children found many other ways to demonstrate the fervency of their patriotism. Many Southern girls recorded their patriotism in their diaries, saving their most vitriolic entries for Southern girls with Northern sympathies, and in particular those who had fraternized with Union soldiers. At the beginning of the 1863 winter term, Cora Owens seemed surprised that "Mollie Parker, Union as she is, looked sweet & even pretty to me," perhaps because she heard Mollie singing "The Bonnie Blue Flag." She disapproved when another girl primped for visiting Federal officers (Hume, April 30, 1863). Nannie Haskins, a teenaged Tennesseean, endured the Federal occupation of her hometown with gritted teeth, sprinkling her diary with a hard-shell patriotism that few adults could match. She complained about the arrogance and cruelty of Federal officers and wartime fraternization by some of her schoolmates with the occupiers, but fell especially hard on those who failed to do their duty. Early in 1862, she attended a party at which the only "young gentlemen" were "fireside rangers"—men who had evaded military duty—"and I had almost *as soon* see so many Yankees" (Underwood, 181).

A much less private form of political rhetoric appeared in the *Newark High School Athenaeum,* a handwritten student newspaper whose motto—"United We Stand, Divided We Fall"—broadcast the political principles of its student editors. With a typical schoolboy combination of humor and seriousness of purpose, the boys covered the election of 1864 between Lincoln and the Democrat nominee General George B. McClellan with two articles. One was a fairly straightforward description of rowdy electioneering in Newark, while another turned the canvass into a biblical parody. "Now it came to pass in the third year of the reign of Abraham the president," it began, "in the eleventh month on the third day of the month, that all the people on the north of the line, even the great line of Mason Dixon, gathered themselves together . . . to elect men who should go in and out before them, and who should speak for them." It went on to describe "Unionists"—the "part adhered to Abraham"—and "Copperheads"—the "part adhered to him not"—and the former's victory over the latter, after which "they had no more courage with which to contend against Abraham and his people." In a more serious vein, the editors attacked slavery's "long catalogue of crime and blood-shed on the one side and of helpless suffering on the other." In a fashion reminiscent of the long, history-laden political speeches of the day, one writer explained the history of slavery in North America and blasted the South "for the course it has pursued in raising the traitors' hand against the Government" (*Newark High School Athenaeum,* September 1864).

Of course, choosing sides marked the beginning, not the end, of a child's Civil War journey. Although the patriotism of Northern children and youth, unthreatened by invading enemies and generally unburdened by belt-tightening shortages and inflation, normally deepened as the war surged toward its bloody denouement, the sheen wore off for many Southerners.

Rabid Partisans among Their Playmates

Susan Bradford's diary and memoir detailed the hardships faced by her extended family as the war closed in on them. In the war's first autumn, Susan announced in her diary that "war has come home" to the neighborhood with the news of the death of a family member, a young officer she called "everybody's darling" (Eppes, 159). Halfway through the war Susan accidentally saw two deserters shot by a firing squad. It happened as she walked past the town green, where, as always, soldiers were standing around. "I always look at the soldiers," she wrote, but she regretted her friendly glance this time, because while she was looking "the squad fired and the deserters fell dead." She felt "perfectly awful" and "didn't think it ought to be done. So many are killed in battle and lives are worth more than that." Maybe, she worried, they had "meant to come back." The scene haunted her, and she predicted that "I shall not sleep a wink tonight" (ibid., 207–208). Susan nevertheless grimly continued to support her nation, defending its decision to go to war: "The South did not want this war. We fought for our rights, we resisted oppression and now we are crushed and conquered" (ibid., 272–273).

Choosing sides marked the beginning, not the end, of a child's Civil War journey.

Perhaps the event that most represented for Susan Eppes what the South had lost occurred just after the surrender of the Army of Northern Virginia at Appomattox, when a band of twenty or so African American children came up to her house singing the anthem most popular among Northern children, "We'll hang Jeff Davis on a sour apple tree" to the tune of "John Brown's Body." Infuriated, Susan chased them off the yard with a carriage whip. Later, she confessed, "For the first time in all my life I have laid hands in violence upon a *negro*" (ibid., 279–280).

As the war ended, Bradford might have been discouraged, depressed, and defeated, but as a mature woman writing a confidential memoir framing excerpts from her girlhood diary, she took on a nostalgic, even jaunty tone reflecting her steadfast patriotism to the Southern cause. She introduced her diary/memoir with a little poem:

> Life is a mixture of sorrow and joy,
> There is no bliss without alloy,
> There's never a rose without its thorn,
> No mortal has yet to perfection been born;
> But the dear OLD FOLKS are morally sure
> That all was perfect in DAYS OF YORE.
> (ibid., 1)

As events later in the century demonstrated—the rise of the solid Democratic South, the troubled and often violent state of race relations, the continuing influence in the former Confederacy of states' rights ideals—the political lessons learned by children during the war remained deeply engrained in their minds as they grew up.

PRIMARY SOURCES:

Egan, Maurice F. *Recollections of a Happy Life.* New York: George H. Doran, 1924.

Eppes, Susan Bradford. *Through Some Eventful Years.* Macon, GA: J. W. Burke, 1926.

Furness, Marion Ramsey. "Childhood Recollections of Old St. Paul." *Minnesota History* 29 (June 1948).

Hume, Cora Owens. Diary. Filson Club Historical Society, Louisville, KY.

Miller, Andrew James. *Old School Days: A Memoir of Boyhood.* New York: Abbey Press, 1900.

Moore, Martha Josephine. Diary. Frank Liddell Richardson Collection, Southern Historical Collection, University of North Carolina at Chapel Hill.

Newark High School Athenaeum. New Jersey State Historical Society, Newark, NJ.

Steele, Samuel A. *The Sunny Road: Home Life in Dixie during the War.* Memphis: n.p., 1924.

Underwood, Betsy Swint. "War Seen through a Teenager's Eyes." *Tennessee Historical Quarterly* 20 (June 1961).

SECONDARY SOURCES:

Becker, Carl M. "'Disloyalty' and the Dayton Public Schools." *Civil War History* 11 (March 1956).

Doyle, Elisabeth Joan. "Nurseries of Treason: Schools in Occupied New Orleans." *Journal of Southern History* 26 (May 1960).

Marten, James. *The Children's Civil War.* Chapel Hill: University of North Carolina Press, 1998.

Chapter Fifteen

What a Difference a War Makes: A Northern Boy and a Southern Girl

November 1864 was a busy month for Gerald Norcross, who lived with his prosperous family in Boston, where his father was a store owner and Republican alderman. Gerald recorded a number of events in his diary, including a "Grand torchlight procession" of bands, drum corps, militia units, and "Union" clubs from all over the city in honor of Abraham Lincoln. Patriotic illuminations and transparencies glowed in support of the Union, a young woman portraying the "Goddess of Liberty" stood motionless in a window, roman candles and other fireworks lit the sky. It was an entirely satisfactory evening for a young boy (Norcross, November 5, 1864).

Just a week later Gerald went to Boston Common to see a make-believe battle between miniature ironclads. Unfortunately, the model of the *Merrimac* broke down, the tent covering the pond created a rather dreary atmosphere, and the little cannons fired in the demonstration were less than impressive. "On the whole," Gerald complained, "it was a sham" (November 11, 1864). Just before Thanksgiving, Gerald attended the National Soldiers and Sailors Fair, where he saw models of exotic ships from all over the world, viewed trophies from Virginia battlefields, and bought a book and some shells. In between these outings, Gerald read books about the Civil War, witnessed classmates give patriotic addresses on "speaking day" at school, and staged battles with his paper soldiers.

While young Gerald was enjoying a Civil War childhood that can only be described as exciting, a girl just his age was having her world turned upside down by that same war. Carrie Berry, a resident of Atlanta for all of her young life, also kept a diary during this period, but her November 1864 was much different than Gerald's. Having survived the siege and the Battle of Atlanta, the Berry family now had to endure the city's occupation by Yankees and its eventual burning. Unlike the overwhelming majority of Atlantans, the Berrys were not forced to leave their home when Union forces began their march to the sea.

A typical scene from one of the massive sanitary fairs held throughout the North
(Library of Congress)

Carrie's November was spent saying good-bye—to the friendly Northern sergeant who had guarded their house and to friends and relatives moving to other
places—and, at least temporarily, worrying about what the future would bring.
On the same night of Gerald's worst war-related episode—the hopelessly lame
simulation of the fight between the USS *Monitor* and CSS *Virginia*—Carrie and
her family "were fritened [sic] almost to death" when "some mean soldiers set
several houses on fire in different parts of the town" (Berry, November 12, 1864).
She could not go to sleep for fear her own house would be next, and she spent
the next several days watching Yankees methodically burn the city until theirs
was among the handful of homes still standing. On the same day that Gerald
spent some of his pocket change on souvenirs at the Soldiers and Sailors Fair,
Carrie told her diary, "Papa and Mama say that they feel very poor" (November
22, 1864). The ten-year-old had spent her days chasing the family's last hog
(driven off by soldiers) and contemplating having only bread to eat; "plundering

about" the ruins of the city, trying to find anything that they might be able to use; and sifting through the ashes for nails (November 18, 1864). To top it all off, she had to help her sister bury a pet guinea pig.

Perhaps nothing better shows the extremes of home front experiences during the Civil War than the diaries of these two children, both of whom turned ten in 1864. A crude measure of how the war affected them is material: at one point Gerald counts over 300 items in his collection of curiosities and well over 100 books, in addition to the vast array of

"Some mean soldiers set several houses on fire in different parts of the town."

other toys and possessions he refers to in his dairy: countless paper soldiers; a toy village; baseball, hockey, and ringtoss equipment; and several board games. Not surprisingly, Carrie mentions only a doll or two—indeed, she goes six weeks in the fall of 1864 without mentioning play at all—and celebrates her tenth birthday by ironing clothes and running for the bomb shelter. At one point, she is ecstatic when a resourceful aunt somehow obtains a bunch of grapes.

Gerald's and Carrie's wartime diaries provide very simple but telling representations of the home front experiences of all Americans. In the South, although cities like Atlanta and Richmond briefly prospered because of military and government activities, in general, life got steadily harder. Food became so scarce in some places that residents rioted, roads and railroads wore out, inflation made it difficult to buy even the most basic goods, schools often closed, many newspapers had to stop publishing, and a large percentage of women and children had to go to work simply to survive. The North, on the other hand, generally prospered during the war. Although there was a period of economic distress just after the war started, factories and farms produced record quantities of manufactured goods and food (because they grew so much wheat and corn, Northern farmers could even export grain to Europe during the war). Schools and universities flourished, fast-growing cities like Chicago expanded their street and sewer systems, and migrants continued to move to the West. By the end of the war, many Southern cities lay in ruins, the plantation economy was destroyed, and most people were living a hand-to-mouth existence. By contrast, most Northerners, aside from those families who had lost loved ones, were probably better off at the end of the war than at the beginning. The diaries of Gerald and Carrie present these contrasts in microcosm.

Gerald faithfully kept his diary throughout the war, writing two or three lines every day. More a catalog of events and possessions than of inner feelings—after all, Gerald was just a little boy—it nevertheless illustrates the variety of ways that the Civil War bloodlessly invaded the Northern home front. Gerald reported the books he read, the games he played, the war news he heard, and the myriad

A house badly damaged during the Battle of Atlanta in 1864
(Library of Congress)

other ways that he participated in the home front experience of war. Gerald's reading included *The Swiss Family Robinson* and volumes from Jacob Abbott's famous "Rollo" series: *Rollo's Vacation, Rollo at School, Rollo at Play, Rollo Learns to Read, Rollo Learns to Work*—and so forth. He also ventured into more exciting dime novels about the war: *Old Hal Williams; or, the Spy of Atlanta* and *The Vicksburg Spy; or Found and Lost.* Later, he read Oliver Optic's "Soldier Boy" and "Sailor Boy" trilogies and Charles Coffin's *Days and Nights on the Battlefield.*

When he was not reading or studying, Gerald played familiar games like hockey, ringtoss, marbles, hide-and-seek, tea party, "Old Maid," and baseball (he played shortstop), as well as more obscure—and possibly improvised—games like "Put up Blondin," "Squat where you be," and "Bar the door." Like children everywhere and in every time, Gerald loved to collect things. He packed scrapbooks with pictures and autographs and once counted 333 objects in his "curiosity" collection. They included rocks, shells, furs, bones, and the sorts of things than any self-respecting boy of his time might gather and cherish. He also acquired a number of toys and souvenirs related to the war, such as American flags, slivers of metal from warships, a revolver cartridge, a sliver of glass from a bottle used in christening a warship, a miniature cannon that fired peas, and a piece of hardtack his father brought home from a trip to Washington. He also seemed amused by two war-related Valentines, one to "a Military Bobadil" and the other "to a raw recruit" (Norcross, February 14 and 17, 1862).

In addition to the normal run of midcentury amusements and entertainments—he attended a circus, went bowling, enjoyed a panorama-travelogue of the Great Lakes, viewed a stereopticon presentation on European monuments, and vacationed at the seashore with his family—Gerald also took part in all sorts of activities related to the war. He

The Civil War bloodlessly invaded the Northern home front.

watched army regiments parade through the city and drill on Boston Common and was impressed by the governor's inspection of the assembled soldiers, especially "the first platoon," which was "dressed like General Putnam's men in the Revolutionary War" (June 12, 1862). He was, however, a little disappointed when the "Ancient and Honorable Artillery" showed up without their cannon. He went to the harbor to view an ironclad that was passing through and had his picture taken with the crew of a visiting Russian ship sent by the czar to show his support for the Union.

The teachers at Gerald's school kept the boys' minds on the war whenever possible. As in most schools of the time, Friday was "speaking day," when boys recited poems or excerpts from famous speeches. Gerald delivered John Greenleaf Whittier's "Barbara Frietchie" one day (after practicing for his mother's friends the previous evening) and, on another, part of an essay called "War Sometimes a Duty." One of his teachers frequently read war news to the assembled boys, who were also asked to sing patriotic songs like "The Star-Spangled Banner," "Rule Columbia," "Rise and Break the Chains That Bind Us," and "Battle Song." Upon hearing of the fall of Richmond, the headmaster led the boys in three cheers for Generals Grant, Sherman, and Sheridan, President Lincoln, and the African American soldiers. School let out early the next day and the boys celebrated by shooting off firecrackers and watching the fireworks at Chester Park later in the evening.

Gerald shared the dreams of most Northern and Southern boys to take a more active part in the war. He regularly drilled with a boys' company with the grandiose title of "Garibaldi's Guards," after the Italian leader who was much in vogue during the period. The only campaign mounted by the "Guards" came when they interrupted their drill one day to explore an abandoned house rumored to be haunted. Gerald expended most of his martial ardor, however, when he and his friends made armies of paper soldiers out of kits they bought at a local toy shop and named their commanders for local officers. The tiny armies fought dozens of battles and sometimes went on "foraging" parties. On some occasions the boys would stab at the battle lines with a sharp knife; other times they would try to bowl over the opposing armies by blowing on them and they even kept lists of the names of the "killed" and "wounded" men.

One of Gerald's fellow "commanders" in these faux battles, the somewhat older Bill Tryon, crossed the line between imaginary and actual war when in mid-1864 he lied about his age, took the alias "W. W. Roe," and joined a "100 day" regiment without his father's consent. Gerald mentioned but did not comment on the incident, although a couple of months later he received a letter from the absent teenager. Bill returned unharmed later in the fall and picked up where he and Gerald had left off in their imaginary battles (July 20, 1864). Even this dramatic intersection of the real war with Gerald's life had a happy ending.

If Gerald's war was characterized largely by attendance at patriotic and military ceremonies and displays and the acquisition of an ever-expanding collection of toys and books and other possessions, Carrie Berry's war was marked by constantly shrinking resources, growing responsibilities, and increasing danger. As Gerald's childhood was made richer by the fun and excitement, Carrie's childhood, for a time, simply disappeared. In fact, the most striking thing about the portion of Carrie's diary that covers the Atlanta Campaign is the extent to which, aside from occasional references to dolls and friends, it does not seem to describe the life of a little girl at all.

A constant accompaniment to Carrie's record of daily life in besieged Atlanta was the fighting going on outside the city—so common and so plainly described that a reader can almost hear the distant guns. Although the first diary entry was dated August 1, Carrie preceded it with a brief paragraph that set the scene for the next couple of months:

> Gen. Johnston fell back across the river on July 19th, 1864, and up to this time we have had but few quiet days. We can hear the canons [sic] and muskets very plane [sic], but the shells we dread. One has busted under the dining room, which frightened us very much. One passed through the smokehouse and a piece hit the top of the house and fell through but we were at Auntie Markham's, so none of us were hurt. We stay very close in the cellar when they are shelling. (Berry, Preface)

Indeed, they lived so close to the fighting that Henry Beatty, a cousin in the Confederate army, could wander in from the firing line to have Carrie grind the precious coffee beans that he had captured from a Yankee. The radius within which the Berrys lived for several weeks was the distance they could cover in a mad dash to their bomb shelter, and household chores and infrequent outings were planned around the shelling. About a week into her diary, Carrie and her father attended church for the first time in a month. The afternoon was so quiet

What a Difference a War Makes: A Northern Boy and a Southern Girl

"it all most seems like [a] Sunday of old" (August 7, 1864). As the fighting intensified, her cousin, Henry, stopped by again, begging the family to move away from the fighting. Carrie's diary is full of entries recording near misses when shells and grapeshot pocked the backyard, rattled through the roof, and blasted beds in which no one, luckily, was sleeping. Eventually Mr. Berry moved his family to a house farther downtown, where the cellar was bigger and safer. Still, by August 23, three weeks after Carrie began her diary, she complained, "I get so tired of being housed up all the time. The shells get worse and worse every day" (August 23, 1864).

Sometimes a glimmer of hope lightened Carrie's mood. Henry, in a fit of wishful thinking, assured the family that the "Federals would [not] be here much longer to torment us and I hope that it may be so for we are getting very tired of living so" (August 16, 1864). On the morning after an unusually loud night of gunfire, Carrie awoke expecting "the hole town would be torn up." She was glad to hear that the noise had, in fact, been made by Confederate guns; as a result, "we have been very well content all day" (August 18, 1864). A few days later, Henry came to report that the Yankees had left their entrenchments. The family spent a "delightful day" anticipating their move home (August 26, 1864). After a quiet week, during which Carrie pined for her friends and neighbors to return home so church and school could start up again, the bubble burst. The Yankees had not left at all; the fighting had simply moved farther away and the rebels had been beaten. Word came that the Confederate army would evacuate the city the next day. Worse news came the same day: Henry had been badly wounded and was not expected to live.

September 2, the day Northern troops took possession of the city, was full of excitement and scenes of chaos. The previous night had been disrupted by Confederates blowing up their ammunition before they retreated. Worse, soldiers and civilians alike had been "trying to get all they could before the Federals come. . . . They have ben running with saques of meal, salt and tobacco. They did act ridiculous breaking open stores and robbing them." A few blue-coated cavalrymen dashed into town later in the day, followed by infantry. Carrie was grateful that "they were orderely and behaved very well," predicting that "I think I shall like the Yankees very well" (September 2, 1864). Over the next few weeks, although Carrie fails to mention him until he departs with the army, the family gained "a very good friend" in the Union sergeant who had lived with them—and, no doubt, helped protect their house from destruction (October 30, 1864).

Military setbacks were only a part of the home front experience for the Berrys. Amid the noise, stress, and shortages of all but the plainest food, Carrie found herself working like an adult. After the Union army took over Atlanta, the Berrys lost their only slave, Mary, "but we can do very well without her," Carrie vowed. "I will have to go to work to help Mama" (September 7, 1864). Carrie spent much of her time knitting and taking care of her little sister, but also helped her father—getting blisters when she helped him tack a mattress for her bed. Most of her work revolved around housekeeping: cooking, ironing, sewing, and caring for her sister. On September 16, she spent most of the day ironing, but then "had hollowday"—playing for the first time in nearly six weeks (September 16, 1864). With most Atlantans gone and her cousins and aunts leaving, too, Carrie was overwhelmed with loneliness. The workload lessened a bit when her mother hired a black woman to help out, and Carrie was able to do a little reading and make a few doll clothes.

Military setbacks were only a part of the home front experience . . .

Adding to their misery was the uncertainty that came when General Sherman ordered everyone to leave Atlanta. The demand "broke all into our [ar]rangments" and caused Carrie to moan "We are all in so much trouble" (September 8 and 9, 1864). Indeed, Mr. and Mrs. Berry had already been so upset that, according to their daughter, Mama "can't do any thing" and "Papa says he don't know where on earth to go" (September 10, 1864). Somehow they mustered the energy to begin packing, but before they were forced to move Mr. Berry managed to find some sort of business in town that would allow him to stay. It was a great relief to the family that they did not have to move, but the arrangement—which Carrie never explains—posed problems later in the fall, when the Federals departed on their march to Savannah and the Confederates reoccupied Atlanta. At one point, Mr. Berry was put on trial, apparently because he was suspected of collaborating with the enemy, and Carrie feared he would have to go to the army, which he did not do.

The departure of the Yankees marked another difficult period in Carrie's diary. November was filled with trauma, fires, and looting, but by the end of the month, Atlantans had begun drifting back into the city. Despite the destruction and the continuing spiral of bad news from the war, Carrie was allowed to become a little girl again. She started studying her lessons on her own and, early in the new year, began attending Miss Maggie's School for Girls. She was able to play from time to time with Ella, the only one of her friends left in the city, and she could look forward to Christmas, which was celebrated with a tree, home-made cakes and presents, and a singing party. And, on December 7, she welcomed another sister into the family when her mother gave birth to Maggie. The return to a relatively normal childhood accelerated in the spring of 1865, when Carrie reported snowball fights, taffy pulls, the reopening of church and Sunday school, staying up late playing piano and singing, receiving a Valentine card from a boy named Eddy Adamson, and crowning a May queen. By the time the Confederate armies began surrendering in April, the war was quite distant. She neglected to mention Lee's surrender at Appomattox, reported briefly on the "Armistice" and her hopes for peace, and complained about the Confederate soldiers passing through on their way home and about the arrival of Union forces once again. Her transformation from home front warrior to young girl on the cusp of adolescence was, by that time, nearly complete. By Christmas 1865, life was back to normal: the family celebrated with candy, nuts, and apples, and Carrie received "a good many presents," including a doll, a doll basket, hair oil, cologne, and a silver quarter (December 25, 1864).

Obviously, not all Northern children had as secure, happy, and interesting a wartime childhood as Gerald Norcross. Many were forced to take fathers' places in their families' economies. For instance, with her father and older brothers gone to the war, Anna Howard was nearly overwhelmed with the work required to maintain a backwoods Michigan homestead and with teaching in a country school; fifty years later she still remembered that life as "a strenuous and tragic affair" (Shaw, 52–53). Seven-year-old Eddie Foy, the future comedian, helped his widowed mother make ends meet by blacking boots and by performing with a wandering fiddler in the streets and taverns of New York City, Brooklyn, and Jersey City.

Of course, many Northern children lost fathers, brothers, and uncles to wounds and disease. Yet their homes virtually never became battlefields. They would not have to live through the kind of crisis that faced fifteen-year-old Sue Chancellor in May 1863, when two of the largest armies ever assembled in North America battled for control of the tiny crossroads where her family's house and a tavern perched. At a crucial point in the battle, Sue, her mother, and several sisters had to flee from the basement of their burning home and dash across a yard littered with dead and wounded soldiers. "The woods around the house were a sheet of fire," wrote Sue, "the air was filled with shot and shell; horses were running, rearing, and screaming; the men were amass with confusion, moaning, and praying." Somehow, although they lost virtually everything they owned, none of the Chancellors were injured in the battle that bore their name (Chancellor, 137–146).

The experiences described in the diaries of Gerald Norcross and Carrie Berry stand at opposite ends of the spectrum of home front life. Gerald's boyhood was positively enhanced by the excitement of war, his schooling was uninterrupted, and his family circle remained intact. Carrie, at least during the several months on either side of the battles around Atlanta, constantly worried about her family's and her own welfare, rarely had enough food to eat (she wistfully wrote on her tenth birthday that she hoped that by next year "we will have peace in our land so that I can have a nice dinner"), could spare only a few moments here and there for play, and had to work many hours a day just to keep the household functioning. Given these diverse circumstances, it is not surprising that, in the decades after the Civil War, most of those Southern children of war who wrote about their childhoods would recall the conflict as tragic, deadly, and life shattering, while most Northerners who grew up during the Civil War would, if they wrote about it at all, recollect the war years as exciting and dramatic—a source of pride in country and in the roles they and their elders played in putting down the rebellion.

PRIMARY SOURCES:

Berry, Carrie. Diary. Atlanta History Center, Atlanta, GA.

Chancellor, Sue M. "Personal Recollections of the Battle of Chancellorsville." *Register of the Kentucky Historical Society* 66 (April 1968): 137–146.

Norcross, Gerald. Diary. American Antiquarian Society, Worcester, MA.

Shaw, Anna Howard. *The Story of a Pioneer.* New York: Harper & Bros., 1915.

SECONDARY SOURCES:

Marten, James. *The Children's Civil War.* Chapel Hill: University of North Carolina Press, 1998.

O'Connor, Thomas H. *Civil War Boston.* Boston: Northeastern University Press, 1997.

Chapter Sixteen

Playing Soldier: Phip Flaxen and the Watermelon War

A skirmish in an otherwise quiet sector of the Confederacy. A small squad of gunmen rise over a creek bank, viewing enemy lines. When the time is right, the captain calls, "Fire! One and all." A soldier falls, another screams, "Lord, he is killed!" The "boys with the guns began to fire and . . . the pop, pop was fierce." It is over in a few moments; although casualties are light on both sides, the "boys" are clear victors (Morrow, 41–42).

The annals of the Civil War are filled with accounts of sharp, violent, but obscure actions such as this one. However, as told by D. F. Morrow in his memoir *Then and Now: Reminiscences and Historical Romance, 1856–1865,* this is not a battle between Yankees and rebels, but between a curmudgeonly farmer and Captain Phip Flaxen's company of boy soldiers. The issue is not states' rights, but "watermelon rights." The boys' enemies are not Northern abolitionists, but Sam Canahan, a newcomer to the rural community that clustered near Burnt Chimneys Muster Ground in Rutherford County, North Carolina. Contrary to local custom, Sam and his son Tad had vowed to keep their prized watermelon patch free of marauding boys, who normally had the run of the small melon fields most farmers maintained in those days, and even had declared at church one Sunday that they were prepared to defend their patch with guns! Local boys, naturally, took this as a challenge, and Flaxen and his cohorts immediately began plotting a campaign to put Sam in his place and to reestablish their rights to poach anyone's watermelons at any time.

Faced by a challenge to their customs and beliefs, these young boys borrowed the rhetoric of the sectional conflict and responded in the way that their elders had two years before: they demanded their rights and resorted to military action to claim them. In so doing, they joined thousands of young boys and girls in incorporating the terrible war raging around them into their play. Phip and his men may have been deathly serious about their campaign to regain their watermelon stealing rights, but their actions resembled those of less sanguinary peers, who mustered their own military companies, learned the manual of arms,

181

*The martial fervor documented by romanticized images like this inspired
many young Northerners to form their own "boys companies."
(Library of Congress)*

fought imaginary battles, and played "hospital." Play is one way that children
have always socialized themselves to political, social, and even economic values, and the Civil war obviously had a huge impact on children's play.
Throughout the North and the South, children managed their fears, sought to
join in the great crusades that everyone talked about, and aimed to become—or
at least sometimes to act like—grown-ups, but at a safe distance.

Even before the war, at one time or another, most midcentury American boys
formed their own mock militia units and played army. In family portraits and
magazine illustrations, they often posed with military toys and props. During the
war, artists frequently depicted boys and a few girls brandishing swords, wearing
military caps, and banging on miniature drums. Children naturally gravitated
toward the thousands of makeshift parade grounds that sprang up after Fort
Sumter to watch their fathers and brothers and neighbors become Union or
Confederate soldiers. Whenever they had the chance, they joined the martial fes-
tivities. When a home guard company finished drilling in Richmond, several
companies of little boys scrambled onto the field. Boys in Culpeper County
formed a sort of shadow company that practiced alongside their local heroes, the
Little Fork Rangers, while in the first months of the conflict the older girls at
Wesleyan Female College in Macon formed their own student company. The half

*Little boys—black as well as white—enthusiastically march alongside
grownups going off to join the Confederate army.
(Hulton Archive)*

dozen sons and daughters of Reverend William Ward matched step for step the
eager young men he collected in his study to teach the rudiments of drill, substituting broomsticks and fire pokers for muskets. "We could shoulder arms, carry
arms, right-about face, guide right, and guide left, right wheel, left wheel, march,
double-quick" and "keep step beautifully," bragged his daughter (Ward, 32).

Oddly, Southern black children often joined their young white masters in
playacting war. Madison Brinn, a young slave in Kentucky, longed to be a soldier. "I didnt care what side," he remembered as an old man. "I jis' wants a gun
and a hoss and be a sojer." Slave children eagerly watched local companies drill
and sometimes exhibited the same kind of hero worship of Confederate officers
displayed by white Southern youngsters (Rawick, vol. 4, pt. 1, 171). Whenever
the white children on the Ward plantation drilled, so did the black children, who
served as privates to the white "officers." On another plantation, white boys
threatened their black playmates with dire consequences if they refused the
parts of despised Yankee soldiers.

Children in the North also converted their play to a war footing. According to
an early history of the war in Illinois, once the war had begun, "each school had

its play-ground transformed into a parade-ground, while small drums, miniature cannon and harmless small arms were the playthings of the nursery" (Eddy, 75). This was certainly true in Galena, where Julia Dent Grant recalled, as "the men were holding meetings and calling for volunteers," the "boys were playing at war, wearing military caps, beating small drums, guarding the crossings, and demanding countersigns." The most famous boy soldiers in the United States lived at the White House, where Tad and Willie Lincoln organized "Mrs. Lincoln's Zouaves"—reviewed on at least one occasion by the commander in chief himself—mounted a log cannon on the White House roof, and frequently court-martialed a Zouave doll, which they would then execute and bury with full military honors (Simon, 89).

"But I made a tent of my sheets, and with a broom for a musket, drilled myself till I was so tired that I fell asleep."

A young Yonkers, New York, girl who proudly referred to herself years later as a "tomboy" was so enamored of her brother's colorful Zouave uniform that she tried to convince him to take her along. He thought she was joking, but, undaunted, she obtained a soldier's cap, canteen, and drum and practiced beating it as she marched "up and down the path in front of our house . . . until every head in the street must have ached." When she thought herself ready, she journeyed, all alone, into New York City to talk to her brother's colonel. He hoped he would agree to take her as the "daughter of the regiment." He declined, however, and when she returned home her worried and angry parents sent her off to bed. "But I made a tent of my sheets, and with a broom for a musket, drilled myself till I was so tired that I fell asleep" (Gilder, 202–210).

Short of enlisting in the army, many children tried to make their war play as real as possible. A group of Cincinnati boys picked up abandoned flintlocks from a local militia armory and promptly formed firing squads to "shoot" helpless little boys forced to act the parts of "spies" and "deserters." They also pounded little mud and wood Fort Sumters to bits with cannon made of old brass pistols and blew up Jefferson Davis effigies made out of potatoes (Beard, 102, 151). Southern boys combed deserted army camps for broken guns and lost cartridges. One boy wrote years later that he would "practice target shooting by the hour, thinking I would some day have to practice shooting at the enemy if the war continued a few years longer." He also enjoyed shooting off a miniature brass cannon that could fire minié balls a few hundred yards, and with three or four friends, played "cavalrymen" on their old farm horses (Ashby, 208–209).

Not all children focused on the violence of war. Far out on the prairies of Iowa, a family of children accompanied their father to war meetings and then recreated the speeches and songs for their mother when they returned home. A

Playing Soldier: Phip Flaxen and the Watermelon War

Massachusetts boy constructed a child's version of a panorama by coloring illustrations from *Harper's Weekly* and pasting them together. As he rolled the series of war scenes from one wooden spool to another, he narrated the events they portrayed to his audience of young neighbors and relatives. Charlie Skinner, a budding theatrical manager, produced epic tragedies with the help of family members and playmates that featured soldiers and sailors, as well as slaves, planters, and overseers, in settings that ranged from Southern plantations to Libby Prison to Seminary Ridge to gunboat decks.

Southern children acted out a whole different set of experiences than Northern children. Nannie Belle Maury's mother overheard her small daughter mimicking the women she had watched deal with various wartime scenarios. One day, when a little friend asked her how she was feeling, Nannie replied, "I don't feel very well this morning. All my niggers have run away and left me." On another occasion, her mother overheard her declare, "Upon my word an [*sic*] honour, Sir, there are no letters and papers in this trunk at all"—the exact words of protest her mother had uttered to a Federal guard on the way out of Fredericksburg some weeks before (Parmelee, 89).

But the more violent side of war always lurked behind the children's play, and some parents, understandably, worried. "Almost their entire set of plays have reference to a state of war," fretted Virginian Margaret Junkin Preston. Her five-year-old son, George, covered the whole gamut of military experiences in his play, staging marches and battles with paper soldiers, taking prisoners, building hospitals with blocks and corncobs and ambulances with chairs, and administering pills to his rag dolls. "He gets sticks and hobbles about," recorded his mother in her diary, "saying that he lost a leg at the Second Battle of Bull Run; tells wonderful stories of how he cut off Yankees' heads, bayoneted them, &c." Occasionally he told his mother good-bye, explaining that his "furlough is out and he must go to his regiment again." Her three-year-old "also kills 'Lankees,' as he calls them, and can talk war lingo almost as well as George. . . . They can tell all about pickets, cavalry, cannon, ambulances, &c." On one occasion, her children and their little friends interrupted a paper doll dance when imaginary Yankees suddenly appeared and the paper soldiers had to dash off to fight them. Mrs. Preston no doubt spoke for many mothers when she complained that "the thought of war is never out of our minds. If it could be, our children would bring it back by their plays!" (Allan, 158–159, 179).

If any of the adults who observed the gang of Burnt Chimneys, Virginia, youngsters mount a military campaign remarked on the poignancy of boys playing at soldier in the midst of a great and bloody war, Decatur Franklin Morrow failed to record it in his 1926 memoir. Indeed, *Then and Now* is long on romance and adventure, but short on reflection, and is more a wartime history of the community in which he grew up, and in which he apparently resided for most of his life, than it is a real memoir of childhood. Morrow peppered his narrative with local color and his personal version of the history of the War Between the States—along with gratuitous criticism of evolution and liberal religion, which had come to a head in the famous Scopes trial in Dayton, Tennessee, just a year before his book was published. Like the flood of memoirs, autobiographies, and other writings about the Civil War and about life in the South before the war, Morrow's reflects a rose-colored and good-humored tone throughout.

Published by one of the leading wartime and postwar Southern publishing houses, J. W. Burke of Macon, Georgia, the book is, as its subtitle insists, a "Historical Romance." Morrow even includes a "cast of characters" and the publisher inserted grainy, posed photographs of particularly dramatic scenes. Although Morrow does offer glimpses of everyday life—spinning, certain customs of the time, descriptions of the simple country school he attended—he is much more interested in two main plotlines: love affairs among various young men and women in the community; and the nefarious activities of local Unionists, spies, and slaves who threaten to cause an uprising among the bondspeople of the county, scheduled, it was widely believed, for December 13, 1863.

Morrow seems to be a good-natured, kindly old gentleman telling his simple stories of intrigue, war, and boyhood. Yet, like most Southern memoirists, he also felt compelled to explain his section's commitment to slavery and to relate his own relationship to the institution. His family owned a plantation and, obviously, at least a few slaves, but most of the slaves he wrote about belonged to other white families. "Old Charles" was the carriage driver and butler for the local aristocrat, Colonel Lightfoot, who so trusted Charles that he allowed him to carry a gun and go out with the Home Guards company to patrol for deserters and spies. Charles and his wife, Rena, represented that class of reliable and contented slaves that Southern whites liked to think they owned. On the other hand, another of the Colonel's slaves, "Old Tobe," belonged to a much tougher class of slaves. He and his wife, Nell, frequently ran away and had to be dragged back to the plantation by slave patrols. Tobe joined a local Unionist, Sid Gitsum, and the outside agitator, Pope Gaines (who pretended to be a Confederate from South Carolina), in fomenting the slave revolt and in causing trouble in the area.

Morrow justifies slavery when he details the respectful and kind ways in which the local aristocracy treated their slaves—and in his approving description of the harsh and sometimes cruel overseers who had to literally whip the "class" of slaves "who did the coarser and harder work . . . many of whom were semi-barbarians, who were just recently brought from the jungles of Africa and sold by the Yankee traders to the Southern planters." These newcomers—smuggled into the United States despite a five-decade-old ban on importing slaves from outside the country—"had naturally to be civilized and taught to work." The harsh treatment was "no doubt better than they had been used to in their own native land," for many had been saved from cannibalistic tribes and other terrors of the continent. The strictness, and even brutality, that characterized some overseers' practices did make them into "good servants" and contributed to their development by the

The grizzled, tobacco-stained Unionist Sid Gitsum was not only "uncouth" but also "'cussed' a lot."

early twentieth century into a "highly cultivated and civilized" group, "especially so when you compare them to the natives of Africa even today." As a result, Morrow concludes, "this so-called inhuman treatment of the Southern planter and overseer was for that race, no doubt but a blessing in disguise" (Morrow, 58–59).

His memoir is not really about slavery—his racist and stereotype-ridden comments about the institution fill only a few pages—and a reader can easily be captivated by this story, written by a nostalgic old man, about the exciting events he witnessed as a little boy. Morrow sets up his book like a late-nineteenth-century dime novel. The grizzled, tobacco-stained Unionist Sid Gitsum was not only "uncouth" but also "'cussed' a lot." His opponent in a famous fight at the Muster Ground was the "gallant young Southern Aristocrat," William Buster; Buster was half of one of the love matches that developed amid the tribulations of war. There are midnight raids, harrowing chases, and even a "shooting affair" at which one of the suspected spies, Pope Gaines, is killed. Even the main characters' dogs get into the action. After a particularly enthusiastic rally for the Confederacy at the Muster Ground, Gitsum appears with his dog, "Yank." Morrow and his ten-year-old friend, Tom, with Tom's dog—inevitably named "Dixie"—confront Sid, and a dogfight ensues. Boys gather round, yelling encouragement and singing the song "Dixie," but despite their moral support, the larger Yank gets the upper hand. His master fares worse, however, after the arrival of Buster, who, after enduring harsh words and a few Unionist oaths, thrashes the "yellow Yankee Scallawag" (ibid., 37–47).

This is the opening salvo in the war between the neighborhood's loyal Confederates and Unionists, which has nothing to do directly with the raid on the watermelon patch, but certainly reflects the same kind of willingness on the part of Southern patriots to stand up for what was right and to take sometimes drastic action to enforce those rights. Like youngsters all over the South, the young boys of this rural neighborhood had often gathered to watch the grown-ups drill at the Burnt Chimneys Muster Ground, which had been used by local militia units for years. When the war began, they naturally formed their own company, led by a local squire's son, twelve-year-old Phip Flaxen. Phip was a dynamic leader and vigilant captain, who "was on the job all the time." Although it is not clear whether or not Morrow was part of his boys' brigade— the boys who made the daring raid on the watermelon patch seem older—it is clear that the younger boys in the area idolized Phip and his comrades.

Like many boys and girls his age, Phip "had heard much of States' Rights among the men and neighbors and was taught to believe that the men had the right to defend States' Rights and if they did why should not boys defend and protect their right to the watermelon patch?" Why not, indeed; on the same Sunday that Sam Canahan rashly declared that no boys would be allowed to take melons from his patch, Phip gathered "his boys" in a council of war and began planning the attack, scheduled for Tuesday night. They would meet at a cross-roads just a mile upriver from Canahan's patch; Phip ordered the boys to load their shotguns with powder and peas. All the boys realized that this was a different kettle of fish than the "chicken fights and camp suppers" they usually attended. It was dead serious: "the boys' Watermelon Rights had been assailed by Canahan and his son, in public . . . and in the presence of lots of the meeting house folks, . . . and something must be done." Phip warned the boys at the meeting not to tell a soul, but to get the rest of the company together by advertising a great "feast and fishing party." His sergeant—Morrow's buddy Tom— spread the word to absent members, and the attack was on for July 30, 1863.

The ten boys who belonged to the company gathered at the crossroads after dark, checked their equipment, and marched quietly to the river, where they confiscated a neighbor's boat and floated downstream toward their target. Morrow declared, "there are some things hard to do in life and one of those" is for boys "to keep quiet while on their sail down the river." Yet, for these boys, play had at least temporarily crossed over into something more serious, and they remained silent. When they reached their objective, they tied the boat to an overhanging willow tree and took positions along the four-feet-high riverbank. A small squad hustled into the watermelon patch to secure the five biggest and best melons, which were stowed on the boat. That was the signal for the boys to erupt into the "rebel yell," which would attract the attention of Sam and Tad Canahan. The boys cocked their guns and leveled them at the watermelon patch. Then they waited for the inevitable counterattack.

They did not have to wait long. The Canahans crept out of their house, shotguns in hand, followed by their mangy old dog. The dog sniffed along the riverbank and began baying; the boys found themselves giggling, despite the seriousness of the situation. Sam's gun accidentally went off, startling Captain Flaxen, who slipped on the sand, whereupon he gave the command to fire. The boys' guns roared; the Canahans dropped their guns, frightened by the pellets peppering the ground all around them, and retreated into their house. The victors rowed with their juicy trophies to their embarkation place, returned the boat to its mooring, and proceeded to the crossroads, where they prepared a supper of "corn dodgers," chicken, and, of course, watermelon.

The aftermath of the story included an interview of Captain Flaxen by Annie Lightfoot (whose boat they had borrowed); he admitted to having used it, and she rewarded his truthfulness with a watermelon treat. The next Sunday, Sam Canahan had his own tale to tell, about the "crowd of . . . fifty men, all with guns," who he and his son had run off after killing "three or four" of them. Of course by then, most of the neighborhood knew the real story of the watermelon raid, and Sam Canahan's boasts rang even more hollow than before.

Morrow concludes that "such was some of the sports in the days of the sixties and the customs of the country in the South at that time." Phip and his friends "were not bad boys, but in fact good ones, as can be seen from the fact that their captain did not want to hurt old Sam, his boy or dog." More importantly, by putting an annoying braggart in his place, they displayed the principles for which their fellow, if older, Southerners were fighting on the real battlefields of the Civil War (ibid., 65–76).

There was an underlying seriousness to the series of episodes. Although Morrow maintains a jovial tone throughout, this adventure of spies, dissenters, and discontented slaves ends at the "Battle of Big Ivey," where the small band of plotters is finally brought to ground and their leader, Pope Gaines, is killed. Just as the boys reestablish their rights to the watermelon patch, their elders reestablish control over their community.

Similarly, the fine line between a child's pastime and youthful misbehavior often surfaced in their military play. Other boys, like Phip and his gang, moved beyond innocent pastimes, activities that few adults found to be as harmless or even positive as the watermelon raid. The boys of Wytheville, Virginia, formed companies with names like the "Baconsoles" and the "Pinchguts," and carried on a war one newcomer thought was "too much like the big war that had been going on so long" (Robertson, 72–74). They blasted away at one another with sawed-off muskets and, like guards in many prison camps, rifled the pockets of captured foes. The boys of Richmond, recalled one young man who grew up in the middle of the Confederate capital, formed "as many clans as the seven hills" on which the city was built. "They had all caught the fighting spirit, just like the new soldier boys" (Wilkins, 23, 41–42). Their battles became so violent that police had to break them up.

Adults generally discouraged such behavior, perhaps because, for some boys, there was such a fine line between faux and real military service. Of course, thousands of underage boys ended up in the armies of both sides, especially in the manpower-strapped Confederacy. Dozens of cadets at the Georgia Military Institute fanned out to train recruits at county seats and training camps throughout the state, while late in the war, boys as young as fourteen joined "Home Guards" companies, which were assigned the task of clearing out nests of bandits and deserters in isolated parts of the South.

For some boys, there was such a fine line between faux and real military service.

The line between play and politics was even more transparent for one boy in the spring of 1861. Ernest Wardwell, who before the war had frequently fought imaginary battles and had, himself, organized a boys' company, joined the mob attacking the 6th Massachusetts as it marched through Baltimore on its way to Washington. Although he started the day an ardent Southerner, the Yankees' "gallant bearing" impressed him, and he eventually jumped into the marching column and volunteered to carry a Massachusetts sergeant's rifle. Swept along with the regiment as it was attacked and then returned fire, the teenager ended up enlisting and rising to the rank of captain (Towers, 427–446).

Morrow does not wax philosophical about the implications of the collapsing boundaries between childhood and adulthood, but his memoir nevertheless tells us a lot about the Southern home front: rather unwittingly, it seems, he displays the fractures in Southern society, especially in those parts of the Confederacy where slavery was a less vital part of the economy. It tells us something about the contours of the peculiar institution; both the "good" slave Charles and the "bad" slave Tobe enjoy surprising amounts of freedom within their bondage. Moreover, it shows us that even children internalized the sectional issues that had dominated the lives of Southerners long before Civil War children were born, as well as the way in which the war monopolized their childhoods.

PRIMARY SOURCES:

Allan, Elizabeth Preston, ed. *The Life and Letters of Margaret Junkin Preston.* Boston: Houghton Mifflin, 1903.

Ashby, Thomas A. *The Valley Campaigns: Being the Reminiscences of a Non-Combatant While between the Lines in the Shenandoah Valley during the War of the States.* New York: Neale, 1914.

Beard, Dan. *Hardly a Man Is Now Alive: The Autobiography of Dan Beard.* New York: Doubleday, Doran & Co., 1939.

Eddy, T. M. *The Patriotism of Illinois: A Record of the Civil and Military History of the State in the War for the Union, Vol. 1.* Chicago: Clark & Co., 1865.

Gilder, Jeannette Leonard. *Autobiography of a Tomboy.* New York: Doubleday, Page, 1904.

Morrow, D. F. *Then and Now: Reminiscences and Historical Romance, 1856–1865.* Macon, GA: J. W. Burke, 1926.

Parmelee, Alice Maury, ed. *The Confederate Diary of Betty Herndon Maury, 1861–1863.* Washington, DC: Privately printed, 1938.

Rawick, George P., ed. *The American Slave: A Composite Autobiography.* 19 vols. Westport, CT: Greenwood, 1972–1974; supplement, ser. 1, 12 vols., 1978; supplement, ser. 2, 10 vols., 1979.

Robertson, George F. *A Small Boy's Recollections of the Civil War.* Clover, SC: G. F. Robertson, 1932.

Simon, John Y., ed. *Personal Memoirs of Julia Dent Grant.* New York: G. P. Putnam's Sons, 1975.

Towers, Frank, ed. "Military Waif: A Sidelight on the Baltimore Riot of 19 April 1861." *Maryland Historical Magazine* 89 (Winter 1994).

Ward, Evelyn D. *The Children of Bladensfield.* New York: Viking/San Dune Press, 1978.

Wilkins, B. H. *"War Boy": A True Story of the Civil War and Re-Construction Days.* Tullahoma, TN: Wilson Bros., 1990.

SECONDARY SOURCES:

Bohannon, Keith. "Cadets, Drillmasters, Draft Dodgers, and Soldiers: The Georgia Military Institute during the Civil War." *Georgia Historical Quarterly* 79 (Spring 1995).

Conrad, James Lee. *The Young Lions: Confederate Cadets at War.* Mechanicsburg, PA: Stackpole Books, 1997.

Randall, Ruth Painter. *Lincoln's Sons.* Boston: Little, Brown and Company, 1955.

Chapter Seventeen

Oliver Optic's Civil War: Northern Children and the Literary War for the Union

"Never since the days of the Revolution," declared an editorial in the juvenile magazine *Student and Schoolmate* early in 1863, "have the courage and fortitude of the American people been so severely tried as at the present time. We seem to be making no real progress in the suppression of the rebellion. Defeat and disaster follow defeat and disaster so rapidly, that we are not permitted to recover from the effects of one, before we are confronted by another." Yet Americans had not—must not—give up. "The Old Flag still, and more than ever before, means freedom," and God, "the Father of all men . . . will lead us to a more holy and perfect peace than we have ever known before" (February 1863, 61).

The writer of this stirring and pious passage was William Taylor Adams, better known as Oliver Optic, the prolific author and editor of children's magazines and books who fought the literary war for the Union from his post as editor and chief writer for *Student and Schoolmate.* Born in Medway, Massachusetts, in 1822, Adams had been a teacher and school administrator before the war; he became a professional writer in the 1850s and, at the height of his popularity two decades later, earned thousands of dollars per short story. He wrote over a hundred books—many of them published originally as serials in monthly magazines—and thousands of stories, essays, and editorials. After leaving *Student and Schoolmate* following the war, he published *Oliver Optic's Magazine: Our Boys and Girls* for several years in the 1870s. His books covered a wide gamut of topics, from seafaring to slavery, but were united in their author's commitment to providing stories with a moral—and a little excitement. An advertisement for one of his books declared that "Boys and girls have no taste for dry and tame things; they want something that will stir the blood and warm the heart." Although he would often be criticized early in his career for the degree to which adventure overcame moralism, and later in his career for the stilted quality of his writing, Optic may have been the most popular writer for youth from the middle of the nineteenth century until his death in 1897. He played a major role in the transition of popular literature for children and teenagers from the didactic and calm style of the antebellum years to the more exciting—even lurid— approach favored by writers for youth by 1900, and in the pages of *Student and Schoolmate* and the books he wrote in the early 1860s, he contributed more than any other author to helping Northern children understand the causes and progress of the Civil War.

Young Northerners had a wide variety of literary options available to them during the Civil War, ranging from the Sophie May stories for little children, such as "Little Prudy's Captain Horace," to the high-minded works of Louisa May Alcott, to the exciting and decidedly lowbrow dime novels produced by the firm of Beadle and Adams. Twenty of the 100-page, $.10 novellas published during the war featured Civil War themes. They focused almost exclusively on individual loyalty and courage, particularly by Southern Unionists fighting overwhelming odds to save the Union, to preserve their fortunes, and, in nearly every book, to marry a beautiful woman—or, in some, a handsome Union officer. The improbable coincidences and startling plot twists inherent to the genre lent themselves especially to stories of espionage and secret societies. In addition to providing eye-popping adventures, these cheaply made books showed that most Southerners, when push came to shove, would stay true to themselves and to their country.

No wartime author was more popular, patriotic, or productive than Oliver Optic. Under his editorial command, *Student and Schoolmate* published articles, editorials, fiction, poems, and even games that revolved around the war. Although Optic did publish other kinds of fiction and nonfiction, the war preoccupied him and his magazine far more than it did other well-known publications like *The Little Pilgrim* or *Our Young Folks*. Moreover, his two trilogies, known as the "Army and Navy Stories," chronicled the adventures of twin brothers Tom and Jack Somers and set the standard for exciting and patriotic war fiction.

Optic's novels were less politically charged than his writing for *Student and Schoolmate*. They did represent the wartime writers' interest in chronicling young boys' longing to contribute to the war effort. Although many authors were content to let their characters play their parts to save the Union by staying at home, where they acted patriotically, played war games, and raised money for the soldiers, the Somers boys—age seventeen when the war began—are thrust into the thick of the action. Although they were much younger than the average soldier or sailor, Tom and Jack represented the common soldiers and sailors in the Union military effort (although each becomes an officer before the war ends). Optic introduced *The Soldier Boy*, the first in the set of books about Tom, as "a narrative of personal adventure, delineating the birth and growth of pure patriotism in the soul of the hero," and as a portrait of a "true soldier, one who loves his country, and fights for her because he loves her; but, at the same time, one who is true to himself and his God" (Optic, *The Soldier Boy*, 5–6).

Optic's books followed a strict formula. Each presented elements of military life and tradition, introduced a squad of loyal sidekicks and dangerous enemies, allowed Jack or Tom to demonstrate their martial skill and bravery in a large unit action, and then set the hero free to operate deep behind enemy lines, where he experienced a round of captures and escapes, met sympathetic Southern Unionists, finished his mission, and made his way back to safety, where he received a promotion that led him to similar adventures in the sequel. Tom and Jack operated more or less alone, relying on their own skills, only a few close friends, their courage and patriotism, and their virtue—qualities found in virtually every story and novel for children during the middle third of the nineteenth century. A fairly typical plot drives *The Yankee Middy*. In this second volume about Jack, the naval recruit, he stumbles into a conspiracy to divert captured contraband goods to the Confederacy. His foe, a Confederate spy named Phil Kennedy, is also Jack's competitor for the lovely Kate, a Union commodore's daughter. While attempting to foil the plot, Jack is captured but escapes; his pursuit of his military and romantic rival ends in a rousing hand-to-hand struggle. Jack mortally wounds Kennedy and his crew overcomes the Confederates. Afterward, Jack reads the Bible to the dying rebel spy, establishing closure for the repentant rebel and a moral for young readers.

Although the twin trilogies were quite popular and stayed in print for decades—with a major reissue in the 1890s—Optic's real passion during the war remained *Student and Schoolmate*, where his words became lightning bolts aimed at Confederates, slave owners, faltering Northerners, and anyone or anything that threatened the Union. "We like to see children who shout for the Stars and Stripes, for the Union, for the Constitution," he declared from behind his "Teacher's Desk," his monthly column. "Let them be loyal always and everywhere; not only to the country, but to their parents and teachers—to God and themselves" (December 1862, 428–429). Although his writing may seem hopelessly moralistic to modern readers, Optic clearly rejected the apolitical, careful writing for children that flourished before the war, when even Sunday school magazines published by Northern religious denominations avoided controversial topics like slavery. Optic's martial and partisan approach, his no-holds-barred hatred of Southern ideals and of slavery, and his insistence that writing for children should be entertaining as well as educational made him a widely read exception to the mainstream of children's authors. The war infused him and his magazine with energy and purpose, politicizing, informing, and exciting readers

Underage soldiers like Austin Johnson of the 16th Massachusetts, who was killed at Gettysburg, provided the plots for the inspiring short stories of youngsters' heroism that filled Northern children's magazines. (Medford Historical Society Collection/Corbis)

through fiction, features, poetry, songs, and games whose specific goal was to create patriotic and pious young Northerners.

A sampling of the kinds of pieces that Optic published show just how much the war dominated his thinking and writing. He had several purposes to his wartime writing: he wanted to educate, politicize, and mobilize the young readers of his magazine. Many of the articles were straightforward descriptions of army life; in fact, Optic devoted two six-part series to educating readers about army operations and the experiences of common soldiers. Charles C. Coffin's "Letters from the Army" showed the daily life of soldiers in camp. Two years later, a more ambitious series called "Campaigning" focused on the organization and administration of units ranging in size from a regiment to an entire army. In an era when the peacetime army of the United States rarely reached 12,000 men, the size of Civil War armies, which often climbed above 100,000 soldiers, must have seemed incredible to children and adults alike. Articles like these helped make the unimaginable scale of the war more comprehensible—"what a lesson of system" concluded one description of an army deploying into the line of battle (August 1864, 48). They also taught Northern children new words like "pickets," "flank attacks," "foraging," and "Sanitary Commission." As Optic wrote in one of his editorials, "the war has increased our vocabulary, and words which are now used and understood by all, would have been unintelligible two years ago" (March 1863, 93). Optic and his authors filled his informational pieces with such jargon, as in the second part of "Campaigning," where children read that

> The Cavalry hold the outposts on most distant picket points, because they can travel faster to warn of the enemy's approach; and when they are driven in, it gives the Infantry outposts time to get into position to meet the coming foe. If the Infantry pickets are outnumbered and driven in, too, then the Artillery, which is always posted so as to sweep all the approaches to the town or fort where our pickets have all fallen back, pour in grape and canister upon the advancing foe, the Infantry being drawn up in the line of battle just behind the Artillery, ready to meet the enemy as he rushes up with the purpose of capturing the pieces. (August 1864, 48)

The last two installments of "Campaigning" offer a little of the adventure that characterized the "Army and Navy" trilogies showing a picket guard of Yankees fighting a skirmish with Confederate cavalrymen and more of Optic's frequently expressed racial and political attitudes. Despite the strategic insignificance of the affair, readers witness vicious rebels looting bodies and attacking wounded, defenseless Yankees, and meet an intelligent and helpful African American contraband. Even more important, however, was the application of prewar ideas

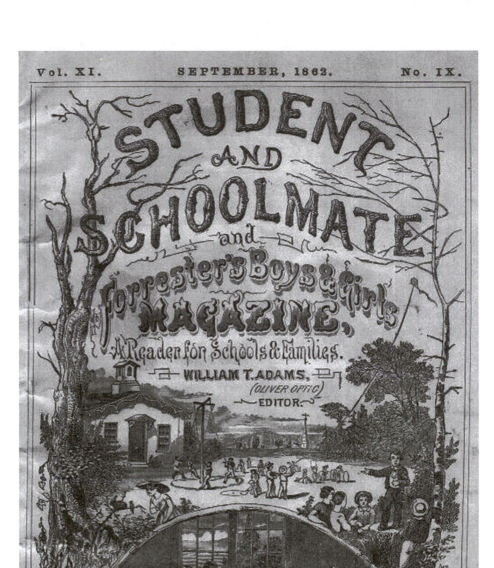

A Student and Schoolmate *cover for 1862 (Library of Congress)*

to the war—the importance of order, hierarchy, and admiration and respect for legitimate authority. Furthermore, the officers in these articles function coolly and courageously, despite "all the tumult, confusion, slaughter, and sacrifice" that surround them. All of this would inspire confidence among youngsters back home, especially those worried about fathers and brothers in the army, and encourage their patriotism (October 1864, 110).

Optic also showed boys acting out the martial behavior that they read about in boys' companies and simulated battles. A brief but not atypical example is a little story written for *Student and Schoolmate* by Christie Pearl, "The Fort and How It Was Taken." The story opens with the miniature soldiers drilling with broomsticks for guns, a coffeepot for a drum, and paper hats with colored streamers for uniforms. From a nearby sidewalk comes an insulting "Hurrah for the broomstick regiment," shouted by a passing group of schoolgirls. The company forms a line of battle and charges the hecklers, who scatter—except for "one bold, black-eyed girl," who sets her back against a wall and declares defiantly, "come on, boys, I ain't afraid of you." She is taller and a little older than the boys, who nevertheless level their broomsticks and issue a series of "unearthly" sounds "representing the 'bang!' of the guns." When that fails to dislodge her, they snatch her hat and demand her surrender. When they ask her on what terms she will submit, she commands them to drill in front of her for fifteen minutes and return her hat. Then she will leave them alone. They agree, march through their permutations, and she runs off (August 1862, 273–274).

This friendly and nonthreatening approach to war and war play was certainly in keeping with the attempts of magazines to win the devotion and loyalty of their young subscribers. Like many of his fellow editors of children's magazines, Optic tried to create a kind of extended family of readers and authors with a section that offered games, correspondence from subscribers, and personal commentary. Optic's "Teacher's Desk" was used to remind "our young readers of the fact that they live in historic times; in a period whose every day will be a page for future ages to read." His editorials tried to prepare the boys and girls who read them for the possibility of future sacrifice: "The days that try men's souls are upon us," he declared early in 1863, borrowing a phrase from Thomas Paine, "may we be equal to the occasion!" Northerners had barely suffered in the war—"except that our young men leave their happy homes for the battle-fields of the Union, and our hearts are occasionally wrung by the tidings of their loss"—but the coming year might require greater "sacrifices of comfort and plenty." If patriotic Northerners were challenged, "let us show our devotion to the great cause by suffering without a murmur. Above all, let us be true to God, true to ourselves, true to the historic character our fathers bequeathed to us" (February 1863, 61).

Not all of Optic's editorials called for sacrifice and courage. One urged children to overcome the common misperception that to be obedient was "degrading." Comparing naughty children to the Southern states who had seceded from the Union, Optic contrasted them to the Northern states, who "we commend . . . and call . . . loyal, simply because they are obedient." This huge political lesson could also teach children about their own small lives: "What is good for States and nations is certainly good for little boys and girls. . . . Obedience is the first lesson we learn as citizens" (December 1862, 428–429).

Other pieces explained common words as they applied to the conflict; he spent one brief editorial defining "copperhead," which was not only a snake, "quite as dangerous as the rattlesnake," but with "no rattle to warn the passerby that he means to strike a deadly blow." Similarly, those Northerners who out of avarice, a lack of courage, or misguided loyalty to the South fought the Union in

"What is good for States and nations is certainly good for little boys and girls. . . . Obedience is the first lesson we learn as citizens."

subtle and cowardly ways—complaining about government policies, failing to support President Lincoln, working to undermine the war effort—"lurk[ed] in the dark places of the land, ready to strike at the National existence whenever an opportunity is presented." They were as bad, if not worse than Confederates, who at least were open in their desire to destroy the Union (March 1863, 93).

An even more unique offering in *Student and Schoolmate* was the monthly playlet called a "dialogue," many of which related to the war. Some were straightforward accounts of stirring wartime episodes; others were political allegories with heavy-handed morals. Boys might identify with the young heroes of "Union Boys in Kentucky," which in addition to presenting the common Northern belief that the South, and the border states in particular, was filled with Union loyalists who hated slave owners and loved the Union, also borrowed from real life in showing a company of boy soldiers defending their turf. Published in the spring of 1863, a few months before the Confederates were finally driven for good from the soil of this deeply divided state, "Union Boys" begins with a dozen boys setting out to play army, only to find that their fort, tent, homemade boat, and other facilities had been destroyed for the third time by the Confederate soldiers posted in their neighborhood. "No more fun for us as long as this war lasts," complains one of the boys. The boys sit around bad-mouthing their enemies—"the rebel soldiers are scoundrels,—that is what they are!" declares one—and whipping themselves into a frenzy. "I won't bear it any longer," one announces, "let us assert our rights and get up a rebellion! If I could have my way, I would drive every soldier out of the city." He and the others talk themselves into "strik[ing] a blow for freedom." They practice their marching, put on their makeshift uniforms, and march on the Confederate headquarters to talk to the general in charge—none other than that irascible rebel, Braxton Bragg. There they have to endure insults and stonewalling from an insolent sentry, who says that the general "has better business than listening to a parcel of good-for-nothing boys like you." General Bragg eventually does see them, however, and uncharacteristically promises that their playgrounds will be protected from now on. The final scene shows the boys celebrating their triumph: their leader has been promoted to "major general," they sing "Yankee Doodle," and several suggest that they are ready for the real army. Finally, one of their number reports that the Confederates are preparing to abandon the town—and the boys, of course, take credit for the sudden departure of their sworn enemies (May 1863, 151–156).

Less entertaining and more political in tone was the two-part dialogue, "The Comedy of Secession," which recounted the secession crisis and the first year of the war as though it were a disagreement among the students at an exclusive girls' school. The revolt of an unruly gang of girls with names like "Louisa Anna," "Caroline," and "Flora Dee" at "Madam Columbia's" girls' school, the "Union Seminary," obviously stood for the Southern states' attempt to break up the United States. In addition to their obvious reliance on puns—a nineteenth-century vice indulged in by writers for adults and children alike—dialogues embraced the period's love of satire. For example, the hard-drinking and profane Confederate fire-eater Louis T. Wigfall of Texas would be made "Chaplain," and General P. G. T. Beauregard, one of the Confederacy's most popular generals early in the war, would be "dancing master" of the new "Confederate Seminary." Like most dialogues, "The Comedy of Secession" is filled with references to political and military events and personalities that subscribers to wartime children's magazines would have easily recognized. After all, such historical allusions, diplomatic references, and constitutional arguments had long dominated headlines, pulpits, and parlors. For instance, in act 2 the girls representing Massachusetts and Rhode Island struggle with Southern girls to keep Miss Mary Land in the Union Seminary, a reference to the troops from New England who helped hold Baltimore and Maryland for the Union in the spring of 1861. Miss K. Tucky (Kentucky) also displays serious reservations about secession, and her Northern friends call on her traditional moderation and willingness to compromise in convincing her to remain in school (August 1862, 279–283; September 1862, 314–319).

Dialogues were meant to be acted out at school or in the home; it is impossible to tell how many children actually sliced the pages from their *Student and Schoolmate* and produced the short plays that appeared every month. However, there is some evidence that another regular feature in Optic's magazine was used by readers—the "Declamation" pieces that appeared in virtually every issue. These were short passages from famous speeches and patriotic poems, verses from sentimental songs, or bits of essays designed to be performed in public. Students were also commonly required to present some sort of speech or presentation on Friday "speaking days," where they performed their own compositions or published pieces well known to contemporary as well as modern readers, such as "Barbara Frietchie," "Sheridan's Ride," or the tearjerker "Home News in Battle Time," which described in heartbreaking detail the last minutes of a mortally wounded Yankee, who asks his corporal to read a letter from his wife and children one last time.

Optic did not publish "Home News in Battle Time"—it actually appeared in *Forrester's Playmate* during the bloody summer of 1864—but the declamation pieces he included were equally stirring. That they were intended for public performance is obvious from the fact that each was accompanied by a chart of ten numbered gestures—ranging from extended right or left arms (numbers one and three, respectively), to right arm raised three-quarters or straight up (numbers six and seven), to the poignant posture of both arms hanging at the speaker's side, with palms showing forward (number ten). The numbers of the appropriate gestures were placed at meaningful spots in the declamation piece; performers were also advised where to raise their voices and which syllables to emphasize.

A sampling of just two of the pieces published by Optic indicates their overwhelmingly pro-war and pro-Union points of view, as well as the fervent patriotism they were supposed to inspire. The famous war song, "We are Coming, Father, Abraham, Three Hundred Thousand More," originally published in the *New York Evening Post*, referred to President Lincoln's new call for troops in the summer of 1862. "We leave our plows and workshops, our wives and children dear . . . to lay us down for freedom's sake, our brother's bones beside" (September 1862, 312–313).

For those students who wanted to avoid the inevitable singsong of a poem, there were prose excerpts like the conclusion of Edward Everett's massive three-hour speech at the dedication of the cemetery at Gettysburg. "God bless the *Union*"—speakers were supposed to emphasize "union" with both hands upraised—"It is dearer to us for the *blood* of those brave men shed in its defence. The *spots* [turning slightly to the left, hand extended] on which they stood and fell; these *pleasant* heights. . . ." Everett goes into an extended description of the landscape on which the battle was fought, but young speakers' emotions no doubt rose as they reached the climax:

As we bid farewell to the *dust* of these [point right hand to ground] *martyr-heroes*, that [raise both arms, bent at elbows, hands at ear-height] *wheresoever* throughout the civilized world the accounts of this great warfare are read, and down to the *latest* period of recorded time, in the glorious annals of our common country, there will be no [stretch high with right hand] *brighter* page than that which relates to [dramatically raise both hands to sides] THE BATTLE OF GETTYSBURG. (March 1864, 88–89)

For all the drumbeat and bugle-type articles and stories published in *Student and Schoolmate,* Optic certainly recognized that the values, patriotism, and obedience he preached to his readers might lead to loss and sacrifice. Children could contribute to the war effort—indeed, they must contribute to the war effort—and their sacrifices would help them learn valuable lessons about life as well as nudge the Union along to victory.

Adult and juvenile magazines alike were filled with maudlin images of the child victims of war. A common genre within the literature of loss was the "dead drummer boy" story, poem, or picture. Optic actually published a poem based on a true story about a fifteen-year-old drummer who died of exposure on the field after the Battle of Fort Donelson. More frequent, at least in Optic's magazine, were teary poems of orphaned and noble children. Optic did not apparently write poetry himself, but he did offer a couple of poems about wrecked families and sacrificial youngsters. "The Soldier's Little Daughter" was the story of a man who comes upon a little girl—"a little bird unblest with wings"—one cold, rainy night. She's begging, for "mother has been dead a year/And father's gone to war." She has lost her job and has had nothing to eat for a day. He takes her in, feeds her, learns that her name is Nellie Grover. At that moment, glancing at a newspaper story about a recent battle, he spots the phrase, "shot through the heart, a private, William Grover." This is, of course, a wonderful and terrible coincidence; as the little girl drifts off to sleep, "unto my soul there came a voice"— the voice of the father, asking him to care for his child. He accepts the challenge, of course, and the poem ends on this bittersweet note (April 1862, 131). An equally sad story presented the story of "The Soldier's Baby" in rhyming couplets: "A baby was sleeping, Its mother was weeping, Pale vigil was keeping, For slumber had fled." The mother was weeping because her husband, she had just learned, had been killed in battle. The poem is told just after the news arrived, when the child is innocent of the knowledge of its loss; all that would change soon: "Too young to know sorrow, Or life's woes to borrow, Must learn some to-morrow, Its father is dead" (August 1865, 230).

These sound a bit fatalistic, but the pieces in *Student and Schoolmate* calling children to arms—figuratively, not literally—were generally more reader-friendly.

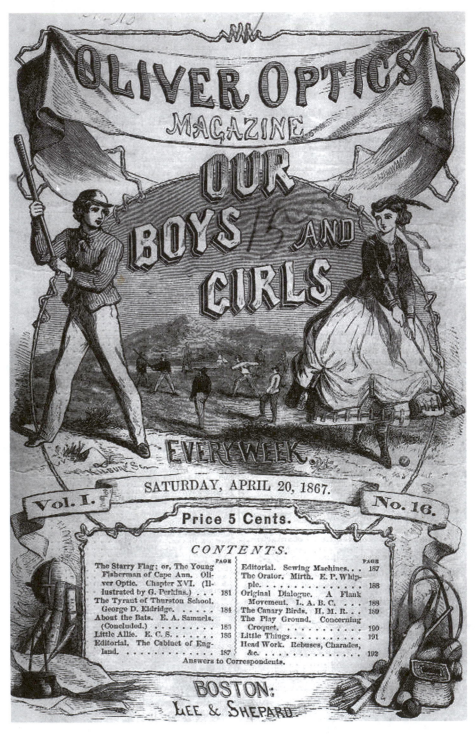

This 1867 cover of Oliver Optic's Magazine: Our Boys and Girls *features boys playing an early form of baseball and girls playing croquet. (Library of Congress)*

Most of the normal child-related home front activities were included: a family of young children tenderly pack little reminders of themselves, warm socks, and a Bible in a box for their father serving in the army; the only child of a poor widow gives up her most prized possession—a kitten—to be sold at a local sanitary fair to raise money for hospitals; a gaggle of well-to-do children gather old but still usable clothes for Southern contrabands. All of these stories showed Northern children how to contribute in their own modest ways—and within their own means—to the Union war effort. They also taught them that it was noble to sacrifice, to be generous, to take part in any worthy cause. Indeed, the youngsters in "The Contraband" learn that the hard way, for at first they joke around, filling the box with useless items and clothes they no longer care for. The frivolity and careless philanthropy is soon ended when their father clears his throat and asks them if they had given away anything they wanted or needed. "No! No! Not one!" they shouted. Their flippant mood shifts when he scolds, "then you have not given properly. Your clothes may keep the 'contrabands' warm, but they will bring no additional warmth to your own hearts. You must make sacrifices in order to reap the benefit of giving." The children realize their error, of course, and quickly repack the box with some of their favorite and most practical clothes (Pearl, "The Contraband," 47).

That mixture of philanthropy and valuable lessons learned was characteristic of much writing for children in the mid–nineteenth century. Modern readers may sense, however, that Optic's heart was elsewhere; he preferred to educate his readers about the politics of war and to spice up the drab moralism of antebellum writing for children with stories of adventure and battle. He remained better known for his Civil War tales than anything else he wrote; his 1870s successor to *Student and Schoolmate, Oliver Optic's Magazine,* occasionally revisited the Civil War long after most of its competitors had gone on to other things, and his "Army and Navy" trilogies remained popular for the rest of the century with brand-new editions issued in the 1890s. For many Northern children, Oliver Optic was no doubt their main source of information about the war. Rejecting the prissy sentimentality of prewar children's writing—up to a point—Optic injected excitement and patriotism into the reading material of children and youth.

PRIMARY SOURCES:

Note: Unless otherwise noted, all cited dates refer to issues of *Student and Schoolmate.*

Burr, C. Chauncey. "The Soldier's Baby." *Student and Schoolmate* 12 (August 1865): 230.

Everett, Edward. "Extract from the Oration of Edward Everett, at Gettysburg." *Student and Schoolmate* 13 (March 1864): 88–89.

Optic, Oliver. *The Soldier Boy; Or, Tom Somers in the Army.* Boston: Lee and Shepard, 1863.

———. "Teacher's Desk." *Student and Schoolmate* 11, 12 (1862–1863).

Pearl, Christie. "The Contraband." *Student and Schoolmate* 11 (February 1862): 47.

———. "The Fort and How It Was Taken." *Student and Schoolmate* 11 (August 1862): 273–274.

"The Soldier's Little Daughter." *Student and Schoolmate* 11 (April 1862): 131.

"Three Hundred Thousand More." *Student and Schoolmate* 11 (September 1862): 312–313.

"Union Boys in Kentucky." *Student and Schoolmate* 12 (May 1863): 151–156.

SECONDARY SOURCES:

Avery, Gillian. *Behold the Child: American Children and Their Books, 1621–1922.* Baltimore: Johns Hopkins University Press, 1994.

Kelly, R. Gordon, ed. *Children's Periodicals of the United States.* Westport, CT: Greenwood, 1984.

MacLeod, Ann Scott. *American Childhood: Essays on Children's Literature of the Nineteenth and Twentieth Centuries.* Athens: University of Georgia Press, 1994.

Marten, James, ed. *Lessons of War: The Civil War in Children's Magazines.* Wilmington, DE: Scholarly Resources, 1999.

PART IV

African Americans and the War

Chapter Eighteen

Havens and Hellholes: Challenges and Opportunities in the Contraband Camps

As Union troops clung to their southeastern Virginia toehold at Fort Monroe in the spring of 1861, their commander, General Benjamin Butler, had a problem: slaves forced to work on nearby Confederate fortifications were running away and sneaking into his lines. No one in the federal government had yet decided about the status of fugitive slaves; should they be sent back to their owners, should they be cared for by the army, should they be considered free people? Butler, ever the pragmatist, cleverly declared the escaped bondspeople "contraband of war" and promptly "confiscated" them under international rules of war. Although Congress later passed a series of acts further refining federal policy toward slaves, the basic approach—and the term by which they were known—were set during that first spring and summer of war.

Butler also established the contours of those escaped slaves' lives. He gave them the material resources to survive but also immediately put them to work. Their escape paid dividends right away; Butler once boasted of the arrival of a dozen black men who had just that morning been working on a Confederate battery that had fired on his men. Although at first the status of the escaped slaves was rather nebulous, it soon became clear that they would not be returned to their masters, and as U.S. government policy evolved during the next two years, those African Americans who managed to get into Union lines were, for all intents and purposes, declared free men and women. By July 1861, at least 900 had run, walked, and rowed into Butler's lines, and the flood tide of bondspeople flowing to freedom never crested.

Over the next four years, untold thousands of African American refugees fled to Union army posts and occupied territory, with over 10,000 streaming into the lower four counties of the Virginia peninsula alone. Fifteen thousand contrabands had fled to South Carolina's Sea Islands even before the arrival of the additional thousands trailing General William T. Sherman's army in the spring

Black refugees entering Union lines (National Archives)

of 1865. Crowded enclaves located at strategic spots along the Mississippi River, from Cairo, Illinois, all the way south past Vicksburg, housed over 50,000 refugees. The population was constantly shifting, but agents for the army and for philanthropic societies estimated that at any given time tens of thousands of former slaves were living in contraband camps that sprang up wherever Union armies established posts. Women and children dominated the population because so many of the men were absent as workers or noncombatant soldiers. Nearly half of the 2,000 residents of a camp near Murfreesboro, Tennessee, were children, while 2,500 women and children—the families of a regiment of black soldiers—clustered around Clarksville, Tennessee. President's Island, near Memphis, held over 5,600 women, children, and old men in 1864, while out of just under 2,000 contrabands in a camp near Helena, Arkansas, about 800 were school-age children.

Some of the camps grew into functioning villages, with schools, churches, and shops lining bustling streets. "Freedman's Village," built on the site of Robert E. Lee's property in Arlington, Virginia, was built to relieve the severe crowding among free African Americans in the District of Columbia. Slaves had begun slipping into the district from Virginia soon after the war began, but with the abolition of slavery in the capital a year later, the number of refugees and otherwise homeless African Americans had grown to as many as 10,000 in 1863. Early arrivals were housed in the Old Capitol Building and in other camps established east of the present capitol. Crowding, a smallpox epidemic, and the need to find productive work for the contrabands led officials to open Freedman's Village across the Potomac in late 1863.

The area, near what would become Arlington National Cemetery, had already become the final resting place for 6,000 soldiers. Houses and other buildings abandoned by the former owners could house 200 families who paid $3 a month to live in the whitewashed, story-and-a-half duplexes. The village also included workshops for training women and children; other men and women earned $10 per month for working on government farms. A school operated by the American Tract Society and furnished by the Boston School Board educated 150 students; a chapel was built for the use of the freedmen; and the hospital boasted a death rate about half that of the contraband camps in the city. In addition to the superior living conditions, the residents of Freedman's Village had one of the best views in Virginia. Men, women, and children who had been slaves just a few years or months before could now behold the valley of the Potomac as the great river wound its way toward the capital—a view enjoyed seventy years earlier by George Washington and, on the eve of the war, his foster son's daughter and her family—Mr. and Mrs. Robert E. Lee.

Although the view was far less spectacular, the contraband camp created at Corinth, Mississippi, had a reputation similar to Freedman's Village. When Corinth was captured by Union forces in the spring of 1862—and then successfully defended from a Confederate counterattack later in the fall—it became a haven for thousands of African Americans fleeing plantations in northern Mississippi and Alabama and southern Tennessee. Although General Ulysses S. Grant was in command of the district, the inspiration for creating a well-planned and safe harbor for the shipwrecked souls washing up within Union lines lay with a young chaplain named John Eaton. The old army barracks in which the first wave of contrabands were living soon filled up. The crowding worsened when the War Department established a policy forbidding African Americans from being transported upriver, where midwestern whites had no interest in competing with inexpensive black laborers or in living near their families.

Eaton set out to make the camp a model of its kind and he succeeded. The contrabands themselves built log cabins to replace the tents in which they had at first lived. Streets were laid out, houses were numbered, and the little town was even divided into wards. Like Freedman's Village, the camp at Corinth soon had a school, hospital, commissary, administrative office, and a log church. Within a few months, some of the African American men had been organized into a militia of sorts, relieving white troops of the necessity of guarding the

A cartoon depicting the evolution of an African American from a slave, to a freeman, to a soldier, to a martyr for the Union cause (Library of Congress)

camp. A number of American Missionary Association workers came to Corinth to teach and to preach; by summer 1863, there were nearly 400 pupils attending the school. The Union Christian Church of Corinth, as the missionaries called their little chapel, regularly attracted hundreds of worshippers—who could also enjoy the preaching of four black ministers recently escaped from slavery—and more than 300 children participated in the Sabbath School estab-

*Freedman's Village, a model contraband camp located on land now occupied by
Arlington National Cemetery (Library of Congress)*

lished later in the year. Families were also encouraged to grow their own food in
individual gardens; a little cotton field and a large field of vegetables for the hospital were also maintained. The Corinth "camp" had become, by the summer of
1863, a fully functioning little town of which any New Englander would have
been proud.

Most contrabands did not experience such well-organized and truly improv-
ing environments, however. A description of a contraband camp by a teacher
sent in late 1863 by the New England Freedman's Aid Society to a refuge near
Beaufort, South Carolina, shows a more typical living arrangement than the
frame houses at Arlington and the cabins at Corinth. Union raids on plantations
along coastal rivers freed hundreds of African Americans who crowded into
small camps comprised of makeshift hovels. The tiny village near Elizabeth
Botume's school contained about a dozen buildings, each divided into four
rooms in which entire families (some with as many as fifteen adults and children) lived. Low benches, a single table, and bunk beds nailed to the wall were
the only furniture; clothes and other belongings hung from the bunks.
"Outwardly," Botume wrote, the cabins "represented the poorest and most mea-
gre animal existence" (Botume, 50–51).

Most occupants of the camps faced even worse conditions, with material dep-
rivations rivaling if not exceeding those of their time as slaves. Sometimes army
quartermasters sold rations and supplies intended for freedpeople on the black
market. Medical care in the camps was sporadic, at best, and in 1864, Congress
eliminated funds for treatment of contrabands, leaving army surgeons to care for
the seriously ill with woefully inadequate resources—and then only if they
wanted to. Cornelia Hancock worked at the contraband hospital in Washington,

D.C., before shipping out to a school in the South. She left a chilling description of the rudimentary care provided to the former slaves and of the rough surroundings in which they lived.

In a letter encouraging Northern supporters to contribute to the care of the former slaves, Hancock promised to "depict our wants in true but ardent words, hoping to affect you to some action." Her letter listed numerous hardships and difficulties: "If I were to describe this hospital it would not be believed." Located north of the city "in an open, muddy mire," in this place "are gathered all the colored people who have been made free by the progress of our Army." The overburdened hospital cared for "all cripples, diseased, aged, wounded, infirm, from whatsoever cause." Their patients included black army teamsters beaten nearly to death by white soldiers; mothers dragging sick and dying children into camp after agonizingly long journeys from northern Virginia; two boys with broken legs after a fall from a wagon. Up to fifty sick, injured, or simply exhausted men, women, and children arrived each day; one morning an ambulance discharged five abandoned children recently dismissed from the smallpox hospital. Sick and sore, they had no one to take care of them until Hancock swooped them up and found a tent and some cots. At least one baby was born daily, but nurses "have no baby clothes except as we wrap them up in an old piece of muslin . . . This hospital consists of all the lame, halt, and blind escaped from slavery" (Jaquette, 33–35).

As these accounts suggest, the quality of life in the camps varied greatly, sometimes because of decisions made by politicians. When he was military governor of Tennessee, future president Andrew Johnson refused to issue tents to contrabands during the winter of 1863, claiming that it would make them too dependent on the government. In some places, freedpeople set up housekeeping in old packing crates, tobacco barns, sod huts, and, if they were lucky, abandoned houses. Single rooms sometimes housed six families. The crowding took a heavy toll. Out of the 4,000 black refugees living in Helena, Arkansas, in 1863–1864, about 1,100 died. In Memphis, 1,200 out of the 4,000 contrabands died in only three months, while the camp at Natchez—also holding 4,000 refugees—suffered a nearly 50 percent mortality rate in 1863. One report out of Vicksburg in the summer of 1863 called the camp at Young's Point "a vast charnel house" with "thousands of people dying without well ones enough to inter the dead." To make matters worse, Confederate guerrillas frequently attacked isolated and defenseless contraband settlements, sometimes kidnapping and selling men, women, and children—each of whom brought as much as $100 on the slave market (Bigelow, 39).

As is so often the case with impoverished families, children bore the brunt of the hardships faced by the contrabands. Two hundred African American children in Nashville could not attend school because they had to work—often simply for food—or because they literally had no clothes to wear. Everywhere contrabands gathered, white observers recorded horrifying vignettes: in Washington, just before the end of the war, a nine-year-old girl supported her mother and younger siblings by selling rags; a dozen freedpeople huddled in a stable on Capitol Hill included a young girl with consumption, a motherless boy with pneumonia, and an infant dying of malnutrition; another group of six children, the oldest only twelve, lived in a shed with no fire or food and wearing only rags. An agent for the Cincinnati Contraband Relief Commission described Davis Bend, Mississippi, in early spring 1864, where, in an open cattle shed, he found thirty-five "poor wretched helpless negros [sic]." The band consisted of a nearly blind man, five women, and twenty-nine children all under the age of twelve. The appalled Northerner went on to detail unimaginable poverty and horror:

> One of the Women had the small pox, her face a perfect mass of Scabs, her children were left uncared for except for what they accidentally rec[eive]d. Another woman was nursing a little boy about 7 whose earthly life was fast ebbing away, she could pay but little attention to the rest of her family. Another was scarcely able to crawl about. They had no bedding. Two old quilts and a soldiers old worn out blanket comprised the whole for 35 human beings. I enquired how they slept, they collect together to keep one another warm and then throw the quilts over them. There is no wood for them nearer than half a mile which these poor children have to toat [sic] . . . hence they have a poor supply, and the same with Water . . . the only vessel they had to carry it in was a heavy 2 gallon stone jug, a load for a child when empty. . . . They were filthy and will all probably have the small pox and a number of them likely [will] die. (Rowntree, 122)

Freedmen and women who survived these brutal conditions faced other challenges. Contraband of all ages had to work in return for the security, rations, and housing the army provided. By the age of ten or twelve, as they had as slaves, freedchildren took their places in the fields alongside older African Americans. At times, the reports of missionaries and plantation administrators displayed the kind of cold-blooded accounting and bottom-line thinking that would have warmed the prejudiced hearts of Southerners who frequently invoked the stereotype of Northerners as money-grubbing and heartless. One government agent, using an accounting scale that would have been familiar to most slave owners, reported that of the 9,050 contrabands on the 189 plantations on the Sea Islands, 3,619 were children unable to work in the fields, while another 335—boys about the age of twelve—were considered one-quarter hands. Women and children, who received only half wages or less, comprised well over half the workers on many Union-run plantations. At the very least,

THE (FORT) MONROE DOCTRINE.

*An ambiguously rude cartoon constructing a play on words with the
Monroe Doctrine and Fort Monroe, where in 1861 General
Benjamin Butler first declared escaped slaves "contraband of war"
(Library of Congress)*

children worked as caretakers for their younger brothers and sisters while their mothers labored in the fields.

One trait shared by all contraband camps, even the most humble and most dangerous, was the presence of some sort of school. Most black refugee children and a number of adults did manage to spend at least some of their time in school, often splitting morning and afternoons between work and class. It was not uncommon to see babies and toddlers snoozing on the porches of schools while their older sisters and brothers studied inside. Almost as soon as they reached Federal lines, African Americans began attending school. From their beginnings in 1861, educational efforts on behalf of former slaves grew quickly. A contraband opened one of the first schools for black students in Norfolk, Virginia, in the fall of 1861; two years later there were twenty-one teachers in eleven schools with 3,000 day and night students of all ages. Scores of freedmen's aid societies as well as individuals, missionary associations, the army, and others were sponsoring or even staffing schools throughout the occupied South; over 1,400 men and women were teaching in 975 schools in the year after the war ended. Schools ranged in size from a few girls being taught by the nine-year-old daughter of a Union army surgeon on the veranda of a Corinth hotel to the 1,422 in public schools run by the U.S. Army in New Orleans and more than 14,000 in schools operated in rural parishes in Louisiana.

African Americans opened the first schools for contrabands in the Tennessee towns of Nashville, Columbia, Springfield, and Pulaski. A few children, mainly in Virginia, North Carolina, and Washington, found themselves in the classrooms of African American teachers. Some, such as "Uncle" Cyrus White, who taught school in Beaufort, South Carolina, for several months in 1863, William D. Harris, a plasterer, and his assistant, Amos Wilson, who taught in Grosport, North Carolina, were former slaves. In fact, the American Missionary Association's (AMA) first school opened under the leadership of Mary Smith Peake—the free daughter of a white man and a mulatto woman—in Norfolk. The school Peake operated in Brown Cottage would later become Hampton Institute, alma mater of Booker T. Washington and other notable black leaders. Most of the more than two dozen African American teachers employed by the AMA, however, came from the North. Edmonia Highgate of Syracuse, New York, had lectured and raised money for the AMA before the war and had taught in the Binghamton public schools; she became a teacher and principal in Norfolk during the war. Her colleague, Sara G. Stanley, came from Cleveland via Oberlin College. A teacher at the AMA school at Camp Barker in Washington was a former slave but had been an educator and writer in Brooklyn, New York, for twenty years before joining the AMA. Only a handful of freedmen teachers came from the South.

The relationship between white teachers and black students confronted contrabands with another challenge: trying to understand Northern white people. Apart form Northerners' idiosyncrasies, young contrabands were fascinated by what motivated them. Their relationships were not based on economics; these were the first whites the freedchildren—and most of their parents—had ever known who valued the former slaves' interests over their former masters' interests. This did not automatically make them fast friends. Early in Laura Towne's long stay in the Sea Islands, when she and three other white women rode onto a plantation, "the children screamed and ran to hide at the sight of white faces" (Holland, 62). A similar scene greeted Elizabeth Hyde Botume when she arrived at her first school in Beaufort, South Carolina. Although the porch had been "crowded with children, all screaming and chattering like a flock of jays and blackbirds in a quarrel," when the children spotted her "they all gave a whoop and a bound and disappeared." After several attempts, she finally captured "one small urchin, who howled vociferously, 'O Lord! O Lord!,'" which brought out the other children. Eventually she got them seated and, over the next few months, they came to trust her (Botume, 41–43).

The gulf between Northern whites and freedmen often closed after these sometimes humorous first contacts, but, like the relationships that formed between Northern soldiers and slave children, those between Northern missionaries and teachers and their African American students were charged with ambivalence. Part of the problem stemmed from the Northerners' race and class perceptions. Most teachers hired freedmen as servants, rarely socialized with African Americans, and distrusted the emotional religion they observed in black churches. Some exhibited much more extreme racism. When a young black girl said good morning to a teacher who worked with Towne, the teacher threatened to slap her. Another teacher rarely held classes and paid little attention to her students when she did, simply declaring that they could do whatever they pleased. Even simple communication could pose problems. A former slave in Texas recalled how his Northern teacher "didn't talk like folks here and didn't understan' our talk." Black children also played pranks that youngsters through the centuries have reserved for new teachers: they switched their names from day to day or made up new ones—like Stonewall Jackson—much to the dismay of the confused teachers (Rawick, vol. 2, pt. 4, 184).

Some Northerners were very critical of the personal traits and behaviors of the freedmen, as though they expected them to convert instantly to middle-class, white, Northern values and habits. Even when they understood the causes of the freedmen's lethargy and seemingly lackluster efforts to change, they could not help being judgmental. Their comments inevitably took on a moralistic tone. A Quaker missionary described the contrabands coming into the Union lines near Norfolk early in 1863 as "almost wholly destitute of clothing, covered with vermin, and extremely ignorant, and incompetent for noble, self-originating action of mind or body, uneducated in principle too as they ought to enter freedom through the path of moral restraint" (Swint, 24). Even Cornelia Hancock declared disapprovingly that "their standard of morality is very low" (Jaquette, 35).

Although one must be careful in drawing evidence from only one side in a complex relationship formed between representatives of what were really very different cultures, it is clear that the white Northerners who encountered contrabands were stunned at the effects of slavery on slaves. One worker on the Sea Islands testified that there was little affection between parents and children: "there is no real domestic life. . . . You cannot get civilization into their houses; they live like pigs, on a fearfully low plane of life." An army officer in Florida complained that the families of black soldiers under his charge had "no disposition to work or to endeavor to provide for themselves; but are satisfied to draw their support from the government & live in idleness" (Berlin, 226, 248).

An idealized illustration of a Freedmen's Bureau classroom in Richmond following the war (Library of Congress)

Comments like these must be taken lightly. Of course, most of the white men complaining of the supposed laziness of the wives and soldiers would have heartily disapproved of their own wives working in the fields. Also, many of the more moralistic and harsh comments were written just after initial meetings between missionaries and contrabands; first impressions frequently softened as the Northerners came to know their pupils and employees. Yet the often harsh responses of Northerners when they first encountered former slaves do help explain the racial attitudes held by even the most sympathetic Yankees and demonstrate the great gulf that separated former slaves and their Northern allies.

Eventually, however, teachers and students usually learned to get along, at least superficially. Black adults became valuable assistants and even friends, and the children came to love at least some of their teachers. They "would fain worship us, the little things," reported a teacher in Norfolk, whose students "like to handle us, to pull at our hoops, and hang about us" (Swint, 81–82). After teaching contrabands in New Bern, North Carolina, for several months after the end of the war, Nellie Stearns exclaimed, rather enigmatically, "I declare I never think but I am black too when I am with my scholars" (Stearns, November 5, 1865).

Most contraband camps were temporary affairs that broke up whenever Union troops moved on or local commanders or politicians ended their support. Freedman's Village made way for more Union soldiers' graves, and the camp at Corinth was dismantled and its residents transferred to Memphis when the Union army marched south. Yet contraband camps were a key element of the home front experience for former slaves. The camps became, for the thousands of men, women, and children who entered them, scenes of great contrasts: they provided first glimpses of freedom—but their abysmal health conditions also ended the newly free lives of many African Americans before they had fairly begun. They offered the first chance for many former slaves to work for wages— but the Northern managers insisted on treating many of those workers like slaves. They provided venues for an introduction to education—but also exposed freedpeople to the condescension and racism of some Northerners. Finally, although the whites and blacks who lived and worked in the camps might not have realized it, the camps provided a kind of "rehearsal" for the politically charged race relations and sometimes conflicting goals that would characterize the period of Reconstruction and the decades that followed.

PRIMARY SOURCES:

Berlin, Ira, et al., eds. *Freedom: A Documentary History of Emancipation, 1861–1867; Ser. I, Vol. III: The Wartime Genesis of Free Labor: The Lower South.* New York: Cambridge University Press, 1990.

Bigelow, Martha Mitchell. "Vicksburg's Experiment in Freedom." *Journal of Mississippi History* 26 (February–November 1964).

Botume, Elizabeth Hyde. *First Days amongst the Contrabands.* Boston: Lee and Shepard, 1893.

Holland, Rupert Sargent, ed. *Letters and Diary of Laura M. Towne: Written from the Sea Islands of South Carolina, 1862–1864.* Cambridge, MA: Riverside Press, 1912. Reprint, New York: Negro Universities Press, 1969.

Jaquette, Henrietta Stratton, ed. *South after Gettysburg: Letters of Cornelia Hancock, 1863–1868.* New York: Thomas Y. Crowell, 1937.

Rawick, George P., ed. *The American Slave: A Composite Autobiography.* 19 vols. Westport, CT: Greenwood, 1972–1974; supplement, ser. 1, 12 vols., 1978; supplement, ser. 2, 10 vols., 1979.

Rowntree, Henry. "Freedmen at Davis Bend, April 1864." In *Journal of Mississippi History,* edited by James T. Currie (May 1984).

Stearns, Nellie F. Letter. Manuscript Division, Perkins Library, Duke University, Durham, NC.

Challenges and Opportunities in the Contraband Camps

Swint, Henry L., ed. *Dear Ones at Home: Letters from Contraband Camps.* Nashville: Vanderbilt University Press, 1966.

Holland, Rupert Sargent, ed. *Letters and Diary of Laura M. Towne: Written from the Sea Islands of South Carolina, 1862–1864.* Cambridge, MA: Riverside Press, 1912. Reprint, New York: Negro Universities Press, 1969.

SECONDARY SOURCES:

Engs, Robert Francis. *Freedom's First Generation: Black Hampton, Virginia, 1861–1890.* Philadelphia: University of Pennsylvania Press, 1979.

James, Felix. "The Establishment of Freedman's Village in Arlington, Virginia." *Negro History Bulletin* 33 (1970): 90–93.

Mohr, Clarence. *On the Threshold of Freedom: Masters and Slaves in Civil War Georgia.* Athens: University of Georgia Press, 1986.

Walker, Cam. "Corinth: The Story of a Contraband Camp." *Civil War History* 20 (March 1974): 5–22.

Chapter Nineteen

Testing the Boundaries: Slave Lives in the Confederacy

James Hayes endured most of his life as a slave in Texas. During the Civil War, when his master and his master's son went off to fight, James became, in a sense, the head of the household. Many years later, he told an interviewer of his obvious affection for the "women folks" on his plantation and of his concern for them after the white men went to the army. One of James's duties was to pick up the mail in nearby Marshall, and whenever he returned from town, the mistress and her daughters "run to meet me, anxious like, to open de letter, and was skeert to do it." One day James brought home a letter, "and I could feel it in my bones, dere was trouble in dat letter." Young Master Ben—the eldest son—had been killed. "When de body comes home, dere's a powerful big funeral and . . . powerful weepin's and sadness on dat place."

Despite the tragic death of the young master, Hayes maintained that during the war, day-to-day life on the plantation went on "like always, 'cept some vittles was scarce." The slaves "didn't know what de War was 'bout," and apparently were not particularly interested. "I guess we was too ign'rant," Hayes said. "De white folks didn' talk 'bout it 'fore us." When the war ended and their master returned home, the slaves joined in the celebration, singing and dancing with the "white folks." According to Hayes, when they learned that they were free to leave, "none of us knows what to do, dere warn't no place to go and why would we 'uns wan' to go and leave good folks like de marster? His place was our home." Most of the slaves chose to stay until the master died in 1866 (Rawick, vol. 4, pt. 2, 126–129).

A very different but no less telling example of the ways that whites and blacks shared the Civil War occurred on another plantation. Isom Norris, who turned seventeen the year the war ended, was a good friend of his master's son, "Little Massa Joe," who told Isom one day, "you is goin' to be free as I is wen de war is over." Isom refused to believe him and said, "Little Massa Joe, if I gits to be free as you is, de fus' thing I'se goin' to do is give you a whipping." The young slave doubted he would ever have the chance to carry out his half-teasing promise.

Yet, one morning, Joe called to Isom and told him that he was, indeed, free. Isom yelled and "jumped right straddle of Little Massa Joe, and threw him down and give him a few licks wid my fist," fulfilling his vow. Reflecting the boys' friendship and the new order of things, Joe "tuk it as a big joke, and did not do a thing to me, but he laughed at me gettin' so happy cause I wus free as he wus" (ibid., supp. 2, vol. 8, pt. 2, 934).

As this simple story shows, African Americans found themselves thrown, along with their white "families," into the anxiety, the hardships, and sometimes the danger spawned by the war. Although many black Southerners fled to Union lines, the majority had no choice but to wait out the war with their masters, while masters had no choice but to rely on their slaves even more than they had in peacetime. The loyalty of African Americans in the Confederacy was rarely discussed openly—indeed, throughout the long history of slavery, whites had been loathe to discuss publicly the attitudes of the people they owned. At the same time that slave owners comforted themselves with the belief that their own servants were loyal and that they were perfectly safe living among dozens or even hundreds of men and women being held against their will, local and state governments passed ordinances and laws restricting slaves' movements and establishing slave patrols intended to ensure the subjugation of slaves. Moreover, whenever slaves actually fought back—or when rumors sped through a town suggesting that a revolt was being planned—governments and mobs initiated savage reprisals.

In 1822, a free black named Denmark Vesey was convicted of plotting to lead an uprising of Charleston slaves; thirty alleged conspirators were hanged. In the aftermath of the 1831 Nat Turner uprising in southeastern Virginia, during which fifty whites were killed, perhaps 200 slaves were executed in Virginia and North Carolina on suspicion of taking part in Turner's or in other insurrection plots. In the summer of 1860, a series of mysterious fires in north Texas convinced whites that a slave insurrection was taking place; mobs hanged as many as twenty people, including several whites suspected of helping the slaves. Finally, rumors of an insurrection in the Natchez area just after the war began inspired a crackdown against local slaves that resulted in the hanging of perhaps forty and the deaths of several slaves who died while being whipped during interrogation. Obviously, the loyalty of their slaves was an issue of extreme importance to Southern whites.

Few slaves left first-person accounts of their experiences, but one source offers a glimpse into the lives and thoughts of slaves. In the 1930s, in addition to building airports, highways, parks, and other major construction projects, the Work Projects Administration (WPA) of President Franklin D. Roosevelt's New Deal conducted more than 2,000 interviews with former slaves. Filed away in

Confederates wanted to believe that their slaves would remain loyal during the war; this cartoon shows a slave hiding her master from the Yankees. (Corbis)

state and federal archives, forty years later, they were finally edited by George P. Rawick and published in three sets numbering a total of forty-one volumes titled *The American Slave: A Composite Autobiography.* Historians of slavery, the Civil War and Reconstruction, and of black culture after the war have long used these sources, while acknowledging their shortcomings. Most of the interviewers were white; the former slaves often seem to be answering questions with the kind of information that they believed the white people wanted to hear. The interviews were not tape-recorded, so the "oral histories" published by Rawick are actually reports or recreations of interviews rather than word-for-word transcripts. The teachers, amateur historians, and unemployed journalists hired for this job attempted to re-create the "negro dialect" spoken by the elderly men and women, littering the accounts with such minstrel show words as "dey" and "dem." Some interviews were edited, with the worst examples of cruelty and heartache removed (although this varied from state to state and the second set of volumes, published in 1978, restored the entries). Most important of course, a lifetime had passed since the events they described had taken place. No doubt memories had faded and perceptions had dulled in the seventy years between the end of slavery and the hour or two they spent with their interviewers.

Yet, despite all their shortcomings, the interviews in *The American Slave* offer the closest thing to an authentic version of slavery from the point of view of the African Americans who lived through it. The details, the emotions, and the complexities of the relationships that formed between slaves and slave owners are revealed. Some of the interviews are barely comprehensible; others are clearly the product of articulate, thoughtful men and women; some are sheer poetry. Taken together, even with all their flaws, they are the best source for understanding the experiences of slaves on the Confederate home front.

> *Obviously, if slaves had chosen to, they could have wreaked havoc on the Confederacy.*

Obviously, if slaves had chosen to, they could have wreaked havoc on the Confederacy. Few revolted openly, however. As it had been throughout the long history of slavery, the most effective form of resistance occurred when slaves simply ran away. Their responses were more complicated, however, than simply to stay or to go. Even those slaves who chose to remain on their plantations reacted to the war in many different ways, and by the end of the war, white Southerners—at least those perceptive enough to take seriously the African Americans with whom they shared their lives—had come to realize that the feelings, beliefs, and attitudes of slave men, women, and children were far more complex than they had thought possible.

Many slaves performed faithfully during the war. "The negroes, as a general thing," reported one newspaper soon after Appomattox, "have acted very well towards their owners and the white residents of the South, during the disturbed condition of the country for the last four years." A few joined "the invaders," but only because of their "ignorance and the superior control of the white man." With the confidence that had helped whites rationalize slavery for generations, the editor asserted that the "war has demonstrated . . . that the idea of negro insurrections, once so prevalent, is a humbug" (*Marshall (Texas) Republican*, June 2, 1865).

A few slaves gratified whites' confidence and expectations by actually going to war to tend horses, nurse the sick and wounded, or act as personal servants to their masters. A few were wounded or killed; some even took up arms against the Yankees. Some slaves provided even more dramatic evidence of their loyalty. When Federals captured his master, William Byrd walked all the way from Virginia back to his master's plantation in Texas and waited until after the war to be freed. Henry Smith marched with John Bell Hood's Texas brigade through the siege of Petersburg, where his master's son was killed. Henry buried him and carried his belongings back to the plantation in Texas, where he continued working after freedom until his white family died. A number of teenaged slaves accompanied their masters to the army and served them faithfully throughout the war. Cicero Finch, only thirteen when the war began, cooked for and maintained the equipment of four of his master's sons, stole pigs and chickens for them, and nursed them when they were sick or hurt. During battles, he and other servants acted as stretcher bearers, and in one battle he was slightly wounded by a shell burst.

Slaves also supported the home front war effort. African Americans in Houston raised $40 for sick soldiers with a grand ball in July 1862, and two Negro tableaux held in Austin in April 1863 raised $450 for Texas soldiers. Their most important contribution though was working on the farms and plantations of the Confederacy. As one freedman recalled, the slaves "kept de work on de plantations going, for dey had to keep on livin' an' some one had to do dis work." Few slaves considered escaping from the Bexar County place where Felix Haywood worked, because, he recalled as an old man, "we was happy." Life "went on jus' like it always had before the war. . . . We get layed-onto time on time, but gen'rally life was . . . just as good as a sweet potato" (Rawick, vol. 4, pt. 2, 131–134).

Slaves were not unaware of the threat they posed to Southern society, however. "If every mother's son of a black had thrown 'way his hoe and took up a gun to fight for his own freedom along with the Yankees," one declared, "the war'd been over before it began." Nevertheless, "we couldn't help stick to our masters. We couldn't no more shoot 'em than we could fly" (ibid., vol. 4, pt. 2, 134). Martin Jackson's father offered a grimly prophetic argument for remaining faithful: "He kept pointing out that the War wasn't going to last forever, but that our forever was going to be spent living among the Southerners after they got licked" (ibid., vol. 5, pt. 4, 14).

Slave children's loyalties were as complex as their parents'. Young slaves, especially, often identified closely with their white owners because these masters and mistresses were the locus of authority, the source of material well-being, the bestowers of treats and gifts, and the dispensers of plantation discipline. So, not surprisingly, many young African Americans found themselves, at least on an emotional level, siding with the South. At times they sympathized with their Confederate families almost instinctively. "All four of my young massas go to do war," recalled Lorenza Ezell; one was killed and two others were wounded. When the youngest was brought home with a shattered jaw, Lorenza was "so mad I could have kilt all de Yankees. . . . I hated dem 'cause dey hurt my white people" (ibid., vol. 4, pt. 1 and 2, 29). One boy exacted revenge on the Yankees who had raided his master's plantation by hiding with a handful of rocks in the bushes near a section of road that passed immediately under a tree with a hornet's nest hanging from one of its branches. When the soldiers "come by gallopin' I throwd an' hit that big old hornets nest. The way

*Members of a local Home Guards company checking slaves' passes
near the Mississippi River (Corbis)*

they piled out on them soldiers. You could see em fightin' far as you could see
em wid their blue caps. The horses runnin' and buckin'." Well satisfied with
himself, the boy told his master, who scolded him, "for he said if they had seen
me they would [have] killed me" (ibid., vol. 8, pt. 2, 140–141).

Another little slave boy loyally defended his white family against all comers.
After Yankees captured Jefferson Davis and his family, they sent Jim Limber,
the free black boy rescued on a Richmond street by Varina Davis, to Union
General Rufus Saxton, an old friend of the Davises posted at Beaufort, South
Carolina. Jim stayed for several weeks and was cared for by teachers and missionaries working with the freedmen. One of the teachers working there recalled
Jim's confusion and the "scorn and distrust" with which "he looked . . . upon all
around him." Vainly hoping that he would soon be reunited with the Davises, he
fought with the other black children when they sang the unofficial national
anthem of Civil War children in the North, "We'll hang Jeff Davis to a sour apple
tree." After one scuffle, Jim vowed that if "he were a man he would kill every
one of them" (Botume, 182–190).

Testing the Boundaries: Slave Lives in the Confederacy

Even many years after the war, a number of slaves seemed proud of their Southern heritage. An old man named Jeff Davis, born in 1862 in Arkansas, was, of course, named for "de fust an' only President of de Confederacy." He remained defiantly "proud of my name, 'cause dat wus a sure great one what I is named after" (Rawick, vol. 8, pt. 1, 118).

Few adult slaves displayed that kind of unconditional loyalty, partly because the conditions they faced during the war made difficult lives even more unbearable—although one slave declared in his WPA interview, with words indicating that he considered himself as much a Confederate as his master, "We wan't beaten, we wuz starved!" (ibid., vol. 6, 50). Slaves found old routines upset and provisions scarce, and many suffered at the hands of cruel overseers hired to replace absent masters. When Andy Anderson's master joined the army, he hired an overseer named Delbridge to manage his Texas plantation. The new man immediately cut rations and demanded more work and, Andy recalled, "he start de whippin's" when the slaves faltered. For making the lives of the slaves so miserable, claimed Andy, "I guess dat Delbridge go to hell when he died, but I don't se how de debbil could stand him" (ibid., vol. 4, pt. 1, 15). While the white folks had to give up tea and coffee, the slaves on at least one plantation had to give up everything but corn bread, mush, and potatoes, with a single meat ration each week (ibid., vol. 3, pt. 2, 171–172). One slave recalled that a number of children and old folks living near his plantation died because food was so scarce and sickness was so plentiful; the rest, "simmer[ing] in their misery," lived on whatever they could scrounge from the fields and forest (ibid., vol. 2, pt. 2, 217).

Even worse conditions faced those slaves forced to build Confederate fortifications. Because few slave owners voluntarily offered their slaves for work on Confederate defenses and even fewer free Africans Americans volunteered for the grim duty, the Confederate and state governments impressed slave laborers and conscripted free blacks, who could be required to work for 180 days or be fined $100. As a result, thousands of slaves and free blacks dug trenches, built forts, and installed gun emplacements for the rebels. When the Union army invaded southeastern Virginia in the spring of 1862, for instance, more than 1,300 slaves were put to work on the defenses.

The owners of slaves working for the army commonly complained of the harsh conditions their human property had to endure, and accounts of poor and scanty rations, disease, punishing work schedules, and abusive discipline occasionally appeared in Confederate newspapers. Even before the major Union offensive of 1862, a correspondent for the *Richmond Examiner* found appalling conditions at the "Negro Engineer Hospital." "Stench and filth abound in intolerable quantities," he reported, "and the poor Negroes are dying off like penned sheep. . . . It is a disgrace to humanity to behold their utter neglect." A year later, conditions had not yet improved. "We doubt if the government is aware of the treatment of Negroes, sent by the patriotic planters of the counties to work on fortifications around Richmond," the *Examiner* scolded (Brewer, 153–154). Fed only three-quarters of an ounce of meat and a few ounces of unleavened bread and water three times a day, the slaves were expected to put in long hours of heavy, sometimes dangerous labor. Many planters complained about the feeble condition in which their slaves returned home, while others castigated the government for failing to pay for those slaves who died.

Despite the poor treatment of those who were impressed or conscripted, only a small percentage of slaves had to work for the army, and, in fact, slaves shared many of the same home front concerns as white Southerners, including a constant thirst for news. Masters and mistresses tried to shield information about the war from their slaves. When a slave in Arkansas had a vision just before war began of "soldiers fighting in the heavens," his owner threatened to "take him out and beat him and make him hush his mouth," because "if they got such talk going 'round among the colored people, they wouldn't be able to do nothin' with them" (Rawick, vol. 8, pt. 2, 44). Nevertheless, slaves were often able to glean bits of war news. A handful could read newspapers or even the letters they fetched from the post office; others listened in on the white folks' conversations. J. W. King said that "some of de men on de plantation would slip up to a open winda at de big house at night and . . . lissen whut was read from a letter" (ibid., supp. 2, vol. 6, pt. 5, 213–214). Despite their distance from the battlefields on which Mr. Lincoln's army fought, they instinctively grasped what was at stake in the white men's war. Around late-night fires, Abram Sells recalled, the older men would crouch, "stirrin' the ashes with the pokes and rakin' out the roast taters. They's smokin' the old corn cob pipe and homemade tobacco and whisperin' right low and quiet like what they's gwineter do and whar they's gwineter go when Mister Lincoln, he turn them free" (ibid., vol. 5, pt. 4, 14).

More than a few slaves chose not to wait and began exploring the evolving relationship with their masters. A Houston newspaper complained in January 1865 about the insolence of the city's blacks. They uttered obscenities in the presence of children, refused to yield roads or sidewalks to white ladies and puffed "vile" cigar smoke in their faces, and bought illicit liquor from white merchants. The editor accused masters of being "altogether too lenient . . . and too regardless of their [slaves'] behavior" (*Houston Tri-Weekly Telegraph,* January 24, 1865). One slave plundered the home of a woman whose husband was in the army, then burned it down to escape detection. Other whites faced decidedly aberrant—if less violent—behavior, with some slaves coming and going as they pleased, refusing to be disciplined, and even borrowing horses and mules for evening rides.

Freed African Americans had to find new lives in a South that had been devastated by war. (Bettmann-Corbis)

As the war hurtled to a close and slavery became doomed, some slave owners nevertheless clutched at hopes that the institution would survive the war. This was especially true in Texas, the Confederate state farthest from the worst fighting and isolated from breaking news. Hopeful and desperate planters—like the family from an earlier chapter, the Stones of Mississippi—had transported tens of thousands of their best slaves to the Lone Star State to preserve their most valuable property from Union troops invading nearby states like Louisiana and Mississippi, but also came from as far away as Virginia or South Carolina. A Mississippi slave remembered having to walk along the side of the road on the way to Texas, because so many wagons were going the same way; "it look like everybody in the world was going to Texas" (Rawick, vol. 7, 221). The forced emigration often separated families, as children and old people were left behind and only healthy young men taken along. Slaves who became ill, even women about to deliver babies, were literally left at the sides of roads. Elvira Boles came to Texas with her master in 1865, "a dodgin' in and out, runnin' from de Yankees" all the way from Mississippi (ibid., vol. 4, pt. 1, 108).

The movement of slaves to the Confederate frontier continued until war's end, and even then Texans, at least, maintained the illusion that they would somehow retain their human property when the fighting ended. As late as May 1865, weeks after Lee's surrender at Appomattox, owners of runaway slaves still offered rewards of up to $500 in Confederate currency. Even after news of the end of the war reached this far corner of the Confederacy, the *Texas Republican* confidently predicted that the Thirteenth Amendment would not even be ratified. Emancipation would be a social, economic, and moral disaster for both races, and would "naturally" be followed by "vagrancy, filth, disease, and crime" among the freedmen. The *Republican* asserted that Texans, at least, should be allowed to keep their slaves, especially since most owners, "actuated by an attachment for the race," still held them as late as mid-June 1865 (*Marshall (Texas) Republican,* January 15, 1865).

Despite these pie-in-the-sky hopes, slavery had been effectively destroyed in Texas and everywhere by the time Union General Gordon Granger declared Texan slaves free on June 19, 1865—a date still celebrated in many states today as "Juneteenth." Although battlefield victories, federal legislation, and a constitutional amendment were obviously the most powerful frontal attacks on the peculiar institution, the slaves who tested the boundaries of slavery throughout the Confederacy had fought from within slavery to free themselves. The struggle for power and survival between the slave owners and the enslaved not only was a constant tension on the Southern home front but also contributed subtly to undermining the Confederate war effort and provided slaves with a taste of the freedom that would come with the end of the war.

PRIMARY SOURCES:

Botume, Elizabeth Hyde. *First Days amongst the Contrabands.* Boston: Lee and Shepard, 1893.

Houston Tri-Weekly Telegraph, January 24, 1865.

Marshall (Texas) Republican, January 15, 1865, and June 2, 1865.

Rawick, George P., ed. *The American Slave: A Composite Autobiography,* 19 vols. Westport, CT: Greenwood, 1972–1974; supplement, ser. 1, 12 vols., 1978; supplement, ser. 2, 10 vols., 1979.

SECONDARY SOURCES:

Aptheker, Herbert. *American Negro Slave Revolts.* New York: Columbia University Press, 1943.

Brewer, James H. *The Confederate Negro: Virginia's Craftsmen and Military Laborers, 1861–1865.* Durham, NC: Duke University Press, 1969.

Testing the Boundaries: Slave Lives in the Confederacy

Campbell, Randolph B. *An Empire for Slavery: The Peculiar Institution in Texas, 1821–1865.* Baton Rouge: Louisiana State University Press, 1989.

Cimprich, John. *Slavery's End in Tennessee, 1861–1865.* Tuscaloosa: University of Alabama Press, 1985.

Jordan, Winthrop. *Tumult and Silence at Second Creek : An Inquiry into a Civil War Slave Conspiracy.* Baton Rouge: Louisiana State University Press, 1993.

Robbins, Peggy. "Jim Limber and the Davises." *Civil War Times Illustrated* 17 (November 1978): 22–27.

Chapter Twenty

Free to Learn: Educating Freedpeople

The description of an army camp would have caused most Civil War soldiers to laugh out loud: it was "near the pine woods, and the air is full of the sweet fragrance of the pine-trees"; the "tents are placed in straight and even rows . . . like the streets of a city"; the entrance to each tent was "arched with boughs from the trees" and labeled with the letter of the company to which its occupants belonged. The tour continued into one of the tents, although the archetypal soldiers who shared it—John Christian and Tom Black—were away. Their supper dishes were washed and neatly stacked on a table they had built. John's "well rubbed and worn" Testament lay in plain view; the narrator was gratified to find that one of the occupants was a Christian. The absence of a second Testament suggested that Tom could not read, but upon spying the "Picture Lesson Book" the narrator guessed that John was teaching Tom to read—"that is right, Tom; though you are forty years old, it is never too late to learn" (September 1864).

Under the book could just be seen "a little paper" called *The Freedman*, which was one of the many publications created for the Southern market by Northern publishers during the Civil War. This was the lead story in an early issue of *The Freedman*, which represents one of the least-known facets of life on the Confederate home front: the efforts of African Americans to achieve liberation through education with the help of Northern philanthropists. Before the Freedmen's Bureau, before the Reconstruction amendments, and before Southern states controlled by radical Republican politicians established public schools for former slaves, Northern men and women established makeshift schools for African Americans, bringing the gospel and the three R's to the occupied South.

Just after the Civil War ended, a book-length summary of the activities of Northern philanthropies included an entry on the New England Freedmen's Aid Society, which sponsored many of those teachers. "The office of these teachers," stated the brief chapter, "was not altogether to 'teach' in the ordinary sense—that is, to set the pupil a lesson, to see that he learned it, and then to hear him

235

recite it." Their real purpose was to educate the freedmen in a far larger sense, for "the negro had quite as much to unlearn as to learn. All the teachings of slavery were to be wiped away. He needed a knowledge which lay far beyond the alphabet; his poverty in book-learning was not his worst deficiency." The catalog of poor habits and lax morals—which Northerners were very careful to blame largely on the effects of enslavement—led missionaries to believe that slaves "needed lessons of industry, of domestic management, of thrift, of truth, of honesty" (Goodrich, 367–368, 370).

The report proudly stated that in the South, whenever missionaries and teachers met freedmen, "We find him naked, and we clothe him; ignorant, and we instruct him; without employment, and we give him the materials to earn a livelihood." With a metaphorical flourish straight out of the New Testament, the report declared, "We find him wounded and bleeding by the wayside, left half dead by thieves who have robbed him of all he possessed; ours is to bring him to the inn at Jerusalem, and take care of him" (ibid.).

These self-styled good Samaritans were often the first Northerners—except for soldiers—that Southern African Americans ever met. As Northern armies began invading the Confederacy almost from the beginning of the war, a less sanguinary but more revolutionary invasion followed the armies nearly everywhere they went. The tiny corps of teachers and missionaries who journeyed south to educate, reform, and "civilize" the men, women, and children redeemed from slavery turned the Southern home front upside down, challenging most of the South's most basic assumptions about race. The images of black children and adults alike crowding into ramshackle schoolhouses and churches, sharing slates and ragged books, eagerly learning from sometimes hesitant, sometimes imperious, and always curious Northerners were optimistic balance weights to the more familiar scenes of carnage and destruction spawned by the war.

Of course, slaves had long treasured the bits of learning they secretly gleaned; because teaching a slave to read or write was illegal throughout the slave states, many took tremendous risks to memorize a few phrases or words from the Bible. Others went much further. When Frederick Douglass's mistress began teaching him his ABC's, she opened a whole new world to the young slave. Her husband stopped the lessons as soon as he discovered them, but his speech—at least as recalled by Douglass many years later—inspired in the young slave an awareness of the power of education. "Now, if you teach that nigger (speaking of myself) how to read, there would be no keeping him. It would forever unfit him to be a slave. He would at once become unmanageable, and of no value to his master." Of course, that was exactly what Douglass wanted, and although the lessons with his mistress were halted, he continued to teach himself to read, almost daring his master to stop him. Since that point in his life—

he was about twelve—Douglass lived in Baltimore, he had unusual freedom, and he contrived to make friends with "all the little white boys whom I met in the street," converting them into teachers. He carried his dog-eared books with him wherever he went; he also learned to trade bread from his master's kitchen with the boys in return for brief lessons in reading and writing (Blight, 57, 60).

Long after Douglass escaped from his bondage and had become one of the greatest spokespersons against slavery, African Americans fought for public education for themselves and for all Southerners in the years following the Civil War. Indeed, equal access to education was a hallmark of the Civil Rights movement of the 1950s and 1960s. The beginning of the campaign to begin to bring the more than 3

Frederick Douglass (National Archives)

million African American slaves into American culture through formal schooling began less than a year after Confederate batteries fired on Fort Sumter, as ministers, adventurous young women, and other Northerners—including a handful of African Americans—headed south in the wake of advancing Federal armies.

Their novice students invested a great deal of emotion, effort, and pride in their education, expecting it to make a real difference in their lives. A New England Freedmen's Aid Society teacher in North Carolina interrupted a group of black children playing raucously on a church pew. The irritated missionary asked them, "What good does it do you to come to school?" They stopped playing, and "one of the most roguish . . . replied, 'If we are educated, they can't make slaves of us again.'" Reading and writing became both a symbol of their emancipation and a shield against slavery. Some freedpeople attached an almost spiritual significance to education. Once, a group of children attended the funeral of a classmate. Standing in a ring around the grave, they began singing their ABC's over and over. Clutched against their chests were alphabets or other school books, which their teacher took as "proof that they consider their lessons as some sort of religious exercise." In fact, most of the teachers who those freedmen, women, and children encountered in schools and churches also made that connection, and it was through that mixture of piety and book learning that former slaves first came to know how their Northern "saviors" perceived them and what they expected of their black students (*Extracts of Letters,* 13; Preston, 65–67).

For all the good intentions reflected in the campaign to educate the freedpeople, a certain ambiguity underlay the relationship between teachers and pupils. Although committed to a fairly abstract notion of racial equality, Northern philanthropists also tended to treat their students, simply put, as children. The notion that slaves were little more—at least intellectually—than children had been a paternalistic fraud for generations. Teachers often treated even adult freedpeople with the same exasperated patience reserved for naughty, slightly slow children. The cultural gap that separated whites from blacks in mid-nineteenth-century America was not bridged in classrooms throughout the South.

That same chasm of condescension appeared in the educational materials used in those schools. Many black students were taught from traditional Northern textbooks such as the famous *McGuffey's Readers,* but many learned from publications written expressly for freedmen and freedwomen. The American Tract Society brought out a number of instructional materials, ranging from a brief pamphlet called *First Lessons* to "The Ten Commandments Illustrated" and two dozen short "Tracts for Beginners" printed in large type. Spiritual lessons were as important as temporal ones. The *United States Primer* provided "elementary educational" information along with verses from scripture, while several sets of cardboard flash cards featured the alphabet, short lessons in grammar and spelling, and the Ten Commandments. One set of cards, designed so they could be seen by the hundreds of students crowded into the barns and churches that often served as schools, measured three feet by four feet and was imprinted with biblical phrases in huge letters. The Society reported that in 1864, 300 sets of these cards were in use and that 20,000 copies of *First Lessons* and 24,000 copies of the *United States Primer* had been sent to freedmen's schools.

But the American Tract Society, which had been distributing tens of thousands of evangelical tracts in the United States and abroad every year since the early nineteenth century—and claimed to have distributed 800,000 tracts totaling 10 million pages just a few years before the Civil War began—published a number of other instructional aids for teachers of Southern blacks. Among them were *The Freedman's Spelling-Book, The Freedman's Primer,* and *The Freedman's Second* and *Third Reader.* Although the bulk of the content of these books was indistinguishable from most antebellum spellers, primers, and readers, they also contained material directed specifically at former slaves. Abraham Lincoln was the great emancipator, but black heroes and heroines like Toussaint L'Ouverture, leader of the Santo Domingo slave revolt, Frederick Douglass, and

*Phillis Wheatley, the eighteenth-century slave and poet often featured in textbooks
written for former slaves (Library of Congress)*

the poet Phillis Wheatley were presented as examples of humility and hard
work. Poems and stories about African American soldiers highlighted their
bravery and patriotism. Like other publications for the former slaves, spelling
and grammar lessons drew heavily on scripture and on the moral platitudes common to prewar Northern textbooks: work hard, mind your manners, know your

place. The Tract Society, while applauding emancipation, avoided any overt political statements regarding voting or civil rights.

Less gingerly in her approach to the status of freedpeople was Lydia Maria Child, whose *Freedman's Book* included biographical sketches but also the writings of African Americans like Wheatley, slaves named "Mingo" and George Horton, and the former slave Harriet Jacobs. Her book offered examples of African Americans seeking and achieving intellectual and spiritual equality with whites. Child certainly encouraged freedpeople to become thrifty, moral, and hardworking, yet the role models she held up before them included the astronomer Benjamin Banneker, Wheatley, L'Ouverture, and Douglass. These men and women frequently appeared in other freedmen's publications as notable African Americans, but Child emphasized their independence and achievements rather than their acceptance of white middle-class values. In addition to abolitionist speeches and essays on the Emancipation Proclamation, Child also offered a polite yet defiant letter from a former slave to his former master. Child clearly meant her selections to show African American readers that freedom meant more than the opportunity to become servants and laborers for white folks. Child's approach though was rare in the world of educational materials for the freedmen.

At once typical but also unique, one of the more remarkable publications for African American men, women, and children was the American Tract Society's *The Freedman*, which appeared in January 1864 and ran until early 1869. It was widely distributed, with 600,000 copies produced during 1865–1866 alone. Despite its tone, which very much resembled that of mid-nineteenth-century schoolbooks, the four-page monthly targetted an adult audience. One story featured black soldiers eagerly studying their copies of the little paper. Grown-up readers were also advised, when they were finished with their copies, to give *The Freedman* "to the children as a reward for diligence and good conduct." Indeed, missionaries in the South reported that their adult students did share their papers with the children.

The format of the paper resembled that of a juvenile periodical or Sabbath school paper: brief vignettes, writing drills, simple reading and arithmetic lessons, poems, prayers, and general information about geography, nature, and history. The Ten Commandments appeared in every issue, and articles, stories, and exercises highlighted traditional values, including thrift, hard work, forethought, temperance, honesty, and perseverance. The freedmen had to learn that, along with their freedom, came certain responsibilities. As one writing example intoned, "But what is it to be free? . . . I am free to be a good and noble man, and not an idle, bad, worthless fellow" (April 1865). No antebellum schoolbook could have stated more clearly the aims of American education or reflected the concerns of whites about the place that former slaves would fill in American society.

Many of these stories contained no reference to race. In fact, the first illustration featuring black characters other than the terrorized Africans from an article on the slave trade or as young students in the masthead did not appear for nearly a year and a half. Most of the articles could have run in any one of the two dozen or so wartime magazines published for children in the North. Not only did most of the pictures in the magazine feature white adults and children, the clothes and toys and other signs of Northern affluence must have seemed fantastic to African Americans accustomed to living in one-room cabins with dirt floors, to eating out of rough-hewn bowls with crude implements, and to playing with toys made of corncobs and walnuts. The January 1866 issue featured a front-page illustration with a family of five boys and girls, happily observed by their loving parents, playing with a top, a doll, a rocking horse, a toy house, tiny wooden animals, a book, and a puppet, among other toys.

Yet several characteristics differentiated *The Freedman* from publications designed for white audiences. Although books and magazines for white children rarely mentioned race, *The Freedman* was filled with information about Africa and about African Americans. These articles sought to educate the freedmen about their common heritage and to create a community of black men and women in America. "A Scene in Africa" painted a rosy picture of the freedmen's homeland, "a beautiful land, where the sun shines very brightly, and many fine trees and fruits grow which we do not have." Yet white invaders had long threatened this verdant place. In the picture that accompanied the story, white slave traders chase down African toddlers, who are "carried off, and stowed away in the dark hold of the vessel, to be . . . sold into wearisome bondage." Yet that bondage, the article promised later, would soon end. "Through all these years, God has had his eye of mercy upon the African race, and in his own time and way has designed to bring them up out of their deep sorrow." The war is his instrument to "deliver the people from their cruel wrongs" (June 1864).

But Africans were more than victims. An early story featured "Faithful Yanko," a slave who saved the lives of the family to whom he belonged. During a "fearful storm upon the ocean," the passengers and crew of a badly damaged vessel are forced to abandon ship. When it is discovered that there is not room enough on the lifeboats for everyone, Yanko, "noble, brave man that he was," gladly gave up his seat for his owner's children (April 1864).

More common were articles providing upbeat accounts of modern-day African Americans. A brief sketch described "a striking scene" in the U.S. Supreme Court: the appearance of an (unnamed) black lawyer, the first to be allowed to argue before the Court (June 1865). The "Intelligence" section

"THE FREEDMAN'S BUREAU".

Wartime work of African Americans grew into the postwar Freedmen's Bureau;
this Currier & Ives print presents a positive image of that impulse.
(Library of Congress)

*The Freedmen's Bureau is savagely attacked in this campaign poster for the
1866 Pennsylvania gubernatorial election, in which John White Geary,
the Republican candidate, defeated the Democratic nominee Hiester Clymer.
(Library of Congress)*

boasted of the large number of black men joining the Union army and of their
soldierly behavior and battlefield exploits. The men of the 1st Alabama, for
instance, refused to drink, refrained from profanity, maintained clean and
healthy encampments, and eagerly attended the schools established in every
company in the regiment. During the Overland Campaign in 1864, declared *The
Freedman,* virtually no black soldiers had fallen out of the line of march, in contrast to white soldiers, nearly half of whom had failed to keep up. A front-page
article featured a short history of black heroes of the American Revolution and
assured readers that the typical black soldier was still "proving himself a
patriot" while at the same time "preparing by education to be a true man, and a
worthy citizen" (August 1864). The 54th Massachusetts, declared an article in
April 1864, had won the day at the Battle of Olustee, Florida. As the Union
attack faltered, it advanced at the "double-quick . . . and saved the left from
being turned, in which case the whole force would have been annihilated." In
commemoration of exactly that kind of heroism, and in a sly twist on the kind of

story problem that frequently appeared in Confederate arithmetic texts (such as, if one Confederate can kill seven Yankees, how many Yankees can seven Confederates kill?), *The Freedman* asked, "if the freedmen should kill, or take prisoners, 394 of the rebels who numbered 462, how many would be left to run away after the battle?" (March 1865).

Accounts of African Americans' accomplishments, patriotism, and good habits no doubt bolstered the confidence of black students. Missionaries were quite aware that the former slaves had a long way to go before they would fit completely into American society, and a number of articles tried to help them understand their place in the free world. With virtually no exceptions, they were advised to work hard, remain humble, and seek the grace of God. One article began with the children's rhyme, "All work and no play makes Jack a dull boy," but actually illustrated the value of the second line: "But all play and no work makes Jack a mere toy." The author went on to recall seeing five boys playing in a yard one morning; when he passed later in the day, they were still there, panting and tired from a day of nothing but play. They next day he gave them some work to do, and they learned that a day of work was just as pleasurable as a day of play. "God made us to work," he declares to them at the end of the story, "and no one feels pleased in his own heart, who does not live for some use. It will make you feel like men to work" (April 1864).

Some of this advice simply provided basic facts of life, and some of it assumed an extraordinary amount of ignorance on the part of freedpeople. An extended paragraph published in June 1865, for example, explained to its readers that the earth was round. A few months later, another article carefully explained that the year was "di-vi-ded in-to four sea-sons: Win-ter, Spring, Summer, and Aut-umn," while yet another described snow for readers who had never lived in the North (April 1864). Another explained the lengths of months, days, hours, and minutes. "People who have never read or studied books," began yet another, "know very little about this world and its inhabitants." The article went on to describe Chinese, but the opening sentence no doubt represented the attitude of most Northerners toward the freedpeople (June 1865).

A number of stories and articles stressed the importance of good hygiene and good habits, both in terms of building character and in terms of preventing disease. In this sense, the editors of *The Freedman* were simply encouraging their readers to conduct themselves in the same ways that editors of myriad religious and educational books urged their readers to behave. An article on African American soldiers in military hospitals stressed that soldiers who practiced temperance became well much more quickly.

But a number of these tidbits of advice seemed to be directed toward countering the kind of behavior that slave owners—that whites in general—tended to associate with slaves. Slave owners frequently complained that their slaves abused livestock; "Theodore and the Rabbits" featured a little boy who learns his lesson after torturing a litter of bunnies (June 1865). Addressing the poor state of cleanliness among the freedmen—not surprising, considering their poverty and the habits ingrained after lifetimes living in one-room shacks— "Keep Clean" used the example of a cat to urge black men and women to take regular baths. "Nice people . . . will not like to come near you, if you are not tidy" (July 1865). The article about China described briefly a few religious practices among the Chinese, then stated, "Does it not seem strange and silly to us, that they should do such things?" Of course, whites had long mistrusted the emotional Christianity of slaves and believed that their piety was undermined by ridiculous superstitions about "haunts" and healers. "But we must not laugh at them, but pity and pray for them." The missionaries going to Asia "shall tell them of a better way" (June 1865).

Some missionaries, worried that slaves would actually live down to the vicious stereotype that once freed slaves would no longer work, frequently hammered at the idea that freedom from slavery did not mean freedom from responsibility or from the necessity of doing an honest day's work. "What is it to be free?" a narrator asked a group of boys. "We are free to work for whom we will, and get our pay for it," says one, while another adds, "we will save up all we can get to buy a farm." "Good," the narrator exclaims, "look out that you do not lose all you earn in some bad way. . . . Do not buy rum with it, or that vile weed to chew that can but make you sick. If you give up your pay, let it be for something that will do you good" (May 1864). Simply having money was not enough; it was better to earn it. "Work for your money, boys; and it will prove a blessing" (January 1865).

Thrift was a major component of a well-educated person—white or black— at least according to mid-nineteenth-century texts. It was also one of those characteristics that slaves had supposedly lacked. "Let Nothing Be Lost" was the title of one article: "These are the very words of the Lord Jesus" after he fed the multitude with loaves and fishes. Readers were urged to care for their clothes so they lasted longer than they might otherwise; Christians should tell themselves, "Now I am going to see how long I can make this coat last, for I want some Sunday clothes for my little Rachel." It went on to remind freedmen that bread crumbs could feed chickens, spoiled milk was good for pigs, scraps of cloth could make quilts, bits of wood and paper could be used for kindling—the list of items that could be reused ranged from old nails to twine. "So gather up the fragments," the article concluded, "that nothing be lost, and teach your children to do so too" (September 1864). As part of its insistence that virtue and piety depended on thrift, *The Freedman* waged a campaign against the use of tobacco—partly because of its effects on the health of men and boys who

A representation of a noble Freedmen's Bureau agent protecting freedmen
from a mob of white Southerners
(Library of Congress)

smoked or chewed it, but primarily because of its effect on their pocketbooks. "A boy fills his pipe and he sees only the tobacco," began one vignette, 'but *I* see going into that pipe *brains, books, time, health, money, prospects* . . . things which are priceless are carelessly puffed away in smoke" (December 1864).

Females were taught to be good wives; one writing exercise packed a lifetime of domesticity into a brief paragraph when it asked a fictional "Jane," "Do you know how to make a nice cake?" and then declared baldly, "If you do not, you are not fit to be Sam's wife." Moreover, "if you do not know how to work—to wash and scrub and cook and sew—you will not make a good wife." Indeed, "a good wife is one of the best gifts that God can give to a poor man" (August 1864).

The author of "Two Thoughts" recounted a story he had read in a newspaper of a little slave boy who greeted the Yankee troops liberating him and his family with the words, "I'se free! I'se free! I an't gwine to rock de cradle no more, ca[u]se I'se free!" The editor was disturbed for two reasons: at the boy's notion that the freed slaves no longer had to work, and at the language he used to express his joy. "You are no longer bought and sold and owned, like cattle," he wrote sternly. "But this boy is just as much bound to" work "as he was before, is he not?" The author was glad that the boy was free, for now he could go to school and learn how to speak correctly. Rather than shouting "I'se free," he will say "I am free." He will say "the" for "de" and "Because" for "case" (August 1865).

Part of knowing their place in the world also meant appreciating just how much Northern whites had sacrificed for the sake of the slaves. *The Freedman* often invoked a sense of obligation toward Northern whites, who had contributed money, established schools, and supported the effort to emancipate the slaves with their lives. Kind Northern teachers appeared frequently in stories and articles. In one, a white woman searches "through the unnumbered and dirty tenements" of a contraband village "for a poor colored woman who needed help" and ends up encouraging one little black girl to help teach another one how to read (July 1864). The caption for an engraving of a white soldier hugging a little girl explained "How glad he is to see his little Mary!" Although "it was sad to see men die in battle . . . it was to make us free." A picture of a young white boy accompanied a patriotic poem that began "I am a soldier's little boy, My father's gone to fight" and went on to explain the cause for which the father was fighting and the sacrifices he was willingly making (April 1864).

No schoolbook or Sunday school tract of the period would be complete without at least one poignant story of a child who displayed the pious philanthropy to which most adults could only aspire. Little Meta, a four-year-old white girl living in the North, had "loved to hear about the freed children," and enthusiastically sent clothes to contraband camps. Sadly, she died, but the money she left behind was sent to a freedmen's school, where it was used to purchase classroom maps (February 1865).

Even more direct was an article illustrated by a white woman rocking her baby to sleep, which reminded readers of the sacrifices made by the wives and children of the soldiers fighting to save the Union and to free the slaves. "The love and sympathy of your friends at the North, and the prayers and blood given so freely in your behalf by your white comrades," *The Freedman* pointedly remarked, "should be a strong motive for you to exert yourselves to the utmost that you may prove worthy of it all." At one point the author stated "Every Union soldier is fighting for liberty. He is fighting for *your* liberty, colored man and woman, and for the liberty of your children and your children's children. He fights that your race may be forever delivered from the shackles of slavery." The best way to repay those soldiers who had sacrificed so much—who had died to make them free—was to become the best people they could possibly be. "The love and sympathy of your friends at the North, and the prayers and blood given so freely in your behalf by your white comrades, should be a strong motive for you to exert yourselves to the utmost, that you may prove worthy of it all." And "the surest way to elevation is *by goodness.* Be honest, sober, diligent and patriotic" (November 1864).

Institutions were also applauded for their the devotion and contributions to the well-being of the freedmen and women. The United States Christian Commission, the American Tract Society, the American Missionary Association, and Northern abolitionists and Freedmen's Aid Societies all received frequent mention for their efforts on behalf of the former slaves. One article featured a picture of a top-hatted man with a basket of books handing them out to well-scrubbed white soldiers. He was, according to the article, the "secretary" of the American Tract Society sent to the South to distribute inspirational reading material and textbooks to soldiers and freedmen and women—including *The Freedman* (May 1865).

Even a superficial reading of *The Freedman* and other American Tract Society publications reveals that, despite their good intentions, they often relegated the former slaves to a status inferior to Northern whites. Many of the most prominent characters—real and fictional—are slaves, servants, or underlings of one kind or another. Yanko, who saved his master's children, was a slave. By ignoring politics and emphasizing obedience and piety, *The Freedman* and the schoolbooks produced specifically for freed blacks undercut their hard-won freedom. By assuming the worst about the morals and intelligence of their readers, they projected a condescension and ignorance that would contribute to the sorry state of race relations in the United States for many generations. Indeed, at times the rhetoric of the liberators resembled the rhetoric of the enslavers. In a June 1864 article on the evils of the slave trade and the war's ending of slavery, *The Freedman* declared that the freedom spawned by the war would give African Americans "the opportunities of education which they could never perhaps have enjoyed in their own land; for there the light of the gospel has scarcely yet dawned."

Yet the efforts of the American Tract Society and of the missionaries and teachers who used its publications had other, more positive results. In their emphasis—however condescending—on the basic humanity of African Americans, in their attempts—however stilted—to show freedpeople of all ages their common history and contributions to the Union war effort, and in their urging—however biased by middle-class assumptions—of the freedmen to meet high standards of behavior, these books and papers provided a counterpoint to the racial ideas of Southern whites.

PRIMARY SOURCES:

Blight, David W., ed. *Narrative of the Life of Frederick Douglass, an American Slave: Written by Himself.* Boston: Bedford/St. Martin's, 1993.

Free to Learn: Educating Freedpeople

Extracts of Letters of Teachers and Superintendents of the New-England Freedmen's Aid Society, 5th Ser. Boston: John Wilson & Son, 1864.

The Freedman. New York: American Tract Society, 1864–1869. Unless otherwise noted, all date-only citations refer to issues of *The Freedman.*

Goodrich, Frank B. *The Tribute Book: A Record of the Munificence, Self-Sacrifice and Patriotism of the American People during the War for the Union.* New York: Derby & Miller, 1865.

Preston, Elizabeth Ware, ed. *Letters from Port Royal, 1862–1868.* Boston: W. B. Clarke, 1906. Reprint, New York: Arno Press, 1969.

SECONDARY SOURCES:

Morris, Robert C. *Reading, 'Riting, and Reconstruction: The Education of Freedmen in the South, 1861–1870.* Chicago: University of Chicago Press, 1981.

Richardson, Joe M. *Christian Reconstruction: The American Missionary Association and Southern Blacks, 1861–1890.* Athens: University of Georgia Press, 1986.

PART V

Aftermaths

Chapter Twenty-One

"That Such a Thing Could Ever Happen": The Death of a President

November, 1963: the unthinkable happens and the entire nation spirals into grief and confusion and anger. The news arrives in many different ways: some hear it from Walter Cronkite, others from radio announcers interrupting the latest pop hit. Some learn the terrible truth from neighbors over picket fences, from teachers, from coworkers coming late to staff meetings, from stricken voices on the telephone. "The President is dead." The memories of that day and of the following several days would remain with Americans for the rest of their lives. The assassination of John F. Kennedy is one of the first great national catastrophes illustrated by television images: shaken newscasters, somber processions, and little John John bravely saluting his dead father. Many saw the equally troubling on-air murder of Lee Harvey Oswald.

Presidents had been assassinated before. William McKinley was mortally wounded in Buffalo in the summer of 1901; James Garfield died at the hands of an assassin in 1881. Civil War–era Americans witnessed a course of events eerily similar to those of 1963, even including the hunt for and killing of the assassin. Although they lacked the immediacy of television, of course, the memories of the men, women, and children who were alive in April 1865—drawn from real life or from fanciful engravings in illustrated weeklies—seem, in a sense, to have been even more vivid than those of their great-grandchildren, unbound by the limitations of black-and-white picture tubes. Harvard professor Bliss Perry wrote long after the event that, "I have never met a man old enough to recall Lincoln's death who did not remember precisely where he was and what he was doing." Bliss was four, playing with an eight-year-old girl outside her father's saddle shop. For him, the most striking part of that long-ago moment was her understated, childlike, but entirely appropriate words: "I think it's just as mean as it can be" (Perry, 60).

253

THE MARTYR OF LIBERTY

*One of hundreds of paintings, engravings, and
sketches of Lincoln's assassination
(Library of Congress)*

Although measuring the precise effects on Americans of Lincoln's death is, of course, not an easy task, it goes without saying that the assassination of Abraham Lincoln had far-reaching ramifications for the United States. It certainly thrust Andrew Johnson, the wrong man, into office at exactly the wrong time. It left lingering feelings of mistrust toward the South among many Northerners. It most likely extended the time it took to remold the nation into a single entity. It may have contributed to the sad course race relations would take over the next century.

Even before all of those issues would be resolved—or even raised—Americans had to confront the fact that the man who had led them through fire to glory, that the man they had just recently rewarded with a new term in office, would neither join them in the celebrations marking the end of the bloodshed nor lead them through the difficult days of Reconstruction. As a kind of punctuation to the war itself, the assassination was one last trial for the residents of the Civil War home front to endure. Their wide variety of reactions ranged from the typical and expected to the unique and surprising, reflecting shock and grief, anger and politics, piety and profanity, generosity and gentleness.

They would always remember where they were when they heard the news and how those around them responded to it. "They said in the family that it was absurd—that I was too young—that I could not possibly remember the night Lincoln was shot," wrote Mary Adams French sixty years after the war. "But I could, and I did." She was sleeping in her parents' room and with them was awakened by a policeman tapping on the bedroom window. Her father clambered out of bed and threw open the blinds. Mary heard the policeman cry in the style of a newsboy, "President Lincoln assassinated! Dead! Seward stabbed!"

(French, 161–164). The images of the next few days blurred over the decades between that morning and Mary's memoir, but she never forgot the striking scene of the policeman at her parents' window.

Many took the assassination personally. A Wisconsin family was in the middle of moving to a new farm, but were so demoralized that they lost the energy to unpack the boxes strewn around the new house! A little to the south, upon hearing the news from a neighbor they happened to meet at a country crossroads, an Iowa farm family was overcome by a "feeling of depression and sorrow," according to one of them. "His death seemed like a personal loss in the family" (Mott, 3–4).

It was unnerving for children to see their parents become so upset, so confused, so paralyzed by events that, after all, although tragic, happened very far away, to a man they had never met. For the first time in their lives, they saw grown men crying in public. Anna Robertson, better known decades later as the painter Grandma Moses, drove with her family into a nearby town on the fateful day. The first indication that something was wrong was the black mourning bunting tacked to shops and houses. Anna heard a storekeeper tell her mother that the president had died, then her mother cried, "Oh, what will become of us now?" (Kallir, 18–19). Similarly, the future journalist Ida Tarbell could never forget her normally calm mother, "burying her face in her apron" and "running into her room sobbing as if her heart would break" (Tarbell, 11).

As is so often the case, small details stood out in children's memories, unrelated to the event itself but reflecting the excitement and sadness that surrounded it. One child recalled being fascinated by the curiously snakelike sound of Booth's purported declaration as he leaped from the president's box in Ford's Theater, "s-s-sic-s-s-s-semper-r tyr-r-r-rannis-s!" (Sessions, 36). Another was captivated by the badges everyone wore that featured the martyred president's picture framed in red, white, and blue, while another recalled newsboys calling out the stunning headlines, bundles of black-bordered papers stacked at their feet. A girl heard a friend say, while viewing one of several funeral processions held for the president, "that's the kind of coffin I'm going to get for my mother" (Neely, 11).

Grown-ups tended to have larger issues to manage. Newspaper editors and preachers used their figurative and real pulpits, respectively, to comment on the sudden change that the nation was going through and to lash out at the supposed perpetrators. The *New York Herald*'s Easter Sunday edition noted that "The sun set last night upon a jubilant and rejoicing people. The whole nation was exhilirated [*sic*] with the success which had attended our armies in the field and the final overthrow of the rebellion. It rose this morning up on a sorrow-stricken people" (*New York Herald,* April 16, 1865).

Lincoln's letzte Stunde. | Lincoln's last hour. | La dernière heure de Lincoln.

A multilingual version of Lincoln's deathbed (Library of Congress)

In addition to sorrow, one of the natural responses to the assassination was anger. One correspondent described the anger that swelled in the street outside the boardinghouse into which Lincoln had been carried to die: "A conflagration of fire is not half so terrible as the conflagration of passion that rolled through the streets and houses of Washington on that awful night" (Turner, *Beware the People Weeping,* 26–27). A man who mindlessly shouted that he was glad that it had happened was assaulted, nearly stripped of his clothes, and had to be saved from lynching by armed policemen; another yelled his support for Jefferson Davis and was nearly lynched. Not surprisingly, other members of the Booth family of thespians, once it became known that the triggerman had been John Wilkes, became targets of public anger. John's brother Junius was in Cincinnati; mobs tore down playbills for his production and besieged his hotel for four days. Later, he was briefly imprisoned by the government.

Although Junius's stay in jail was short, politicians and public figures of all kinds called for harsh retribution against the conspirators and against Confederate leaders, who must have been involved, they believed. Many advocated the razing of Ford's Theater, as though destroying the scene of the assassination would somehow alleviate the pain it symbolized. Members of the acting company and stage crew of *Our American Cousin* came under suspicion as the notion that a far-ranging conspiracy gained currency. Worse were the intemperate, even mad, suggestions that the South be depopulated of whites and repeopled with freed slaves and that copperheads be summarily executed. One Pennsylvanian asked the government if he could please have the pleasure of executing Jefferson Davis when he was captured!

Ministers reflected—and, no doubt, some fanned—a little of this anger when they preached sermons full of Old Testament fire and brimstone, castigating Southerners, slavery, and anyone who had not believed deeply in the holy war that the Civil War became, at least in retrospect. The assassination was, in the words of the Reverend W. H. Benade, the nearly inevitable product of rebellion: "And, thus, did the rebellion prove itself, by its own last act, to have been all a murder, clothed in the dark and filthy rags of a lie, the very child and image of him who was a 'murderer and a liar from the beginning'" (ibid., 78). Only blood would due to soften the blow: "Let the leaders of the rebellion, or a suitable number of them, be tried, sentenced and executed for treason . . . then justice having had its place, and the majesty of the law having been honored, mercy may have its exercise, and the people of the rebellious states be forgiven" (ibid., 88).

But the North's mood calmed surprisingly quickly. Charges against leading Confederates were soon dismissed, and, in fact, there was little violence following the assassination, once the conspirators were rounded up and Booth himself was killed. There would be a quick military trial and a quicker execution of the three men and one woman deemed most responsible for the murder, but for the most part Americans moved beyond the death of their president. Perhaps the prospect of peace did, after all, quiet their sometimes irrational anger; perhaps four years of bloody conflict, and the hundreds of lives lost, put the death of one man—no matter his station in life—into perspective; perhaps, with spring arriving and planting to be done, with fathers and sons and brothers finally returning from the army, with life going on for most Americans, the will to continue to agonize over the assassination waned.

There were, of course, rituals to be completed before the assassination—and the victim—could be laid to rest. Nearly the entire North could say good-bye personally during the grand tour that took the bodies of Lincoln and of his son Willie, who had died three years earlier at the age of eleven, back to Springfield, Illinois, for burial. The "Lincoln Special" included a locomotive boasting a large picture of Lincoln, wreathed in garlands, on its cowcatcher. Thousands of people gathered on the streets to watch the coffin carried to and from government buildings, where it lay in state in a number of cities. Ten thousand people viewed the body in Baltimore, 300,000 in Philadelphia, and perhaps half a million in city hall in

Reward poster circulated by the U.S. War Department for Lincoln's assassin and two of the coconspirators (Library of Congress)

"That Such a Thing Could Ever Happen": The Death of a President

New York City. The train crept halfway across the continent on the route traveled by Lincoln on his way to Washington from Springfield to take office in early 1861. Moving at no more than twenty-five miles per hour—and sometimes as slowly as five—the train was viewed by huge crowds wherever it went. Even the smallest towns turned out in force to catch a glimpse of the car carrying their deceased leader. Frequently ribbons of black material arched over the tracks, placed there by mourners from nearby towns.

By the time Lincoln's body reached Chicago on May 2, nearly two weeks after leaving Washington, his skin had become discolored, upsetting some observers. A local undertaker applied rouge, chalk, and amber to restore the president's face to its natural hue. The deterioration in the cadaver's condition did not, however, stop Chicago from pulling out all the stops when it staged one of the biggest of the many funerals and memorial services held to honor Lincoln. Thirty-seven thousand people joined the funeral procession down Michigan Avenue, 10,000 schoolchildren wore black mourning sashes, and even Lincoln's horse, "Old Bob," sported a black mourning blanket. Lincoln's coffin rested on a three-tiered, arched platform that cost $15,000 and was carried on a funeral carriage that featured a stuffed eagle on the roof and a team of ten horses—wearing mourning dress, of course. The next day, the "Lincoln Special" completed the last leg of the journey to Springfield, where the body was transported to the tomb in a gold, silver, and crystal hearse lent to Lincoln's hometown by the city of St. Louis.

Although children made up a large percentage of the crowds lining streets and waiting in lines—one teenager spent an entire day, evening, and early morning making three trips past the casket in the U.S. Capitol—they also found their own ways of processing their grief. On Nantucket Island, the mother of nine-year-old Mary Starbuck returned from the local memorial service to find the first floor of their big old house decorated for the occasion. Mary and a friend had rummaged through Mrs. Starbuck's sewing bag and had hung black and white ribbons, garlands, ties, sashes, half-finished clothes, and rags from all the windows and doors that they could reach in an old-fashioned mourning custom. A group of teenaged boys belonging to Unionist families in Covington, Kentucky, donned their Sunday suits, pinned tintypes of the dead president edged with black cloth onto their lapels, and went around town ordering neighbors to close their blinds and attach to them black ribbons designating their grief. The news reached St. Johnsbury East, Vermont, on Anson Hopkins's fourteenth birthday, but the ruined day was salvaged when he and a friend were given the important job of tolling the bell in the steeple of the Methodist church all day long. "We were really quite heroes that day," he recalled, "in our imaginations at least!" (Hopkins, 1–2).

259

One family of children sought to exorcise their grief by falling back on one of their favorite pastimes. Children often "play" through their fears and hopes by acting out the terrors and nightmares that haunt them, and when Henry Wadsworth Longfellow's children and their neighbor and playmate, Henrietta Dana, learned of the murder, they naturally "were stunned with amazement and vague terror . . . that such a thing could ever happen in our civilized age, in our own free country, to our own good and dear President." Even news as terrible as this could not keep the boys and girls down for long. "Our love of the dramatic came to our rescue," wrote Henrietta, "and as descriptions of the scene of the assassination began to appear in the daily papers and illustrated weeklies, with one heart and mind we rushed to stage the scene in our outdoor theater." The theater to which she referred was the east veranda of Craigie House, Longfellow's residence in Cambridge, Massachusetts.

Henrietta Dana—who would later leave a charming account of her childhood and her intimate knowledge of Longfellow and other prominent Bostonians—was the daughter of Richard Henry Dana, a lawyer and author of *Two Years before the Mast*. Henrietta's childhood was characterized by a close acquaintance with many of the leading lights of Boston society and of Republican and antislavery politics. The abolitionist firebrand Wendell Phillips and the radical Republican, Senator Charles Sumner, were frequent visitors to the Dana household; Harriet Beecher Stowe was one of her mother's dearest girlhood friends. Henrietta's father was one of the lawyers deeply involved in defending fugitive slaves in the 1850s and had been injured in the celebrated attempt to rescue the fugitive slave Anthony Burns. As an adult, she wrote "how thrilling it was for an eight-year-old child . . . to find out that right in her own State and city the very things she had read about had been going on . . . Succoring fugitives, underground-railroading, rescues, escapes, trackings, kidnapings and renditions into slavery" had all occurred in her hometown—and her father had been in the thick of them (Skinner, 169).

She had been a Republican long before she could vote, which was hardly surprising, since her father had helped organize the Massachusetts branch of the party. During the 1864 campaign, "we were all agog over the re-election of Lincoln," and the family attended at least one Republican torchlight procession. From the window of an upstairs hotel room, she could look down "upon the moving masses of men and boys . . . with the flaring torches, the gay colored lanterns, floats, and illuminated transparencies with their mottoes and slogans, the blare of brass bands, the crowds cheering and whistling, or shouting the choruses of popular war-songs" (ibid., 173–174).

But the excitement and drama of politics and history were merely distractions. Most of Henrietta's time was spent at Craigie House, where she shared the

A mourning card memorializing the martyred sixteenth president
(Library of Congress)

Longfellow children's tutor. Although the elderly poet was a committed Republican and a friend of the same movers and shakers who frequented the Dana household, he nevertheless "shrank from the details of a fraternal war and wished to keep its shadows from darkening his children's minds." Miss Davie, their teacher, was English, and she had no problem keeping the war at arm's length, at least in the classroom. She did, however, show the children pictures of Lincoln's second inauguration in March 1865 and discussed the end of the war with them in early April. "Then, in the midst of this relief and rejoicing came . . . the sudden black tidings of the assassination of Lincoln! The country was engulfed in a whirlpool of horror, of lamentation for a wise and good man and of anxious forebodings for a future for which there seemed no settled policy, no guiding light" (ibid., 23–42).

Like it did for so many Northerners, the assassination focused the entire war—including the dramatic political and legal wrangling of which she knew her father had been a part—for Henrietta. Lincoln had helped to give meaning to the war, through his actions, through his ability to articulate the causes for which Federal troops fought, and in his intensity and commitment. His death "seemed, like an earthquake, to knock away from under us all sense of stability and direction, leaving us dizzy and terrified." She and her friends, like much older Americans, had to respond somehow, to make their own sense out of the assassination (ibid.).

So, faced with unthinkable news, the children made a play of it. The veranda became the presidential box in Ford's Theater and the croquet lawn became the stage on which scenes from *Our American Cousin* were enacted. The older girls, who had followed events more closely and had more knowledge of the events leading up to and from the murder, directed and took the best roles, while Henrietta, the youngest, got only "the dummy roles which no one else wanted." The tallest girl played Lincoln as he entered the presidential box waving to the applauding audience, although Henrietta had to play Lincoln in the passive role of target and victim. The children played out the whole drama: the shooting, the stabbing of Major Rathbone, the leap onto the croquet lawn (stage)—paper cutter in hand, shouting "*Sic semper tyrannis*"—the escape and chase, and the trapping and shooting of Booth. The eight-year-old Henrietta had to act out the last moments of the "lonely, crippled, hunted fugitive" taking refuge in the stable at the rear of the house. The rest of the cast, playing the posse in hot pursuit, soon surrounded the hideaway; even Longfellow's "small fat Skye terrier" represented "a brace of manhunting bloodhounds." The posse shouted and jumped about, the dog barked, and Henrietta, overwhelmed with the scene and with her surprising empathy for the trapped criminal—"rather a lonely and even terrifying role for" an eight-year-old—was on the verge of tears. They played out the scene, however, and Henrietta's memoir went on to other topics, just as Americans had to move on to new phases in their lives (ibid.).

Even as the nation mourned, there were those who took a longer, more commercial view of the tragedy. Within a few days, souvenirs and even toys appeared to commemorate the life and death of the sixteenth president. Predictably, the firm of Currier & Ives, which had spent the war producing wildly popular prints of military and other scenes of the war, published its own colored versions of the assassination, the death, and the funeral of President Lincoln. A number of pieces of sheet music were issued in the weeks after the assassination, ranging from William Willing's "The Flag Is at Halfmast: A Quartet," to a funeral march played at various stops along the route of the train returning the slain president's body to Springfield, to "The Death Knell Is Tolling: A Requiem to the Memory of Our Late Beloved President Abraham Lincoln." One ballad that stood out in the crowded flurry of Lincoln songs and dirges was "The Assassin's Vision," which described the crime from the diabolical and doomed point of view of the assassin. "As he hurried away from the scene of death, On his brow were looks of despair; Before him! Around him! The evening's breath, Told him God's vengeance was there!" Indeed, the song ends oddly triumphantly: "'Vengeance is mine!' saith God in his might" (Turner, "The Assassin's Vision").

An unusually effusive and rather unique item was a children's puzzle made of twenty-four rectangular wooden blocks. Each featured four different images, which could be constructed into five different designs: a "Children's Monument," a "Freedman's Monument," and a "National Monument," all to the slain president, a "National Monument" to George Washington, and a "Presidential Monument." The "Children's Monument" included several illustrations: Lincoln's portrait, Lincoln reclining (apparently lying in state), and members of his family. Most of the blocks were filled with text, which began "Great and immortal chieftain! Though cold and silent, thou art not dead"; went on to promise, "We are but children, yet thou hast a warm place in all our hearts. When our parents speak of the great and noble, they whisper thy name with reverence, and tell us to emulate thy virtues"; declared that "By patient, persevering toil, thou didst crush the viper treason, subdue the great rebellion, and give liberty to four millions of people"; and concluded "Thine shall be a fame sublime; And the virtues of thy soul; Shall, in triumph, onward roll, Until men and nations, free, Blend they name with LIBERTY." Interestingly, cheap photographic prints of the conspirators, including photographs of their hooded bodies hanging from the gallows, were also popular in the weeks following the assassination (Schwartz, 262).

The nature of the American system of government, the quick swearing in of the dead president's successor, the necessity of dealing with myriad problems posed by peace, and the excitement of the return of relieved veterans all contributed to a surprisingly rapid return to normality. Yet memories and questions lingered. At least one child was haunted by nightmares inspired by those popular posters featuring pictures of the hanged conspirators, especially Mrs. Surratt's "long billowing skirts gruesomely fluttering about her dangling legs" (Reese, 76).

Ida Tarbell responded more deeply. She had watched her parents decorate their house with black crepe and had shared their grief over the death of the president. "From that time," she wrote much later, "the name spelt tragedy and mystery." She wondered "Why all this sorrow over a man we had never seen, who did not belong to our world—my world? Was there something beyond the circle of hills within which I lived that concerned me? Why, and in what way, did this mysterious outsider concern me?" (Tarbell, 12).

In some ways, Tarbell's question—felt as a child, articulated as an adult—was a hard one to answer. When Walt Whitman memorialized Lincoln's death with a poem late in 1865, he no doubt helped at least some Northerners to explain that meaning to themselves. Although he later commented that he was almost sorry to have written it because he grew tired of audiences always requesting him to read it, "O Captain, My Captain" is an emotional and memorable evocation of the grief and sense of loss with which Americans responded to Lincoln's death.

Lincoln's funeral procession in New York City (Library of Congress)

O Captain! my Captain! our fearful trip is done,
The ship has weather'd every rack, the prize we sought is won,
The port is near, the bells I hear, the people all exulting,
While follow eyes the steady keel, the vessel grim and daring;
But O heart! heart! heart!
O the bleeding drops of red,
Where on the deck my Captain lies,
Fallen cold and dead.
(Whitman, 262–263)

The poem's popularity stemmed in large part from the fact that it recalled the sudden sadness of the days immediately following the assassination, the intermingling of grief and pomp in the ceremonies and funerals and other occasions surrounding the death, and especially from the sense that the man who had led the country through perilous times would never reach that peaceful shore. Americans would feel the same way in 1945, when Franklin D. Roosevelt would die just before the United States reached the promised land of peace. A closer parallel, no doubt, was 1963, when, after the death of John F. Kennedy, Americans shared a sense of innocence lost and looked toward a decade filled with promise but also with difficulty. For the Civil War generation, when they thought about it years later, Lincoln's death marked an end of one era and the beginning of another—a period of ragged political reconstruction, phenomenal industrial growth and pressing economic problems, and of growing international power and gnawing global responsibilities. The Civil War home front would become the front lines in this uneasy transition.

PRIMARY SOURCES:

French, Daniel Chester. "A Child's Memory of Lincoln." In *When I Was a Child,* edited by Edward Wagenknecht. New York: Dutton, 1946.

Hopkins, Anson Smith. *Reminiscences of an Octogenarian.* New Haven: Morehouse and Tyler, 1937.

Kallir, Otto, ed. *Grandma Moses: My Life's History.* New York: Harper & Bros., 1946.

Mott, D. C. *Fifty Years in Iowa.* Marengo, IA: Marengo Republican, n.d.

Neely, Anne E. Sterling. *Just Me: An Autobiography.* New York: Macmillan, 1939.

New York Herald, April 16, 1865.

Perry, Bliss. "The Butterfly Boy." In *When I Was a Child,* edited by Edward Wagenknecht. New York: Dutton, 1946.

Reese, Lizette Woodworth. *A Victorian Village: Reminiscences of Other Days.* New York: Farrar and Rinehart, 1929.

Sessions, Ruth Huntington. *Sixty-Odd: A Personal History.* Brattleboro, VT: Stephen Daye, 1936.

Skinner, Henrietta Dana. *An Echo from Parnassus: Being Childhood Memories of Longfellow and His Friends.* New York: Macmillan, 1929.

Tarbell, Ida M. *All in the Day's Work: An Autobiography.* New York: Macmillan, 1939.

Turner, J. W. "The Assassin's Vision." Cleveland: S. Brainard's Sons, 1865.

Whitman, Walt. *Leaves of Grass.* Philadelphia: David McKay, 1891–1892.

SECONDARY SOURCES:

Chesebrough, David B. *"No Sorrow Like Our Sorrow": Northern Protestant Ministers and the Assassination of Lincoln.* Kent, OH: Kent State University Press, 1994.

Harrell, Carolyn L. *When the Bells Tolled for Lincoln: Southern Reaction to the Assassination.* Atlanta: Mercer University Press, 1997.

Schwartz, Thomas F. "Grief, Souvenirs, and Enterprise Following Lincoln's Assassination." *Journal of the Illinois State Historical Society* 83 (Winter 1990).

Steers, Edward, Jr. *Blood on the Moon: The Assassination of Abraham Lincoln.* Lexington: University Press of Kentucky, 2001.

Turner, Thomas Reed. *Beware the People Weeping: Public Opinion and the Assassination of Abraham Lincoln.* Baton Rouge: Louisiana State University Press, 1982.

Chapter Twenty-Two

Out at the Soldiers' Home: Union Veterans

"It was a very sightly world," wrote Elizabeth Corbett of the place she called home: the National Home for Disabled Volunteer Soldiers (NHDVS), Northwestern Branch—which everyone in nearby Milwaukee, Wisconsin, called "the Soldiers' Home." Corbett cataloged the oaks, maples, chokecherry, elm, and pine trees crowding the hills and valleys of the Home grounds. Apple trees burst into color and exuded delightful aromas. Roads wound over knolls and through glades. "Lawns green and smooth as a golf course" sprouted gorgeous foliage sometimes arranged to spell "GRANT" or "SHERIDAN" (Corbett, *Out at the Soldiers' Home*, 4). Willow trees lined four small ponds, with rowboats—also named for Union generals—available for hire. Gravel walks encircled formal flower beds and a cast metal statue of the goddess Flora. Completing the scene of Corbett's 1890s childhood were the three swans living on the largest of the four little lakes, a tame black crow, friendly squirrels who would eat nuts from the hands of the residents, and, in cages, two large eagles and a badger.

Long before the post–World War II practice of institutionalizing the less fortunate members of society in colorless glass and concrete boxes, the U.S. government chose to house its disabled, elderly, and otherwise needy veterans of the Civil War in grand buildings placed in beautiful settings. Although retired members of the regular army and navy had for many years been supported at the Soldiers' Home near Washington—where a frame house provided temporary lodging for Abraham Lincoln from time to time during the war—the NHDVS was the first large-scale government program dedicated to caring for a specific segment of the population. Even before the war was over, the government acknowledged that something would have to be done about the soldiers so maimed and weakened by wounds or disease that they would not be able to support themselves. The United States Sanitary Commission had established "soldiers' homes" during the war—temporary hospitals and way stations for wounded and weary soldiers—but Congress decided that a more comprehensive effort must be made to care for the battered survivors of the war.

The need was great. As the U.S. Army quickly demobilized following the defeat of the Confederacy, a host of social problems faced returning veterans. Many soldiers, especially those discharged late in 1865, were unable to find work, while homelessness and addiction to pain killers like opium and its derivative, laudanum, plagued others. Many Americans believed that ex-soldiers were disproportionately represented in the growing prison and jail populations; in Lancaster County, Pennsylvania, a postwar increase in crime was fuelled largely by returned veterans who committed nearly half of all offenses, especially "moral" and property crimes. These conditions were exacerbated by well-publicized incidents of rioting, lawlessness, and general misbehavior by mobs of ex-soldiers and a fairly generalized fear among employers that veterans would make poor and untrustworthy workers. Some veterans were actually reduced to begging, while newspapers frequently described their destitution and reported despondent veterans' suicides. Perhaps 200,000 were fully or partially disabled by wounds or disease.

Many soldiers . . . were unable to find work, while homelessness and addiction to pain killers like opium . . . plagued others.

Despite cheerful accounts of plucky veterans overcoming their disabilities—left-handed writing contests were held in the years just after the war to show the adaptability of men who had lost their right arms in the war—it was clear that something had to be done. The federal government responded to the financial and health crises facing the saviors of the Union with a pension system for disabled and, later, aged veterans that, by 1885, comprised 18 percent of the federal budget. In the spring of 1865, Congress had established a system of federal "asylums" for disabled veterans. These homes, along with the billions of dollars in veterans' and widows' pensions, comprised the largest single extension of "welfare" benefits to Americans prior to the mid–twentieth century. Over the next several years, the Board of Managers of the National Asylum—later Home—for Disabled Volunteer Soldiers created branches in Milwaukee, Wisconsin; Dayton, Ohio; Togus, Maine; and Norfolk, Virginia, with five more added in subsequent years. In May 1867, the first company of men moved out to a ramshackle collection of farmhouses on a 400-acre site just west of Milwaukee. Within twenty years, over 1,300 men lived at the Home. A massive building program created a pleasant village a half hour's carriage ride from Milwaukee. By the 1880s, the main building, completed in 1869, towered gothically over a pleasant village that included barracks, houses for staff and their families, a chapel, a post office, a fire station, a library, a grand house for the "governor" of the institution, a recreation hall and beer garden, a theater—

complete with a stained glass window featuring General Ulysses S. Grant—and a growing forest of simple white grave markers.

This was the "sightly world" where Corbett lived with her family. Her father was a civilian official of the Home (although he was often called "Major" by the men), who had moved his family to a house built just for them on the Home grounds in 1891. "Bebby," as Elizabeth was called, was three at the time; her brother, Dick, was two; and sister Gay was born soon after the move. They grew up surrounded by old soldiers and aging staff members, exploring the drives and woods and ponds, observing the extremes of human nature among the veterans as well as the visitors who regularly tramped about. The children attended school in the city, and Bebby would later attend the University of Wisconsin in Madison, but until her father left his post for a job in Milwaukee in 1916, she called the Home "home."

Soon after her family left the NHDVS, Elizabeth moved to New York, where she lived for nearly fifty years and authored more than forty books, a few volumes of nonfiction and several books "for girls." Some were best-sellers and a couple were made into movies. She based some of her fictional characters on people she had known in her girlhood; one of her most beloved characters, the Mrs. Meigs who appeared in three different novels, bore a striking resemblance to the wife of the Home chaplain of the early twentieth century. A quarter century after departing the Home, Corbett penned her most personal book, *Out at the Soldiers' Home*. Mostly memoir, it was a fond but clear-eyed look at the lives she and her family made among the old soldiers. Partly history, it vividly captured the twilight years of some of the men who had won the war to save the Union. Written on the eve of World War II, at a time when the nineteenth century's "greatest generation" was nearly gone, it remains one of the best accounts of what the government tried to do for its veterans and of how those veterans responded.

The Home had established itself as a prominent feature of the landscape of Milwaukee County long before the Corbetts appeared. Guides to the city traditionally featured illustrations and detailed descriptions of the beautiful grounds. In 1877, *Milwaukee Illustrated* described the Soldiers' Home as "one of the most attractive sights Milwaukee affords." Most descriptions of the Home focused on the beautiful hills and groves that surrounded the sprawling physical plant. Summer or winter, it was, as a newspaper article gushed, "a place of great beauty by nature, vastly improved upon by the work of man" (*Milwaukee Illustrated*, 28–31). The grounds were "enchanting" on summer days, with their "far blue vistas, the wide stretches of high-way, velvety turf, odorous shrubbery and variegated beds of flowers." Even on cold days in late fall, the brightly colored leaves and "tantalizing effects of light and shade" in the distance made for a stimulating and gracious ambiance (*Milwaukee Sentinel*, October 28, 1888, and September 16, 1869).

Union veterans pose with their wartime commander, William Tecumseh Sherman (center).
(Library of Congress)

Officials nurtured the Home's parklike elegance. In 1871, for instance, they invited city residents to come out and enjoy the Home's new pleasure boat, while in 1875 alone, a dance hall, a bandstand, three summer houses, two water closets, and a new street gate were built; new and existing roads were graveled and graded; and 600 shade trees were planted along the paths and drives criss-crossing the grounds. The Home governor acknowledged that improvements not only benefited the old soldiers by beautifying their surroundings but also made their lives less monotonous by attracting visitors and tourists.

On one occasion the governor inadvertently raised one of the major problems facing the men at the Home. Although many residents held part-time jobs at the Home as security guards, janitors, gardeners, and servants for the officers and their families, most of the men had a lot of time on their hands. There were a few distractions: literary societies, a small Home band, the increasingly regular funeral ceremonies, traveling musicians and theatrical companies, and other activities, but as Corbett recalled years later, many filled their empty hours by drinking, a habit she called "that great resource of veterans" (Corbett; Papers,

Out at the Soldiers' Home: Union Veterans

Elizabeth Corbett to Enos Comstock, September 8, 1943). The men could buy beer at the Home saloon, but for hard liquor they turned to the establishments located just outside the grounds, which Corbett compared to "the lowest type of waterfront saloon[s]" (Corbett, *Out at the Soldiers' Home,* 74–75). In 1896, for instance, over thirty clustered within a few blocks of the Home's two entrances. Veterans were clearly attracted to dives boasting familiar names like "Lincoln," "Sheridan," and "Sherman." A *Milwaukee Sentinel* correspondent claimed that "the baser sort from the city" haunted these saloons, shrewdly getting veterans to buy them drinks and then, after the old men were "stupidly drunk on vile whiskey," robbing them in the street (*Milwaukee Sentinel,* June 29, 1884).

Although drinking was obviously a discipline problem, it was also one of the worst health problems facing officials . . .

The convenience of these drinking establishments had rather inevitable consequences. Being "drunk" and "under the influence of liquor," two separate violations of Home regulations, regularly accounted for nearly half of all incidents. Although most men ran afoul of the rules rarely or not at all, others seemed to be in trouble all the time. Frederick Richards, for instance, was charged with thirteen alcohol-related offenses in less than three years. On separate occasions he was caught drunk off the Home grounds, in the main building, in the cemetery, and in his quarters. Another, John O'Brien, racked up nine offenses between late 1888 and the fall of 1889.

Although drinking was obviously a discipline problem, it was also one of the worst health problems facing officials at the Home. Hospital records from the 1880s suggest that at least 14 percent of all cases of disease or injury was related to drinking. Attending physicians sometimes merely wrote "alcoholism" to describe a patient's condition, but most cases were more complicated. Patrick King came into the hospital with double pneumonia on November 3, 1883, after a "protracted debauch of 7 days" and died less than three days later. The surgeon blamed his death on "long continued periodic sprees." Drinking aggravated existing conditions such as heart disease, asthma, insomnia, and digestive problems; resulted in falls down stairways, on sidewalks, and in quarters; caused sudden, outdoor blackouts that led to frostbite during bitter Milwaukee winters; and caused psychological problems so severe that some men—suffering, perhaps, from "softening of the brain" as the Home surgeon liked to put it— had to be put in restraints, placed in the insane ward, or transferred to the asylum for insane veterans in Washington. John Van Gent, "being a constant drinker," jumped out of a two-story building on Spring Street (just north of the Home), suffered a compound fracture of both bones in his lower right leg, had it amputated, and died of infection a week later. Walking home late one night after spending the evening drinking on National Avenue, George F. Conn died when he fell, hitting his head on the porch of a house (Marten, 275–294).

Although Corbett wrote plainly about the problems posed by alcohol abuse at the Home, she clearly preferred to think about the veterans in a different way. Indeed, as a member of the Home community, she could get close to the veterans in ways that completely eluded the 60,000 visitors who thronged the grounds of the Soldiers' Home every year. Tourists seem to have maintained their distance from the residents, although they may literally have tripped over a few of them lying about on the grass. Elizabeth Corbett reported that their reclining bodies littered the grounds on most fair days. If visitors had looked more closely, they would have noticed the old men who made up the colorful core of the genteel institution. Corbett compared them to Dickens's characters in their eccentricities and special interests. They rarely bathed and frequently swore but also fondly offered visiting youngsters tasty Smith Bros. cough drops.

Apparently less fond of the cherry-flavored treats than her children, Corbett's mother sometimes ran out of patience with the old men who worked around the house. Sometimes they would paint themselves into corners; they would insist on cleaning huge floors with a single pail of dirty—and growing dirtier—water; the man who delivered ice kept trying to open the screen door, letting in clouds of bugs. Mr. Corbett "always made excuses for the old soldiers," telling his wife, "You don't know what you'd do if you were old and alone in the world" (Corbett, *Out at the Soldiers' Home*, 18). Generally, his daughter reported, he was extremely kind and sympathetic in the penalties he meted out for infractions of Home rules. However, he drew the line when one of the old men refused to bathe. Inmates were required to take a bath once a week, but some managed to avoid it by running the water during their allotted time in the bathhouse, only to emerge dry and just as dirty as when they entered. These "hard cases . . . preferred the guard-house . . . to the horrors of bathing." When one particular veteran applied for admission, everything seemed to be in order until he discovered that he would have to take a bath every week. "I ain't had a bath since I fell in the river at the Battle of Shiloh"—some thirty years earlier—"and I'll be God damned if I'm goin' to begin now." With that he walked out and never came back (ibid., 19).

Elizabeth and her siblings were hardly judgmental in their evaluation of the peculiarities of the old soldiers. Indeed, they regarded the eccentricities of the men "as a show put on for their special benefit" (ibid.). Corbett cataloged their offbeat hobbies: collecting burnt matches, manufacturing and wearing counterfeit medals, "curing" deadly diseases, and proposing marriage to women visitors, inevitably claiming to have run away to become drummers in the Union army as little boys. Some were accomplished whittlers, especially, Corbett believed, those who had been prisoners of war with too much time on their hands. They could carve tiny baskets out of peach pits, a folding knife and fork out of a stick, and hat racks, bootjacks, and towel bars out of larger blocks of wood. One of these wonderfully clever craftsmen even made a foolproof mousetrap that, before it finally wore out, caught hundreds of mice. A few men considered themselves writers. An original work by one of the residents, a temperance play called *Jerry the Lush,* was actually performed by clerks and officials' children in the Home theater, with the playwright taking three of the lead roles. Another writer wrote an epic poem in heroic couplet, with twenty-four cantos filled with supernatural references and deep thoughts. Yet another man perfected a patent medicine "cure" that he tried to market, complete with advertising leaflets. Most men, however, spent their spare time in the billiard hall or in the library, silently reading newspapers and the small collection of books reserved for the use of veterans.

Although the veterans were highly individualistic, they also took on certain characteristics when they acted as a group. One of Elizabeth's favorite pastimes was attending the various "shows" that appeared at the Ward Memorial Theater, built with the money given to the Home by a grateful philanthropist. The theater booked as many traveling and local performers as possible, paying for them out of the profits from the Home store and beer saloon. Each troupe or act would play a matinee and an evening performance to which the soldiers received free admission. Elizabeth remembered them as a "difficult audience" with "their own standards. They liked girls, gaiety, and jokes. They despised anything talky or highfalutin'; most dramatic conflict and practically all pathos bored them" (ibid., 79). Whenever a show was scheduled, the inmates began lining up at least an hour before the doors opened. They waited more or less patiently, although they seemed to cough more than most audiences. Bebby and Dick "had an imitation known as 'The Soldiers' Chorus,' which they were not encouraged to give before company" (ibid., 80).

Oddly, even though they would wait quietly in their seats for an hour before a show started, the veterans' patience vanished as soon as the curtain went up. "All at once their time became extremely valuable to them. If the show failed to please, they did not linger in the hope that it might get better." They simply rose and left, in groups, whenever the spirit moved them. "They did not wait for the end of a scene, nor even for the end of a speech." In some extreme cases, the actors had to perform half a play to a nearly empty house. The soldiers particularly liked farces—Elizabeth remembered now-forgotten plays like *A Bunch of Keys* and *A Milk White Flag* as especially favored—but hated anything that might be considered serious or socially redeeming. Mr. Corbett had managed a theater in Milwaukee before taking the job at the NHDVS, and he agreed with the old soldiers that the purpose of an evening of entertainment was, indeed, entertainment, and he tried to book "a minstrel show or a musical play with lots of dancing" as often as possible. Once, however, another officer talked him into inviting a popular lecturer to the Home, who illustrated his talk with lantern slides. Proving that the men failed to read closely the posters advertising such occasions, even before he had finished his introduction, one old soldier sitting nearly in the front war clambered out of his seat, staggering over the knees of the other men in his row, and stomped out the door, "remarking at the top of his lungs, 'Well, if you're goin' to keep on a-talkin' all night—!'" (ibid., 81).

But one perennial favorite, despite its age and somber and uplifting message, was *Uncle Tom's Cabin*, which, even forty years after the Civil War, was still being done in theaters, town halls, and tents throughout the country. Companies performed the old chestnut at the Home fairly regularly, and with exciting incidents like Eliza fleeing across the icy Ohio River and various fights and escapes; the comedy in the scenes with Topsy and Miss Ophelia; and two touching death scenes—Little Eva and Uncle Tom himself—it was a natural for the old soldiers, who "always stayed through it" (ibid., 87). One particularly poor acting company came when Elizabeth was in her teens; although the play had always been one of her favorites, she grew bored with the lackluster acting and hackneyed production. Most of the soldiers agreed; although they remained in their seats, "they didn't seem to be much affected by the show." But then Corbett spotted one of the three or four African American veterans, a former slave, who lived at the Home. "The tears were running down his poor old black face and splashing off unheeded," Elizabeth wrote. "He wasn't seeing actors or listening to lines: he was watching the drama of his race's servitude." It was one of the most meaningful moments Elizabeth experienced in her long Soldiers' Home childhood (ibid., 91).

One other veteran stood out in Elizabeth's memory. Although she was quite fond of the old soldiers as a group, the family got to know a few very well. They worked around the house or in her father's office; some were, of course, friendlier and more accepting of children than others, and they became special favorites of Elizabeth, Dick, and Gay. The veteran who took the place of honor in her memoir was a man named Smithy—Jason Smith, actually—who for a number of years drove the children to and from school in Milwaukee, where they attended the "model" school at a local college. Unlike many of the veterans, "he was genuinely kind-hearted and obliging; besides, he loved to tease prickly females." Only in his fifties when he entered the NHDVS, Smithy had been a barber and had worked with horses after the war. He was fun to be around and had a "way of putting things that made you remember it." For instance, he kept track of how much money other veterans owed by how many glasses of beer it would buy. He liked a glass of beer; once, when he showed up at the Corbett house (he actually lived in the basement), he was just beginning to sober up and he stated forthrightly to Elizabeth's not entirely approving mother, "Well, I guess you know where I've been!" He took a special liking to Gay, who he taught to ride Mac, the old carriage horse. Although he had inherited the family farm, he never visited it; when he wrote a nephew about it, the younger man wrote back, "Dear Uncle

"The tears were running down his poor old black face and splashing off unheeded."

Jason, We hadn't heard from you in so many years, we thought you was dead" (ibid., 252). Nonplussed, Smithy decided to leave the farm to Gay—although he failed to make the appropriate changes in his will in time.

Smithy drove for the Corbetts upward of a decade and became one of the most memorable veterans, for his kindness and generosity—and because he saved Bebby's and Dick's lives one chilly spring day. The half-hour trip into the city took them over a macadam road in disrepair, a rutted, muddy lane, and a viaduct and a bridge. In these early years of the twentieth century, automobiles had just begun to make their appearance, and when the trio passed a stalled car, the old horseman Smithy just had to yell "Don't you wish you had a horse?" Down the road a bit the carriage crossed a railroad tracks, where an engine snorted ominously. Mac, the horse, started and broke into a run. Smithy pulled on the reins, but the harness broke, slapping the horse on its rump, causing him to think he was being whipped to go faster. Bebby and Dick— eighteen and seventeen years old, respectively—hung on tight, hoping Smithy could get the beast under control. Suddenly Smithy cried "Dick!" Dick sprang to his feet and grasped the reins; together, they began to slow the frightened horse down. They had reached the bottom of a hill where the road narrowed and a new excavation had been dug for a sewer installation. There wasn't room for the careening carriage to pass and Smithy made a split-second decision: he pulled with all his might on the right-side rein, forcing the horse toward a building. The horse stopped, the carriage tipped over. Dick and Bebby, in the backseat, were unhurt, but Smithy was pulled off the front seat and trampled by the horse. He died the next day. The story of the old veteran's heroism and death was, in a sense, Corbett's tribute to all of the men she knew and loved at the National Home. The story is the climax of her memoir; it ends with her bittersweet comment that Smithy "lies buried there in the cemetery under one of the uniform headstones," with his name and the number of his company and his New York regiment. "Smithy gave his life for the children whom he loved. He sleeps in a soldier's grave. Somehow, I feel that he earned it twice over" (ibid., 247–257).

Absent from Corbett's memoir, for the most part, are references to the truly and severely handicapped men who survived the war. Most veterans—even most disabled veterans—did not end up in Soldiers' Homes of any kind. By the turn of the century, just 2 percent of all veterans, North and South, were living in any of the federal or state homes built for them. Like the survivors of most wars, Civil War veterans by and large melted back into the population from which they had come. Those most ravaged by disease and injury died during the first few years after the war. Most Americans thought of veterans, when they thought of them at all, on occasions like Decoration Day or the Fourth of July, when members of veterans organizations like the Grand Army of the Republic gathered to march once again as the saviors of the Union. No one knew—at least no one talked about it if they did know—about the horrifying psychological effects the war had on some of the men who had endured combat conditions. Hints of what we now call "post-traumatic stress syndrome" appear in NHDVS hospital records as "nervousness" or other fairly benign words, but in insane asylums around the country angry, confused men reflected the horrors of war for a generation after the guns fell silent.

Those men, however, were not necessarily Elizabeth Corbett's veterans. "Her" men were the stoic, gruff, and entertaining old guys with whom she spent upward of a third of her life. That life was made possible by a federal government forced, by the scale of the war it had fought against the Confederacy, to introduce programs and accept responsibilities inconceivable in 1861.

PRIMARY SOURCES:

Corbett, Elizabeth. *Out at the Soldiers' Home: A Memory Book.* New York: D. Appleton, 1941.

———. Papers. Milwaukee Public Library, Milwaukee, WI.

Milwaukee Illustrated. Milwaukee: Charles Harger, 1877.

Milwaukee Sentinel, June 29, 1884, October 28, 1888, and September 16, 1869.

SECONDARY SOURCES:

Dean, Eric T., Jr. *Shook over Hell: Post-Traumatic Stress, Vietnam, and the Civil War.* Cambridge, MA: Harvard University Press, 1997.

Kelly, Patrick J. *Creating a National Home: Building the Veterans' Welfare State, 1860–1900.* Cambridge, MA: Harvard University Press, 1997.

Logue, Larry M. *To Appomattox and Beyond: The Civil War Soldier in War and Peace.* Chicago: Ivan R. Dee, 1996.

Out at the Soldiers' Home: Union Veterans

Marten, James. "Nomads in Blue: Disabled Veterans and Alcohol at the National Home." In *Disabled Veterans in History,* edited by David A. Gerber. Ann Arbor: University of Michigan Press, 2000.

McConnell, Stuart. *Glorious Contentment: The Grand Army of the Republic, 1865–1900.* Chapel Hill: University of North Carolina Press, 1992.

Rosenburg, R. B. *Living Monuments : Confederate Soldiers' Homes in the New South.* Chapel Hill: University of North Carolina Press, 1993.

Chapter Twenty-Three

Children of the Battlefield: Soldiers' Orphans

Thanksgiving, 1863. Although the war continues to coat the land in blood, a shift has begun in the North, where a higher purpose—the elimination of slavery, made official at the beginning of the year—has given the war new meaning, and where Abraham Lincoln's brief remarks at the dedication of the National Cemetery at Gettysburg just over a week before have quietly reminded Americans of the war's great aims. Today the Northern states celebrate a Thanksgiving Day set by the president, who in his proclamation included a plea for Americans to remember in their prayers "all those who have become widows, orphans, mourners or sufferers in the lamentable civil strife in which we are unavoidably engaged" (Basler, vol. 6, 497).

At the governor's residence in Harrisburg, Pennsylvania, Governor Andrew Curtin is getting ready to attend Market Square Presbyterian Church when he hears a knock at the door. When he answers the door, he finds two small children asking for food. He asks them why they must resort to begging. They reply that their father had been killed in battle, that their mother is also dead, and that they have no friends or relatives who can help them. The visitation of these soldiers' orphans haunts the governor, who fidgets through the Thanksgiving Day church service and finally declares—in the kind of complete sentences and dramatic phrasing known only to admiring histories—"Great God! Is it possible that the people of Pennsylvania can feast this day while the children of her soldiers who have fallen in the war beg bread from door to door?" In the months following this fateful Thanksgiving, Curtin begins to create a system of homes for war orphans, which he pushes through the legislature in 1864 (Heiges, 110).

Curtin found his personal inspiration for promoting the welfare of soldiers' orphans in this possibly apocryphal encounter with two little children whose names and genders were left unrecorded. A larger call to action came from Abraham Lincoln, who again vowed, in his Second Inaugural Address, to care for "him who have borne the battles, and for his widow, and his orphan." Many Northerners were inspired to do just that. Congress established small pensions for disabled soldiers and the families of soldiers who died in their country's service. All over the country, state legislatures fulfilled Lincoln's promise by creating soldiers' orphans' homes and schools. Southern war orphans did not enjoy a similar outlay of resources; there were no institutions created specifically to house or educate the children of Confederate soldiers. While Northern orphans benefited from a developing conception of the role of government as an agent of social welfare, Southern orphans became part of a very different aftermath of the war: they were central components of a nostalgic reverence for the glorious and tragic Confederate past.

"Is it possible that the people of Pennsylvania can feast this day while the children of her soldiers who have fallen in the war beg bread from door to door?"

War orphans in both sections became patriotic symbols of the war and potent reminders of the deaths of hundreds of thousands of good men on both sides. Despite the differences in the experiences of Northern and Southern orphans, this confluence of patriotism, politics, and philanthropy in both sections marked a significant change in the lives and assumptions of Civil War children.

The most famous orphans' home grew from a nationwide campaign to find the most famous soldiers' orphans. They were the children whose melancholy faces stared from the photograph clutched in the hand of an unidentified soldier found dead on the battlefield at Gettysburg. The sad tale came to a Philadelphia physician and volunteer army surgeon named J. Francis Bourns who, apparently knowing a good story when he heard one, helped to publicize the incident. A little over three months after the battle, a *Philadelphia Inquirer* headline asked, "Whose Father Was He?" In describing the poignant last glimpse of his children's picture by the unknown soldier, the article declared, "How touching! How solemn! What pen can describe the emotions of this patriot-father as he gazed upon these children, so soon to be made orphans!" The reporter described the children and asked newspapers throughout the country to spread the news. Many newspapers and journals simply reprinted the original *Inquirer* story; others published their own accounts. One was the *American Presbyterian*, which ran a story late in October. Several days later, a subscriber in Portville, a village in western New York, passed the article along to a friend, who passed it along to another friend, who passed it along to Mrs. Philinda Humiston, the mother of eight-year-old Franklin, six-year-old Alice, and four-year-old Frederick—and the wife of Amos Humiston, the unknown soldier. The Humiston youngsters were quickly dubbed the "Children of the Battlefield."

The poignant photo caught the imagination of the Northern public, which bought thousands of prints of the photograph produced by Dr. Bourns, proceeds

Soldiers' orphans living in the homes built for them in Northern states were often required to wear military-style uniforms. (Corbis)

from which were intended for the widow and her children. Northerners also eagerly purchased copies of the song "The Children of the Battle Field" by James G. Clark, winner of a poetry contest sponsored by the Philadelphia branch of the United States Sanitary Commission. A traditional tearjerker whose cover also boasted the now-famous picture of the three orphans, its third verse went like this:

Upon the Field of Gettysburg
The full moon slowly rose,
She looked, and saw ten thousand brows
All pale in death's repose,
And down beside a silver stream,
From other forms away,
Calm as a warrior in a dream,
Our fallen comrade lay;
His limbs were cold, his sightless eyes
Were fixed upon the three

Sweet stars that rose in mem'ry's skies
To light him o'er death's sea.
Then honored be the soldier's life,
And hallowed be his prayer. (Clark, "The Children of the Battle Field")

Although there were a few errors in the song—Humiston had died in a brickyard in Gettysburg, not beside a "silver stream"—the song was quite popular. The composer announced he would dedicate the money earned by his sentimental piece to "the support and education of the Orphan Children." Soon a campaign was under way to establish a national orphanage for soldiers' orphans, promoted by Sabbath Schools around the country. By 1866, the former Gettysburg headquarters of Major General O. O. Howard, Humiston's commanding general, had been purchased and nearly two dozen children were living there, including Franklin, Alice, and Frederick Humiston and their mother, who worked as chief seamstress. The family left after a few years, but for a decade after its founding, seventy orphans resided at the National Home.

Three hundred soldiers' orphans were living in county infirmaries and that as many as 2,000 others were homeless . . .

Although the Humiston children and the idea of creating the National Homestead caught the imagination of a Northern public longing for a silver lining to bloody war news, most homes were established by state governments. Pennsylvania, Illinois, Kansas, Minnesota, Indiana, Iowa, Wisconsin, Rhode Island, Connecticut, and New Jersey all established state-supported institutions in the years immediately after the war. Some began as small, private schools or homes that state governments eventually took over. Others, as in Ohio, originated as projects supported by Republican politicians and veterans. Outraged when he discovered that 300 soldiers' orphans were living in county infirmaries and that as many as 2,000 others were homeless, Governor Rutherford B. Hayes of Ohio called on the Grand Army of the Republic and other veterans to convince the legislature to pass a controversial orphans' bill in 1870. Single-minded governors in Wisconsin and Pennsylvania, building on their reputations as the special friends of soldiers, helped win legislative funding for homes in their states. Orphans in Indiana originally lived in the state-sponsored soldiers' home, until a separate institution was established in 1870. A grant from the Camden and Amboy Railroad provided seed money for the New Jersey home, while the Pennsylvania Railroad contributed the original $50,000 for soldiers' orphans' schools in the Keystone State. Eventually, more than fifteen separate schools contracted with the state to provide homes and education for Pennsylvania's war orphans.

In the decades following the end of the war, soldiers' orphans frequently appeared in public as reminders of the sacred duty of Americans to follow through on their collective responsibility. No less than veteran survivors, they became living monuments to the Federal cause. The public could attend year-end examinations at the orphans' homes if they wanted to make sure their tax dollars were creating well-educated and orderly citizens, but more important were the ceremonies and events that focused on the patriotism reflected in the children's plight. In fact, one of the most effective uses of orphans for political ends came shortly after the war when, in a well-orchestrated effort to solidify support for several boarding schools in Pennsylvania already housing soldiers' children, a regiment of orphans invaded Harrisburg in March 1866. After marching in military order from the depot into the state capitol, they entertained and successfully moved politicians to action with patriotic and religious songs, speeches, and earnest pleas for help. Their message: patriotism and justice could be achieved by supporting these worthy offspring of devoted patriots.

The orphans' appearance at the "entertainment" held for members of the legislature was a marvelous brew of public relations, patriotism, and poignancy. Students from several of the Pennsylvania soldiers' orphans' schools crowded into the Hall of the State House of Representatives to show legislators that their generous appropriations were doing good work and that their benevolence reflected the promises made by Abraham Lincoln and by Governor Andrew Curtin to care for the Union's orphans. Criticisms leveled recently at the homes had suggested that they had not been cared for properly and that state money had been wasted. As one official suggested, this event gave lawmakers a chance "to decide for yourselves whether the . . . ready obedience they yield, and the fine healthy countenances they exhibit do not indicate reasonable care and success in their management thus far" (Ceremonies at the Reception of the Orphan Children of Pennsylvania Soldiers).

The children took over at that point, singing songs evocative of the war that had ended less than a year before: "Rally around the Flag," "Tenting on the Old Camp Ground," and "The Dear Old Flag," a song about slaves singing of freedom, and a tune with a pointed reference to their own plight, "Uncle Sam Is Rich Enough to Send Us All to School." Individual students delivered short speeches, which emphasized not only the patriotism of their deceased fathers and the responsibility of the state to care for them but their own humble origins and the chance the orphans' schools gave them to improve their lots in life. A boy named Stanley Booz explained that because of their parents' poverty, they had not attended school much before the state took them in. "Our fathers had

the misfortune to be poor men, and could not afford even to buy books and clothing suitable for us to attend school regularly." But despite their meager
resources, "they were patriotic men and sacrificed their lives in defence of their
country and its sacred liberties." Then, in an extraordinarily direct plea for aid,
Stanley declared that their fathers' contribution to preserving the Union "makes
us feel that we have a claim upon our noble State, and to look to it for support,
protection, and above all for a good education." This was not only a duty for the
taxpayers of Pennsylvania but also a good investment, for "we expect to be able
to earn our own livelihood, and also to become useful citizens, and honorable
members of society" with the help provided by the state (ibid.).

The link between the soldiers' sacrifice and the state's responsibility to their
children—a connection made in every state where politicians and philanthropists fought to create institutions for soldiers' orphans—was articulated in a
poem written by a friend of the orphans and "spoken with feeling and pathos" by
one of the boys. It told of a cozy family circle broken by the father's departure for
the war. In their last "united prayer," the father had pledged "My service to my
country, my children to her care." When "the fearful, crushing news" came of his
death in battle, the family was left with nothing "but his vacant chair beside our
lonely hearth." The poem pointedly asked, "Shall not the land they died to save
fulfill the sacred trust?" and implored the lawmakers to aid the orphans "in our
martyred fathers' names." A subsequent speech by one of the boys asked,

> Our fathers . . . where are they? Ask these, my bereaved schoolmates. Go from one
> to the other and ask, "where is your father?" and they will tell you. One will
> answer *mine* died in camp; another, *mine* was killed at the battle of Fair Oaks;
> another, *mine* was a color bearer, and was shot through the heart while boldly
> pressing forward with the country's flag at the "battle of the Wilderness"; in death,
> he grasped the starry banner as if to die beneath its folds were "far more sweet";
> another will answer, *mine* fell at the battle of Petersburg; another, *mine* was
> starved to death in Andersonville prison; and others will answer, *mine* fell at the
> battle of Gettysburg. (ibid.)

"Are these sad tales," the boy asked, "and do they touch a tender chord in
your fatherly bosoms and enlist your sympathies?" The children's portion of the
program ended with the song, "The Orphan's Prayer."

Adults made equally forthright demands for support. "Legislators!" pleaded
the principal of one of the homes represented at the capitol, "be just and liberal
towards the bronzed veterans who saved the nation's life, and towards the children of those who fell in her defence, and you can safely trust her protection
against either foreign foes or domestic traitors to them, independent of standing
armies or special guaranties" (ibid.).

Children of the Battlefield: Soldiers' Orphans

The orphans' trip to Harrisburg worked wonderfully, and the Pennsylvania system of orphans' schools became one of the largest such institutions in the country. Of course, at a time when only the "deserving poor"—even youngsters—were believed worthy of aid from local, state, and federal governments, the nation expected something in return for their beneficence. This point was alluded to throughout the dramatic appearance of the Pennsylvania orphans at the state capitol; one of the boys promised that if the state continued to support the orphans' schools, "we shall make every effort to . . . become . . . useful members of society; and, though we are averse to war, yet, if needed, we, the soldiers' orphan boys, are willing and ready, *like* our fathers, to rally 'round the flag, and like them—TO DIE FOR OUR COUNTRY" (ibid.).

No one knows how many soldiers' orphans were actually called in future wars to die for their country, but while they lived at the schools and orphanages created for them, they were required to contribute to the well-being and patriotic tone of the institutions. At most homes orphans labored in gardens, workshops, and kitchens to help pay their room and board. They were also frequently brought out on patriotic occasions. At the first Memorial Day ceremony at Arlington National Cemetery in 1868, orphans of Union soldiers spread flowers over 12,000 graves. Children at the Gettysburg National Homestead traditionally participated in local Decoration Day celebrations, strewing flowers on the graves at the National Cemetery while chanting an ode beginning "Lightly, lightly, lovingly tread/O'er the dust of the patriot dead" (Collins and Stoufer, 29–32). They also commemorated the Battle of Gettysburg with a program on the anniversary of the last day of the battle, with the girls clad in white dresses with blue sashes and the boys in military-style uniforms, complete with miniature guns. Orphans also appeared when Pennsylvania's battle flags went on display in Philadelphia in 1866 and at Pennsylvania Governor John F. Hartrauft's inauguration in 1873. Students at the New Jersey school brought tears to the eyes of the administrator, when, wearing red, white, and blue badges, they sang patriotic songs at a flag raising on Independence Day. Drill teams and bands from other homes participated in GAR (Grand Army of the Republic) encampments and in dedication ceremonies for war monuments.

Administrators of the Northern soldiers' orphans' homes peppered their reports with the rhetoric that had been so successful in awakening citizens to their duty to war orphans. A year after the war ended, the director of the Soldiers' Children's Home in New Jersey wrote in his report to the legislature that "We have to-day an unbroken circle of healthy, happy children—orphan children whose fathers fell on almost every battle field, consecrating the soil of every southern state." The memory of these heroes "is green in the hearts of our people, and the principles for which they sacrificed their lives, form yet the foundation of our government." He concluded his introduction to the report by promising to mold the orphans into "useful, happy men and women" and reminding public officials that "their homes were desolated and broken up to save ours." If only the lonely deaths of fathers whose final thoughts were of their children could have been eased with the knowledge of "how kindly his children would be cared for [by] the state; would it not have thrown a ray of brightness even over Libby and Andersonville?" (*Report of the Directors of the Soldiers' Children's Home,* 1243, 1245).

Orphans of Union soldiers spread flowers over 12,000 graves.

Of course, thousands of Confederates had died in prison at Elmira, New York, Camp Douglas in Chicago or at Johnson's Island on Lake Erie, and at others, not to mention thousands more in battle, and soldiers' orphans were just as common in the defeated Confederacy as they were in the victorious Union. Grinding postwar poverty and a long-standing distrust of government-sponsored institutions discouraged Southern states from establishing homes for children of their deceased soldiers. Some men had tried during the war, however. Several legislatures considered and even passed bills to create orphans' homes, scholarship funds for the children of dead soldiers were organized, and local institutions were established for the care of orphans in several places. In Charleston, orphans shared quarters with the widows and mothers of Confederate soldiers, while Richmond finally established its own city orphanage, partly because of the large number of soldiers' orphans living in the former Confederate capital.

Confederate soldiers' orphans were clearly not forgotten. Organizations like the United Confederate Veterans, the United Daughters of the Confederacy, the Sons of Confederate Veterans, the Children of the Confederacy, and even the Ku Klux Klan vowed to protect and to educate the children of Confederate heroes. They sponsored scholarships, held essay contests on Southern topics, campaigned to abolish the Lincoln's birthday holiday, encouraged "junior historians" in Southern schools, and established children's auxiliaries to ensure that rebels' orphans, not to mention subsequent generations of Southern children, gained a necessary appreciation for the sacrifices and valor of Confederate soldiers.

Perhaps even more than in the North, Southern orphans became symbols of their section's cause, joining the long-suffering wives of Confederate soldiers as paradigms of virtue and Southern patriotism. A contemporary account of the opening of the Charleston home for the "Mothers, Widows, and Daughters of Confederate Soldiers" suggests that Northerners did not have a monopoly on the rhetoric of patriotism and sacrifice. When it opened in late 1867, a large crowd "thronged the spacious parlors of the building . . . amid the most profound feeling. A hush as of the presence of the dead seemed to rest upon all; the awe of a place already consecrated by the use to which it was set apart." Later, the account averred that "the Southern soldier had left those who were dear to him to the care of a grateful people, whose solicitude should, as far as might be, supply and compensate for his loss." The home in Charleston "was the reply of the ladies of Carolina to the last sigh of the soldier; it was a proof that they accepted the trust" (*City of Charleston Yearbook*, 362–363).

Ultimately only a few orphans were ever residents of the home in Charleston or anywhere else; Confederate orphans had to settle for being poster children of the Lost Cause. No single person reflected this obsession with the real and symbolic sacrifice of Southern children more than the only surviving child of General Thomas J. "Stonewall" Jackson. Born only a few months before Jackson's death and pushed by her mother Mary Anna Jackson into the Lost Cause limelight, Julia Jackson's short life was dominated by her status as the daughter of one of the Confederacy's greatest heroes. Although she never spoke in public, she was a guest of honor at scores of monument dedications, receptions, and Confederate reunions, starting at the age of twelve with the unveiling of the Jackson statue in Richmond. She constantly received gifts honoring her father and was the subject of a best-selling photograph labeled, "Julia, Daughter of Stonewall." She died suddenly at the age of twenty-six, but her young children often took her place at numerous Confederate ceremonies.

The Confederacy's emotional outpouring for the children of her glorious dead never really ended; like other elements of the Lost Cause, it lingered well into the twentieth century. Most Northern institutions housing soldiers' orphans had much shorter lives, however. Some homes survived by welcoming orphans of soldiers from later wars; others became the primary state agency for the care of all sorts of orphans. Many redefined their missions to include children of disabled soldiers or of veterans too poor to support their families. Yet most closed after a few years or after a generation or two. The Connecticut home, for example, had only forty-one residents just a year or two before its demise in the mid-1870s, which its administrator attributed at least partly to a decline in contributions and interest on the part of the state's residents. More than 200 girls and boys lived in the New Jersey home in 1870, but the number had dwindled to 75 when the home closed six years later. One of the few homes built expressly for African American orphans, the Shelter for Orphans of Colored Soldiers and Friendless Colored Children in Baltimore, had the resources to provide for only about a dozen children at a time.

Sometimes simple politics led to a home's demise. Democrats fought what they believed to be an intrusion of the state into the lives of private citizens and complained about the cost of the homes. The bustling home for Wisconsin orphans, located in an old army hospital in the state capital at Madison, held between 250 and 300 children throughout its several years of operation, but when a new Democratic legislature took over in 1874, they promptly cut the program from the state budget. The institutions were frequently criticized for the same reasons orphanages had always been criticized: the children were working too hard and studying too little; they would be better off if they were "placed out" in families; large, impersonal institutions were no place to raise children.

Critics also looked closely at the administration of the homes. Accusations of misbehavior on the part of the children and of inadequate care prompted a special committee to investigate the New Jersey Soldiers' Children's Home in 1872. They concluded that most of the allegations were false, but the home closed four years later. As early as 1874, the Illinois home had already survived numerous investigations. Yet the institution was plagued by frequent accusations of harsh treatment and poor management during its long history. The privately owned, profit-driven Pennsylvania system of orphans' schools was ripe for a wide array of abuses. The beginning of the end for them came with an 1886 exposé in the *Philadelphia Record* of corruption, profit-mongering, and ill-treatment. Income-producing work in shops and on farms was emphasized over education, critics charged. A newspaper campaign, a damning state investigation, and the withdrawal of support by the GAR led to the closing of most of the schools by 1892.

The most shocking revelations came from an unlikely place: the National Homestead in Gettysburg. Rumors of abuse and embezzlement began leaking out in the early 1870s, an investigation was launched, and residents were stunned to learn that the allegations were true. Residents of Gettysburg were stunned to hear of children kept in the "dungeon"—an unventilated, dark basement room—for minor infractions; of boys and girls confined with ankle and wrist shackles; of girls forced to wear boys' clothing for punishment and other children going without shoes, even in winter; of orphans having to work as servants to the staff, performing backbreaking and menial duties; of a one-armed teenager who acted as a kind of enforcer for the matron by bullying the rest of the children into submission. Ultimately, Rosa Carmichael, the matron, was convicted, fined, and thrown out of town and others were also implicated in the widespread mistreatment of the children. Even the kindly Dr. Bourns, who had headed the Board of Trustees throughout the home's existence, found his reputation besmirched and his welcome worn out. Indeed, the Humiston children believed for the rest of their lives that their mother had never seen a penny of the profits from the sale of the children's photograph. Despite a waiting list of orphans needing homes, the National Homestead closed in the fall of 1877.

Despite the sad and ironic demise of the National Homestead and other homes for soldiers' orphans, the movement to care for the young victims of the

Civil War proved to be an important aftermath of the war. The nation extended its obligation to citizens who fought in its wars to boys and girls who had never set foot on a battlefield. In the North, this evolving sense of grateful duty reflected a growing conception of the role of government in people's lives; in the South, it was part of the fierce yet comforting dedication to the memory of those who sacrificed all for a lost but noble cause. In both sections, the connection of children to the memory of the war indicated yet another way in which the home front was a central part of the larger war.

PRIMARY SOURCES:

Basler, Roy P., ed. *Collected Works of Abraham Lincoln*. 9 vols. New Brunswick, NJ: Rutgers University Press, 1953–1955.

Ceremonies at the Reception of the Orphan Children of Pennsylvania Soldiers, Who Perished Defending the Government by the Governor and the Legislature in the State Capitol. Harrisburg: George Bergner, 1866.

City of Charleston Yearbook, Appendix. Charleston: n.p., 1885.

Clark, James Gowdy. "The Children of the Battle Field." 1864.

Report of the Directors of the Soldiers' Children's Home to the Senate and General Assembly, for the Year 1866. Trenton, NJ: n.p., 1867.

SECONDARY SOURCES:

Collins, Mary Ruth, and Cindy A Stouffer. *One Soldier's Legacy: The National Homestead at Gettysburg*. Gettysburg, PA: Thomas Publications, 1993.

Dunkelman, Mark H. *Gettysburg's Unknown Soldier: The Life, Death, and Celebrity of Amos Humiston*. Westport, CT: Praeger, 1999.

Heiges, George L. "The Mount Joy Soldiers' Orphan School." *Papers of the Lancaster County Historical Society* 48 (1944).

Veder, Robin. "'Julia, Daughter of Stonewall': Julia Thomas Jackson." *Virginia Cavalcade* 46 (Summer 1996).

Chapter Twenty-Four

Up from Slavery: African Americans after the War

"The first knowledge that I got of the fact that we were slaves, and that freedom of the slaves was being discussed, was early one morning before day, when I was awakened by my mother kneeling over her children and fervently praying that Lincoln and his armies might be successful, and that one day she and her children might be free" (Washington, 5).

This passage, which appears very early in Booker T. Washington's famous autobiography, suggests that the boy who would become one of the great African American leaders was not made aware of his bondage until his freedom had become a possibility. Only nine when the war ended, Washington experienced all the challenges facing former slaves in the aftermath of war. His memoir, written when he was the "Wizard of Tuskegee," a respected educator, the spokesman for a conservative but determined approach to black equality, and a shrewd behind-the-scenes political operator, was designed to underscore the grinding cruelty of slavery and the difficulties freedpeople faced after their emancipation. It was also intended to show the efficacy of his own program rising to equality through hard work, self-reliance, and economic progress—rather than the more confrontational and politically oriented campaign promoted by such leaders as W. E. B. DuBois.

Nevertheless, Washington's description of the obstacles he and his family faced in the years after the Civil War, and of the successes he achieved, details many of the forces that shaped the lives of the freedmen and freedwomen who entered the brave new world of a post-slavery United States. The antipathy of whites, their own lack of education, a Southern economy mired in a generation-long depression, and families scattered by slave auctions and wartime escapes were among the challenges African Americans had to overcome. Their goals were simple: to gain an education, to prove that the racist assumptions of whites were wrong, and to become full-fledged members of the American community.

Booker T. Washington was only five when the state in which he was born, Virginia, seceded from the Union, so he remembered only fleeting images of the

Booker T. Washington
(Perry-Castaneda Library)

war years. He feared going into the woods, for slave quarter folklore had it that rebel deserters would cut off the ears of any black boys they found. He also recalled that one of his chores was to operate the pulley-driven fans hanging above the dining room table; he especially appreciated the chance to glean war news from the whites folks' dinner conversation. Since African Americans already subsisted on simple, cheap food, wartime shortages had more of an impact on whites than on slaves. The conflict, however, did touch the plantation: one of the master's sons was killed, while two others were wounded. Billy, the dead son, had been the slaves' favorite, for as a boy he had often played with the young slaves and, as an adult, he had intervened on their behalf with his father. He was deeply mourned.

But no one mourned the end of slavery. The slaves had known their redemption was near for months: "Freedom was in the air," remembered Washington. Confederate deserters and discharged soldiers passed by daily, while the slaves' "grape-vine telegraph" flashed with the good news from the front "night and day." As the slaves sensed their day of freedom growing nearer, "there was more singing in the slave quarters than usual. It was bolder, had more ring, and lasted later into the night" (ibid., 13–14). Emancipation came in the form of a U.S. Army officer, who read the Emancipation Proclamation and made a little speech. Washington's most vivid image of the moment of freedom was of his weeping mother, bending down to explain to him what the words meant.

Up from Slavery: African Americans after the War

Not surprisingly, the newly freed slaves launched into a spontaneous celebration, with singing, dancing, and feasting. But that lasted only a few hours, Washington recalled, as the ramifications of being free began to dawn on the freedmen: "There were the questions of a home, a living, the rearing of children, education, citizenship, and the establishment and support of churches. Was it any wonder that within a few hours the wild rejoicing ceased and a feeling of deep gloom seemed to pervade the slave quarters?" The noise quieted and the men and women who now had to make their own ways in the world began to plan, at least for the immediate future. "Gradually," Washington wrote, "one by one, stealthily at first, the old slaves began to wander . . . to the 'big house' to have a whispered conversation" with the master to arrange at least temporary housing and employment (ibid., 16).

Some slaves recalled the moment of emancipation with the kind animal imagery that peppered their traditional, homespun stories—the kind of stories that came down to the present day as the "Uncle Remus" tales featuring "Br'er Rabbit" and "Br'er Fox." Jenny Proctor remembered that "We didn' hardly know what he means. We jes' sort of huddle 'round together like scared rabbits." Even after they knew they were free, "didn' many of us go, 'cause we didn' know where to of went." On a North Carolina plantation, at least one family was too frightened to leave. They were "jes like tarpins or turtles after 'mancipation," one remembered. "Jes stick our heads out to see how the land lay" (Litwack, 212–213).

This mixture of unleashed joy and worried reflection described by Washington characterized the responses to freedom of most African Americans, who immediately began trying to create "free" lives for themselves. Their first step was often to seek out family members. Sometimes this was relatively easy, as husbands and wives who had lived on different plantations only a few miles apart simply decided to move in together. For many families, however, the process was much more difficult, for their spouses or children had been sold away years before, or had been separated from them during the chaotic war years, as masters desperately tried to remove their most-prized slaves from the paths of Union armies.

Some freedpeople asked officers working for the Freedmen's Bureau—a government agency whose full name was the Bureau of Freedmen, Refugees, and Abandoned Lands—to write letters to former masters or to relatives asking for information about long-lost family members. Others posted advertisements in African American newspapers in both the North and the South, such as this one bought by a couple in Nashville:

$200 Reward. During the year 1849, Thomas Sample carried away from this city, as his slaves, our daughter, Polly, and son, Geo. Washington, to the State of

Mississippi, and subsequently, to Texas, and when last heard from they were in Lagrange, Texas. We will give $100 each for them to any person who will assist them, or either of them, to get to Nashville, or get word to us of their whereabouts, if they are alive. (ibid., 232)

Sometimes efforts to find family members worked; mostly they did not. When they did, poignant reunions were followed by equally touching weddings, as men and women legalized marriages that had never been recognized under the slave codes.

This understandable drive to reconstitute families contributed to the impression among whites that all of "their negroes" were on the move.

This understandable drive to reconstitute families contributed to the impression among whites that all of "their negroes" were on the move. It seemed during the months immediately after the end of the war that the roads were filled with former slaves walking or riding in rattletrap wagons, trying to get from one place to another. Some felt that only by moving could they enjoy true freedom. As one old slave preacher declared at a bonfire-lit meeting in Florida, "You ain't, none o' you, gwinter feel [really] free till you shakes de dus' ob de Ole Plantashun offen yore feet an' goes ter a new place whey you kin live out o' sight o' de gret house. . . . You mus' all move—you mus' move clar away from de old places what you knows, ter de new places what you don't know, whe[re] you kin raise up yore head [without] fear o' Marse Dis ur Marse Tudder" (ibid., 296).

In actuality, however, most slaves did not move far. Many only temporarily took to the road, seeking family members, returning to the farms or plantations of former masters where friends or fond memories drew them. In the end, a majority of slaves remained as wage laborers or tenants on the plantations where they had been living when freed. Perhaps 10 percent of former slaves moved into towns and cities. Despite the famous migration of thousands and of "Exodusters" to Kansas and other western states in the 1870s and a trickle of migrants to the North, the mass of freedpeople remained in the rural South.

Slave owners had never really appreciated the strength of slave society, but historians in the last thirty years have argued that one way slaves coped with the abuse and violence and limitations on their lives was by creating strong, vibrant communities, united by remnants of their African cultures, by religion, and by an insistence on forming families in the face of tremendous obstacles. In many cases, the collapse of slavery caused freedpeople to lose that sense of community in the confusion and uncertainty that followed emancipation. They got a head start on forming new bonds, informed by the assumptions of freedom rather than slavery, by participating in celebrations that inspired a sense of confidence and gave closure to lifetimes of slavery. At the most basic level, freedpeople celebrated their new status by resisting discipline, ignoring plantation rules, or even pillaging their former owners' property. More organized expressions of jubilation occurred in Southern towns and cities after their occupation by Union troops or after news arrived of the Confederate surrender. Four thousand black residents of Charleston held a spontaneous parade before 10,000 spectators. The procession offered visions of the past as well as the future. It included a mock slave auction, a "slave gang," and a coffin draped in black and labeled "Slavery Is Dead." Also joining the celebration were groups of black artisans carrying their tools, African American fire companies, the brass band of a black infantry regiment, and black schoolchildren chanting "We know no caste or color" (Deas-Moore, 29–30).

African Americans would continue to nurture a sense of community by celebrating emancipation; indeed, June 19, the date in 1865 that slavery was formally abolished in Texas, is still celebrated as "Juneteenth" in many parts of the United States. Their path to freedom was, as those who had worked in cotton fields might have said, "a tough row to hoe." Perhaps the most important inhibiting factor was the continued intransigence of Southern whites, who desperately fought to prevent African Americans from enjoying any of the fruits of freedom.

Just after the war, Southern legislatures imposed "Black Codes" to reassert white control over their former slaves. They were often slightly revised versions of the old "slave codes" that had limited slaves' rights to travel about the countryside, testify in court, own property, carry guns, buy or possess alcohol, gather together without white supervision, and learn to read and write. A new form of restriction, the so-called "apprenticeship laws," affected children and young men most directly. Although their stated goal was to care for black orphans, the law actually allowed governments to bind children to planters as laborers—"apprentices"—for years at a time. Inevitably, there were abuses; officials falsified birth records of former slaves or took advantage of the fact that few slaves actually knew their exact date of birth. As a result, many young men and a few women who were actually adults were apprenticed to employers as "children." Many of the supposed "orphans" had one or more parents who understandably did not want their children bound out to a white family. Youngsters rarely received the education, financial settlement upon completion of the indenture, and skills necessary to practice a trade promised them under the law. As a result, thousands of black children, teenagers, and young adults remained in de facto slavery for years after emancipation.

In addition to the legal and extralegal manipulations by which whites tried to deprive former slaves of their rights, there was an epidemic of violence perpetrated by whites against African Americans. After more than two centuries in which Southern whites knew exactly how much a black person was worth—the amount he or she would demand at a slave auction—African Americans had suddenly become, literally, "worthless" to Southern whites. Their vaunted paternalism withered with astonishing speed and, at least in the immediate aftermath of the war, when feelings were running high and former masters felt abandoned by their supposedly "loyal" servants, comments like those of one South Carolina woman were not uncommon: "If I could get up tomorrow morning and hear that every nigger in the country was dead, I'd just jump up and down" (Litwack, 276).

African Americans all over the South slept in the woods to avoid marauding night riders . . .

The ocean of blood shed in the postwar South suggests that at least some whites tried to make that angry woman's dream come true. Thousands of documented and many more undocumented attacks on African Americans by whites occurred during Reconstruction, while the period from the late 1880s through the 1920s saw thousands of murders of innocent black men falsely accused of assaulting white women. The violence came in a number of forms: street fights, ambushes, lynchings, and outright executions. Schools were burned, and white and black teachers—many from the North—were beaten or killed. Two riots in 1866 killed dozens and injured hundreds; in New Orleans a mob attacked a procession of delegates to a convention promoting suffrage for African Americans, while in Memphis whites rampaged through black neighborhoods that had grown rapidly during the Civil War and just afterward. African Americans all over the South slept in the woods to avoid marauding night riders, and hundreds fled from counties when violence reached epidemic proportions. In their nearly nightly attacks during one eleven-month period in York County, South Carolina, Klansmen murdered eleven people and assaulted 600 black men, women, and children. Some incidents were gothic in their horror. Twenty-five blacks were dragged out of a Houston church in 1875, slaughtered, and then drawn and quartered.

Although the scale of violence was horrifying, the most persistent problem facing former slaves was the difficulty of achieving economic freedom. African Americans, like their white fellow Southerners, were held down by the devastated economy of the conquered Confederacy. For generations, Southern plantations had fueled much of the economic expansion of the United States; cotton had accounted for over half of all exports for several decades before the war,

Up from Slavery: African Americans after the War

while sugar, hemp, and rice were also important cash crops. However, the destruction of fields and livestock, the disruption of the labor supply—with a quarter of a million white men dead and slavery abolished—the ruined transportation system, and the simple fact that European countries like England and France had found new sources of cotton in India and Brazil led to a decades-long depression. Prices for most Southern products remained below—sometimes far below—prewar levels until late in the nineteenth century. Property values plummeted, but with so little cash in circulation, few black or white Southerners could purchase land. When African Americans attempted to take a step toward land ownership by convincing planters to let them farm plots of land on shares—this would allow a family to support itself while growing a little cotton on the side to build up a nest egg with which they could buy their own place—the resulting system of "sharecropping" became a trap for hundreds of thousands of black families. (It should be noted that many white farmers were forced into sharecropping, too; over half of all whites in Georgia were tenants by the end of the century.)

Legal discrimination, violence, economic depression: this triple-threat challenge to the freedom of African Americans proved to be nearly insurmountable to most former slaves. Yet a few managed to drag themselves up from slavery, and one of the most remarkable success stories was Booker T. Washington, whose life in the aftermath of war showed how slaves' home front struggle to *gain* freedom became a postwar struggle to *enjoy* freedom. His determination to receive an education, his insistence on becoming economically independent, and his acceptance of help from a few well-placed white people formed a philosophy that by the late nineteenth century had become the core of one of the most important responses by African Americans to the racism of Southern whites.

Washington recalled in his memoir that "there was no period of my life that was devoted to play." From his earliest memories, "almost every day of my life has been occupied by some kind of labour." Even the youngest slaves had to spend at least part of their days performing work. "Trash gangs" picked up litter and weeded gardens, boys and girls delivered food and water to hands working in the fields, somewhat older girls cared for babies and toddlers or helped in the "big house" kitchen, boys assisted groomsmen and slave craftsmen (Washington, 4). Although most other slaves did remember enjoying leisure time playing games, fishing, or making their own toys, Washington's point that even little children were considered economic commodities on a plantation was true for all slaves.

Even though Washington wished he had been able to play—"I think I would now be a more useful man if I had had time for sports"—as a boy he placed more importance on another childhood "right" of which young slaves were deprived:

learning to read and write. He knew of schools, because sometimes he carried his young mistresses' books to school. From the door, his glimpse of "several dozen boys and girls in a schoolroom engaged in study made a deep impression upon me." Those brief visions of another world left him with "the feeling that to get into a schoolhouse and study in this way would be about the same as getting into paradise" (ibid., 5–6).

Work and schooling dominated young Booker's life after slavery, which began when his stepfather called for his wife to join him in West Virginia. He had not been around much during Booker's childhood, perhaps for a day or two at Christmas, but his mother's deep-seated desire to reestablish her fractured family led her to take her two boys over the mountains to a little town near Charleston, West Virginia. They pulled their meager possessions in a cart, but the boys walked most of the several hundred miles, camping out every night.

When they arrived at Malden, they found the stepfather working in a salt mine and living in a tiny cabin much like the one they had left on the old plantation. Yet, Washington recalled, it was worse in that the crowded conditions—there was a motley collection of poor blacks and whites living in extremely close, makeshift quarters—led to a filthy environment made worse by the constant "drinking, gambling, quarrels, fights, and shockingly immoral practices" (ibid., 19). Despite his age, Washington's stepfather got him a job at the salt furnace, which meant getting up at four in the morning. He soon moved to a coal mine, which Washington loathed and feared. He hated how filthy the work made him and tended to get lost in the confusing, pitch-black passages in the underground mine.

Despite the backbreaking, sometimes dangerous work, one desire animated the boy's life, a desire kindled during his fleeting visits to the white children's school: "From the time that I can remember having any thoughts about anything, I recall that I had an intense longing to learn to read." Any chance he had, any sliver of time without work, he gained "book knowledge." His first foray was pathetic and practical: he learned that figures and letters represented certain meanings when the foreman wrote big numbers on the salt barrels to keep track of how much each worker produced—"18" was his father's identification number. As an adult Washington recognized this simple exercise as the first time he learned that abstract symbols could represent concrete ideas and meanings. Soon after, he begged his mother to get a book for him. "How or why she got it I do not know, but in some way she procured an old copy of Webster's . . . spelling-book," from which he soon learned the alphabet. This put him ahead of all the other black people he knew, for no other African American of his acquaintance could read (ibid., 20).

More opportunities for learning surfaced, as, "in the midst of my struggles and longing for an education," a young black man from Ohio moved to Malden.

He could read, and at the end of the day would frequently read from newspapers for a large crowd. "How I used to envy this man!" Washington wrote. Apparently his appearance was something of a catalyst, for the black community decided to open a school. They found another young African American, a former soldier, to teach it. Students paid a small fee and promised to take turns "boarding" the teacher, a treat for all the men, women, and children seeking an education (ibid., 21).

This put him ahead of all the other black people he knew, for no other African American of his acquaintance could read.

Unfortunately, family finances forced Booker to quit day school; from that time on, most of his boyhood education in that mining town took place at night school. He had to find the teachers on his own, sometimes hiring them for one night at a time. Sometimes he had to walk several miles after work just to recite his lessons. "There was never a time in my youth, no matter how dark and discouraging the days might be, when one resolve did not continually remain with me, and that was a determination to secure an education at any cost" (ibid., 27). He was aided in that cause by his work ethic, which impressed a difficult Yankee lady who employed him as a servant for more than a year. Lifted from the squalor of the workers' cabins, Washington grew accustomed to performing his chores at a very high level; neither a spot of dust nor a speck of lint was allowed to gather in the fastidious household where he worked. When he finally gathered the courage—and the money—to apply to Hampton Institute in Norfolk, Virginia, he claimed that he was admitted because he did a good job of sweeping a classroom. Hampton, one of the most famous institutions of higher learning for African Americans at the time, combined rigorous, practical learning with an even more practical insistence that its students work as part of their education and their tuition.

Washington grew to manhood at Hampton, and he gave most of the credit for his later success to a single person: General Samuel C. Armstrong, the former Union officer who was the head of Hampton. As a celebrity in his own right, as someone who had, as he admitted, the good "fortune to meet personally many of what are called great characters, both in Europe and America," Washington nevertheless declared that "I never met any man who, in my estimation, was the equal of General Armstrong," who he called "a perfect man" and "superhuman." Armstrong taught Washington the value of strength of character, of refusing to admit the possibility of defeat, of the necessity to endure pain and hardship before achieving success. The students at Hampton "worshipped" him; Washington believed "there is almost no request that he could have made that would not have been complied with" (ibid., 39–40).

In addition to the exemplar of General Armstrong, Washington learned a number of other simple but vital lessons at Hampton: the importance of bathing, not only in contributing to good health, but also "in inspiring self-respect and promoting virtue" (ibid., 41); the absolute centrality of hard work—Washington's entrance-exam sweeping of a classroom led to his paying for room and board by working as a janitor; the value of having a patron, such as the kindly Mr. S. Griffitts Morgan, a New Englander who General Armstrong recruited to pay Washington's tuition.

Washington's philosophy as an adult—his map for raising his race up from slavery—can be traced directly to his experiences as a slave and as a young boy growing to manhood in the postwar South. He sought out and admired white men and women who could help him, who could see him without the blinders of race. He believed from the bottom of his heart that only hard work and respectability would allow African Americans to make something of themselves in a society controlled by white men. He reacted against the squalor and shortsightedness of the lives led under slavery and in the salt mines by promoting cleanliness, rational planning, and training in useful occupations. His boyhood experiences—discovering the orderly lifestyle of the New England woman for whom he worked in West Virginia, figuring out how to sleep in a bed with two sheets in the dormitory at Hampton, coming into contact with the earnest young men and women at Hampton—all contributed to his future personality and choices.

Grateful to have escaped the legal bondage of his childhood and the economic bondage of his youth, Washington believed he had found a way to raise his people from their centuries of degradation and hopelessness. Other former slaves, however, took very different routes to different forms of independence. Hundreds of thousands of ex-bondsmen became active in politics, joining "Union League" organizations throughout the South and voting overwhelmingly as Republicans. They elected thousands of "their people" to public office, where they served as county judges and state senators and members of the U.S. Congress and lieutenant governors of Southern states. Black legislators held brief majorities in Mississippi and South Carolina; one congressional district in North Carolina continued sending a black representative to Washington well into the 1880s. For the first time in their lives, Southern blacks could testify in court against white people and possess firearms—which some used when they fought back against white mobs or when, in several states, they were allowed to join state police forces.

The explosion of freedom that corresponded with radical Reconstruction—when sympathetic Republicans in Congress supported the opening of Southern society with often punitive measures carried out against former Confederates—

turned the world upside down for a few years. A Texas newspaper complained a few years after the war that "the reign of niggerdom has commenced," when

> Negro juries sit upon the rights of white men . . . Negroes go to political meetings and crowd around respectable white ladies, elbowing their way every where. Negro balls are held in the capitol, and Negro schools are examined there. Negro processions parade our streets, by day and by night, with bands of music and flags. Negroes are in the hall of the House of Representatives. . . . They boldly say that they are to rule the country (*Austin Tri-Weekly State Gazette*, June 29, 1868).

Unfortunately, this halcyon period for black civil rights was blasted by violence and poverty and the loss of interest among Northern whites. The torch bearing the flame of equal civil and political rights passed to Northern blacks—men like W. E. B. DuBois, who had never been a slave—who began to construct an alternative to Washington's more conservative approach.

At one point in Booker T. Washington's moving account of his difficult childhood, he declared that "The Negro boy has obstacles, discouragements, and temptations to battle with that are little known to those not situated as he is. When a white boy undertakes a task, it is taken for granted that he will succeed. On the other hand, people are usually surprised if the Negro boy does not fail. In a word, the Negro youth starts out with the presumption against him" (Washington, 26).

On the other hand, Washington admitted, American culture in the late nineteenth century had come to measure success "not so much by the position that one has reached in life as by the obstacles which he has overcome while trying to succeed." As a result, when a white boy strives and fails, he suffers disgrace and condemnation. When a black boy—for whom expectations are much lower—manages to rise above his station and make something of himself, his rewards and his stature are inevitably greater, at least in his own community (ibid., 29).

Washington's approach to race relations was deemed by many to be excessively conservative; he seemed too willing to give whites what they wanted and too unwilling to stir controversy in the movement to obtain equal rights for African Americans. His analysis of the obstacles facing blacks in the aftermath of the Civil War, developed, no doubt, in light of his own remarkable victory over poverty and racism, strikes a chord. One of the primary challenges to being black after the Civil War was that everyone assumed you would fail, or at the very least, that your success would be a long time coming. This was the world into which emancipation thrust Southern African Americans: the main challenge of their Civil War "aftermath" was to create a blank slate—a fresh start—and then to propel themselves into a more secure future.

PRIMARY SOURCES:

Austin Tri-Weekly State Gazette, June 29, 1868.

Washington, Booker T. *Up from Slavery: An Autobiography.* New York: Doubleday, Page, 1901. Reprint, Garden City, NY: Doubleday, 1963.

SECONDARY SOURCES:

Deas-Moore, Vennie. "I've Got Something to Celebrate." In *Jubilation! African-American Celebrations in the Southeast,* edited by William H. Wiggins Jr. Columbia: McKissick Museum, University of South Carolina, 1993.

Litwack, Leon. *Been in the Storm So Long: The Aftermath of Slavery.* New York: Knopf, 1979.

Rable, George C. *But There Was No Peace: The Role of Violence in the Politics of Reconstruction.* Athens: University of Georgia Press, 1984.

Scott, Rebecca. "The Battle over the Child: Child Apprenticeship and the Freedmen's Bureau in North Carolina." *Prologue* 10 (Summer 1978).

Williamson, Joel. *The Crucible of Race: Black-White Relations in the American South since Emancipation.* New York: Oxford University Press, 1984.

Chapter Twenty-Five

"True Soldiers of the Southern Cross": Confederate Women and the Lost Cause

When the *Charleston News and Courier* published a collection of memoirs detailing the experiences and contributions of Southern women during the Civil War, the paper declared somewhat hyperbolically that "our women died a hundred deaths, died day by day and almost hour by hour." The editors were speaking metaphorically, of course; few white civilians actually died as a direct result of the Civil War, even in the South. Yet the publication of what became a book-length testament to women's roles in the Confederate war effort was an admittedly meager effort to recognize these "true soldiers of the Southern Cross." Although they were given "no ribbon or star" to wear as "the badge of their nobility," this book would "give the public . . . some faint idea of what they saw and what they did, what they hoped and what they feared, in those exciting times which are gone forever" (*Our Women in the War*, frontispiece).

The stories had originally been published as a newspaper series under the title "Our Women in the War." At a time when publications like the *Confederate Veteran*, the *Southern Historical Society Papers*, and *Century Magazine* were pouring forth wartime memoirs by Civil War soldiers, the *News and Courier* had begun to sample the reminiscences of Civil War women. Indeed, the editors acknowledged that, until now, "every point of view" of "the Confederate War and its incidents had been fully described." The women's tales revealed

> that no Confederates were more worthy of our loving remembrance than those who bound their warrior's sash when he went forth to fight; who suffered worse than death, a thousand times, when battle raged loud and long; who were stung and wounded by privations that the hardy soldier never knew, and who, besides, were exposed to the injuries and taunts of the infamous raiders who, during and after the war, visited Southern homes and stripped them of what was holiest and dearest. (iv)

303

The stories show that Southern women suffered and endured pain "such as no other nation of such women has ever known since the world began" (ibid.).

The articles, which appeared in no particular order, referred to specific incidents ("The Taking of the Arsenal," "The Sack of Columbia," "The Fall of Richmond"), to certain kinds of wartime conditions ("The Costumes of War Times," "Starvation in the Valley of Virginia," "Refugeeing in Barnwell"), or to certain kinds of women's work ("The Hospitals at Danville," "Hospital Memories"). Other subjects included children's play, wartime weddings, the experiences of officers' wives, and faithful slaves. Throughout, Southern women appear as unwilling warriors but ardent patriots, peaceful but proud, patient but forthright.

These qualities made them perfect exemplars of the Lost Cause, a movement that borrowed its name and its tone from the vain efforts of Scots to win their independence from England. The term was first applied to the Confederacy by Edward Pollard, the acerbic editor of the *Richmond Examiner*, in his history of the war published just a year after the guns fell silent. The Lost Cause grew over the decades following the war to include a full range of pro-Southern beliefs and values: the commemoration of the heroism of Confederate soldiers, an insistence that the war had been fought to preserve constitutional principles rather than slavery, and a nostalgic desire to return to the halcyon prewar plantation days. A wide array of publications and organizations—the Southern Historical Society, *Confederate Veteran Magazine, The Land We Love*—projected myriad conflicting images and attitudes. Southerners formed associations to fund Confederate monuments, preserve Confederate graves, and found homes for disabled and aged Confederate veterans. The United Daughters of the Confederacy, the United Confederate Veterans, and other groups memorialized the sacrifices of the men and women of the Confederacy by celebrating Confederate memorial days, holding essay contests and granting scholarships, and holding reunions of former Confederates and their families. The Lost Cause reached a crescendo between 1880 and 1910, but continued to exert a major influence on Southern society and politics for years afterward.

The attitudes of proponents of the Lost Cause reflected numerous points along a pro-Confederate spectrum: a respect for the past on the part of some groups became dogmatic allegiance to such Confederate icons as the famous battle flag that became a symbol of resistance to the Civil Rights movements in the 1950s and 1960s; a romantic but relatively benign appreciation of the supposedly more manageable relationship between the races under slavery was flanked by virulent racism expressed in the lynchings that spread like an epidemic through the South between the 1880s and 1920s; a grudging admittance that the South was finally defeated by larger armies, and a government with greater resources pro-

Women attending Confederate graves in Charleston, South Carolina
(Library of Congress)

duced a bitter, deep-seated resentment against all things Northern and against all efforts by the federal government to influence conditions in the South.

Much of the extremism associated with the Lost Cause, however, would come later. During its first generation, the women who had fought the war on the Confederate home front led the way, forming cemetery and memorial associations, protecting the honor of their husbands and fathers, and promoting their own version of the events of the war years. Their campaigns and their publications made public the contributions, adventures, and nightmares they had experienced as daughters, wives, and mothers.

The articles in *Our Women in the War* are not simply narratives and chronicles. Rather, they reveal the desire—the need—of the female veterans of the Southern home front to make sense out of their experiences, to add meaning to events that were made even more frustrating and horrifying because of their ultimate futility. The eighty women who contributed to the book had not simply

Their efforts comprise one of the great and enduring aftermaths of the Civil War.

responded to the editors' initial invitation to "tell their whole story, in their own way" (iv). Instead, *Our Women in the War* represents the efforts of many Southern women, in publications ranging from tiny newspaper articles to self-published chronicles to regionally distributed memoirs to reminiscences of prominent women (often produced, ironically, by Northern publishing houses), to seek recognition for their roles as home front warriors during the War Between the States and to shape the way that succeeding generations would remember their roles. Their efforts comprise one of the great and enduring aftermaths of the Civil War.

One of the themes that emerges from the essays is that women dreaded the coming of war. Indeed, a common thread in Lost Cause ideology was that the North had been the aggressor, forcing the South into a war it had not sought but would not turn from. One Alabama woman had "imbibed a horror" of war from reading books and from hearing family stories about the American Revolution, "and from my earliest years dreaded lest I too might live to see one." While the boys and men sought another war in which they could prove themselves, she could see only the "dark and suffering side." As a result, the "constant predictions of a civil war" filled her "with all the old childish dread" (273).

But, as Abraham Lincoln sighed in his Second Inaugural Address, "the war came," and the women of the South were more than up to the hardships, oppressions, and other challenges that life on the Confederate home front threw their way. Many of the stories recorded in *Our Women in the War* revolved around the ways that wartime conditions affected their roles as wives and mothers. Many concerned themselves with the traditional role of keeping the home fires burning—literally—and maintaining farms and households, educating and feeding their children, managing slaves, desperately clinging to notions of propriety and status. Even those women who proudly recorded their achievements outside the home focused on their work as nurses—a necessary and, in its own way, gender-role-shattering job, but one that nevertheless relied on domestic skills and sensibilities.

As a result, *Our Women in the War* should be seen as more than a chronicle of women's work. Read in a slightly different way, the following sampling of three women's stories provides a record of how Southern women remembered their own wars, and a map to how they wanted their contributions and experiences to be remembered by others a generation after the shooting stopped.

A general kind of "hunkering down" occurred throughout the South, especially in those areas in the path of approaching Union armies, and Emma Stroud's memoir displayed the endurance and stamina she needed to maintain a grip on her emotions and sanity. Although her husband did not have to go to the army, he was often on business or—at least once—under arrest by suspicious Union troops. As a result, his wife and family frequently had to deal with crises on their own.

Mrs. Stroud recalled the opening months of the Vicksburg Campaign in late 1862, when Union troops arrived at their home on Walnut Bayou in Louisiana. With a son in the army and a couple of daughters still at home, the fifty-something Emma could not have known the depths of the challenges she would soon face. The Strouds hid all their firearms—including Mr. Stroud's favorite, "old Betsy"—to the accompaniment of a miles-away cannonade that set their windows rattling. "We lived in constant dread, for we hourly expected a visit from some scouting party." When the Yankees finally arrived, surrounding the house and storming the sitting room, pistols drawn, Emma had the chance to show her metal, refusing to tell the intruders where their valuables were hidden. After a grinning raider uncovered their cache of arms—a slave revealed that they had been hidden under turkey and duck nests—and teased, "your ducks and turkeys sit on formidable eggs," Emma retorted, "I only wished every Southern turkey, duck, chicken and hen could hatch such 'eggs,' and that each one could be made useful in killing a Yankee" (17).

An autumn of "constant visitation by scouts from Grant's army" encouraged the Strouds to move with their few remaining slaves to a place farther west, near Milliken's Bend—which, by Christmas, put them yet again in the path of the Union troops encircling Vicksburg. On one memorable raid, Emma returned from a visit to friends to find her husband gone and her farmyard occupied by 200 bluecoats and, she estimated, 1,000 runaway slaves from other plantations. Her slave owners' sensibilities were shocked to see the easy drinking and fraternization among the black and white invaders. Worried sick about her husband and "almost paralyzed with fear," she entered her house, which had been thoroughly ransacked: "I found trunks broken open, drawers pillaged, furniture turned over" and "everything scattered around." Her pantry had been stripped of Christmas cakes, her smokehouse emptied of the meat of forty just-slaughtered hogs (18).

She appealed to an apparently drunken Yankee officer—"drinking whiskey," she pointedly remembered, "with my slaves . . . to protect myself and daughters from the insults of the drunken crowd. He replied with a terrible oath, "that it was not his business in the South" to protect women and children. Emma knew she needed to get her little daughters away from this place, but was unwilling to traverse Yankee and runaway slave-infested territory alone and at night. "Clasping my children in my arms I kneeled down in the piazza and prayed, as I had never done before, that God would not forsake me in my trouble." She believed her prayers were answered; a "gallant federal officer" soon rode into the yard and asked her if the men were bothering her. She reported the insults and robberies that had occurred, and the officer—an Iowa colonel—immediately ordered the men to leave and stood guard on the veranda until the entire division had passed by. The colonel apologized for the behavior of the troops, and, Emma recalled twenty years after the events of that frightening evening, confessed "that if he had known the South had to be conquered by such cruelties as he had seen inflicted on defence-less old men, women and children, he would never have enlisted for the Union" (18).

The family survived this raid—Mr. Stroud returned home on foot a day later, a little shaken but unhurt after a brief imprisonment by the Northerners—and decided to move to Texas. Before the plan could be carried out, however, the last remaining slaves, even Reuben, the loyal foreman, vanished in the night. Stroud nearly collapsed, crying, Emma remembered, "Oh! wife . . . What shall we do?" After witnessing the behavior of the runaway slaves she had encountered just a short time before, Emma had, it seemed, half expected their own slaves to leave:

> The poor man was greatly distressed, as he could not bear for any one to even hint that his slaves would leave him, he being an indulgent, kind master, treating them as children. I threw my arms around him, and told him we could work, and still be so happy, without the Negroes—that it was only a question of time, when they would be free, and that the present was a good opportunity to begin to learn to wait upon ourselves. (19)

So began the Strouds' lives in the post slavery South. Stroud cut some wood and built a fire and the women—Emma, her daughter, and two friends staying with them—"marched in a body to the kitchen and . . . prepared a breakfast . . . not worth bragging about." Yet Emma recalled a small sense of victory; it was the first meal she had ever prepared without help from a slave (19).

The last two years of the war held more of the same for the Strouds. Another sudden raid exposed the family to more angry soldiers—crowds of stragglers rooting around under the house for valuables, a soldier pointing a pistol at the defiant Mr. Stroud and threatening to "blow his brains out"—and further sapped the resources of this once-affluent family. Stroud took his surviving cattle to the West, and, alone, Emma tried to carry on. One of her loneliest and most frightening moments came when a group of African Americans barged into her house and demanded that she free the little eight-year-old slave girl who had been left behind when the older slaves fled. When she refused, they "cursed me" and promised to return with a squad of Yankee soldiers who would no doubt burn her house down. Confronted again with an unexpected challenge to her beliefs and assumptions, Emma navigated a swamp back to the home of an "Irish . . . hermit," where the girl would be safe. Returning to the house, "I crept behind the outhouses every moment expecting to be shot; still I determined to enter my house and boldly walked in" (20).

> "*I crept behind the outhouses every moment expecting to be shot . . .*"

Raiders continued to take away her property; during one of several subsequent moves, Emma had to leave behind all of her furniture. She was finally reunited with her husband in Delhi, Louisiana, where they remained in safety for the final months of the war. Only then could Emma let down her guard, and only then did it become apparent just how much stress she had been under and how high had been the psychological and physical toll of her adventures. "For months I had been under continued excitement, which kept me from sinking under my troubles; when this excitement was gone I fell sick, and for months I was kept in my room" (21).

Emma's story is full of contradicting experiences and attitudes, the logical outcome of a person whose life is rocked by catastrophe and unexpected hardship. Her brief memoir reflects a number of the lessons common to the ways that Southern women wanted to remember their wartime experiences. Her confidence in the inherent goodness of human beings is shattered and then restored, and her perception of the basic depravity of the common Yankee soldier is confirmed. She temporarily becomes the stronger partner in her marriage, bolstering her husband's confidence until he is able to resume his place as head of the household. She briefly and bitterly mourns the loss of her slaves—and of her sense that she really understands this race of servants—but quickly determines to make the best of the situation. She reveals moral as well as physical courage, but acknowledges the burden of presenting a strong front.

Even women who found roles in the Confederate war effort outside the home frequently used stereotypically feminine skills and demeanors to accomplish their feats. At least a few insisted on remembering those contributions as steps toward a kind of liberation, albeit within safe boundaries. Indeed, when "Miss I. D. M." of Columbia, South Carolina, described the efforts of the "Young Ladies Hospital Association," she referred to meetings at which committee chairwomen would turn their backs to the room while reading reports and minutes, so unused to public speaking were the women of that time. "Pity the benighted girls of '61," she urged the "advanced young women of the present

*Confederate veterans at a Confederate memorial late in the nineteenth century
(Library of Congress)*

day! They had scarcely ever even heard of an emancipated woman, and a female
lecturer or public reader was beyond their powers of imagination" (3).

But the author—who retained enough of that public shyness to reveal only her
initials—clearly sought to have Columbia women's creation of a local hospital for
Confederate soldiers seen as an innovation in the care of soldiers and organization of public philanthropy. She went so far as to claim that the Columbia
Wayside Hospital was "the first of its kind in the world," quoting an 1873 address
in which a rather paternalistic but authoritative-sounding South Carolina physician stated "with justice and pride" that the "credit of originating" the system of
caring for sick and wounded soldiers in the Civil War as well as in the European
wars fought since then "is due to the women of South Carolina" (4). Their organization, which began in a single room in the state capitol but soon expanded into
a full-blown hospital, reached 75,000 patients.

The hospital grew out of the Young Ladies' Hospital Association, which, after
the First Battle of Bull Run, was the vehicle by which teenagers and unmarried
young women hoped to make their marks for the Confederacy. "What memories
are recalled of laughter and fun," recalled Miss M., "of sighs and tears, or sobs
and agony." The youngsters "were unused to labor, but willing minds made up for

their lack of skill, and it was wonderful how soon they learned to cut out and make up homespun shirts, knit socks, roll bandages, &c., and before long many a box of substantial comforts was sent to the boys in the army from the girls at home" (3).

Larger needs, however, soon became apparent. The growing number of sick and wounded soldiers coming home from the army during the winter of 1861–1862 required attention, as there were no facilities available for men who had to wait for transportation to their homes. Columbia was merely a stop, not the final destination, for most of them, and many seriously ill or hurt men had to wait hours or days to continue their journeys. Individual women would sometimes meet the trains and care in whatever way they could for the men, but there was no regular system of organizing material or human resources. A local clergyman suggested to the Young Ladies' Hospital Association that they might be able to help. "The idea seemed to them a good one," recalled Miss M., "and the suggestion was immediately acted upon" (4).

The first "Soldier's Rest," as it was called initially, was in a single room. It soon became apparent, however, that these meager accommodations would not be enough and a larger space was created at the train depot. Another change occurred soon after the rest was established; women and a few men took over the organization. Unwilling to allow their young daughters to be exposed to the "grim work to be done, ghastly sights to be seen, [and] horrors to be endured," the elders "wished to spare the young hearts, already becoming too familiar with sorrow, everything which it was in their power to do." The Soldier's Rest was rechristened the Wayside Home (and later Hospital), and a committee of men and women took over its operations, "leaving to the girls . . . the esthetics of the Hospital" (4).

Although at first they were outraged—"What are the esthetics of a hospital, we would like to know"—the girls eventually settled into preparing and serving food and coffee and providing cheer and good comfort (4). The decidedly grimmer jobs of washing soldiers who sometimes came straight to the hospital from battlefields, of dressing wounds, and of helping the men put on clean clothes fell to the mature women and men who had taken over the operation. Soldiers were given supper, a clean, safe bed, and breakfast before they were sent on their way, although the seriously ill sometimes stayed longer.

Like Louisa May Alcott, Walt Whitman, and scores of other Civil War nurses in the North and South who told their stories, Miss M. offered a few "Pathetic and Humorous Incidents." She told of the wagon with the "forest of crutches" traveling down the street that ran past the hospital, of the father who came to carry the remains of two of his sons home for burial, of grievously injured men begging to be sent home rather than stay on a few extra nights, of sickbed and deathbed conversions, of steadfast courage in the face of suffering, and of loyalty to the Confederacy despite overwhelming odds.

Miss M.'s tale of the origins of these short-term care facilities for Confederate soldiers—which were, indeed, created in hundreds of towns and cities across the North and the South during the Civil War—contains a number of elements of Southern women's memories of their contributions to the Confederate war effort. Those who formally joined the Confederate war effort liked to be considered veterans of the struggle; like Miss M., many hoped to be remembered for their innovative responses to the national emergency. Other considerations were also important: they fought their home front war without giving up propriety; without crossing gender roles; without losing their faith in the power of kindness, cleanliness, and intentions to do good even in a world ravaged by war.

The women's side of the Lost Cause commemorated a number of different ways in which female Southerners wanted to be remembered. Emma Stroud's first priority—and the actions from which she drew the most satisfaction—was simply enduring: preserving and protecting her family, which for thousands of women was in itself a key factor in the success or failure of the Confederate war. The girls and women of the Young Ladies' Hospital Association stepped outside their homes in innovative and truly useful ways, but not outside their traditional domestic responsibilities as caretakers and nurses. A relatively small number of women left behind traditional roles almost entirely, making their own way in a war-torn world.

Virginia Dade recalled her life as a young woman working in a government agency in Richmond, where she and her sister Fanny roomed in a large boardinghouse with over a dozen other women and a handful of men unfit for military duty. Virginia and her sister were on their own, without the protection of male family members—or any other men, for that matter. They contributed directly to the Confederate war effort and faced the wartime challenges alone.

At the center of Virginia's essay is the fall of Richmond in April 1865, but she also recorded what life was like in the crowded rebel capital, providing a glimpse of the urban version of the endurance test that was life on the Southern home front. The city was jammed not only with soldiers and government workers but also refugees and the families of Confederate soldiers. Rents were astronomical and inflation pushed prices for necessities to impossible levels: $300 for a barrel of flour, $13 for a pound of beef, $40 for a pound of coffee, and $80 for a pair of shoes. As a result, Virginia wrote, "we had to practice the closest economy even in the veriest necessaries of life, counting out the potatoes for dinner and the grains of coffee for breakfast, when we were so fortunate as to have the grains to count" (99).

The stress of living so near the edge was tempered somewhat by the exciting sights and sounds of the city. Richmond's role as the seat of Confederate power and as the target of Yankee attacks meant that her salons, offices, and boardinghouses buzzed with rumors. Virginia heard them all, and wrote that Sunday "was always a day prolific of startling rumors," probably because most workers had the day off and the leisure to indulge in gossip (99). The rumors intensified as the Union noose around the Confederacy tightened in the spring of 1865, and when the worst possible news—that Lee's army had collapsed and that Richmond was to be abandoned—was confirmed in that first week in April. Virginia, Fanny, their married sister (whose husband was away in the army), and her small children were cast into situations that they had never before encountered, testing resources and providing an impressive trove of home front "war stories."

Virginia took the lead in getting her small band of women through the crisis. In addition to witnessing the fires that ravaged huge swaths of Richmond and sadly watching Union troops occupy the city, she had to provide in a number of ways for her all-female family. She put up a brave front—"though I spoke hopefully . . . a nervous shiver came over me and my limbs were so tremulous and weak that I thought I should fall" (100). It was a bad moment, but her determination—and a shot of brandy—got her through it. She quickly gathered her family and set about improvising a plan. A strange calmness came over them as the last of the Confederate troops left town; that night, "as I have heard is often the case with a criminal on the night before his execution, we soon fell into a profound slumber, though our last waking thoughts were filled with visions of black-faced, blue-coated ruffians, with savage yells and gleaming sabers" (101).

It did not go nearly that badly for Virginia and her little band, but she had to extend herself far beyond the normal social and economic roles of Southern women. With fire approaching their neighborhood, she organized some of the women and children into a fire brigade to keep the roof wet, then commanded a "foraging expedition" of the younger children, who marched with her through the burning streets to her sister's abandoned house, where they rescued as much food as they could carry (103). Later, she volunteered to carry out "the daring enterprise" of obtaining "protection papers" from the provost marshal— this was supposed to ensure that no Union troops damaged or otherwise threatened their home—and, still later, joined the "hungry throng" of Richmonders jammed into the "ration office" to get their allotted portions of "codfish, fat pork and yellow meal" (105).

Virginia and her sisters and nieces survived the fall of Richmond and even the Confederate collapse that followed. Moreover, Virginia could take comfort—a comfort that no doubt grew as the years passed and the fear and heartbreak of wartime Richmond faded—from her very direct contributions to the Confederate war effort, and from her successful attempt to go it alone during her country's crisis.

Constrained by Victorian conventions, Southern women hesitated to promote their own roles in the Confederate war effort. By the 1880s though, at least a few apparently ached to tell their stories. As Mrs. Pauline Dufort of Charleston suggested in her essay, "Now that years have passed since the sullen clouds of fratricidal war have rolled back and the azure sky of peace again droops like a liquid canopy over our Southern, sunny land, it well becomes the patriotic women of the South to embalm in song and story the heroism of their sex during that terrible struggle" (49). Women of the Lost Cause wanted their contributions to be remembered in the context of fairly traditional Southern behaviors. The war had threatened the very foundations of their society, had shaken gender roles, and had upset generations of social and racial assumptions, but Southern women were proud to have persevered, sustaining their families and society and remaining true to their gender and their country.

Much has been written about the extent to which the Civil War changed the lives of Southern women. Many were forced to take over farms and plantations, others—especially single women and young girls—worked outside their homes in Confederate government offices or in munitions factories (dozens were killed and injured in an explosion at an armament factory in Richmond in 1863). Obviously, many Southern women, including, no doubt, some of the contributors to *Our Women in the War,* found their lives forever changed by the loss of husbands and fathers, the destruction of property, and the economic dislocation of the war and Reconstruction. The majority of Confederate women, despite the pressures placed on them during the war, remained ensconced in traditional home front roles—and, at least in the essays written by a sampling of women throughout the South during the generation after the war, that is how they wanted to be remembered.

Just as soldiers seek to shape the ways in which their actions are interpreted and appreciated by succeeding generations, Southern women insisted on projecting their own perceptions of how and why they contributed to the Confederate war effort. By joining the politically and racially charged Lost Cause, women ensured that, at least for them, the war would never end. The immediacy of the stories in *Our Women in the War* suggests the extent to which even home front experiences were seared into the minds and memories of Confederate women—and indicates the importance they placed on their own roles in the war. The statues for which they raised funds, the cemeteries of Confederate soldiers they carefully tended, and the books and articles they wrote years after the war became their memorials.

Confederate Women and the Lost Cause

PRIMARY SOURCE:

"Our Women in the War": The Lives They Lived; The Deaths They Died. Charleston, SC: News and Courier Book Presses, 1885.

SECONDARY SOURCES:

Clinton, Catherine. *Tara Revisited: Women, War and the Plantation Legend.* New York: Abbeville, 1995.

Foster, Gaines M. *Ghosts of the Confederacy: Defeat, the Lost Cause, and the Emergence of the New South.* New York: Oxford University Press, 1987.

Wilson, Charles Reagan. *Baptized in Blood: The Religion of the Lost Cause, 1865–1920.* Athens: University of Georgia Press, 1980.

Chapter Twenty-Six

The Devil's Civil War: The Stories of Ambrose Bierce

The doomed man stands on a makeshift gallows attached to a bridge spanning an Alabama creek; he thinks of his family and plans a desperate escape—which occurs when the rope breaks and he plunges to the rushing water below. Freeing his hands, he ducks the rifle fire from the stunned guards on the bridge, and after a hard day's and night's travel he staggers into his front yard, where his wife awaits. "As he is about to clasp her he feels a stunning blow upon the back of the neck; a blinding white light blazes all about him with a sound like the shock of a cannon—then all is darkness and silence!" (Hopkins, 53).

The stream is Owl Creek, the dead man is Peyton Farquhar, the story is one of the most famous fictional accounts of the Civil War, and the author is Ambrose Bierce. Generations of Americans have read that story in high school and college literature anthologies; many, no doubt, have missed the earlier foreshadowing—the pressure on his throat and "streams of pulsating fire heating him to an intolerable temperature" just before Farquhar supposedly regains consciousness in the water below the bridge. Once alerted, however, to the "ironic" nature of the ending, students check Bierce's name off their list and move on to Mark Twain or Robert Lowell or some other Gilded Age literary figure (ibid., 48).

Bierce's stories have not traveled well over the years; they are gimmicky, with trick endings and gratuitously sad and maligned characters. Most people remember him, if they remember him at all, as the author of the devilishly satiric *The Devil's Dictionary*. He was, of course, much more than that. Unlike his contemporary, Stephen Crane, Bierce wrote about the war from personal experience. An eighteen-year-old shopkeeper, Bierce enlisted in the 9th Indiana regiment and campaigned in western Virginia early in the war. He rose through the ranks, fighting as a sergeant major at Shiloh and Stones River. Promoted to second lieutenant, he became a staff officer, drawing maps and performing other duties through Chickamauga, Missionary Ridge, and the opening days of the Atlanta Campaign. At Kennesaw Mountain, Bierce suffered a head wound that was slow to heal. Although he returned to duty in time to participate in the battles at Franklin and Nashville, he asked for a discharge and left the army early in 1865.

Bierce began writing for newspapers in San Francisco, Washington, D.C., and, for a time, London. He was writing a column called "Prattle" for William Randolph Hearst's *Examiner* by 1887. Although he was not known for his Civil War stories, he wrote just over two dozen of them through the years, a number of which were published in his 1891 collection, *Tales of Soldiers and Civilians*. Their graphic depictions of violence and fatalism; their dour and cynical take on warfare in general and the "War of the Rebellion" in particular; and their tragic, hapless, and duty-blinded characters were something of a shock to readers.

> *"A blinding white light blazes all about him with a sound like the shock of a cannon—then all is darkness and silence!"*

A precursor to Crane's realistic approach to Civil War combat, Bierce wrote of war not as a grand adventure, although some of his characters believe it to be one before they experience it, and not as an occasion for pride or national honor, although a recurring theme is the folly of such attitudes. This ran counter to almost everything Victorian Americans believed about war—at least what they suggested they believed in their fictional accounts, public demonstrations, and personal narratives of the war years. Perhaps the most evocative statement of these ideas came from the pen of Oliver Wendell Holmes Jr., who declared that "the generation that carried on" the Civil War—his generation—had been "set apart by its experience. Through our great good fortune, in our youth our hearts were touched with fire. It was given to us to learn at the outset that life is a profound and passionate thing" (Posner, 86–87).

Accustomed to drum and bugle memoirs and histories of the war, late-nineteenth-century Americans in both the North and the South expected to read about heroes dying nobly for worthy causes. Bierce gave them precious little of that. Instead, his characters, dying squalid deaths for dubious reasons, were buffeted by bad luck and worse generals. His stories were filled with realistic detail like this rousing and chilling description of hand-to-hand fighting between small squads of enemies, who had no time to reload their guns; the Yankees thrust with bayonets, the rebels swung rifles as clubs. "The sound of the conflict was a clatter like that of the interlocking horns of battling bulls—now and then the pash of a crushed skull, an oath, or a grunt caused by the impact of a rifle's muzzle against the abdomen transfixed by its bayonet" (Hopkins, 87).

The protagonists and antagonists caught up in this vicious fighting were privates and lieutenants, spies and martinets, pompous politicians and fatalistic

Ambrose Bierce (Corbis)

common soldiers. Among the sometimes humorous, often pathetic, and virtually always tragic characters Bierce invented for his Civil War stories were a philosophical Yankee spy named Parker Addison, chatting with his captor about the nature of death and life; the smooth-faced orderly who reluctantly agrees to don women's clothing to trick a fatuous and evidently lonely staff officer; a frantic captain whose company suffers a single casualty on the fringe of a battle—aside from the captain himself who, undone by stress, plunges his sword through his breast; a ghostly scout who waves his company away from the spot of a rebel ambush—an hour after he was killed; the generally silly Brigadier General Jupiter Doke, a bumbling braggart of a brigade commander whose farcical military career is told through a series of confusing dispatches and exaggerated newspaper stories; and a little deaf boy wandering the backwash of the Chickamauga battlefield among a small army of horribly disfigured and wounded soldiers.

But Bierce's most shocking stories turned the nature of the way Americans thought about war on its head: duty carried to extremes; glory reserved for the so-called leaders who stayed safely behind the lines; courage rarely rewarded. Three selections illustrate Bierce's unusual—for the nineteenth century—approach to telling about the war. Each offers stark descriptions of warfare's reality, while at the same time presenting a slightly unreal and decidedly macabre prospect.

"A Horseman in the Sky" begins with a peaceful scene in the fall of 1861, with a young soldier dozing near a road in western Virginia. Lying flat on his stomach, his head nestled on a bent arm, the soldier has fallen asleep "at his post of duty." If detected, the former officer Bierce reminds his readers, "he would be dead shortly afterward, death being the just and legal penalty of his crime" (ibid., 97). The spot at which he slept offered a panoramic view of the cliff falling away below the road and of the wooded valley in which five regiments of Union infantry rested. The road by which the boy was posted—the road that this small army would traverse after dark—led to a Confederate encampment. Obviously, the exhausted young man had let down his comrades, leaving them vulnerable to discovery and attack.

This was no ordinary Union soldier, Bierce explains. Carter Druse was the only child of one of the most affluent families in the mountains of western Virginia, raised in luxury by loving parents. Yet when the war broke out a few months before the story begins, Carter had spoken plainly to his father: "A Union regiment has arrived at Grafton. I am going to join it." This was not unusual in this maverick region of the Old Dominion; two years into the war, it would officially be admitted to the Union, breaking away from the Confederate portion of the state to become West Virginia. In this case it broke apart a family. "Well go, sir," the elder Druse said, "and whatever may occur, do what you conceive to be your duty. Virginia, to which you are a traitor, must get on without you. Should we both live to the end of the war, we will speak further of the matter" (ibid., 99).

The boy did join the Yankees and had done his duty—up to the point where he slipped into slumber alongside this crucial road. When he awakes—"what good or bad angel came in a dream to rouse him from his state of crime, who shall say?"—he finds himself confronted with a scene that, at first, gives him "a keen artistic delight." Farther along the cliff was a man on a horse, peering into the valley that sheltered Carter's comrades. "Motionless at the extreme edge of the capping rock and sharply outlined against the sky," the rider sat his horse "with the repose of a Grecian god carved in the marble which limits the suggestion of activity" (ibid., 99). Carter's momentary delight in the sheer nobility of the scene is cut short by the realization that the man wore the gray uniform of a Confederate officer and that from his vantage point he might easily spot the hidden Federals below.

Druse carefully brings his rifle to bear on the horseman, cocks it slowly and quietly—and then the Confederate turns his head as if to look directly at Carter. The young soldier pales, loses his concentration, and drops his head to the ground, nearly overcome with the intensity and danger of the situation. He soon recovers and resumes his soldierly duty, "conscience and reason sound." He knows he cannot hope to capture the mounted enemy; any movement on his part will simply cause the scout to gallop back to warn his unit, with terrible consequences for the unsuspecting Union soldiers below. He glances at the valley floor; perhaps the Confederate has seen nothing—but a foolish officer has allowed his men to water their horses from a stream in plain view of anyone posted at any of the surrounding mountains. The man has to be killed.

Carter lowers his aim to the horse, and just before pulling the trigger, remembers his father's parting words: "Whatever may occur, do what you conceive to be your duty." He conquers whatever qualms had made him hesitate and pulls the trigger.

A few minutes later, a sergeant creeps up to Carter's position, wondering what he had fired at.

"A horse," Carter answers. "It was standing on yonder rock—pretty far out. You see it is no longer there. It went over the cliff."

"Was there anybody on the horse?" asks the sergeant.

"Yes."

"Well?"

"My father."

The sergeant rises to his feet and walks away, shaking his head, and uttering, no doubt, the words—or something like them—that Bierce hoped would leap into the minds of his readers: "Good God!" (ibid., 102–103).

Carter Druse plainly did his duty, in the military sense. However, the suggestion is clear that, if he had only stayed awake, he might not have been faced with the choice of killing his father or betraying his regiment. This kind of ironic twist—Druse fails in his responsibilities, only to be forced into a terrible decision to make up for his failure—is one of Bierce's most commonly employed techniques.

"A Horseman in the Sky" also reveals another of Bierce's interests: the issue of loyalty in the South. His characters frequently come from divided families like the Druses. Reflecting the war within the war that plagued areas like Kentucky, Tennessee, and western Virginia, many of the stories take place in border regions shared by Unionists and Confederates.

Another such story is "The Affair at Coulter's Notch," which also features a sadistic commanding officer and an underling's nearly fanatical and ultimately destructive devotion to duty. It begins with a general's order for a colonel to have one of his officers, Captain Coulter, place his battery in the narrow notch of a craggy outcropping in order to fire on a dozen Confederate guns in a clearing below. Coulter would have to bring up one gun at a time, for there was no room for the entire battery. The colonel, who had frequently extolled Coulter's skill as an artillerist and bravery as a man, suspects that the general had, for some reason, taken a disliking to the young officer. He also knows that the Confederate guns are actually merely a rear guard for the retreating rebel army and believes that this action is unnecessary. Worried that his praise for Coulter may have doomed him, but recognizing that there was nothing else he could do, the colonel gives the order.

Coulter replies, "slowly and with apparent effort," asking if the enemy guns were near the house. A little surprised, the colonel nods in the affirmative. "And it is—necessary—to engage them? The order is imperative?" The captain had paled and his voice had become "husky and broken" (ibid., 17). His superior, hoping in vain that the general will rescind the order, nearly has Coulter arrested to relieve him of his burden. Coulter sends for his battery and nudges his horse up into the notch, where he raises his binoculars to scan the target. Soon a gun and caisson caroms to a stop, and a well-disciplined gun crew unlimbers the cannon, wheels it into the notch, and fires their first shot.

The stirring and surrealistic description of the action was not, according to the author, "intended to relate in detail the progress and incidents of that ghastly contest—a contest without vicissitudes, its alternations only different degrees of despair." The desperate odds—twelve Confederate guns against a single Union gun—made the notch a hell of smoke and activity. "To the end the Federal can-noneers fought their hopeless battle in an atmosphere of living iron whose thoughts were lightnings and whose deeds were death" (ibid., 18). The notch "seemed the crater of a volcano in thundering eruption" in which successive gun crews—as, one by one, the Yankee guns are destroyed or dismounted from their carriages—fight savagely and with great effect on the Confederate guns and gunners near the house in the clearing.

When another colonel requests permission for his infantry to open fire on the Confederate guns—they are, in fact, within easy range—the general inexplica-bly refuses. As Coulter's colonel observes the action, he chats with the adjutant general of the brigade, who informs him that Coulter was a Southerner, that ear-lier in the war the general had actually been posted near Coulter's home when he had met Coulter's wife and when some sort of trouble had developed between them. "She is a red-hot Secessionist," says the adjutant, "they all are, except Coulter himself, but she is a good wife and high-bred lady" and had apparently complained to headquarters (ibid., 20). The general was transferred to a new unit—and then had demanded the transfer of Coulter's battery to the general's division.

The colonel realizes what has been done and, "eyes . . . blazing with a gen-erous indignation," rides over to the notch to order the withdrawals of Coulter's guns. He is shocked at the destruction, the blasted guns and dead horses and torn bodies. The men "looked like demons of the pit," stripped to the waist, bloody, stained black with smoke, loading and firing like automatons. When one fell, another leaped into his place. "The colonel observed something new to his military experience—something horrible and unnatural: the gun was bleeding at the mouth! In temporary default of water, the man sponging had dipped his sponge into a pool of comrade's blood" (ibid., 21).

Just as the colonel finally identifies Coulter—"a fiend seven times damned . . . his teeth flashing between his black lips, his eyes, fierce and expanded, burning like coals beneath his bloody brow"—the firing stops. The Confederates have withdrawn from the clearing; the affair at Coulter's Notch is over. The column moves forward, and the colonel takes the "somewhat shat-tered" plantation house for his headquarters. After the staff is settled, an orderly informs the commander that something was rummaging about in the cellar, and is accompanied by the colonel and another staff officer to find out what it is.

They find the motionless figures of a man, woman, and child, cradled in the woman's arms, who they believe to be dead. A shell had crashed through the floor; they see blood on the heads of the man and woman and a severed infant's foot. "Suddenly the man whom they had thought dead raised his head and gazed tranquilly into their faces. His complexion was coal black; the cheeks were apparently tattooed in irregular sinuous lines from the eyes downward. The lips, too, were white, like those of a stage negro. There was blood upon his forehead." No one recognizes him, until the colonel asks him what he's doing there. The man responds that this is his house, and, when pressed, that the others—who really are dead—are "my wife and child." And then, in the twist that magnifies the ironic tragedy of this tale of uncontrolled power, perverse duty, and needless death, he says, "I am Captain Coulter" (ibid., 23).

They find the motionless figures of a man, woman, and child, cradled in the woman's arms, who they believe to be dead.

Bierce often uses the war as a device to show the worst traits of humankind and the ways in which even the noblest men can be trapped between duty and dishonor, and in no story is that more apparent than "The Coup De Grace," which begins with the aftermath of a battle. "The fighting had been hard and continuous; that was attested by all the senses. The very taste of battle was in the air." As far as the eye could see, "among the splintered trees, lay wrecks of men and horses." Stretcher bearers gather the few surviving wounded, and burial parties dump bodies in mass trenches, rarely knowing the names of the men they are burying. The veteran Bierce knew that the reality of battle rarely matched the long straight lines of contemporary lithographs, and that in a big fight battle plans collapsed and units intermingled. "Nine men in ten whom you meet after a battle," he wrote, "inquire the way to some fraction of the army—as if any one could know" (ibid., 59).

The author turns the reader's attention to the battle-stained Captain Downing Maxwell. As the "setting sun straggled redly through the open spaces of the wood," he makes his way into those woods, looking for Caffal Halcrow, his dear friend and a sergeant in Maxwell's company. To the extent that their separate ranks allowed, these lifelong friends had been inseparable, even during the war. Indeed, Halcrow had "nothing military in his taste nor disposition," but when his friend had gone off to war, he had gone, too, just so they could be together. Unfortunately, the major of the regiment was Halcrow's brother Creede, and Maxwell and Creede Halcrow had nourished for many years an antipathy that only worsened when they ended up in the same regiment. Their hatred had reached its climax that very morning, when, in ordering Maxwell to move his company into a particularly dangerous position, he cynically suggested that Maxwell might, given the difficulty of the situation, ask a lieutenant to take over command of the company. The captain could give as good as he got; he suggests that the major go with the company, for "a mounted officer would be a conspicuous mark, and I have long held the opinion that it would be better if you were dead." Later in the morning, the Confederates had driven the entire regiment miles away from its original position, leaving behind the dead and wounded—including Caffal Halcrow (ibid., 60–61).

The object of Maxwell's sad journey on the evening after the battle—which his army had eventually won—is to find his friend, dead or alive. When he finally recognizes the inert form of the still alive but critically hurt sergeant, he notices an odd kind of wound:

> His clothing was deranged; it seemed to have been violently torn apart, exposing the abdomen. Some of the buttons of his jacket had been pulled off and lay on the ground beside him and fragments of his other garments were strewn about. . . . There had been no great effusion of blood. The only visible wound was a wide, ragged opening in the abdomen. It was defiled with earth and dead leaves. Protruding from it was a loop of small intestine.

Maxwell had never seen a wound like this. With horror, he spots "several dark objects moving among the fallen men—a herd of swine," feasting on the dead and still-living victims of the battle (ibid., 61).

Caffal cannot speak, but groans with every breath and shrieks whenever Maxwell touches him. Writhing in pain, his hands clutch leaves and dirt from the small holes he has insensibly scooped out on either side of his body. His eyes seem to be praying for something—and Maxwell fears he knows what it is: a "blessed release" from the pain that had become the only world he knew (ibid., 62).

A sobbing Maxwell speaks his friend's name over and over, then turns away. "A horse, its foreleg shattered by a cannon-shot, lifted its head sidewise from the ground and neighed piteously" (ibid., 62). The act of drawing his pistol and shooting the poor animal between the eyes seems to make up Maxwell's mind. He turns back to Caffal, kneels, and puts the muzzle of the pistol to his friend's head. He pulls the trigger—but he had used his last cartridge on the horse. Hesitating only a moment, Maxwell draws his sword, places it on his friend's breast, and pushes with all his might. The blade plunges straight through Caffal's body. His knees jerk up, his right arm instinctively reaches across to clutch at the blade.

And at that moment, at the point of death for Caffal Halcrow, three men step into view: "two were hospital attendants and carried a stretcher. The third was Major Creede Halcrow" (ibid., 63). The story ends at that moment: the sworn enemies standing over the body of their friend and brother. As in many of Bierce's stories, vital questions remain unanswered; their sudden endings jolt the reader, leaving entirely too many loose ends hanging.

Yet there is an undeniable power to Bierce's visions of war and of human nature. Although his stories seem somewhat formulaic and even predictable to modern readers, they were not to his contemporaries. Bierce relished shocking his readers and going against the grain of his society's commonly accepted values. In his most famous book, *The Devil's Dictionary* (1911), he cast a jaundiced and angry eye at the assumptions of mainstream America with arch definitions and commentary on words and ideas of the time. He tellingly defined war as "A by-product of the arts of peace," and amplified, writing: "The most menacing political condition is a period of international amity. . . . The soil of peace is thickly sown with the seeds of war and singularly suited to their germination and growth." In a sense, Bierce is a dark reminder of the war to later generations; he extends the war's reach to home fronts formed long after the shooting stopped.

Bierce used his short stories to vent his pent-up frustrations with the follies of humankind, to exorcise the demons that often plague veterans of harsh combat, to distinguish himself—his intellect, his detachment, his objectivity—from the pedestrian feelings and emotions of his fellow Americans. He could, however, cast off his bitter, ironic demeanor at times, as he did in 1903 when writing about the burial grounds at a tiny battlefield in West Virginia—a battlefield that he himself had fought on a lifetime before. The casualties had been light on both sides, but a small national cemetery had been created and maintained for the few Union dead who had fallen in this tentative, early engagement. Little had been done for several Confederate graves lying a short walk from their enemies' well-manicured resting places. They were merely indentations in the dirt, with a handful of scattered, incomplete stone markers. Bierce's famous essay, called "The Bivouac of the Dead," ended with a plea to do something for these worthy opponents:

> They were honest and courageous foemen, having little in common with the political madmen who persuaded them to their doom and the literary bearers of false witness in the aftertime. . . . Among them is no member of the Southern Historical Society. Their valor was not the fury of the non-combatant; they have no voice in the thunder of the civilians and the shouting. Not by them are impaired the dignity and infinite pathos of the Lost Cause. Give them, these blameless gentlemen, their rightful part in all the pomp that fills the circuit of the summer hills. (ibid., 139)

Bierce himself was buried in an unmarked grave; even the location is unknown. He may have died in Arizona, but legend has it that he died somewhere in northern Mexico, where he had gone in 1913 to cover the campaigns of Pancho Villa. The stories he left behind changed the ways that writers wrote about war, providing a literary precursor to the bitter memoirs and fiction inspired by the wars of the twentieth century.

The Devil's Civil War: The Stories of Ambrose Bierce

PRIMARY SOURCES:

Bierce, Ambrose. *The Devil's Dictionary.* New York: A. & C. Boni, 1911.

Hopkins, Ernest Jerome, comp. *The Civil War Short Stories of Ambrose Bierce.* Lincoln: University of Nebraska Press, 1970.

Posner, Richard A., ed. *The Essential Holmes: Selections from the Letters, Speeches, Judicial Opinions, and Other Writings of Oliver Wendell Holmes, Jr.* Chicago: University of Chicago Press, 1992.

SECONDARY SOURCE:

Morris, Roy J. *Ambrose Bierce: Alone in Bad Company.* Oxford: Oxford University Press, 1998.

Bibliographical Essay

In addition to the secondary sources listed at the end of each chapter, the following books offer information and analysis about the Confederate and Union home fronts during the Civil War.

Bibliographies and General Works

Historians have, of course, produced countless volumes about the Civil War. They have also produced a number of notable books *about* Civil War books. Among the most useful recent examples of this genre are: James M. McPherson and William J. Cooper Jr., eds., *Writing the Civil War: The Quest to Understand* (Columbia: University of South Carolina Press, 1998); David J. Eicher, *The Civil War in Books: An Analytical Bibliography* (Urbana: University of Illinois Press, 1997); and Steven E. Woodworth, ed., *The American Civil War: A Handbook of Literature and Research* (Westport, CT: Greenwood, 1996). The format of Eicher's work is an annotated bibliography; the other two consist of critical essays on secondary and, in some cases, primary sources.

Four books are the logical starting points for a study of the Civil War era, and each devotes considerable attention to home front issues. James M. McPherson, the dean of Civil War historians, has produced a largely political and military history of the era in *Ordeal by Fire: The Civil War and Reconstruction, 3rd ed.* (Boston: McGraw-Hill, 2001), while Eric Foner's *Reconstruction: America's Unfinished Revolution, 1863–1877* (New York: Harper & Row, 1988) spends more time on racial and social issues. Philip Shaw Paludan's *A People's Contest: The Union and Civil War 1861–1865, 2nd ed.* (Lawrence: University Press of Kansas, 1996) is the starting point for any study of the Northern home front, while Emory M. Thomas, *The Confederate Nation, 1861–1865* (New York: Harper & Row, 1979), covers the Confederacy.

Although each of the chapters in *Civil War America* normally describe a facet of the home front in either the North or the South, a number of historians have examined aspects of the nonmilitary Civil War experience from both Northern and Southern vantage points. They include Alice Fahs's *The Imagined Civil War:*

Popular Literature of the North & South, 1861–1865 (Chapel Hill: University of North Carolina Press, 2001), which deals with magazines and novels produced during the war (including writing for children), and Anne C. Rose's *Victorian America and the Civil War* (New York: Cambridge University Press, 1992), which explores Victorian religious and ethical values and the way they helped middle-class Americans deal with war and its aftermaths. Two sets of essays examine diverse elements of the home front: Maris A. Vinovskis, in his anthology *Toward a Social History of the American Civil War: Exploratory Essays* (New York: Cambridge University Press, 1990), wondered if social historians had "lost" the Civil War; in *Divided Houses: Gender and the Civil War* (New York: Oxford University Press, 1992), editors Catherine Clinton and Nina Silber and a team of historians assert they have not. Finally, Randall C. Jimerson, *The Private Civil War: Popular Thought during the Sectional Conflict* (Baton Rouge: Louisiana State University Press, 1988), suggests some of the ways in which Americans pondered the Union, race, and other weighty issues related to the sectional conflict.

Community Histories: South

Like much social history, the story of the Civil War home front can often best be managed at the community level, and historians have written about the war from the town, city, county, and regional points of view. Examples of general studies of specific Southern communities include: Stephen V. Ash, *Middle Tennessee Society Transformed, 1860–1870: War and Peace in the Upper South* (Baton Rouge: Louisiana State University Press, 1989); Martin Crawford, *Ashe County's Civil War: Community and Society in the Appalachian South* (Charlottesville: University Press of Virginia, 2001); Wayne K. Durrill, *War of Another Kind: A Southern Community in the Great Rebellion* (New York: Oxford University Press, 1990); Ernest B. Furgurson, *Ashes of Glory: Richmond at War* (New York: Knopf, 1996); Richard W. Iobst, *Civil War Macon: The History of a Confederate City* (Macon, GA: Mercer University Press, 1999); William W. Rogers Jr., *Confederate Home Front: Montgomery during the Civil War* (Tuscaloosa: University of Alabama Press, 1999); Daniel E. Sutherland, *Seasons of War: The Ordeal of a Southern Community, 1861–1865* (New York: Free Press, 1995); Steven Elliot Tripp, *Yankee Town, Southern City: Race and Class Relations in Civil War Lynchburg* (New York: New York University Press, 1997); and Brian Steel Wills, *The War Hits Home: The Civil War in Southeastern Virginia* (Charlottesville: University Press of Virginia, 2001). A community study on a very specific topic is Thomas G. Dyer, *Secret Yankees: The Union Circle in Confederate Atlanta* (Baltimore: Johns Hopkins University Press, 1999). A recent example of the spate of state studies is William Blair, *Virginia's*

Private War: Feeding Body and Soul in the Confederacy, 1861–1865 (New York: Oxford University Press, 1998).

The internal conflict that wracked much of the South during the Civil War has provided grist for a number of studies in recent years. William W. Freehling, in *The South vs. the South: How Anti-Confederate Southerners Shaped the Course of the Civil War* (New York: Oxford University Press, 2001), and the contributors to John C. Inscoe and Robert C. Kenzer, eds., *Enemies of the Country: New Perspectives on Unionists in the Civil War South* (Athens: University of Georgia Press, 2001) cover the entire South. So does Catherine Clinton, ed., *Southern Families at War: Loyalty and Conflict in the Civil War South* (New York: Oxford University Press, 2000), another anthology that transcends state and community lines to explore the racial, ethnic, gender, and moral aspects of conflict in the Confederacy. Mark E. Neely takes a look at Confederate policies and practices in dealing with political dissenters in *Southern Rights: Political Prisoners and the Myth of Confederate Constitutionalism* (Charlottesville: University Press of Virginia, 1999), while Noel C. Fisher's *War at Every Door: Partisan Politics and Guerrilla Violence in East Tennessee, 1860–1869* (Chapel Hill: University of North Carolina Press, 1997) is one of the best of the many recent examinations of dissent, disorder, and disaffection in Southern communities, regions, and states.

Southern Women

The study of Southern women during the Civil War era has been a veritable growth industry during the last twenty years, with imaginative and sometimes provocative accounts of material privation, empowerment through hardship and widowhood, gender clashes, racial divides, and the legacy of the war in the lives of women. Among the more important works on Southern women during the Civil War—most of which also integrate the pre- and postwar lives of women into their wartime experiences—are: Victoria E. Bynum, *Unruly Women: The Politics of Social and Sexual Control in the Old South* (Chapel Hill: University of North Carolina Press, 1992); Laura F. Edwards, *Scarlett Doesn't Live Here Anymore: Southern Women in the Civil War Era* (Urbana: University of Illinois Press, 2000); Drew Gilpin Faust, *Mothers of Invention: Women of the Slaveholding South in the American Civil War* (Chapel Hill: University of North Carolina Press, 1996); George C. Rable, *Civil Wars: Women and the Crisis of Southern Nationalism* (Urbana: University of Illinois Press, 1989); and LeeAnn Whites, *The Civil War as a Crisis in Gender: Augusta, Georgia, 1860–1890* (Athens: University of Georgia Press, 1995). An imaginative study that is as much about the way that Southern women remembered and were remembered for their wartime roles is Catherine Clinton, *Tara Revisited: Women, War & the Plantation Legend* (New York: Abbeville, 1995).

Community Histories: North

As in so much writing about the Civil War home front, historians have paid less attention to Northern communities. A quartet of fairly recent books combine political, social, and urban history to portray the effects of the war on the North's cities: J. Matthew Gallman, *Mastering Wartime: A Social History of Philadelphia during the Civil War* (New York: Cambridge University Press, 1990); Louis S. Gerteis, *Civil War St. Louis* (Lawrence: University Press of Kansas, 2001); Theodore J. Karamanski, *Rally 'Round the Flag: Chicago and the Civil War* (Chicago: Nelson-Hall, 1993); and Thomas H. O'Connor, *Civil War Boston* (Boston: Northeastern University Press, 1997). Gallman has also authored a synthesis on the Northern war effort at home in *The North Fights the Civil War: The Home Front* (Chicago: Ivan R. Dee, 1994).

Historians have also examined the relationship between the war and home front institutions, political development, and gender relations. In the North, the emphasis tends to be on ways that Northerners found to contribute to the Union war effort and the ramifications of those efforts for Northern society. The classic study of the economic effects of the war is Emerson Fite, *Social and Industrial Conditions in the North during the Civil War* (New York: Ungar, 1963). Robert H. Bremner's *The Public Good: Philanthropy and Welfare in the Civil War Era* (New York: Knopf, 1980) is a wide-ranging look at the ways that the wartime philanthropy drew on antebellum methods of caring for the less fortunate members of society, while William Q. Maxwell, *Lincoln's Fifth Wheel: The Political History of the United States Sanitary Commission* (New York: Longmans, Green, 1956), as its title suggests, is less concerned with social meanings than with political realities. Earl J. Hess explores the mind of the North in *Liberty, Virtue, and Progress: Northerners and Their War for the Union, 2nd ed.* (New York: Fordham University Press, 1997), while a new collection of essays edited by Paul A. Cimbala and Randall M. Miller, *Union Soldiers and the Northern Homefront: Wartime Experiences, Postwar Adjustments* (New York: Fordham University Press, 2002), shows the many ways Northern civilians found to maintain close relationships with the sons, brothers, husbands, and sweethearts they sent off to the army.

Although rarely as much of a threat to order or to the successful prosecution of the war as in the Confederacy, Northern dissent has also occupied the attention of historians for many years. The best early works on this topic were produced by Frank L. Klement; see *The Copperheads in the Middle West* (Chicago: University of Chicago Press, 1960) and *Dark Lanterns: Secret Political Societies, Conspiracies, and Treason Trials in the Civil War* (Baton Rouge: Louisiana State University Press, 1984). More recently, Mark E. Neely won the Pulitzer Prize for his study of government policies toward dissent in *The Fate of Liberty: Abraham Lincoln and Civil Liberties* (New York: Oxford University Press, 1990). Grace Palladino's *Another Civil*

War: Labor, Capital, and the State in the Anthracite Regions of Pennsylvania, 1840–68 (Urbana: University of Illinois Press, 1990), places the wartime dissent of miners in Pennsylvania in the contexts of ongoing ethnic and labor struggles.

Northern Women

Although, for perhaps obvious reasons, Northern home front women have not been studied in the same detail as Southern women, a flurry of books over the last dozen years has examined the contributions of Yankee women to the Northern war effort and, even more importantly, traced the ways that women's war work politicized and changed them in other ways. See especially Wendy Hamand Venet, *Neither Ballots nor Bullets: Women Abolitionists and the Civil War* (Charlottesville: University Press of Virginia, 1991); Elizabeth D. Leonard, *Yankee Women: Gender Battles in the Civil War* (New York: W. W. Norton, 1994); Jeanie Attie, *Patriotic Toil: Northern Women and the American Civil War* (Ithaca, NY: Cornell University Press, 1998); and Judith Ann Giesberg, *Civil War Sisterhood: The U.S. Sanitary Commission and Women's Politics in Transition* (Boston: Northeastern University Press, 2000).

African Americans

The study of African Americans has been one of the most exciting fields in U.S. history for more than a generation, and the earlier emphasis on the lives of slaves has been followed up by excellent work on the experiences and contributions of African Americans during the Civil War itself. A number of works deal with Federal policies toward the slaves and freedmen in the South and with the activities of Northern philanthropists, missionaries, and planters whose goals often conflicted with those of Southern African Americans. See, for instance: Ronald Butchart, *Northern Schools, Southern Blacks, and Reconstruction: Freedmen's Education, 1862–1875* (Westport, CT: Greenwood, 1980); Louis S. Gerteis, *From Contraband to Freedman: Federal Policy toward Southern Blacks, 1861–1865* (Westport, CT: Greenwood, 1973); Robert C. Morris, *Reading, 'Riting, and Reconstruction: The Education of Freedmen in the South, 1861–1870* (Chicago: University of Chicago Press, 1981); and Joe M. Richardson, *Christian Reconstruction: The American Missionary Association and Southern Blacks, 1861–1890* (Athens: University of Georgia Press, 1986). The best study of the cultures and policies clashing in the wartime South is still Willie Lee Rose, *Rehearsal for Reconstruction: The Port Royal Experiment* (Indianapolis: Bobbs-Merrill, 1964).

Other historians have examined the ways that African Americans made the war their own, especially in the South, where slaves freed themselves and many joined the Union army. See especially Patricia C. Click, *Time Full of Trial: The Roanoke Island Freedmen's Colony, 1862–1867* (Chapel Hill: University of North Carolina

Press, 2001); Clara Merritt De Boer, *His Truth Is Marching On: African Americans Who Taught the Freedmen for the American Missionary Association, 1861–1877* (New York: Garland, 1995); Noralee Frankel, *Freedom's Women: Black Women and Families in Civil War Era Mississippi* (Bloomington: Indiana University Press, 1999); Ervin L. Jordan Jr., *Black Confederates and Afro-Yankees in Civil War Virginia* (Charlottesville: University Press of Virginia, 1995); and Leon Litwack, *Been in the Storm So Long: The Aftermath of Slavery* (New York: Knopf, 1979).

As always, less has been written about the ways that African Americans in the North dealt with the Civil War, but a good starting place is David W. Blight, *Frederick Douglass' Civil War: Keeping Faith in Jubilee* (Baton Rouge: Louisiana State University Press, 1989).

Legacies and Memories

Another booming field in the historiography of the Civil War era deals with the long-term effects of the war on the country's psyche and on the ways that Americans remember their collective history. Nina Silber's *The Romance of Reunion: Northerners and the South, 1865–1900* (Chapel Hill: University of North Carolina Press, 1993) shows some of the ways in which the Civil War generation reconciled after the war, while David W. Blight's award-winning *Race and Reunion: The Civil War in American Memory* (Cambridge: Belknap Press of Harvard University Press, 2001) explores the highly charged issue of race as a factor in postwar thinking. An entertaining, poignant, and sometimes disturbing take on the racial and political ideas reflected in Civil War reenactments and other commemorative activities can be found in Tony Horwitz, *Confederates in the Attic: Dispatches from the Unfinished Civil War* (New York: Pantheon, 1998). Finally, Theda Skocpol's *Protecting Soldiers and Mothers: The Political Origins of Social Policy in the United States* (Cambridge: Harvard University Press, 1992) places the growing influence of the federal and state governments on social welfare programs in the context of wartime and postwar initiatives to aid Civil War veterans and their families. See also Jim Cullen, *The Civil War in Popular Culture: A Reusable Past* (Washington: Smithsonian Institution Press, 1995), and David Goldfield, *Still Fighting the Civil War: The American South and Southern History* (Baton Rouge: Louisiana State University Press, 2002).

Index

Index

Civil rights, for emancipated African
    Americans, 300–301
Civil Rights movement, 237
Civilians
    Ruffin, Edmund, 3–15
    soldier-civilian relations in the occupied
        South, 53–63, 128–129, 307–309
    Southern dissenters, 65–73
    Southern plantation owners as refugees,
        27–39
    women and children surviving the
        Vicksburg Campaign, 41–52
    See also Children
Clark, James G., 281
Clarke, Mrs. Lou, 47
Class consciousness, 150
Clymer, Hiester, 243
Collin County, Texas, 73
Colored Orphans Asylum, New York City,
    151, 152
Columbia, South Carolina, 53, 310–311
Columbia Wayside Hospital, 310–311
Confederacy
    Confederate supporters in the NYC draft
        riots, 156
    disloyalty of Southerners to the, 68–73
    domestic life of grass widows, 17–25
    Lincoln assassination, 256–257
    loyalty of slaves to owners, 223–229
    Northern newspaper depictions of the
        Confederate army, 104
    Ruffin's criticism of, 11
    treatment of war orphans, 286–287
    wartime plight of slaves, 229–232
    See also Southerners
Confederate Veteran Magazine, 304
Conn, George F., 272
Conscription
    conscript evasion, 68–73, 96
    conscription bill, 78–79
    NYC draft riots, 147–157
    slaves preparing Confederate defenses,
        229
Conspiracy theories, 91–92
Contraband camps, 58, 209–220
Conwell, Russell H., 61
Cooke County, Texas, 65–73, 70
Coon, David, 129

Copperheads, 156, 168, 200
Corbett, Dick, 269, 275
Corbett, Elizabeth, 267, 269, 271–276
Corbett, Gay, 269, 275
Corbin, Janie, 128
Corinth, Mississippi, 211
Corruption in orphans' homes, 288
Cotton embargo, 68
"The Coup de Grace" (Bierce) 324–325
Courts martial, 56, 71
Crane, Stephen, 317, 318
Crime, 67–68, 268. *See also* Violence
Crutcher, Emmie, 43
Currier & Ives, 242, 262
Curtin, Andrew, 279

Dade, Fanny, 312–313
Dade, Virginia, 312–313
Dana, Henrietta, 260–262
Dana, Richard Henry, 260
Davis, Jeff (slave), 229
Davis, Jefferson, 66, 228
Davis, Varina, 228
Death
    murder as a commonplace, 37
    suicide, 13–15, 20–21
    See also Casualties
Depression, 17–25
Deserters, 66, 68–73, 169, 292, 308
The Devil's Dictionary (Bierce), 317, 326
Dialogues, of Oliver Optic, 200–202
Diamond, George Washington, 71–72
Disaffection, of Southerners, 65–73
Disease
    in contraband camps, 215
    educating freedpeople about, 244
    hygiene, 243–245, 272, 300
    Vicksburg, 42
Disloyalty, of Southerners to the
    Confederacy, 68–73
"Disperse and retire" proclamation, 77–78
Dissatisfaction, with the war, 82–83
Dissenters, Southern, 65–73
Dix, Dorothea, 113
Donelson, Fort, 100, 203
Douglas, Stephen A., 161, 166
Douglass, Frederick, 236–237, 239, 240
Draft evasion, 68–73, 96

Index

Index

Index

Index

About the Author

James Marten, Professor of History at Marquette University, is the author or editor of several books on the Civil War era and on children's history, including *The Children's Civil War* (University of North Carolina Press, 1998). He is director of the Children in Urban America Project, an on-line archive of documents related to children in Milwaukee.